The Vision Thing

Contemporary politics goes on at a mythic level. This is the provocative argument put forward in this unique book which results from the collaboration of practising politicians, organizational and political consultants, scholars of mythology and culture, and Jungian analysts from several countries.

The first part of the book focuses on leadership and vision, and features a reflection on myth and leadership by former US Senator Bill Bradley. The second part deals with the way the theme of 'the one and the many' works itself out in politics today. From the perspective of 'the many', there are chapters on factionalism, ethnic strife, genocide and multiculturalism. From the perspective of 'the one', there are chapters on the economic myth and gender politics showing how these bring coherence to today's confused political scene, culminating in the suggestion that the modern political psyche is itself in the midst of a rite of passage.

The relevance of the book to the practice and study of politics, mainstream and marginal, cannot be overemphasized and the book will provide stimulating reading for practitioners and students in these areas as well as for those engaged in psychological work such as therapy, counselling or analysis.

Thomas Singer is a psychiatrist and Jungian analyst. He is Chair of the Extended Education Committee of the San Francisco C.G. Jung Institute, and the author of *Who's the Patient Here* and *Portraits of the Young Psychotherapist.*

Contributors: John Beebe, Bill Bradley, Betty Sue Flowers, Judith Grahn, Joseph L. Henderson, Alexander Laban Hinton, Samuel L. Kimbles, Martin Kransey, Thomas B. Kirsch, Betty D. Meador, Renos K. Papadopoulos, Peter Rutter, Andrew Samuels, Craig San Roque, Richard Tarnas, Eli B. Weisstub, David Ulansey.

The Vision Thing

Myth, politics and psyche in the world

Edited by
Thomas Singer

London and New York

First published 2000
by Routledge
11 New Fetter Lane, London EC4P 4EE

Simultaneously published in the USA and Canada
by Routledge
29 West 35th Street, New York, NY 10001

Routledge is an imprint of the Taylor & Francis Group

Typeset in Times by
Keystroke, Jacaranda Lodge, Wolverhampton
Printed and bound in Great Britain by
Biddles Ltd, Guildford and King's Lynn

British Library Cataloguing in Publication Data
A catalogue record for this book is available from the British Library

Library of Congress Cataloging in Publication Data
A catalogue record for this book has been requested

ISBN 0–415–19553–5 (hbk)
ISBN 0–415–19554–3 (pbk)

Three leaders – each very different from one another – have given me the support, inspiration, and courage to make my vision of this book a reality. This book is dedicated to Joe Henderson, Tom Kirsch, and Bill Bradley with deep gratitude. Three family members – my wife, Jane, and children, Eliza and Jimmy – had the love and patience to put up with me while I pursued *The Vision Thing* and I am grateful that they still talk to me.

Contents

List of illustrations xi
Notes on contributors xiii
Acknowledgements xvii

Introduction: the vision thing 1
THOMAS SINGER

PART I
Leadership and vision in myth and politics **19**

Foreword by Thomas B. Kirsch 21

1 **Reflections on myth, politics, and leadership** **23**
Senator BILL BRADLEY

2 **The inner vision and social organization** **29**
JOSEPH L. HENDERSON

3 **The good-enough leader** **34**
ANDREW SAMUELS

4 **The feminine and politics** **50**
BETTY D. MEADOR

5 ***The Wizard of Oz*: a vision of development in the American political psyche** **62**
JOHN BEEBE

6 The politics of transformation: the transformation of politics **84**
ANDREW SAMUELS

PART II
The one and the many in myth and politics **97**

Foreword by Martin Krasney 99

The many 103

7 Arresting Orestes: mythic events and the law **105**
CRAIG SAN ROQUE

8 Factionalism and interethnic conflict: narratives in myth and politics **122**
RENOS K. PAPADOPOULOS

9 Reflections from the back side of a dollar: myth and the origins of diversity **141**
ELI B. WEISSTUB

10 The cultural complex and the myth of invisibility **157**
SAMUEL L. KIMBLES

11 Under the shade of Pol Pot's umbrella: mandala, myth, and politics in the Cambodian genocide **170**
ALEXANDER LABAN HINTON

The one 205

12 Practicing politics in the economic myth **207**
BETTY SUE FLOWERS

13 Cultural transition and spiritual transformation: from Alexander the Great to cyberspace 213
DAVID ULANSEY

14 MOOSE, FOOSE, FAMOSE 232
JUDITH GRAHN

15 Reasonable Woman/Reasonable Man: the emergence of a modern archetype of gender equality in political life **241**
PETER RUTTER

16 Is the modern psyche undergoing a rite of passage? **251**
RICHARD TARNAS

Index 269

Illustrations

FIGURES

2.1	Hobbes' "Leviathan"	28
5.1	The relationship between Dorothy and the Scarecrow	66
5.2	The political relationship between Dorothy and the Scarecrow	67
5.3	The relationship according to hierarchical status and archetype	67
5.4	An auxiliary character axis	68
5.5	The pattern of consciousness emanating from the story	68
5.6	Consciousnesses and their political designations	69
5.7	The characters in relation to their antagonists	71
5.8	The interplay of consciousnesses	74
5.9	Stations in Dorothy's political development	77
7.1	Aborigines sandpainting	109
9.1	The Tower of Babel	142
11.1	Buddha seated in meditation on the coils of a *naga*	172
11.2	Angkor Wat near Siem Riep, Cambodia	181
11.3	Administrative divisions of Democratic Kampuchea, 1975 to 1979	193
13.1	Babylonian conception of the universe	220
13.2	Aristotle's universe	222

Contributors

John Beebe, MD, is an analyst in practice in San Francisco. He has been Co-editor (US) of *The Journal of Analytical Psychology* and Editor of *The San Francisco Jung Institute Library Journal*. He is highly regarded for his scholarly articles on film, as well as for his book *Integrity in Depth*, a psychological study of the archetype of moral wholeness.

Senator **Bill Bradley** was a three-time basketball All-American at Princeton, an Olympic gold medalist, a Rhodes scholar, and a professional player for ten years with the New York Knicks. Elected to the Senate from New Jersey in 1978, 1984, and 1990, he has authored extensive legislation. He has been a leader on tax reform, international economic issues, and the Senate Foreign Relations Committee. A presidential candidate, Senator Bradley has written four books: *Life on the Run*, *The Fair Tax*, *Time Present, Time Past*, and *Values of the Game*.

Betty Sue Flowers is an English Professor at the University of Texas. She was PBS Series Consultant and Editor for *Joseph Campbell and the Power of Myth* and Editor of *Synchronicity: Inner Dimensions of Leadership*. She has collaborated with Bill Moyers on four books.

Judith Grahn is a poet and writer and one of the founders of lesbian feminism. Her book *Another Mother Tongue* is a gay and lesbian history. She has published numerous books of poetry, a novel, a study of Gertrude Stein, a play based on the myth of Inanna's descent to the underworld, and, most recently, a new origin theory, *Blood, Bread, and Roses: How Menstruation Created the World*. She has received the Bill Whitehead award for lifetime achievement in lesbian letters, an American Book Award, and numerous other honours.

Joseph L. Henderson, MD, has been an analysand, student, and colleague of Carl Jung from the late 1920s. He continues to maintain an analytic practice well into his nineties. He is the author of "Ancient Myths and Modern Man" in *Man and His Symbols*, edited by C.G. Jung, *Thresholds of Initiation*, *Cultural Attitudes in Perspective*, and *Shadow and Self*. He has lifelong interests in the archetype of initiation, the role of culture in the psyche, and the anthropological aspects of analytical psychology. For over seventy years he has particularly focused on

Native American mythologies, and remains one of the most innovative and revered of Jung's original group.

Alexander Laban Hinton is an assistant professor in the Department of Anthropology at Rutgers University. He conducted ethnographic fieldwork in Cambodia from 1994–95, focusing on the relationship between culture, psychology, and violence. His articles have appeared in *American Anthropologist*, *American Ethnologist*, and *The Journal of Asian Studies*, and he is currently completing a book entitled, *Cambodia's Shadow: Cultural Dimensions of Genocide*.

Samuel L. Kimbles, Ph.D., is a clinical psychologist, Jungian analyst, and organizational consultant. He is an Associate Clinical Professor at the University of California, San Francisco, and maintains a private practice in Santa Rosa, California.

Thomas B. Kirsch, MD, has authored over forty articles on dreams, the life and work of C.G. Jung, the history of analytical psychology, and the practice of analysis throughout the world. He is the past President of the International Association for Analytical Psychology and has been a roving ambassador for Jungian psychology for many years, travelling to Russia, China, Australia, Korea, and many other countries. He is currently writing a social and cultural history of the origins of the Jungian tradition, to be published by Routledge.

Martin Krasney has had thirty years' experience in the design, development, and leadership of not-for-profit organizations, mostly in the fields of innovative education and social change. He has served on many boards and been Executive Director of the Aspen Institute Executive Seminars. He is currently writing literary fiction.

Betty D. Meador, Ph.D., is a Jungian analyst who practices in Berkeley, California. Her translations of the Sumerian myth and poetry appear in her book *Uncursing the Dark*, and in the forthcoming *Inanna: Lady of the Largest Heart*. She is a past President of the San Francisco C.G. Jung Institute.

Renos K. Papadopoulos, Ph.D., is Professor of Analytical Psychology at the University of Essex, Consultant Clinical Psychologist at the Tavistock Clinic, and Training and Supervising Jungian Analyst in practice in London. He is the Editor of *Harvest: Journal for Jungian Studies* and Chair of the Academic Sub-Committee of the International Association for Analytical Psychology. He is the editor of the four-volume *C.G. Jung Critical Assessments*, co-editor of *Jung in Modern Perspective*, and co-editor of *Multiple Voices: Narrative in Systemic Family Psychotherapy*. As consultant to the United Nations and other organisations, he has worked with survivors of violence and disaster in several countries.

Peter Rutter, MD, is a psychiatrist and Jungian analyst. He also serves as an expert legal witness and does conflict resolution regarding sexual harassment and boundary problems in professional relationships. He is the author of *Sex in the Forbidden Zone*, and *Understanding and Preventing Sexual Harassment: The Complete Guide*.

Andrew Samuels is Professor of Analytical Psychology at the University of Essex and a Jungian Training Analyst in practice in London. He works as a political consultant and lectures on politics and psychology internationally. His books include *Jung and the Post-Jungians*, *The Father*, *A Critical Dictionary of Jungian Analysis*, *Psychopathology*, *The Plural Psyche*, and *The Political Psyche*. His most recent book is *The Secret Life of Politics: Therapy In/Of/By the World*.

Craig San Roque, Ph.D., is a Jungian analyst and President of the Australian–New Zealand Society of Jungian Analysts. He lives in Alice Springs and focuses on the psycho-political problems of Aboriginal interaction with contemporary Australian culture. He is also a poet and playwright.

Thomas Singer, MD, is a psychiatrist and Jungian analyst. He is Chair of the Extended Education Committee of the San Francisco C.G. Jung Institute and author of *Who's The Patient Here*, *Portraits of the Young Psychotherapist*, and *A Fan's Guide to Baseball Fever, The Official Medical Reference*.

Richard Tarnas, Ph.D., is Professor of Philosophy and Psychology at the California Institute of Integral Studies, and Director of its graduate program in Philosophy, Cosmology, and Consciousness. He is the author of *The Passion of The Western Mind*, a narrative history of the western world view from the ancient Greek to the postmodern.

David Ulansey, Ph.D., is Professor of Philosophy and Religion at the California Institute of Integral Studies. He is the author of *The Origins of the Mithraic Mysteries* and numerous articles in publications ranging from *Scientific American* to the *Journal of Biblical Literature*.

Eli B. Weisstub, MD, has served as President of the Israel Association for Analytical Psychology and Second Vice-President of the International Association for Analytical Psychology. He practices Jungian analysis in Jerusalem and has written critical articles on Jungian theory.

Acknowledgments

The von Waveren Foundation, Wilma Messing, and the C.G. Jung Institute of San Francisco Scholarship Fund have all been most generous in lending financial support to this project which began with conferences in Bolinas, California and San Francisco, California.

John Beebe, Marty Krasney, Andrew Samuels, and Eli Weisstub came through with impeccable editorial advice and encouragement, time and again. All of the contributors to this volume were exceedingly generous with their time and ideas. This book would never have come into being without their genuine collaborative spirit.

The Routledge editors – Kate Hawes, Joanne Forshaw, and Imogen Burch – were efficient, professional and most helpful. Ursula Egli's thoughtful editorial and manuscript assistance has been invaluable. Iden Goodman's friendship and wise counsel was ever present.

PERMISSIONS

Acknowledgements

Introduction

The vision thing

Thomas Singer

There are times when politicians stumble into the need to link the political and mythological. They are propelled by a peculiar mix of dire necessity, conscious intention, and a deep unconscious sense of collective need. The title of this book is taken from a phrase born out of just such a situation. Although George Bush had recently "won" the Gulf War and conventional wisdom had it that he was unbeatable in 1992, the President was having trouble communicating with the American people – especially around domestic policy, as so poignantly revealed when he went shopping at a supermarket and didn't know what a bar code was at the check-out counter. The President had lost touch with everyday life and people in his own country. His re-election campaign began to implode. Bush identified part of his problem connecting with a restless electorate as "the vision thing."

"The vision thing" – a phrase that Bush himself had inadvertently coined early in his administration as a self acknowledged problem of articulating a clear vision for the country – had been haunting him for four years. He often joked about it in his speeches in an attempt to defuse the implicit criticism that in fact he had little or no intuition as to where the country was, or ought to be, headed. In a futile attempt to resurrect his lame 1992 campaign, Bush tried to fill the vision gap by referring to a past "vision" of the sunrise of American promise he had when he was plucked from the Pacific as a downed fighter pilot in the Second World War just as in 1988, in his inaugural address, he had sentimentally kindled a future vision "to make kinder the face of the nation and gentler the face of the world" nursed by "a thousand points of light."

Although Bush failed to fill the vision gap in the 1992 election, he did leave us to ponder his legacy of "the vision thing." This book's title was chosen from his aptly awkward attempt to link political reality with archetypal vision – not to mock George Bush, but to acknowledge the awesome difficulty of uniting vision with reality. In truth, "the vision thing" experienced at a personal and collective level attempts to bring together the political and mythological realms through psychological experience. "Vision" is seen with the mind's or spirit's eye and "thing" designates the most basic, concrete stuff of reality. "Vision" and "thing" do not fit comfortably together. It is the rare leader who can put "vision" and "thing" together in a believable way; it is the rare leader who can articulate a true vision that fits with real politics.

ORIGIN OF IDEA

The idea for this "vision thing" book grew out of a conversation I had with Senator Bill Bradley in 1989. Over dinner one night Senator Bradley asked about Joseph Campbell's lifelong study of mythology. Public interest in Campbell was peaking at the time, and Senator Bradley was curious both about Campbell's work itself and the increasing public attention given to mythological themes. He wanted to understand more about the importance of myth in human affairs and, specifically, what was currently capturing the public imagination about the study and insights of mythology. Our talk was not about myth in its popular use as "inaccurate fiction" but about how in some mysterious way a living myth establishes a meaningful link between man, nature, and spirit. In this use of the word, "myth" is the central story a people tells about itself to understand its beginnings, its purposes, and its place in a broader historical and cosmic order. At the heart of Senator Bradley's inquiry were the pragmatic American political questions: "What myth, now? What stories are people telling about themselves and our world now?"

INITIAL DREAM

The conversation with Senator Bradley stirred me deeply, and that night I had what Carl Jung called a "big dream." It seemed to be a comment on the relationship between collective consciousness, as expressed in political reality, and collective unconsciousness, as expressed in myth, vision and dream. I will offer the heart of the dream, though a "private" communication, because I believe that if we are serious about engaging what lies beneath the surface of our individual and collective lives, it is best to begin at home and because my home-made vision became a kind of guide, question, warning and meditation that I kept very much in mind as the themes of this book unfolded. Here is my dream's central section: "I am talking to an ancient sage about the meaning of the rapid changes taking place in the world as the millennium approaches. He has his hands on the skull of a black monastic nun from the early Christian era." The puzzling dream with its hints of an unfamiliar past political history, teased me with its elusive profundity. Over the years of gathering the pieces of *The Vision Thing* it constantly reminded me that the questions the authors of this book are asking are huge, not easily answered, and require a creative imagination that can embrace the profound changes in our political, economic, geographic, and even cosmological reality. The dream reminded me that such upheavals also marked the early Christian era and to my Jungian ears suggests a mystery surrounding something dark, feminine, spiritual and long removed from the world. With the advent of the millennium many prophets are coming forth with crystal-ball prophecies of what is in store for our civilization and planet. They shout at us with enormous conviction about the truth of their ready-made intuitions and fill our heads with utopian promises which are either technological or anti-technological. Black and white, boom or bust prophecies and strangely empty metaphors about our "need to prepare for the twenty-first century" suggest a poverty of ideas as we grapple with the awesomeness of a truly unknown and unenvisioned future.

One California Jungian analyst's meditation on the skull of a black nun from the early Christian era does not provide any better crystal ball. Rather, such a meditation assures us only of the certainty of death; underlines the turmoil and upheaval of a world in rapid transition; and behind it all, evokes the eternal presence of religious mystery. The image, moreover, moves beyond a Christian, Western perspective on these matters. Like a Tibetan monk contemplating a skull in daily religious practice, my "sage" seems to suggest that we can look upon the skull both in the horror of human destruction and as a reminder that death is always our companion in life. As Hamlet knew, our individual lives will soon end in death, and the life of our times will shortly be but a skull in the hands of future generations. Our times are fleeting. Do they matter at all? How can we make them count?

NEGATIVE CAPABILITY

Thankfully, my solution has not been to rededicate myself with firmer, twentieth century resolve, to the pursuit of a unitary saving vision. Rather, in the spirit of the dream, this book seeks to cultivate the art of not knowing. It is the same art that Keats[1] urged for the poet – what he called "the negative capability," by which he meant the deepest receptivity, free from any overriding insistence on a particular point of view. This attitude is quite different from that taken by those who address us with their daily, instant interpretations of political and cultural life. Reality becomes a toy in their hands in which the meaning of events appears to precede the actual unfolding of the events themselves. Perhaps this is the shadow side of our so-called information technology. The more information we receive, the less we really know. It is small wonder that skeptical deconstruction has become the dominant philosophical stance of our times. Retreat into an absurdist position of refusing to ascribe meaning to anything seems like the only reasonable way to escape the tyranny of spin doctors' instant analysis. Perhaps more useful in the long run will not be the refusal to give a definite meaning to anything, but the hard effort of holding open the door to meaning in the hope that it may reveal itself in time. Without that, we are stuck with accepting instantaneous meaning or its opposite, across-the-board meaninglessness. "Negative capability" as receptivity urges holding open the space of not knowing long enough for something authentic to emerge. When we pursue an inquiry about our collective mythological, psychological, and political future, it is an attitude worth cultivating.

The common observation of those who study myth and history is that it is almost impossible to know the myth or myths of the times one is living through. If this is true, why should we even bother to ask the basic question of this book, "What myth(s) now?" One answer is, because the question has already posed itself to us. Perhaps one of the greatest prerogatives of being human is the right to take up unanswerable questions, posed by the facts of our lives. For example, many of us who came of age in the 1960s shared an almost tribal assumption that we were participating in the birth of a new era and that we had even glimpsed the outlines of its universal mythology. How different that time and even the myths we thought we were giving birth to appear now through the rather short lens of a few decades! Very few people of my generation know more than that they aren't in Kansas anymore. Thus, the idea behind this book which began with a straightforward question from a thoughtful politician – "What myth now?" – can also be phrased, "Where are we now?" This is the kind of question that can only be answered through dialogue. The actual work on this book began when the politician's reasonable question engaged the nonrational dream response of a psychiatrist trained to read such compensatory, unconscious communications in the tradition of Jungian analytical psychology. This first exchange between two very different kinds of mindset establishes the basic paradoxes and tensions that the book sets out to explore: conscious and unconscious, politics and myth, reality and vision – all mediated by the psychology of individuals sharing and trying to envision the same collective psyche.

MYTH, POLITICS, PSYCHE

The basic assumption of the book is that there are deep, highly charged, unexplored relationships between mythological or archetypal reality, psychological reality, and political reality. I have sometimes pictured this as a continuum:

myth/archetype ◄——► psyche ◄——► politics

At one end of the spectrum is the purely mythological or archetypal realm with its grand themes of death and rebirth, inner transformation and outer renewal, man and God. At the other end of the imaginary spectrum is the realm of everyday politics with its power plays, deals, persona appearances and deceptions, and a quite substantial knowledge of the practical world. Politicians are at least as adept at shrewdly engaging the reality of the "shadow" as analytical psychologists – even if they do not use the same jargon. In the model I am proposing, psyche sits between and mediates the exchange between myth and politics. Individual fears, aspirations and conflicts are part of this psyche. Psyche also has a collective aspect which carries the conscious and unconscious concerns and values of the group in which the individual lives. It is the tension and interaction between myth, psyche, and politics in the world that this book proposes to explore. In a way, there is nothing new about this exploration. The Upanishads, the Koran, the Bible and just about every other sacred scripture of the world's great religions wrestle continuously with the theme of man as a political animal against the backdrop of deep archetypal encounters with spirit.

So the questions addressed by this book are at once old, timeless and contemporary. Perhaps what makes its way of exploring them new is the psychological effort to render a little more conscious the nature of the tension and interaction between mythological and political realities. Intuition tells us that such relationships are everywhere, nowhere more pronounced than in our culture's media intermingling of myth, politics, and entertainment. The "American dream," for instance, is still a vital myth with deep political resonance. The underlying linkage is self-evident. Indeed, we hardly question that much of American politics is deliberately dressed up to give the appearance of fulfilling the material and social promises of that "dream." What is not self-evident is the conscious teasing out of the relationship between the mythic "dream" and the actual politics because most people are not accustomed to think of myth, psychology, and politics at the same time. But, in my thinking, myth, psychology, and politics are so entwined in the collective psyche – often quite unconsciously – that we might even think of them as bound together in some kind of marriage. Yet, strangely, as with the factors influencing other marriages we have trouble articulating clearly the relationship between them or even talking about them at the same time. The expedient and practical do not mix easily or naturally with the symbolic and inner. And yet myth does not exist without embodiment in politics, and politics always has deep, unconscious origins in the stories of a people and its leaders.

There is an inherent opposition between the kinds of people who are most interested in the inner dynamic of archetypal reality and those interested in everyday politics, just as there is an inherent tension between mythological thinking and political thinking. Both have different modes of perception, of apprehending the world. They represent different ways of being in the world. Put someone who sees the world archetypally in a room with a politician, and the dialogue quickly dissolves into misunderstanding and confusion. For instance, quite savvy and articulate students of politics and history can turn quite dumb when the conversation explores the realm of myth and psyche, as if these "spacey" ideas have nothing to do with the everyday affairs of man. Real discussion quickly breaks down into mutual distrust. Those who are archetypal and psychological in their thinking display disdain for the mundane machinations of the politician, and those who are political in their thinking perceive (quite accurately) that these more rarefied psychologically minded thinkers do not understand how the real world of human deal-making works.

THE COLLECTIVE PSYCHE

Another factor in the tangled relationship between myth and politics is the notion of the "collective psyche." At the heart of this book is the idea that the tension between myth and politics is mediated, intensified, and transmitted by a psyche that is somehow shared by all of us and articulated by a psychology that we hold in common. Carl Jung wrote: "the human psyche is not a self-contained and wholly individual phenomenon, but also a collective one" (Jung 1928: 7–235).[2] The word "psyche" derives from the Greek, meaning "soul," and usually "psyche", like soul, is conceived of as an individual phenomenon. It was Jung's discovery that not only is the individual psyche real, but that there is also a living "collective psyche" which arises out of the group or "collective" experience of human beings, and that this collective psyche has an objective reality beyond the interpretations accorded it by different individuals. It is important to note that the collective psyche is not just real in groups. The collective psyche is alive and operative in the individual as well as a transpersonal force to be reckoned with. Just as the individual psyche gives expression to the ripples of deep personal yearnings, one can picture the collective psyche as providing the strong currents and tides in the ocean of common human concerns. Like ocean currents, they are often imperceptible, unfathomable and moving in conflicting directions. Occasionally, however, collective trends coalesce into large and unpredictable waves that dramatically alter the course of human affairs.

An example of such a potent wave moving through the collective psyche and landing differently in different groups of individuals is the contemporary struggle over what kind of leaders we want to have. A good argument is being made that at least a piece of our present crisis in political leadership is about what kind of "father" (or "mother") should lead us at this time: firm or loose, principled or responsive. There are some authorities whose leadership is solidly rooted in principle and order. They are firm, sometimes stern – but always ground their authority in principle, as befits the father archetype that informs their "patriarchal" behavior. Margaret Thatcher was such a "father." There is another more modern type of "father" whose strength is based on a fluid sensitivity to the changing needs of the family and community. Loose and flexible, his or her fatherhood is based less on principle than on responsiveness. It is fascinating how Republicans (like George Bush) are talking about "compassionate conservatism" and Democrats are trying to show that they are firm on economic matters while still being responsive to social issues. Both parties are trying to find the right balance of firm and loose "fathers", leaders who will be both principled and responsive in their models of leadership. Obviously, the image of leadership in the collective psyche is in flux, and it lands in the individual psyche with different resonances, depending on the kind of fatherhood (and motherhood) one has had, not had, or yearned for.

There are many people who do not believe in an individual psyche, much less a collective psyche. For them, the individual psyche is a Romantic, and before that neo-Platonic hangover soon to be replaced by the rational Aristotlean coupling of neuropsychology and psychopharmacology. Within such scientized monikers, "psyche" is becoming buried in mind's neurology and pharmacology. By scientific rationalists, the idea of a "collective psyche" is often dismissed as mystical nonsense. Those who reject the notions of an individual and collective psyche argue that the attitudes, moods, and values of the population are more accurately explained by the rational social sciences of economics, politics, and sociology which can be measured and tracked by statistics. "It's the economy, stupid!" is sometimes their kneejerk explanation for what is most affecting the electorate. Given the importance of money in our lives, this reduction of political motivation to a material cause makes sense. But not always. The "collective psyche" has a spiritual, *zeitgeist* dimension that is not reducible to sociology or economics. Ask any good advertising man, stock market analyst, political pollster, or sportscaster what moves large groups of people. They may not call it the "collective psyche" by name, but they will allude to an ineffable, mysterious, powerful, non-rational force with currents that run strong and deep and which, more often than not, behaves like an unpredictable beast from the watery depths. Occasionally the beast displays its own uncanny wisdom, even if more often it behaves with the mindless force of a large group of adolescents bombarded with hormones. Yet it always has an idea or value that seems to be energizing it. Analytical psychologists call this the "collective psyche."

VISION AND REALITY

Another characteristic of the relationship between myth and politics is that a tension between vision and reality seems to be wired into the psyche. This inherent conflict is experienced universally in the individual and in the collective or social order. One can say that it is archetypal in the sense that typically patterned behaviors, images and deep feelings emerge in response to the activation of the conflict between vision and reality.

In the life of the individual, for example, most of us have an internal image or vision of what is beautiful. I had a view from our house that looked towards a mountain without a single man-made structure visible. When a neighbor built a new road that cut a white cement line right through the heart of that uninterrupted view, not only was the view of the mountain itself altered, but my inner image of beauty was violated. Such injuries affect one's sense of well-being and lead to some predictably intense emotional reactions. All of us encounter such conflicts between vision and reality every day and throughout our lives – when our vision of what we should be as children or parents collides with what we know to be the reality of our being a child or parent, or when our vision of a "ripe old age" runs up against age's often harsh realities, and even on a daily basis when the fair play that we envision for our roadways is forced to endure the heedless interactions and rude exchanges we in fact discover on our highways.

If the vision we have of our individual lives is challenged at every phase of development by the reality of our natural abilities and the opportunities available to us, so too the conflict between vision and reality is exponentially amplified in collective and political life. The best and worst politicians appeal to what we envision to be a good society or even a "great society." That visionary appeal to an inner image is almost always undermined by the reality of what is possible and real. How many promises of the visionary are made to us everyday through the seductively powerful assault on our collective psyche by images from television, films and especially savvy advertisers who have the art of passing off the visionary as sellable reality down to a science? The impact occurs at subliminal levels where we are conditioned to believe in these promises. The inevitable experience of the gap between these visionary promises and the reality we discover expresses itself in frustration and anger which can lead to either disillusionment and withdrawal or a mobilization to action and the desire "to do something about it." The tension between vision and reality is as wired into the collective psyche as it is to the individual psyche, whether we get our primal stories and images from the village elders of old or the modern transmitters of our shared stories – movies, television, newspapers, and the internet.

Many politicians make a career out of exploiting the tension between vision and reality by rubbing our faces in the discrepancy between what has been promised in visionary terms and what has been delivered in real terms. Others try to help us see and close the gap by offering viable links between the visionary and the real. Perhaps the best of times is when there is a shared coherent vision of the natural, social, and religious order that provides ongoing meaning to the realities of everyday life – however harsh they may be. (The way the country gathered together to make sure "the system worked" in the Watergate crisis might be an example.) One might say that in those times the inherent tension between vision and reality is creative and that the realities of everyday life neither mock unattainable promises of the visionary nor undermine the vision of the whole. Perhaps the worst of times is when a shared vision of the world is disintegrating and the demands of everyday reality are intolerable. (The riots in Chicago at the time of the 1968 Democratic Convention were an example of this.) And perhaps the most exciting of times is when there are competing visions of the world order and the demands of reality are not so harsh and limited that the freedom to experiment is restricted. We may be in such a time now.

In our so-called "postmodern" life rarely is there a shared vision in the collective psyche of what would be best for the social order, and often there is profound disagreement even on what is real. When a President of the United States is reduced to defending himself in public with the statement, "It depends on what 'is' means," it might signal that it is no longer safe to place much faith in our conventional sense of reality. "Is" is one of the most basic things we can say about reality. With little shared vision or even consensus on what is real, the gap between vision and reality widens and we are left to the national pastime of carping disbelief. We indulge in visionary expectations and hyperbole (our fantastic celebrities and super bowls and academy awards) and then delight in the collapse of what we have built up in our collective imagination and what we think reality has delivered to us. Beneath this split between vision and reality, it is important to keep in mind that the most enduring myths as embodied in the world's great religions – Hinduism, Buddhism, Muslim, Jewish, and Christian – have always been able to speak to the deepest yearnings, the deepest sufferings, and the deepest joys of large groups of people. The enduring myths are able to bridge the inherent tension between vision and reality. They are able to connect the deepest truths of human vision to the most mundane levels of reality.

Having affirmed (1) the complex intermingling of myth, politics, and psyche, (2) the reality of the collective psyche, and (3) the inherent tension between vision and reality, it is timely to give an example from our recent political past of how these forces play themselves out. I have discovered that while many can agree in principle with the notion of the interpenetration of myth, psyche, and politics, it is harder to find a consensus in interpretation when one actually examines a specific case history. Everyone seems to bring their own myth and psyche to controversial political conflicts, which perhaps only further illustrates the powerful interweaving of these forces.

MYTH, POLITICS AND PSYCHE IN THE CASE OF HEALTHCARE REFORM

Bill Clinton surprised many people when he came out of nowhere to challenge George Bush in the 1992 presidential elections. Clinton's fresh face and new energy was in stark contrast to George Bush's tired inability to articulate a domestic policy and his failure to convincingly address what he himself called "the vision thing." Clinton's campaign effort gained substantial momentum as he rode a popular wave of disgust with health insurance companies that coupled with his timely call for national healthcare reform. It seemed inexcusable to the aroused electorate that close to twenty (or was it thirty?) million employed Americans did not have basic health insurance. The collective psyche was mobilized for real change and Clinton capitalized on this profound shift in mood to win the election. Emboldened by the mandate for reform and the emerging new myth of men and women as truly equal partners in work/leadership as well as marriage, Clinton turned over the day-to-day task of bringing about healthcare reform to his wife shortly after the election. Together, they vowed to achieve one hundred per cent universal healthcare, not ninety-five per cent.

By many accounts however, the Clintons along with their chief architect of reform, Ira Magaziner, were arrogant, did not listen to their natural allies and refused to compromise even when they were close to achieving most of their goals. The brief window of opportunity for significant reform slammed shut. The insurance companies, which had been on the defensive, were let off the hook and they simply redoubled their formidable resistance to any significant reform. The aroused electorate sank back into apathy. The push for reform collapsed without any tangible accomplishments.

To link the colossal failure of Clinton's national healthcare proposal to the psychic inflation of a relatively young man over-identified with the hero myth takes a little explaining. Clinton wanted to be the dragon slayer. The dragon was clearly the collective power of insurance companies, drug companies, and all the vastly powerful economic interests that were motivated mainly by the desire to preserve profits, not necessarily to provide quality care for the entire population. Like every hero caught in the grandiose self-idealization of an archetypal inflation, Clinton promised and believed that he could slay the dragon and deliver a boon to his suffering nation – in this case, the heroic accomplishment of freeing up healthcare from the clutches of entrenched financial interests and delivering it to a "universal" population. This was the vision that filled many Americans with new hope from the man from Hope.

It is a sad truth that inherent in visionary politics is the tendency towards psychological inflation or grandiosity – a shared grandiosity on the part of the leader and the people. In this case, the inflation turned out to be of mythic proportions and ended in disastrous political miscalculations. This was the reality. The potential creative tension between vision and reality could not hold, and ended in collapse. I think it is reasonable to suggest as a psychological interpretation that not only did Clinton himself become inflated but the Clintons as a couple became inflated, i.e. the couple became caught in the power of an emerging new myth of equal and shared power between men and women (see Peter Rutter, Chapter 15). Together, they suffered the familiar archetypal pattern of such inflations – namely, soaring, visionary dreams ending in total collapse. The emotional and political price that the President, his wife and his administration paid was severe. Many who had harnessed their dreams to the vision of universal healthcare were profoundly disappointed and disillusioned. They held the Clintons personally responsible for the failure of the healthcare reform initiative. Whatever the causes of the collapse might have been, it all came crashing to the ground as many such idealizations of leaders buoyed and fueled by the electorate's dreams are destined to do. The emotional hangover of such mythic visions linked to political failure is anger, cynicism, boredom, and disaffection. The only real measurable change that came from the promise of healthcare reform was a significant but transitory drop in the stock prices of drug companies which bore the brunt of Clinton's initial assault on the dragon of the healthcare establishment.

Several plausible interpretations can be made about the failure of the healthcare initiative, the role of the Clintons in that failure, and which archetypal mythic forces played themselves out in the political struggle. More than one mythic tale can be operating simultaneously in complex political battles. For instance, the epic Grail quest tells of a kingdom which is suffering, a fisher king with an unhealing wound, and a knight who goes in search of the Holy Grail to bring a cure to both. This myth of wounded would-be healer suits the Clinton mythopolitical picture as much as the hero's task of slaying the dragon. It does not take a big stretch of the imagination to think of Clinton as Parsifal going in search of the Grail to bring healing to the kingdom (the crisis in national healthcare) and his own wounded father king (the presidency). In our modern incarnation of the myth, the quest seems to have failed and both the kingdom and the king are still very much in need of healing. Such is the complex intermingling of myth, psyche, and politics in the world – with more than a little economics thrown in.

CIRCUMAMBULATIO

Like politicians, analytical psychologists walk around the same material over and over again. Analytical psychologists call it "circumambulatio." Politicians call it the "campaign platform." Returning to the same issue over and over again is part of the slow digestion process of real integration – whether it be an individual integrating the symbolic material of a big dream over a lifetime or a nation integrating a racially divided population over many generations.

In that spirit, let us return to the starting point of this chapter – my dream of the skull from the early Christian era. The dream begins as a meditation on our own current global transformation with the advent of the millennium. In a sense, the chapters in this book taken as a whole can be viewed as an extended group meditation on the dream image of the black monastic nun's skull – reflections on the dark, mysterious realm of the collective psyche, its past violent upheavals, current traumas and future course. Gazing backward, we see that the early Christian era was a time of enormous turmoil – political, social, economic, spiritual. Even man's view of the cosmos was in flux. We too live in such an age, and the relationship between our deepest beliefs about ourselves and how we should structure our political life (even how to pay for our political life) raises many more questions than there are answers. How do we conceive of ourselves as a local, national, or global community when we have just learned that our sun is only one of fifty billion such stars in the Milky Way, and that the Milky Way itself is only one of more than fifty billion galaxies in the known universe? While our material resources are rapidly dwindling, our economy appears to be strong. The stock-market – especially high-flying technology stocks – is defying all traditional standards of valuation, and there is a healthy fear that what is so high may come crashing down. "Up and down, big and small" play tricks with our sense of value about money, our countries' role in the world, and our shared sense of time and space. Almost daily we are discovering more about how small we are in the vastness of space and how interdependent we are on other nation states – truly a large dose of shifting perspectives for a young nation on a tiny planet.

With the rate of change itself rapidly accelerating and many of life's decisions and problems becoming ever more complex, many desperately search for clearer and simpler answers which are often served up on the twin silver platters of political promises and religious panacea. Single-issue fundamentalism – whether it be clothed in religious or political dogma or both – becomes the order of the day on the right and the left, leaving a beleaguered and bland middle to wade through the muck in uncertainty. Over-simplification seems to be a human being's best and final defense against overwhelming complexity. C.G. Jung said many decades ago that modern man is in search of a myth(s) to live by. Perhaps today it might be more correct to say that postmodern man is in search of a deconstructed myth(s) to live by. Such a search for integrative meaning frequently takes a political form or at least dresses itself up as if it were a political problem – a sort of metaphysical cross-dressing. Actually, the metaphor of cross-dressing is quite apt for a discussion of myth and politics because there is considerable identity confusion when we try to decide what is myth and what is politics and which is dressing up as which. The right to life/pro-abortion debate is a perfect example of how powerful and destructive this religious/political single-issue fundamentalism can become. All of life's complexities get condensed into and filtered through this profoundly disturbing debate and in that crucible, we are asked to choose as if there is only one, clear simple answer.

MYTH AND RITUAL

Let's return to the word myth. Myth's bad name comes from the titillating tales that are used to adorn or denigrate politicians' campaigns, celebrities' lives, nation states' ambitions, or the next-door neighbors' behavior. "Myth" used in its colloquial meaning, usually signifies a misleading fiction or even a willfully distorted falsehood. Our use of it here might lead the reader to conclude: "I know the theme of this book. Politicians can't be trusted. They win votes by weaving myths about themselves and what they are going to do for us if they are elected. They poison the airwaves with tales of the sordid and evil wrongdoing of their opponents. It is all just myths. This book is going to explore the myths that are today's politics." (A previous book with just this aim was called *Reagan: The Man, The Myth.*)

Here, however we are after a different level of mythopoetic perception from that of the false and superficial tales that shower every aspect of contemporary life – politics, sports, entertainment, business. Myth at this deeper level can be understood as the central, unifying story that a group of people tells about itself – about its origins, its place in time and space, its trials and sufferings, and its means of sustaining, renewing, and re-creating itself through its vision of its role in the cycles of history, nature, and spirit. Myth at this level provides the foundation of ceremonial life, social life, and political life.

Politics, for example, is truly gripping when the myth of the times and its political processes are in creative relationship to one another. The Kennedy brothers – Jack with his grace and vision, Bobby with his gutsy existentialism – tapped into the potent mythological undercurrents of the 1960s and helped channel this energy into political activism for a brief, creative burst that ended in the destruction of many lives and dreams. The opposite of this kind of potent alchemy between myth and politics is equally true. Nothing is more enervating to individuals than when the political processes of the body politic and the underlying stirrings of the collective psyche are not authentically related to one another.

Consider for a moment what I have come to call "the politics of empathy." With the growth of psychology as a popular frame of reference, our leaders have been learning that people want them to have feelings and, as a result, more and more politicians have been willing to reveal a feminine or feeling side of their personalities. There is something disturbing about this, because the capacity to manipulate deep emotions and images – what can be called archetypes – has always been the stock in trade of politicians and mass entertainers, who share a certain demagoguery. (Steven Spielberg and Bill Clinton are the perfect couple in this regard.) On the one hand, it is heartening that the collective psyche is moving towards a more genuine expression of compassion and empathy. The problem is that the present political enactment of this feminine archetypal potential ("I feel your pain") doesn't ring true. The words are right but the tears are a crocodile's. Put another way, the persona of empathy is becoming part of the job of political and business leadership. This has given birth to a national industry of politicians and newscasters who serve as "disaster compassion consultants!" Their major function seems to be wearing the mask of compassion at an instant's notice when a plane crashes, a storm hits, or the country witnesses another murderous rampage in horror and fascination. In turn, our leaders as "compassion consultants" receive either higher ratings or more votes or both as a reward for their public display of empathy. As political leaders consciously seek "to connect" with the populace through "the politics of empathy," we become more and more aware of the real "disconnect" between our political processes and deeper mythological yearnings to link man, nature, and spirit. Political pronouncements become empty sound bytes, and fewer and fewer people feel gripped by an authentic intersection of myth and politics. Some politicians have even learned to use the word "vision" as if the repetitious magical incantation of the word itself will create the belief in the electorate that they actually have a vision of the future. But the underlying stirrings of the collective psyche and current political processes are rarely linked in an authentic connection that is believable to the general population.

The same can be said of ceremonial life which is based on mythic foundations. It can be argued that the central collective ritual events of late twentieth-century America have become The Super Bowl, The Academy Awards, and the World Series, which are often more hype than substance, more letdown than exhilarating, more hollow than transforming. At a less grandiose level of modern ceremonial life, there has been a revolution in the conduct of marriages, funerals and almost every other significant threshold ceremony in the past few decades that reflects the desire to link significant life passages in a real and personal way to age-old spiritual traditions. Many people no longer tolerate ceremonies that fail to honor and bring together both the personal and archetypal dimensions of life. They insist on a real connection between myth, psyche, and the important passages of their own lives. When politics fails to make that same connection, people abandon politics.

Women and men are born story-tellers. When their stories are told and enacted in ritual often enough (the Roman numerals of the Super Bowl aspire through their repetition to attain this status), they become legends. And, if these legends in time become the spoken and unspoken backbone of a community's understanding of itself, we are truly in the realm of myth. A group's story of itself – its relation to nature and to the sacred, how its people are to relate to one another, and sometimes, more importantly, how its people are to relate to those who are not part of its beginnings – gets told over and over again and becomes the central thread that binds generations together and gives them meaning and purpose. Whether it be the Jewish or Christian myth, America's twin myths of rugged individualism and the "melting-pot" which have fused into the elusive American-dream marriage of capitalism and democracy, or the apparently dying Marxist–Leninist myth of Communism, these stories become the driving, collective forces in the minds and hearts of its people.

Women and men are also born political animals. As long as they have been telling their stories, they have also been enacting or fighting for their deepest beliefs and yearnings in political action. The contemporary language and discourse of politics seems barren and empty – perhaps occasionally riveting in the same way that we attend to or studiously avoid an O.J. Simpson saga, or witness in awe the enormous roller-coaster of energy that propels a Newt Gingrich's rise and fall from popular grace. Whether it be the "New Covenant" or the "Contract with America," the promises of political platforms are undeliverable, while the pressures fueling the promises are enormous and uncontainable. Our cranked-up society with its incessant emphasis on peak performance creates ever-increasing expectations for athletic achievement, entrepreneurial creativity, stock-market valuations, global high-technology networking, and even higher and higher spiritual attainment. Politicians as performers become empty vessels for filtering these insatiable appetites.

Shards

This project began with a question and a big dream a decade ago and, as I was searching for the right note to sound at the end of this introduction, another moving image emerged from the psyche. The new dream further oriented me to the problem of looking for the underlying myth(s) that might help draw a clearer picture of the contemporary relationship between myth and politics:

> Wearing the robes of Asian Buddhist monks, I am part of an organized tour of Nepal or Tibet. Bill Bradley is a member of the group and is studying the sites with great interest and focus. We enter a vast underground space and soon I get separated from the group and wander around alone, lost and in fear. There is a sense of endless spaces of all sizes and shapes. One of them is a vast sacred place with a vaulted ceiling in the center – built centuries ago. Finally, I stumble out into the daylight, totally alone and profoundly disoriented. I see an information booth staffed by little old lady docents. They see how confused I am as I begin to empty my pockets of many glass shards that I have collected as I wandered from one space to another. The docents seem to know where they are and want to help orient me. As I look up behind the booth, I see signs pointing to Mount Everest and other places and I begin to get a sense of where I am.

Immediately on awakening, I remembered seeing a strikingly beautiful and powerful piece of sculpture by the modern German artist, Anselm Kiefer. Entitled *Breaking of the Vessels*, it is Kiefer's attempt to make sense of the Holocaust as symbolized by *Kristallnacht*, the infamous night when the Nazis smashed the glass out of the windows of Jewish-owned stores in November 1938. Kiefer's art wrestles with the awful intersection of myth and politics in the Nazi era by linking *Kristallnacht* to the creation myth of the Jewish mystical tradition of the *Lurianic Kabbalah*. He has constructed a large sculpture of steel, copper, and hundreds of shattered shards of glass that spill out on to the gallery floor. The sculpture evokes the *Kabbalistic* vision of the "breaking of the vessels," in which the original oneness of creation is shattered into broken fragments. Kiefer physically frames the political atrocity of *Kristallnacht* in the context of this primal breaking of the vessels. The fragments simultaneously carry the divine sparks and symbolize the introduction of evil into creation. The shards are only fragments of what was originally whole.

Senator Bradley's question years ago began my search for a unifying collective myth(s) that might give meaning to contemporary political life. But the dream suggests that in undertaking a tour into the collective unconscious, I become confused, lost and frightened as I travel through vast and tiny underground places. What I find in my pockets as I emerge above ground are little bits and pieces of the divine spark from many traditions, but none of them is whole – although as broken fragments they suggest that there was a time when they were part of a whole. What is orienting, paradoxically, is the knowledge that: (1) there isn't a contemporary unifying, collective myth; (2) there are fragments of what was once whole to be discovered in many places; (3) it is useless to look for a unifying myth in one place or tradition – like politics alone; (4) but one shouldn't give up on the fragments, which allude to an underlying spiritual image of wholeness, bits and pieces of which may be found in many places. Does Mount Everest still stand for that wholeness of Self, in spite of the pollution that now tracks right up to its summit?

STRUCTURE OF THE BOOK

With this further dream message in mind, I want to introduce the vision for the structure of this book. Each author can be thought of as picking up a different shard of glass, from a different place or a different perspective, and telling us what they have discovered.

Part I Leadership and vision in myth and politics

The first part of the book explores the relationship between mythic vision and political reality. It is the challenge of this section to suggest a creative and positive relationship between myth and politics and in the arenas of vision and leadership, despite how difficult it might be for many to believe that leaders have real vision or that myth and politics have much more to do with each other than demonstrating their shared underlying bankruptcy.

Part II The one and the many in myth and politics

Whether we speak in terms of race, gender, economy, psyche, or religious beliefs, we can all feel the pull to experience reality in some sort of profound, age-old tension between what can be called "the one and the many." On the side of "the one" is the deep thirst for a unifying vision of an integrated planet in the face of relentless global homogenization of economy, place, and sensibility. On the side of "the many" is the plea for the sanctity of diversity amidst the awful reality of disintegration at every level of experience from individual, to family, to community, to nation, to the God-image itself.

The many

The more positive side of "the many" we call "diversity," where we dream that all people can sit down at any number of the banquet tables of life and choose from vast and varied menus – that indigenous, unique, and separate cultures can coexist, or commingle, or at the least leave one another alone. At its best, diversity is a dream of difference, respect, cooperation. At its silliest, diversity becomes a euphemistic slogan of insipid political correctness. Enormous psychic and political energy, locally and globally, centers around the theme of diversity whether it concerns the Aborigines in Australia, the blacks in Africa or America, homosexual people throughout the world, women in the workplace, the disabled in public places – all the minorities as defined by whatever differences one can think of. The shadow or darker side of diversity we call "disintegration" which expresses itself in the fragmentation of families, the breakdown of nations, the rise of tribalism, fundamentalism, and factionalism at every level of social organization whether it be in a Yugoslavia or a Rwanda or on a freeway or in a high school in America. This disintegration ultimately results in ungovernable societies without any agreed-upon sanctions. We have come to recognize and fear this phenomenon, and more and more reference is being made to it in the talk of a "Civil Society" which, in fact, reflects the decline of civil society. So much is now being said of the civil society because so much of contemporary life has become so uncivil, and many fear that we are heading towards a global "Balkanization" – the breakdown of civil society on a planetary scale. Apocalyptic visions – the ultimately uncivil world disorder – are the inevitable product of the tendency towards disintegration. With apocalyptic visions and their attendant imagery of chaos, violence and evil we move into the archetypal dimension, and the chapters in this section will move back and forth from myth to psyche to politics.

The one

The positive side of "the one" we call "integration" in which we can imagine the diverse forces in the individual psyche, the nation, the global body politic or even the God-image itself coming together into some sort of differentiated whole. We might go so far as to dream of an individuated planet that is "one." There is a shadow side of this dream of "one" as well. It takes shape in a dark vision of mass homogenization dominated by a global market mentality that reduces all human differences to a "bottom line" formula. Mass media, mass transportation, mass politics, can all reflect this diminished sensibility of life reduced to the lowest common denominator. The frightening vision of "homogenization" is a life of managed care – in health, education, job training, opportunity, culture, and even religious belief. Sameness rules, and that is why the bleak prophetic vision of the world becoming a global "franchise" so haunts us as we travel down any main street in America. It makes *The Man in the Gray Flannel Suit* from the 1950s seem innocuous by comparison.

THE TOUR

What is the collective unconscious brewing up for us as a way of finding meaning in the twenty-first century? This book is a grand tour in time and space of myth and politics in the world as seen through the psyche's eyes of "the one and the many." In these essays, bits and pieces of recombinant visionary myths and political realities can be seen to scatter the landscape of the so-called "global village" like so many shards of Kiefer's *Breaking of the Vessels*. Thoughtful inspection of these shards reveals a recurrent tension between diversity/disintegration and integration/homogenization. The most optimistic vision for the twenty-first century would be a synthesis of the positive aspect of the "many" (diversity) with the positive aspect of the "one" (integration).

But it is highly uncertain whether such a desirable outcome can be attained. The line-up of political possibility runs from the horrors of resurgent ethnic animosities in the Balkans through the flickering hope for accommodation in Northern Ireland to the remarkable, if still fragile, transformation of South Africa. Cutting across the axis of political possibilities is a psychological spectrum that ranges from the commodified dehumanized global trading zone where everything has a price and nothing has a value to a sphere of intensely humanizing peace and compassion, exemplified by the teachings of the fourteenth Dalai Lama.

As the writers in this collection demonstrate, all of these options are alive and vigorous in the world that is now home to more than seven billion of us. At the start of the twenty-first century, the challenge is to value the mythic dimension of life, to nurture the psyche in each individual and every community, and to embrace the leadership that will energize us to choose correctly. It is as true now as it was when the Biblical prophet first proposed it more than three thousand years ago that: "Where there is no vision, the people perish" (Proverbs, chapter 29, verse 18).

NOTES

1 *Oxford Dictionary of Quotations*: Keats quote #21 from letter to his brothers, G. and T. Keats, letter 32, 21 December 1817, reading: "Negative capability, that is, when a man is capable of being in uncertainties, mysteries, doubts, without any irritable reaching after fact and reason."
2 C.G. Jung (1928) "Collective Psyche," *Collected Works*, vol. 7, par. 235.

Part I

Leadership and vision in myth and politics

Foreword

Thomas B. Kirsch

From the origins of psychoanalysis to the later development of analytical psychology, myth has played a central role in depth psychological theory. For Freud it was the myth of Oedipus which was seen as the universal in the child's development. Jung, a decade later, found that behind the dream images of the individual and the hallucinations of the psychotic, there existed a collective level of the psyche which was best described in mythopoetic terms. For the next fifty years Jung's research led him to study various mythological systems which corroborated his hypothesis of the collective psyche and archetypal theory. In the latter part of his life he focused his attention on western alchemy, as he discovered there the missing links between pagan mythology and the dreams of the modern individual.

However, both for Freud and Jung, the investigation of myth was largely an intrapsychic event. From early on Freud gave up on the idea that the fantasies of his patients had any basis in outer reality. Today there is some controversy about these findings, as some investigators would like to reinterpret his conclusions. For Jung there was no question of the reality of the inner world. This was where the archetypes could be most intensely experienced, as described in the chapter entitled "Confrontation with the unconscious" in *Memories, Dreams, Reflections* (Jung 1963). Out of Jung's own experience he developed a technique called active imagination, where one consciously dimmed the ego so that the inner archetypal images could become more alive. At the same time he wrote on psychological types, where he outlined the differences between introversion and extraversion. Jung saw himself as an introvert, and all of his writings emphasized that aspect of personality development. Although theoretically, archetypal theory has both an inner and outer aspect, the inner subjective reality had much more reality for Jung than did its outer manifestation. Thus, those who followed Jung came to analytical psychology because of his exploration of the inner archetypal world.

Jung did have an extraverted side which led him into great difficulties. In 1934 he took over the presidency of the International General Medical Society for Psychotherapy, which at the time had a large Nazi contingent. To this day he has been criticized for his role in that organization during the decade leading up to the Second World War. When Jung was asked about his connection to the International General Medical Society for Psychotherapy, he said that he was a Swiss neutral trying to help German psychotherapy, and that he was completely "apolitical." This apolitical side was the norm among the first generation of Jungian analysts.

After Jung's death in 1961 there has been a gradual shift away from his extreme introverted bias. A major theoretical development has been proposed by Joseph Henderson in his book *Cultural Attitudes in Perspective* (Henderson 1984). Here he writes about the cultural level of the psyche which can be viewed as another layer of psychological reality between the individual and the archetypal. In this layer Henderson defines four different cultural attitudes: philosophic, religious, aesthetic, and social. Those with a well-developed social attitude will probably have a strong involvement in political life.

As analytical psychology has become more a part of the mainstream psychotherapeutic community, the extraverted aspect of life has taken on more meaning. Instead of only speaking about the inner king and queen, we now speak of modern political and cultural figures as representing royal archetypal images. Why else would there be so much interest in Princess Diana? Now archetypes are not only seen in dreams and visions, but they can be spoken of with regard to political, historical, and social figures and events. Jungian analysts like Andrew Samuels, Renos Papadopoulos, Jerome Bernstein, and Walter Odajnyk have all written books on politics in relation to various aspects of analytical psychology. Politics is no longer a taboo subject within the Jungian framework. The chapters in Part I of this book focus on vision and leadership as it appears in myth and politics.

BIBLIOGRAPHY

Henderson, Joseph (1984) *Cultural Attitudes in Perspective*, Toronto: Inner City Books.
Jung, C.G. (1963) *Memories, Dreams, Reflections*, New York: Pantheon Books.

Chapter 1

Reflections on myth, politics, and leadership

Senator Bill Bradley

I was a child of the Cold War. When I was eleven years old I made a diagram of my own private bomb shelter. In that diagram I had a place where I was going to keep my cot, a place where I was going to keep my favorite books, a place for my favorite food, and one for my basketball. My assumption was that after Armageddon there would still be basketball.

That Cold War is over now, along with all of the mythology we built up around it, including my personal mythology of a bomb shelter that would keep a special place for my basketball. The end of the Cold War has been a tremendous liberation from a fear that, while not constant, was often somewhere in the back of our minds. Things are largely better. But the end of the Cold War era poses a fundamental question for American politics: what is the nature of our leadership in the world? For more than fifty years our leadership came primarily from our proven ability to defend other nations from what was seen by many as not only an obvious military threat, but an actual living evil: the communist Soviet Union.

This was the context I had in mind when I first had a conversation with my friend Tom Singer about what happens when the negative organizing force of an entire society dissolves. Our conversation took place shortly after I had come back from a Senate intelligence committee tour of Europe. One of the most memorable moments had been a visit with our European Command in Stuttgart, Germany. As a demonstration of the new openness between our two societies, seven army officers described how they had just returned from observing Soviet military exercises at the invitation of the Gorbachev regime. Although I am certainly not clinically trained, as the officers described what they had seen, they appeared to me to be depressed. What they were describing was how easy it had been to get all at once what they had spent a lifetime learning the skills to obtain, either clandestinely or through piecing together millions of little bits and pieces of information. Suddenly, there it was, all there for everyone to look at.

It struck me that the end of the former Cold War really does have deep and far-reaching impacts on society as a whole. Over fifty years of war, first Hot, against Fascism, and then Cold, against Communism, has profoundly affected everyone's attitude – even all our mythologies – of the world. The impacts are far more than my childhood memory of the bomb shelter, or the fact that increasingly large chunks of our national wealth have been going to build weapons. Ever larger and larger segments of our intelligentsia have been working either to devise those weapons or as part of the large information-gathering apparatus we had to establish for spying on people, places, and circumstances that might conspire to bring about our own destruction. My childhood beliefs, the national defense budget, and our intelligence operations have all been justified by the pervasive rationale that we will have to protect ourselves against the threat of an evil force.

But the ramifications didn't just end there. Some of the related things that happened were unexpectedly good. We built the interstate highway system because of the premise that in war we would have to move vehicles and equipment quickly across the country. It was in reaction to Sputnik, and from the Defense Education Act, that many people I know got college educations. Sometimes there were less favorable consequences – such as the fact that in every American subdivision the streets are so wide. Did you ever think about the reason for that? The answer is that if the Cold War ever turned into a Hot War, every road had to be wide enough for two trucks travelling at fifty miles an hour to pass each other. But the roads are so wide and impersonal that they keep us apart. They impede our sense of community. For example, in cities there is something called "street smarts," which depend on a sense of alleys and byways. It's hard to develop "cul-de-sac" smarts in the suburbs.

The Cold War also hardened our perception of psychological reality into a rigid dualism. You were either against communism or you were not. You were either for a strong military deterrent or you were not. You were either a loyal American or you were not. This dualism infected our politics at all levels of thinking. In fact, the defining characteristic of our politics for so many years has been to say what we are against, not what we are for. What will define our view of reality in the future to replace this rigid either/or? For those who don't want to think through what we are for, and find it easier to be against something, a natural impulse has been to find another source of conflict. We are already seeing that ethnic and religious violence stand poised to replace communism as the world's largest negative force.

Today, the Iron Curtain – at least in Europe – is already being replaced by the "Velvet Curtain." Everything north and east of a line that extends through the Balkans and eastern Poland, down through Rumania and hooking around to Croatia is Roman Christendom. Everything west and south of that is Orthodox Christendom. Coming out from the south is Islam. At the moment, these forces converge in the former Yugoslavia with the tragedy that we see unfolding there. From this point of view, while nationalism is still important, it no longer has the same pull as ethnic religion, which may become the paradigm of future conflicts, and holocausts, in the world.

A counter view says that religious chauvinism and ethnic hatred will be replaced by the desire to become rich. Religious impulses cannot compete with people's desire to have more material things. Some argue that the economic myth of open economies and markets is also the only one that has been truly egalitarian. Either you make it or you don't. That myth is truly global. It accepts the premise of interdependence, and rewards not individualism but a systems approach. Thinking systemically, according to that view, is the only way to succeed in a world of highly competitive individuals and units.

When Tom Singer and I spoke, we raised another possibility. Could people still learn something by reference to the traditional myths that have previously given diverse people around the world meaning in their lives? Myths help to explain why things are the way they are by placing them in a context of the way they've always been.

That further possibility for constructing a post-Cold War point of view – of considering the myths of diverse people alongside the religious and economic forces governing their lives – raised two questions in my mind. Are those diverse myths simply unrelated stories that prepare us for a state of being that enhances our flexibility when we find ourselves living inside different circumstances? For example, Shell Oil Company says it did so well after the oil supply disruption of the mid-1970s because it had rejected "forecasting" long ago. That corporate view no longer took the past and arbitrarily ascribed certain criteria to measure its "performance" from which to predict the future. Instead, Shell engaged its management in a process of developing "possible" stories about the future. The thinking was that, with such stories in mind, there would be an element of flexibility that could accommodate the unforeseen, the truly unpredictable, the untoward event that no forecast could possibly have predicted by only looking at the past. When the oil supply disruption did come, Shell was operating within a story, not scrambling to rethink a failed forecast. Here's the difference: once you are in the story that's being told, you have to ask, "Well, how's this story going to turn out?" By thinking about your experience within a story that's being told, you also have to start thinking about the future in a different way.

Pursuing the possible relevance of myth to our world after the end of the Cold War and the collapse of the "Evil Empire" led me to take up another question with Tom, one rather closer to home: what myth might speak to a practicing politician who is not trained psychologically but who thinks, reads, and feels? My thoughts naturally turned to a version of the hero myth – the belief (often false) that the course of history can turn on one individual political figure. As Thomas Carlyle insisted, great men make a difference in the future of nations and the world. The way they make a difference is by force of will, cunning, and intelligence. They seem to personify their country at a particular time. I believe that there have been three American politicians who through their own lives succeeded in embodying the prominent struggle or trauma of the nation at that particular time.

Abraham Lincoln's embodiment of national trauma was very real. While he was in the White House, a relative of his wife was living with them. Her husband had been a Civil War Officer in the Confederate Army, killed by the northern troops that Lincoln commanded. Every day, when Lincoln came down for breakfast, sitting at the table was the personification of the enemy that he was fighting. Her presence reminded him of how personal the conflict was that he presided over. It underlined the fact that the clashing armies were destructive and deadly. It told him that the goal of war was to reunite. In that sense, he confronted, embodied, and felt moved to heal the national trauma every day.

Franklin Roosevelt did the same thing. In the midst of the Depression, still struggling against the after-effects of polio, he kept his spirits high, maintaining compassion and joy at the same time that he worked every day. His physical circumstances seemed to personify a nation that was flat on its back economically. Yet his jaunty spirit, his eternal optimism, his ability to roll his head back and laugh anew, said to all America that we too could pull through. It was what the country needed to see and to feel.

The last of my three examples would be Robert Kennedy, who through the experience of his brother's loss embodied the trauma that the country itself had experienced post-1963. The country was in bloody conflict abroad in the Vietnam War and at home with anti-war demonstrations on campuses and race riots in the cities. Bobby Kennedy addressed the roiling emotions around these conflicts with a vital understanding and compassion. Yet, unlike his brother Jack, Bobby's style was not particularly attractive. He risked telling the truth in staccato messages that often made people feel uncomfortable. He had the habit of going into an audience and telling people what they didn't want to hear because he knew that there was nothing to gain by failing to do that. He had lost his brother. We had lost a President. It was a new day. And a new chance. And he himself embodied that possibility.

So, there are these three – Lincoln, FDR, and RFK – people who have taken on the nation's woes and symbolically carried them through their own lives. Through their personal embodiment of the nation's struggle and suffering, they told us that they understand. But, there's a deeper, more urgent need, I think, than the rare emergence of the compassionate hero/leader, particularly if our goal is to perpetuate our democratic ideal of individual liberty, social equality, and representative government. For that, the hero myth becomes problematic. Bertolt Brecht in his play *Galileo* has a character who says, "Pity the nation that has no heroes." To which Galileo replies, "Pity the nation that needs them." This political observation reminds us that what happens in our lives as *citizens* is in some cases the foundation on which all else will rest.

Barbara Bush put it well when she said that "what happens in your house is more important than what happens in the White House." Our citizenship occurs within our families and local lives. And yet if you look at our civil society you find that disconnectedness and isolation are increasing and individuals are less willing to reach out to others. PTA membership is down; Red Cross membership is down; Elks, Lions down; JCs down. The traditional voluntary organizations that De Tocqueville said characterized the uniqueness of America have in the last thirty years fragmented and withered to a surprising degree. Some say that new organizations, such as those brought forth by the environmental movement, have taken the place of the old, more conventional organizations. But the new movements have focused primarily on themselves. They have not fostered face-to-face interactions with others, seeking to find what people have in common.

What has been lost is the public square, the place where people can come to work out consensus and find a way to move forward. It is not that they cannot, but that they haven't come together. Here, a hero is not much help. The charismatic leader cannot help us with the decisions about community that our country must make. One cannot deal with the issue of race in America only by having a President who says the right words; the responsibility really belongs to each of us. Yet when was the last time you talked about race with someone of a different race? If the answer is "never," you are part of the problem. And while a President can set a tone on race – a negative tone, as Ronald Reagan did, or a positive tone, as Bill Clinton has – it is only individuals and communities that can truly come to terms with the divisiveness that belonging to one race or another has produced throughout American history: stupidly, wrongly, but embeddedly. From my perspective, this barrier to effective community is an issue of the highest importance.

What can a political person do with the undermining forces that swirl around us today? And, in particular, what can be done in an atmosphere where a real public discourse is destroyed by attack ads and sound bytes that communicate in pre-tested, pre-polled, pre-designed phrases spoken only for the purpose of moving an electorate, like an amoeba, towards an election day in which "it" will register a manipulated verdict? "Not much" is one answer.

But even in such an environment, I think there is an opportunity to face the real issues and speak the truth as one sees it. Many of us recognize that there is probably not a single truth. This leads us to believe that we should speak a view as we see it and seek others who will find common cause with us. That is ultimately why, in a country as big, as diverse, and as complex as the United States, it would be much easier if there were a few guiding myths that would provide the Braille for the blind to follow. Perhaps their availability will light up the path to common ground.

Frontispiece of *Leviathan* by Thomas Hobbes.

Figure 2.1 Hobbes' "Leviathan"

Chapter 2

The inner vision and social organization

Joseph L. Henderson

In my work as an analytical psychologist I am continually aware of a sense of opposition between inner motivation and outer performance in my patients, but also in the life around me among so-called normal people. This is a problem of opposites between an inner image and an outer object. It may be studied in many different ways: as a philosophic problem, an aesthetic problem, a religious problem, or a social problem.

The focus of this chapter is not to write about philosophy, aesthetics, or religion, but about a social attitude for which the image has traditionally been carried by a king and his sacred attributes, the opposite of which is the community over which he reigns. Our modern incarnation of this inner ordering principle has been carried outwardly by the presidency or the prime minister, although both inner image and outer object have suffered enormous fragmentation. The community over which the king ruled was normally obedient, but it could also become a source of protest against too absolute a power, if kingship or the social ordering principle is misused. This ordering principle was well exemplified pictorially by Hobbes' "Leviathan" (Figure 2.1), an image of the king as a superhuman figure whose body is composed of many people comprising a commonwealth. This king has a crown on his head and in his right hand there is a sword, while his left hand holds a crozier. Thus this figure is the embodiment of a unifying power whose authority reconciles church and state with the army, a suitable image of society as it was conceived to be through the seventeenth century.

But this kind of unity began to break up, leaving behind a new diversity represented by a government we call democracy with its blessings and its discontents and interruptions by dictators. Let us look at this in brief perspective. Moving far back in history we know that in feudal periods of all the larger cultures, from Egypt, China, India, up to the Greco-Roman West, mythology and political action were completely unified. Then the early Greek philosophers began to separate myth from society and the different mythological traditions from each other. This paved the way for social consciousness to arise as we know it today.

As you know, Plato wrote *The Republic* which outlined a so-called democratic social system to be ruled by philosophers. But Plato's interest did not remain in the social sphere. His work was influenced by Pythagoras, and Plato also drew upon the mythological resources of the time in which he lived. By adding his own ideas to these other sources, Plato created a body of esoteric knowledge not unlike the knowledge that Jung, in our time, derived from the collective unconscious with its archetypal imagery. However, Plato did not connect the new mythology, the eidola or ideal images, with politics, and his *Republic* remains ungrounded looked at from our modern viewpoint. Like the pre-Socratic philosophers, he did not formulate a truly social attitude as we know it, only a philosophic idea of how government might be conducted.

We have to move into our own culture to understand what it means to have a social attitude that reflects a mythological content. I think of Jean Jacques Rousseau as a man who still speaks to our time showing how a social attitude, which he termed "a social contract," is based on a view that mankind's fundamental nature is mythologically significant. He spoke of mankind as the "noble savage" as a basis for social life to flourish in a democratic modern spirit. It has been fashionable in our times to discredit Rousseau and to make fun of his naive assumption that human nature is only "noble," but he did sense that an underlying pattern of myth allows us to relate to each other with true feeling and not just from political expediency. He was able to help rescue education from the hierarchical structure of the eighteenth century and to become democratic in the sense that the student should not simply be taught to conform to society as the only way to becoming oneself in an organized society.

The relation of mythology to a social attitude is more clearly to be seen in the work of William Blake, a so-called mystic who began as a neo-Platonic philosopher and ended as a socially conscious poet and activist. Unlike Rousseau he was not blinded by the optimism of the Enlightenment and, moving into the nineteenth century, warned of the dangerous course which Western culture was pursuing in the industrial exploitation of natural resources. He wrote of "the dark Satanic mills," those early factories in the midlands of England which were covering the green fields with coal smoke. For Blake it was not just nature or society that might suffer from this development but the strength of the archetypal field itself, with its meaningful dualism and the dynamic search for unity between nature and society.

When we come to the twentieth century and to Jung, whose psychology is the touchstone for this chapter, it would seem that he, like Blake, was a philosophical more than a socially conscious man. But this does not express something important about his personal social history and his place in the *Zeitgeist* of his time. He was an introvert and a more or less conservative Swiss citizen in a country with a long history of functional democracy, uninterrupted by political demagoguery. During the years I knew Jung in Zürich, I learned about the origins of that democracy which helped explain Jung's influence on those who came in contact with him, and that particular Swiss shrewdness which allowed him to formulate his concept, the Shadow, in its archetypal, not just personal, aspect. Empirically I would describe this as the image of an evil we project on to others who do not agree with us, and how necessary it may be to withdraw that image and learn to live with it so as to enter into a more understanding and productive relation to those others.

This is epitomized in the story of Nicolas von der Flüe, the Swiss patron saint who lived in the fourteenth century and was canonized (by Pope Pius XII) in 1947. Brother Klaus, as he was called, had visions that had a profound effect upon him, one of which we would certainly call an image of the Shadow. This was "the head of a human figure with a terrifying face, full of wrath and threats" (*Collected Works* 11: 322). But its frightening aspect is mitigated later by two other visions which are almost the opposite, visions of a benevolent God-the-father-and-son and God-the-mother-and-son. I quote:

> There came a handsome, magnetic man with shining color in his face and a white garment. And he laid both arms on his, (i.e., Brother Klaus'), pressed him close, and thanked him with all the love of his heart because he stood by his son and helped him in his need. There came a beautiful, majestic woman, also in a white garment. . . . And she laid both arms on his shoulders and pressed him close to her heart with an overflowing love because he had stood so faithfully by her son in his need.

Jung comments on these visions as follows:

> The androgyny of the divine ground is characteristic of the mystic experience, an age-old conception that goes back to primitive times. . . . The trinity in this vision, Father–Mother–Son, is very undogmatic. . . . It is nice to think that the only outstanding Swiss mystic received, by God's grace, unorthodox visions and was permitted to look with unerring eye into the depths of the divine soul, where creeds of humanity which dogma has divided are united in one symbolic archetype.

Now, what has this to do with social attitudes or politics? Brother Klaus became a hermit after his visions, and was sought out by many people as a wise man to help them with their problems. Some of these people were important political figures, rulers of one sort or another, or their ministers, asking him to advise them about their national interests. Brother Klaus acted as an adviser and mediator at other more public occasions. The most famous of these was one in which representatives of two Swiss cantons came to discuss their conflict with each other. He told them that they must settle their differences between themselves and support a Swiss Confederacy, and this was the beginning of the stable democracy that was subsequently founded. How did it come about? Presumably because they were forced to acknowledge their own Shadow-aspects projected upon the other canton. I understand that he pointed out to them that if they did not do this they would have no country, because the individual cantons would be swallowed up by more powerful neighbors in Italy, France and Austria, all living under the enduring tradition of kingship. The Swiss had to find within themselves a psychological equivalent of this image of kingship, and Jung, many centuries later, was to call this image the Self, an image that can only be effectively revealed when its Shadow-aspect can be effectively removed.

The terrifying face "full of wrath and threats" was Brother Klaus' image of the Shadow. If he had not become conscious of this and experienced its true nature, he could have become an angry, judgmental person who would have told those canton leaders that they must behave themselves in a Christian spirit and, if they did not, they would simply go to Hell. Instead, the images of two figures representing the Self, the compassionate man and the loving woman, appeared in his vision and allowed him to persuade rather than cajole these people into acting with reason and justice. At the same time he did not leave them with a sense of duty to some higher power but honored their healthy self-interest as a recognition of the ego as well as of the Self. And so he showed them that their worldly survival depended upon this realization and the action to follow.

I have described political communities that are small enough or so geographically contained that their inner visions of social organization are not appropriate for the kind of democracy we experience in the multicultural societies of modern times. But the imagery of the collective unconscious is so varied and inexhaustible that we need not worry if it does not seem to meet all our cultural expectations. Jung was fond of the term *Anthropos* to designate an image of mankind that transcends ethnic or national forms and embraces the totality of what it means to be human. This image can be traced back beyond Europe, Egypt, or China to paleolithic times where the image of a supreme being exerts an ordering effect upon societies where the contrary position would be one of complete anarchy or some other dispersal of cultural values. Marie-Louise von Franz shows pictures in *Man and His Symbols* (Jung 1964: 201) of this *Anthropos* as ancient China's P'an Ku, a "gigantic all-embracing figure (or First Man) shown covered in leaves like a plant grown from nature," and a painting from an illuminated manuscript from India of a Cosmic Lion Goddess riding a lion, made up of many people and animals, holding in her hand an image of the Sun. That those images are not introjected from some local cultural form, but are innate in the human psyche, she points also to Jung's fondness for an "unspoiled form by the Naskapi Indians who still live in the forests of the Labrador Peninsula. These simple people live in isolated family groups so far from one another that they have not been able to evolve tribal customs or collective religious beliefs and ceremonies. The Naskapi hunter has to rely on his own inner voices and unconscious revelations" (Jung 1964: 161). In his basic view of life, the soul of man is simply an "inner companion" whom he calls "my friend" or *Mistapeo*, meaning "Great Man." But this *Mistapeo* is not a personal possession of the ego but belongs to everyone, and therefore his guidance applies to the hunter's relation to both animals and people. It serves an individual but also a social or, as we might say, a political function. "The major obligation of an individual Naskapi is to follow the instruction given in his dreams. . . . Lies and dishonesty drive the Great Man away from his inner realm, whereas generosity and love of one's neighbors and of animals attract him" (Jung 1964: 161).

So here we have some real anthropological and psychological evidence for the innate motivation for living in a democratic spirit which is not to be equated with its doubtful corollary: free enterprise. The latter is always there, but it does not take first place because of its shadowy tendencies to obscure the more basic activity of the Self.

REFERENCES

Jung, C.G. (1933) "Brother Klaus," in *Collected Works*, Vol. 11. London: Routledge & Kegan Paul.

Jung, C.G. and von Franz, M.-L., Henderson, J.L., Jacobi, J., and Jaffé, A. (1964) *Man and His Symbols*, London: Aldus Books Limited.

Chapter 3

The good-enough leader

Andrew Samuels

Psychotherapists and analysts have always wanted to explore the social world and current events. It is not a new fad or fashion. Freud (1920) hoped to understand "the riddles of the world," and Jung (1946) said that therapists "cannot avoid coming to grips with contemporary history." But the world never really turned up for its first therapy session. Maybe the world knew what it was doing, because many attempts to link psychotherapy and social issues have tended to present everything as exclusively psychological, thereby keeping the therapist in control and above the fray. Attempts to put political leaders and other significant figures such as Bill Clinton, Tony Blair, or Princess Diana on the couch as patients have, quite rightly, been criticized and ridiculed.

It is crucial not to confuse or conflate the processes that go on within an individual with what happens on the much more complex level of society. Provided such errors are avoided, psychotherapy and analysis are useful and imaginative tools of social criticism and not self-indulgent psycho-babble. Temptation to analyze prominent people in public should be resisted and, instead, fruitful working partnerships can be forged with people working in other areas – social policy, education, the media, and environmentalism. Therapists and analysts also need to recall that not everything is rosy in their own professional politics and to avoid giving an impression that they have all the answers.

There is no place for psychotherapy in politics on its own, in splendid isolation. Everything depends on achieving sufficient – if uneasy – acceptance for its perspectives, so that eventually, many policy committees and commissions would quite naturally have a therapist sitting on them, at one end of a spectrum of experts which has statisticians at the other end. We should not think in terms of committees of therapists.

Having indicated that it is not my intention to analyze specific leaders, in a spirit of ground-clearing let me indicate some other themes and angles on leadership that I will *not* be pursuing in this chapter. I am not going to get involved in the familiar debate over whether leaders are more likely to be exceptional individuals in themselves or tend to be the persons of the moment. Nor am I going to provide a list of the psychological attributes of a successful leader, which is the kind of empirical project often carried out by academic political psychology (e.g. Iyengar and McGuire 1993). Whilst useful areas of study, these are not my interests. Similarly, in contradistinction to many analysts, I will not be exploring the motivations of citizens who follow individuals leading large movements or parties. Hence, this chapter is not about crowd psychology or large group dynamics in relation to leaders and leadership. Although the word "power" cannot be avoided in relation to leadership, whether in its benevolent or malevolent aspects, this chapter is not a study in power. Nor does it very much concern the ubiquitous, impersonal forces of, for example, globalization or international finance, which contribute so much to the intractability of many social issues and problems. Nor, on this occasion, will I be focusing on what we as citizens might do when faced with the collapse of much of which we had previously taken for granted in the world of politics.

My aim is to stimulate an image-based, hence depth psychological approach to leadership, an approach which, hopefully, will interest general readers as much as professional therapists.

One final introductory point I need to make is to clarify that much of what might sound like *advocacy* in this chapter is in fact *description*. Intellectuals have learned, over the years, that a lot of useful theorizing is in fact nothing more elevated than good description of cutting-edge practice. So what I seem to be contributing to theorizing or thinking about leadership probably reflects what is going on already. Something arises out of what is there, something was hidden in the open. Let me give some further brief examples of this tendency. Machiavelli did not actually advocate what successful princes should do in sixteenth-century Italy. Rather, he can now be seen to have described the actions of the most successful princes of his day. But he was the one who raised it to cultural consciousness, formed it into a discourse. Adam Smith was not advocating what capitalists should do at the end of the eighteenth century. He was describing what the new entrepreneurs and financial manipulators were already doing.

GOOD-ENOUGHNESS

Many readers will know that the British psychoanalyst Donald Winnicott coined the phrase "the good-enough mother," although nowadays people tend to talk about the "good-enough parent." Winnicott had in mind that, after a period in which the mother (or the parent) does her best to meet the omnipotent fantasies and expectations of the baby, there is a time when such a situation is not going to work psychologically or behaviorally for either party. What ensues, at least in Western families, is a kind of graduated let-down or disappointment of the baby carried out by her or his parents. The baby is carefully introduced to the realities of life, in which one cannot have omnipotently determined, magical, hyper-pleasurable satisfaction of instinctual needs. Included is the difficult-to-bear realization that no one is self-created.

How does a parent make the move from being the parent of omnipotent fantasy to the good-enough parent? In my understanding of this, one key way in which parents become good-enough facilitators of their baby's development is by *failing their babies*. At the heart of good-enoughness lies a certain kind of failure. It is this particular aspect of good-enoughness – its linkage to failure – that I want to carefully detach from the world of developmental psychology, from fleshy family life, in order to see whether good-enoughness does have a utility in relation to politics in general and the problem of leadership in particular. We are talking not only about the arts of parenting, but also about the arts of politics when we descry what may be called the middle way, a path that wends its way between an idealizing of the parents (or leaders) on the one hand and a denigrating of them on the other. As it is for the baby in relation to the location of good-enough parents, so it may be for the citizenry in relation to good-enough leaders. Please note: I am not saying leaders are parents – only that, if we want to avoid the extremes of idealization and denigration in relation to leaders, the qualities and processes that go into good-enough parenthood are equally pertinent in a parallel or analogous way. I am trying here to promote a discussion about how to steer a path between these idealizations that we see all too often in extreme form in the quietistic acceptance of despotic, fascistic, and tyrannical leaders, and today's equally striking denigrations, with nobody trusting anybody in positions of authority at all. It seems to me that the issues which Winnicott highlighted – the move away from idealization and denigration, the introduction of a dose of realism in a graduated and copeable-with way – are issues that are highly relevant to the political situation in many Western countries such as the United States and Britain.

LEADERSHIP AND FAILURE

I have suggested that failure is a core element of good-enoughness. I want now to link the idea of failure with the problem of leadership. I will discuss, in turn, (1) failed leaders, (2) the failure in our time of the very idea of leadership, and (3) leadership as the study and practice of failure – leadership as the art of failing. (This template incorporates some of the features of Hillman's (1969) study of failure in clinical analysis.)

I first raised this question of the intimate linkages between leadership and failure at the annual Congress of the British Labour Party in 1994. The reaction should perhaps not have startled me – but it did. There was considerable television, radio, and press coverage of the idea that the image of failure could stimulate interesting discussion of the nature of leadership. Now it is not the be-all and end-all of psychological contributions to cultural debate to be on television. But the reaction made me a little more certain that just placing leadership, failure and good-enoughness in the same frame took some of the shackles off the political imagination.

As far as *failed leaders* are concerned, I trust it is not too reductive to say that, all too often, we witness a failure to achieve good-enoughness. Those leaders commonly agreed to have failed seem to have been perceived as either excessively yet falsely strong figures or, conversely, manifestly weak and indecisive, devoted to pleasing others and hence unable to do whatever they are supposed to do.

Another feature that academic and biographical studies of leaders suggest is that failed leaders seem to have a great capacity for self-deception. The most famous example is, of course, Hitler, who, by 1945, was busy moving non-existent armies around the map of Europe.

Another aspect of leadership that seems to invoke failure, or to suggest that failure is more or less inevitable, is that some people's styles of leadership are just plain wrong for the time in which they live. The way that some individuals want to lead, a way that seems to them almost "natural," does not seem to fit with what the populace is willing to accept.

The last thing I want to say about failed leaders is that riding one's luck seems to be very important for leaders. Machiavelli wrote beautifully about this. He said that one of the main things a prince needs to be able to do is to make use of *fortuna*. *Fortuna* means more than luck; there is also the question of alignment or harmony with the rhythms of the universe, but the modern notion of luck is by no means a trivial concept, especially when considered with leadership in mind, and the stakes are at the life-and-death level.

I now move on to consider the second tranche of my essay into the connections between leadership and failure: *the failure, in our time, of the very idea of leadership*. I believe we are in a strikingly split situation over this whole question of leadership. Our cognitive understanding of the way in which received ideas of leadership have failed us has long overtaken our emotional capacity to manage that realization. We lack the emotional means to manage our understanding that, as Brecht (1962: scene xiii) has Galileo put it, "Unhappy is the country that needs a hero." By now, everybody knows that apparently strong and manifestly heroic leaders are deeply suspect. They are hyper-masculine or macho personages, and, intellectually speaking, we don't want them. They are "male" whatever their sex because, for heroes, the obstacles to be overcome are, in Western discourse, always "female." They are dangerous, whether in the role of savior, explorer, king, philosopher, or warrior. And in the nuclear age in which we continue to live, it is quite clear why they are dangerous. Everybody knows this on the intellectual level. Women know it, for sure. All over the world, women are deeply suspicious of male and, indeed, female heroic leaders and leadership styles that are redolent of heroism. Yet we don't let go of whatever hopes and desires are locked up in such leaders. This is the split, and it would be hubris for anyone to claim to have got over it. The *idea* of the hero will not go away. Even when a leader decides to become a very democratic sort of person, and walk down Constitutional Avenue or play head-tennis with a soccer star, as did Jimmy Carter or Tony Blair, taking deliberately anti-heroic, democratic, man-of-the-people stances, the very deliberateness of such behavior reveals that it trades off the heroic thing. No anti-hero without a hero in mind, at some level. As Bob Dylan put it, "There's no success like failure and failure's no success at all."

Psychology and psychotherapy have something to say about why it is so hard to lose the lead of leader-as-hero emotionally, even while knowing intellectually and cognitively that it is no use at all to have heroic leaders. Broadly speaking, the reason the split exists has to do with identification. Many people feel themselves to be deeply enhanced by the kinds of fantasies that take place in identification with a heroic leader. Erase the heroism and you spoil the pleasures of identification. We come to feel in some way denuded or deprived. So, although we know that the heroic leader is passé, is dangerous, is destructive, that he (or she) leaves out whole sections of the community (who are then excluded from power, and not part of the body politic), it is proving extremely difficult to get beyond heroic models.

One of my aims in raising the idea of good-enough leadership is to see whether there are non-heroic images of leadership that can inspire people emotionally and psychologically in the way that heroic models do. Or, to put it in the language of political process and experience, I want to see whether we can factor into bottom-up, networked, collaborative, organizational models the same kinds of energic charge that we can see all too clearly at work in top-down, heroically led, hierarchical organizations such as the modern state. To use the vernacular, can one make cooperation, participation, and networking sexy, just as the dominant–submissive, heroism-infected, leader-led relationship still seems to exert its strange attraction?

Up to now, I have discussed failed leaders and the failure of the idea of heroic leadership in our time. What about making fuller use of my proposition that failure is at the heart of good-enoughness? *To be a good-enough leader, you surely have to be an artist in failure*! Now, most of our leaders have had enormous difficulty in coming to terms with the inevitability of failure. People have often noted how hard it is for politicians to say that they have changed their minds about something; this seems to be an admission of failure. As Mrs Thatcher put it, "the lady's not for turning." I want to push this observation a bit further. It is also extremely interesting to see how difficult it is for leaders to accept that what they are proposing may well not work out or succeed as planned. To accept that failure comes with the political territory. Accepting this would involve the understanding that leadership requires proficiency in the art of failure.

When Ulrich Beck, the German sociologist, talks about risk societies (1992), he prods us in the general direction of an acceptance of impotence and failure. In the modern – or late-modern – age, governments and leaders often cannot deal with the problems they are faced with because they do not know in advance what the problems are going to be. In Britain, BSE, "mad cow disease," was a classic example of a risk that almost nobody in authority had anticipated. Similar events are going to happen increasingly frequently the more complex and fragmented societies become. Many risks are simply beyond the comprehension and ken of governments to cope with. The uncertainty principle we know about from physics also operates in politics. From this point of view, leadership becomes less and less a question of succeeding in coping with the challenges and the risks that face a modern society and more and more a question of ameliorating the inevitable failure to deal with the risks which society is confronting. So a leader who is artful, a leader who is competent, a good-enough leader, is not a leader who solves things. She or he is a leader who well manages her or his own failure to solve the problems that confront the community. A "can't do politician."

A further, more depth psychological reason why we have to accept that failure is inevitable has to do with the unconscious itself. The human psyche is a source of everything in the world that is creative, benevolent, artistic, spiritual, lovely. It is also the source of everything that is horrible, shitty, aggressive, life-destroying, and spelling planetary destruction. There is a both-ness to the human psyche – perhaps we could call it the "bad-enough" psyche. Now, our both-ness is something with which, politically and psychologically, we have an enormous problem. It has never been easy to accept that there are limits on what can be done in the social realm in the face of the nasty, shadow side of being human. If leadership is the art of failure, good-enough leaders may have to come on stream to say that not only will we fail to do what we want to do, because problems are difficult to solve, but, as human beings, we are flawed problem-solvers, always and already failures in getting things done. Mistakes want to be made.

Let me take this opportunity to add a decidedly political comment to these psychological observations. People of goodwill, good heart, and progressive opinions cannot prevail because there are elements, structures, and institutions which do not wish them to prevail. Politics is not a level playing field and, while the human psyche may have contributed to this state of affairs, it is not a purely psychological problem. In many Western societies, inequalities and discrepancies have been getting increasingly worse. Vested interests, structural imbalances and economic theories mean that, even if Labor or Democratic leaders seek to distribute wealth and work towards social justice, there are forces that will always seriously limit their goals.

GOOD-ENOUGH LEADERS

I now want to outline three images of good-enough leaders. They are good-enough because each image is shot through with incompleteness and an intimation of failure. Please do not identify with these flawed, failed representations, nor try to relate the images to specific leaders or politicians because, actually, *these are not people*, these images of leaders I am drawing. They are fictions, not types. Perhaps one could imagine a single good-enough leader with some or all of these images activated within her or him. But that would be accidental and not central to what I am getting at. The three images of good-enough leaders are those of the erotic leader, trickster-as-leader, and sibling leadership.

First, the *erotic leader*. This is not about what many readers may think it is about. An erotic leader is not a leader who hops in and out of bed with people. Public obsession in many countries with the sex lives of leaders suggests that there is something about the actual, physical, corporeal eroticism of leadership which is worth exploring further. But I have in mind something other than the prurient interests of the mass media. Nevertheless, the concern of the media with the sexuality of leading figures in society generally, not just political leaders, suggests that, as in so many cases, mass consciousness has discovered something of interest. I think that the populace, in its obsession with the sexuality of leaders, is on to something important.

I see the erotic leader as using her or his sexuality to convey to citizens that they (the citizens) are exciting, creative, and autonomous people who can work together cooperatively. Receiving ordinary admiration and warmth is an extremely potent part of psychological evolution and the establishment of self-esteem. Whether the leader does or does not communicate to the people in an almost physically warm way, that the leader admires them is an interesting and neglected aspect of the political process.

My model for this notion is the work I have done on parenting, focusing on what I have called "erotic playback" (Samuels 1989, 1993, 1995). This is the way in which the parent communicates to children of both sexes that they are admirable, physically desirable, and erotically viable creatures. Of course, I am referring only to incest fantasy here and not to the physical enactment of such fantasy. Western societies seem to me to mirror Western families in that the subtle damage and deprivation caused by erotic *deficit* is far less spoken of than that of erotic *excess*. Actual physical incest takes place at an appallingly high frequency and it is important to recognize this and mobilize against it. But something equally central and much more benevolent in sexuality (especially male sexuality) is being overlooked. Moreover, the consequences of an absence of such positive sexuality are also overlooked.

My reference to the erotic includes sex, but has to do with more than sex. It has also to do with harmony, relatedness, purpose, significance, and meaning: *Eros*. As we know from psychoanalysis and Jungian analysis, sexuality is involved or implicated in all of these things in some way and at some level. This means, of course, that ambivalence, anxiety, jealousy, rivalry, and a sense of lack – the rudiments of failure – will also be present in the picture.

How does the erotic leader function? First of all, let me stress that the erotic leader can be a good-enough leader of whatever sex. As I work through what is involved, I will delineate it according to the actual sex of the leader and the actual sex of the citizen, though bearing in mind that sexuality is also a metaphor and that we still know more about men as erotic leaders than we do about women.

The erotic leader not only makes citizens feel good and beautiful at a very deep, almost bodily level. She or he brings out and reflects back the healthy self-love and self-admiration that exists in everyone. Her or his admiration contributes to their feeling honored in their internal diversity, including sexual and other kinds of rivalry with the members of the internal family. Because sexual identity is not a unified, fixed, static, eternal, universal thing, erotic playback as communicated to the citizen by the erotic leader encourages that citizen to think of him- or herself in a diversified way, to come alive and hold together in the mind all aspects of the self: body areas, mental areas, sub-personalities, complexes, ego, id, and superego, public and private, active and passive, political and psychological. Because sex carries such a diversified charge, sexual communication with an erotic leader can lead – encourage – the citizen's recognition of her- or himself as a diversified being, including and perhaps foregrounding that being's inevitable tendency to fail.

Above all, there is something about the way in which sexual processes can switch between submission and domination on the part of the individual involved that make them particularly relevant for a discussion of this particular kind of leader – the erotic leader. Switching between psychological submission and domination is something that is missing from Western polities, no matter the lip-service paid to the supremacy of the ballot-box. Where are the submissive leaders? Where are the dominant citizenries? In our inner lives, and in our relationships, we surely know about this switching. The erotic leader can create a micro-environment in which the citizen can switch between submission and domination in relation to the leader. In Jean Genet's play *The Balcony* there is a special kind of brothel. In it, the police chief can dress up as a criminal and the bishop can wear the garments of a prostitute.

When the erotic leader is male, he makes a female citizen feel other than maternal. I am not saying mothers are not sexy. Mothers *are* sexy. But there is something about female sexuality that can be separated and divorced from the maternal. The male erotic leader works with the female citizen to enable her to go beyond the traditional and socially restrictive virtues of relation and care.

When the erotic leader is male and the citizen is male, what arises between them is what I call "homosociality," which is fraternity in action. We see this in operation in many gay communities which are experimenting with new political and social forms partly in order to come to grips with the challenges presented by HIV/AIDS. There is something very special about the homosociality that a male erotic leader and a male citizen can develop between them.

When the erotic leader is female, and the citizen is male, she offers that male citizen a chance to merge with her, against the prevailing psychodynamic orthodoxy which says that symbiosis and merger with the feminine or the mother is a very bad thing for a man. What we could call ecomasculinism (men who care passionately for the environment) needs a political climate in which female erotic leaders create circumstances where male citizens can merge with them (the female leaders trading off their traditional, earthy representations as women).

What if the erotic leader is female and the citizen is female? Then I think the citizen is offered a very special and different approach to power, rivalry, and competition. Such a couple are not going to be stuck in some sort of false sisterhood. They are going to be rivalrous and competitive with each other. But it is an unusual kind of rivalry, less dominated by male values, and, in its femaleness, not necessarily structured by penis, phallus, or rivalry for possession of them.

To summarize: when the erotic leader is male, he helps females to feel other than mothers and males to participate in homosocial action. When the erotic leader is female, she offers males a chance to merge creatively with her and females a different approach to power, rivalry, and competition from the one that men have laid out. Both sexes of leaders will fail to achieve these goals, as we shall see below.

But there are dimensions to this that go beyond sexuality and individual functioning. Like human sexuality, human society is exceedingly diverse. My further suggestion is that there are links between a full flowering of diverse, plural human sexuality and a full flowering of diverse, plural human culture. These, too, may be activated by the erotic leader. The sense of admiration and respect for the full potential of sexual diversity can cross over into the processes that enable societies to sustain cultural diversity – for example, ethnic or "racial" diversity. Once the collective moves into those areas where sexual desire is in operation, which means that fixed identities and rules cease to play the part that they are supposed to, we are sensitized to and prepared for the challenge of living in and managing a diversified culture.

To summarize once more: the erotic leader makes the citizenry feel good and admired, and that has its own benefits. But there is also a communication about diversity which is on more than an individual level. Of course, I am trying to synthesize a massive body of work on the relations between gender and sexuality on the one hand and ethnicity and raciality on the other (Adams 1996; Bhabha 1990; Chirimuuta and Chirimuuta 1987). Succinctly put, between colonizer and colonized there has always been a kind of masculine–feminine divide. The British were the "masculine" to the "feminine" of the Indians of the subcontinent, or to that of the Irish. Erotic playback from a good-enough erotic leader destabilizes who is masculine and who is feminine. It destabilizes "colonial" relations within particular cultures like Britain or the United States.

As I mentioned, erotic leaders are most definitely not always men. Towards the end of her life, Princess Diana emerged as a kind of erotic leader on the kind of iconic level I am exploring here if not as a person. Here, I do not see Princess Diana as the mere combination of mother and sexual icon which many commentators noted. I see her more as an image of *maternal sexuality*, where the two are already joined. The topic of maternal sexuality is, of course, a highly emotive and tabooed one. The French psychoanalyst Jean Laplanche (1976) posits that "what inspires psychological growth is the seductiveness of the (m)other." By the action of her sexuality and, I would add, via erotic playback, she seduces the growth potential out of the child, who longs to join with her in a relationship and so must "move" and grow in order to do so. For Laplanche, this primary seductiveness accounts for the origins of psyche itself, which is, so to speak, drawn out of the individual by something sexual. Princess Diana certainly drew out our psyches, and this is why it is reasonable to see her not as simply "mother plus sex," but as an image of maternal sexuality itself. When this topic is discussed, the "seductive mother" is often seen as a bad one in the professional literature. Yet without her seduction of and erotic playback to the child there would be no psychic activity or growth. If this overall analysis is in any way pertinent, then Princess Diana's life and death are symbolic examples of the primary seduction of maternal sexuality and erotic playback and we, the public, were (healthily) seduced and led. The public mood at the time of her death contained all the energy you would expect to see when it is drawn out by this kind of erotic playback, which I see as carried by the maternal body. Diana's maternal sexuality and her qualities of erotic leadership quite literally drew out the potential of people.

I will end my outline of the erotic leader by reiterating that leadership played in a good-enough key inevitably involves failure. (It could even be argued that a too successfully erotic leader will inaugurate a special and spectacular order of failure.) Erotic leaders will fail because there are real difficulties for the citizen in taking this type of leader inside her- or himself so as to relate "erotically" to other people in society. Citizens will fail to relate to each other in ways that are congruent with the messages they receive from an erotic leader. So the whole business of erotic leadership will not work as planned. For example, the giving of erotic playback may stay very much the sole property of the leader. Moreover, one cannot just clobber people into feeling better about themselves. In our world, and maybe in all possible worlds, we have to face the fact that many people do not and never will feel good about themselves. Consider how many of Roget's categories for synonyms of "failure" have a personal flavor: inferior, impotence, mistake, insufficiency, lost labor, imperfection, bungling, hitch, loser, loss, insolvency, object of scorn, guilty act.

The second image of a good-enough leader is *trickster-as-leader*. Once again, I need to begin with a clarification. Tricksters in politics are not necessarily identical with the practice of dirty tricks in politics. I am certainly not going to say we need more dirty tricks, sleaze, backhanders, or undeclared interests. Tricksters are legendary or mythic figures, found in many cultures, who tend to defy the laws of reality, the laws of time, space, and place. For the Greeks, the arch-trickster was Hermes, the messenger of the gods, the deity of change, with his tendency to play jokes, to lie, to steal, to cheat, to deny physical and social reality, and to engage in grandiose fantasy. When Hermes steals Apollo's cattle, he drives them backwards to his home stable in order to fool Apollo's pursuing posse. When Apollo tries to capture him, the ropes which are supposed to bind Hermes snake off in all directions. In the Hermes story, when Apollo and Hermes resolve their differences through an exchange of gifts, the links between criminality and creativity are established and celebrated.

In the Middle Ages, carnivals began to take on their present form and there would usually be a subversion of the social hierarchy. An unsuitable person, such as a child or the village idiot, would be dressed up as the bishop. In fairy-tales, we find figures like Tom Thumb taking an anti-heroic role. Parapsychology is full of tricksterish poltergeists who challenge the boundaries of what we take for reality. Animals often represent the trickster in politics (Machiavelli's famous fox is a good example).

Most tricksters, from *Coyote* in North America to *Ananse* or *Eshu* in West Africa, follow this pattern, undermining the prevailing organization of power and even the perceived structure of reality itself. For example, *Ananse* manages to trick the wealthy *Akwasi* so that *Akwasi* actually ends up by ordering *Ananse* to make love to his wife *Aso*.

Anthropologists have suggested that the cultural function of tricksters is to destabilize the social order. Tricksters are in-house revolutionaries. Of course, tricksters' discourse is not nearly as articulate as I am making it sound. They are, after all, according to Jung, symbols of the unconscious itself. Now, when politics becomes little more than dirty tricks and jiggery-pokery, and back-room deals, we are seeing only a tiny and distorted part of the trickster theme in action; much else is simply overlooked if we permit our moralizing zeal to get the better of us. Tricksters enhance our notion of leadership by virtue of their visionary, rule-breaking capacity. They are revolutionary simply because they are not rooted in reality.

Many readers will understandably have a mixed reaction to where I am going with this. I am indeed talking about the political value of the immature personality. I am indeed talking about the political yield that stems from people who have not grown up. I am indeed valorizing the politics of grandiose fantasy. But this is meant to be a politics of play, of unbridled creativity, of Romantic and Bohemian sensibilities. Tricksters are not dictators; they haven't got the attention span. I want to claim tricksters for the political because what they do is dispute what we are entitled to call realism, and what we are entitled to call idealism. They simply do not yet know that there is supposed to be a difference! For them, there is *only* the vision thing.

But tricksters introduce us to more than a visionary politics. Trickster politics involves bringing a dreamy and playful out-of-touchness with reality into politics. I believe this is something that contemporary Western politics needs, and something that requires trickster leadership to bring about. We are talking about ingenuity, improvisation, flexibility, rule-breaking, seeing things differently, doing things differently, not being hidebound, being open to change, being open to failure. This concerns the kind of skills that we sometimes see in the parallel (or "black") economy in Third World countries. If the official statistics told the true story about economic activity in some countries, everyone would have died long ago. But unlicensed unofficial trade is surviving, whether in the shanty towns of Latin America or the villages of Somalia (not to mention north London). Spontaneously formed economic and social organizations are full of tricksterism and need trickster energies to get going.

Western politics places great stress on the formal constitutional structures and decision-making processes. In its devotion to formality, mainstream politics has lost the ability to access these kinds of vital and innovatory dimensions. So, while trickster leaders, as I am thinking about them, certainly have the potential to carry out all sorts of ugly, dirty tricks, they also have the potential to be extremely intuitive, ingenious, improvisatory, and creative in relation to politics.

Trickster leaders will fail, just like the erotic leader will fail. They will fail because anyone who tries to live *exclusively* as a trickster will simply and quite correctly not be trusted, and will be unlikely to achieve high office. Nevertheless, most of us have seen trickster leaders in action: somebody in an organization (often a person low down in the hierarchy) has a crazy idea and everyone thinks yet again that this person is a real liability. Then, suddenly, you find that the off-the-wall remark they made a few weeks before has turned out to be surprisingly worthy of trust. Never forget that it is the solid folk, well placed in the hierarchy, nary a trickster among them, who follow orders, know the ropes, do the cruel and nasty things in organizations, play the power games, perform the back-stabbings, carry out the exclusions – psychotherapy organizations are wonderful examples here. It is the mature, rounded, realistic people who sometimes hold the whole thing back, and often deal out the nasty stuff. It is the apparently harmless visionaries, leaders who may not know too well who they are as people or even that they are leaders, who, every now and again, get results.

There are signs that Western societies are producing more female trickster leaders these days. Sometimes the female trickster enters the political arena by overdoing what is prescribed for women to the point where it is possible to go beyond the restrictions. For example, the mothers of the Plaza de Mayo helped to topple the Argentinian Junta by assembling, dressed in full maternal mourning gear, in the main square of Buenos Aires. They wore the embroidered scarves of bereavement but stitched on each scarf was the name and date of the disappearance of their child or children. The regulations about exchanging such information were evaded. The mothers exploited the good feeling which Argentinians, even torturers, have towards mothers.

Another area where we can see today's female tricksters in leadership roles is in the environmental movement. The equation of women and nature or earth is one of the most oppressive equations for women because culture and power are then left for men. But when the equation is exaggerated and parodied, as in some forms of ecofeminism, a novel kind of energy becomes available for politics. An illustration of this is in Margaret Atwood's novel *Surfacing*, where the female narrator melts into the earth, becoming a hybrid human, animal, ghost – and gains power over her persecutors in the process.

Similarly, we can understand the huge debate in feminist theory over consensual lesbian sadomasochism as part of the politics of the female trickster. The women are involved in a politicized dramatic performance that destabilizes what we think about sex, gender, and society. Viewed as female tricksters, consensual lesbian sadomasochists are doing far more than copying heterosexual power imbalances.

The list of contemporary female tricksters is almost endless. I think of the crop of female private investigators like V. I. Warshawski or sexually open film stars like Sharon Stone with her one-liner that "having a vagina and a point of view is a deadly combination." Perhaps some will say that the struggle for autonomy which characterizes the life of any and every woman in Western (or, indeed, non-Western) societies makes her a female trickster already. Perhaps. But the main point is that the blatant political flavor of the female trickster highlights the argument with which I began: that political cultures need tricksters as leaders and this is far more than a question of truth or falsehood in political conduct.

I am not so naive as to simply say that we need carnival politics and all will be well. But the notion that politics can have a carnivalesque element to it has been around for a long time. In our lifetime we have seen the yippies, the situationists and the whole way in which the anti-nuclear protestors took a symbolic, gestural, tricksterish path. In Britain, protestors knitted a gigantic scarf to "warm" a United States Air Force nuclear base.

The third example of good-enough leadership is *sibling leadership*. Here, I seek a depth psychological way to deconstruct the notion of leadership altogether. What follows is my take on decentralized, non-hierarchical, networked, bottom-up, highly democratic ways of organizing things. I do not discard the notion of leadership, because, in my experience of them, these experimental forms of social organization often founder because they dare not address the problematic of leadership.

Let me begin by asking my readers to review everything in their mind concerning the sibling relationship, especially the brother–sister relationship. Aren't the usual themes of friendship, enmity, attraction, repulsion, alliance, rivalry, rebellion, seeking the favors of the more powerful markedly political themes? And, stemming from the Bible perhaps – Cain and Abel, Isaac and Ishmael, Jacob and Esau – don't siblings usually get a bad press? Conversely, Antigone's story alerts us to the positive, political role that this relationship can play when tyranny is afoot.

In our gender-conscious times, citizens want to play whatever part they like in the political process firmly within the sex that they actually are. This has been especially true for women but is becoming increasingly the case for men as well. I am not just a citizen, I'm a male (or female) citizen. But, if a gender-conscious citizen does not want to engage in a 1960s or early 1970s separatist style of politics, but, rather, wants to work in alliance with members of the other sex who have similar values and aims, what are they to do? We know that male and female agendas are different, so how can one do politics as a man but in alliance with women? My experience is that many people experience this as a problem. They definitely do not want to be bland, sexless citizens, without an acknowledgment of differences, especially different political goals for the two sexes. But at the same time they do not only want to work politically with or support members of their own sex. They tend to shelve the problem and get on with things as best they can.

In part, this happens because, in the West, we lack images and models to foster women and men in doing their politics as women or men but in some kind of explicit and consciously entered-into temporary deal or alliance with the other sex. The aim would be to function openly as a sexed citizen but not as a separatist sexed citizen. This is extremely difficult, yet the need to do it may become more and more pressing in the twenty-first century. Conventional political discourse does not admit this kind of differentiation on the basis of gender and, as I have said, there are virtually no images to help us do it. Romantic love does not really supply useful imagery or a model on which to build a political organization, largely because such love is so incredibly absorbing of the time and energy of the people involved. Marriage really does not work here either, because marriage, as we know, has its own particular and peculiar politics – its own oppressions, its own imbalances, its own property laws.

So I have turned to siblings as an image of an alliance between female and male citizens (though I have not forgotten same-sex sibling relationships, the politics of which, unsurprisingly, has been much better theorized thanks to feminism and lesbian and gay political theorists). I believe the sibling relationship can be taken into politics in the following way. Quite a lot of Western families, however composed, go through the following scenario: When the first child reaches about the age of eleven or twelve, with puberty and adolescence about to hit, something changes in the relationship between the siblings in the family. This happens especially in the brother–sister relationship, but also in same-sex relationships, in which we start to observe a stand-off or mutual ignoring develop. The old, easy *alliance* of the siblings against the parents is no more and is replaced by the well-known phenomenon of adolescence in which the growing individual confronts the adult world alone or with friends. The psychodynamic textbooks tell us this great change occurs because of a fear of incestuous sexuality on the part of the siblings and, of course, this is not wrong. But it is an incomplete explanation and I think there is a special kind of repression to consider. When children reach that age, they start to become a really serious threat to parental and other sources of authority. I believe adults are quite scared of all the potentials – political as much as social – that are contained within the adolescent body. There are good reasons to have such fears. Adolescent bodies are extremely dangerous to adults in every conceivable way. They are dangerous because they are so radical, because their changes are so radical. What happens in particular as adolescence occurs is that the radical potential of the sibling relationship tends to be lost as indifference grows. The alliances that would make a difference in terms of social reality dissolve as the children go their separate ways. Could a society ever win back that radicality?

Central to the idea of siblings as leaders is a politicization or re-politicization of the horizontal dimension of being a sibling. Sexed citizens can access the radicality and autonomy that informs the pre-adolescent children's struggle with their parents. It is a mistake to see rebellion against authority solely located in adolescence. Whilst this might be true for individuals, the opposite happens in connection with the sibling relationship. I am proposing that there is a "natural" political struggle involving children versus parents within the family that we need to know more about. It is a struggle for forms of social justice based on the struggle between the generations of a family. In their ineluctable resistance to parental and societal authority, siblings speak for a decentralized style of leadership that eschews the erection of authority figures (thereby building in its eventual failure, as we shall see below).

There is a psychological linkage between family and society to flesh out here. As far as social reform is concerned, perhaps things change so slowly and with such difficulty because we have depoliticized and depotentiated the sibling relationship in families, which makes it very difficult to establish or re-establish it in societies. This would to some extent explain the psychology of the worldwide onslaught on trade unions and other forms of labor organization right across the Western world in the last twenty-five years. Whether we call it fraternity or sisterhood (or sibling politics), it is feared by those in power and hence not wanted. Sibling politics is far too threatening to conventional ideas of leadership and good order in the political realm.

What I would hope is that sibling leadership would involve networking, non-hierarchical ways of communicating and decision-making without this becoming bland and homogenized into a new approach to management consultancy. As I said, I would also hope that sibling leaders would never deny the existence of other kinds of leaders. By thinking of modern leadership in terms derived from sibling models we undercut the very notion of leadership itself without denying the phenomenon. The rapid and easy exchange of information through the internet might also be seen as a re-emergence of sibling politics on the cultural level. Pre-adolescent siblings do not keep secrets from each other; they coeducate each other. That gets lost in adolescence.

If we were to regard sibling leadership as a mode of leadership, we enter the territory of ambivalence. We are talking a language of temporary political alliance or coalition between citizens of both sexes, not a state of affairs that involves people walking arm in arm (man and woman or two men or two women) up a hill into a rosy sunset. Progressive politics has trouble embracing the ethos of temporary deal-making that capitalists and patriarchs do very well. Politically progressive types have high ideals. They want to agree completely with the people they are doing their politics with. This can lead to disaster, and has tended to prevent several Green parties from fulfilling their potential. Many political activists spend much time and energy on the political equivalents of wanting to be in love, wanting to be married to each other, without realizing that these are the old stories about relationships in action.

I have found it hard to get a discussion going about this ineluctable, unavoidable, unhealable, but potentially radical ambivalence between the sexes. The brother–sister story is a useful and interesting way to start to address the theme, offering the possibility that men and women can do their politics as men and as women, which is what many if not most of them want to do. Regarding ambivalence, although the brother–sister relationship is supposedly a relation of equals, we know that, for diverse cultural and psychological reasons, often it is not. Ambivalence, perhaps the most difficult thing to manage in political terms, is written into the sibling relationship as it is written into social relations generally.

Sibling leaders will also fail. This is because, unfortunately (and I speak absolutely personally here), the siblings, full of radical imagination, all too soon become the parents, full of a new and pressing desire to keep the status quo and even to turn back the clock, retaining power as they go. So sibling leadership, although good-enough in all the ways I have been using the term, fails because the siblings grow up and lose their radical edge.

DRAWING TOGETHER

What I have tried to do is to position some ideas about good-enough leadership against a background of a transformative politics, which I see as something quite powerful from an energetic point of view, but relatively powerless from the point of view of conventional political power and influence. I think that good-enoughness, which is a concept that all therapists and counselors are familiar with, has also got out into the culture, because it steers a middle course between idealization and denigration. Good-enoughness seems particularly relevant to the problem of leadership. I think good-enoughness involves letting people down, which in turn involves certain kinds of failures. If we think about leadership in terms of failure, the results are worthwhile. The three particular images I have wanted to share with readers are of particular fascination to me; others will find other images via which to address the perennial problem of leadership.

BIBLIOGRAPHY

Adams, M. (1996) *The Multicultural Imagination: 'Race', Color and the Unconscious*. London and New York: Routledge.

Beck, U. (1992) *Risk Society: Towards a New Modernity*. London: Sage.

Bhabha, H. (ed.) (1990) *Nation and Narration*. London and New York: Routledge.

Brecht, Bertolt. (1962) *Galileo*, trans. Eric Bentley, London: Methuen.

Chirimuuta, R. and Chirimuuta, R. (1987) *Aids, Africa and Racism*. Burton upon Trent: Chirimuuta Publications.

Freud, S. (1920) "Post-scriptum to a discussion on lay analysis," *Standard Edition 20*. London: Hogarth.

Hillman, J. (1969) *The Myth of Analysis*. New York: Harper.

Iyengar, S. and McGuire, W. (eds) (1993) *Explorations in Political Psychology*. Durham and London: Duke University Press.

Jung, C. G. (1946) Preface to "*Essays on Contemporary Events*," *Collected Works 10*. London: Routledge & Kegan Paul.

Laplanche, J. (1976) *Life and Death in Analysis*. Baltimore, MD: Johns Hopkins University Press.

Samuels, A. (1989) *The Plural Psyche: Personality, Morality and the Father*. London and New York: Routledge.

Samuels, A. (1993) *The Political Psyche*. London and New York: Routledge.

Samuels, A. (1995) "The good-enough father of whatever sex," *Feminism and Psychology* 5(4): 511–530.

Chapter 4

The feminine and politics

Betty D. Meador

The idea that at some historic time women dominated culture politically, economically, and socially is so radical a concept that its mention tends to evoke reactions of fear, rejection, or ridicule. Images of one-breasted, sword-wielding Amazons, devouring mothers, spell-casting witches, seem to overwhelm consideration and abort rational reflection. Yet we are confronted with archeological evidence, spanning thousands of years, of a predominance of female figures and fertility images in cave-wall paintings, rock art, remains of apparent religious buildings, figurines, and portraits (see e.g. Levy 1948; Goff 1963; Mellaart 1967; Gimbutas 1982, 1989). Did women rule in these societies from the Upper Paleolithic, 40,000 BCE, through most of the Neolithic, 7000 to 3500 BCE, in Europe, Asia, the Near East, Africa, even Australia?

This question, perhaps unanswerable, forces us to contemplate the puzzle presented by the raw material. What do all these representations of women mean? Considering that we are looking at a period of over 30,000 years, we can be sure that there is no one explanation. We do know, however, that the predominance of female images gradually gave way, between 3500 and 1600 BCE, to a predominance of representations of males. Writing on the first clay tablet texts appeared in Sumer in about 3300 BCE, at which time we begin to have documents and stories that help explain not only the figurative representations, but also the shape of the culture. We designate the appearance of writing as the beginning of historic time, an assumption unfortunately biased against cultures that had no written texts. Do they not also have history?

The very difficult problem of history before writing is that we have no texts, and we must learn to read the images and other cultural remains in order to grasp meanings in the lives of these ancient people. One popular and coherent explanation of the predominance of female images is that ancient people organized culture around a worldview radically different from the one we assume in the Euro-American western world, in the Islamic population, and in much of the remainder of the globe. That hypothesis, put simply, asserts that our ancestors held up images of women as sacred, and this idea became the central organizing force of society. Many of the thousands of images of women that archeologists have discovered were apparently figures pertaining to religious belief; they represent goddesses.

The fertility cycles of women and the representative goddesses symbolized the processes of growth and decay in all living plants and animals. In other words, the evidence fits societies whose core orienting belief regards the given world of nature as a sacred expression of divine will, a world whose variety and aspects are most aptly symbolized by figures of women as goddesses.

Until very recently this has indeed been considered a radical idea because it is so alien to western scientific mentality. Euro-American culture has as its central deity a single male god, prevailing, all powerful, entirely removed from the vicissitudes of the natural world. He has power over nature. This belief is quite opposite to that of our ancestors, who observed the myriad workings of the divine in all living things. The implications and consequences of these two opposing worldviews demonstrate the power of myth in politics. The first, that of the ancients, reveres the natural world. Its people live as beings among all other beings and phenomena occurring in nature. They devised rituals and beliefs that convey meaning and give structure within the constantly changing patterns of nature and fate. The second, that of most of the modern world, reveres a one true, unrepresentable, male deity who alone has power in the universe. He started it all with a Big Bang. He chose "man" as his helpmate and gave "him" power over plants and animals as well as over women. This god separated human beings from nature and elevated them above the rest of creation.

By itself, neither of these myths seems entirely viable in the complexities of today's world. The nature-immersed ancients, believing all beings to be equal, could require group cooperation and demand submission to norms that would discourage individuality and personal achievement. Conversely, the nature-dominating attitude of the current worldview is a disaster to the planet, and supports a superiority of western males, particularly white males, beliefs that are crippling to women and people of color all over the world.

The story I am painting with a very broad brush is a mythological story, not a solid scientific one that can be firmly established from the data of archeology. It is a story developed from a mythological interpretation of the visual images of prehistory. This method of interpretation evolved in the last one hundred years, as the investigations of Freud and Jung connected mythic drama to the hidden processes in the human psyche, in the unconscious. My story, then, is based on a modern way of understanding individuals and groups of human beings by interpreting their symbolic icons and their mythology.

According to this method, mythic drama is not random but reflects the state of psychological development of the people who believe it. A culture's myth or myths reflect its religious beliefs as well as its political and social forms. C. G. Jung spent his life deciphering mythic images. We can turn to his work for an overview of the influence of myth on the psyche. In his book *Aion* (Jung 1959) he collected the common mythic images of our age and connected their evolution to historical and cultural events across a 2000-year period. This 2000-year *aion* corresponds to the period in which the sun rises in the heavenly constellation of Pisces. Jung presents convincing evidence that in astrology the projection of meaning on to heavenly bodies originates from the same source as mythic imagination, namely the unconscious psyche of individuals and groups.

In describing the myth of the past 2000 years in the west, Jung asserts that the collective psyche has enacted a drama whose mythic theme and backdrop reflect two opposing forces, a myth projected on to the opposite-facing fish in the astrological sign of Pisces. At the beginning of our era, the spring point, that portentous moment of sunrise at the spring equinox, entered the northerly or easterly fish in Pisces. The spring point moved across the first fish's southern edge and entered the tail of the second fish in about the sixteenth century at the time of the Reformation. The spring point has now moved across the southern edge of the second fish and will enter the constellation of Aquarius in the third millennium. By one calculation this event took place in 1997. By another it will happen in 2154.

During the course of this passage through Pisces, the collective psyche developed a story of two hostile brothers corresponding to and represented by the two opposite facing fish. Jung says the dominant symbol of the first fish was the image of Christ. That is to say, the vitalizing archetypal motif, the motif that shaped culture, politics, and religion for the first thousand years or so, was a particular spirituality. In the sixteenth century, as the spring point entered the second fish, known as the Anti-Christ, the vitalizing spiritual archetype degenerated into rationalism, intellectualism, and masculine logos. Thus, the two brothers are hopelessly split into two irreconcilable halves. In other words, the sweep of the prevailing beliefs of a given age are held not simply in an individual, nor in a group of powerful individuals, but in an unconscious, consensual affirmation of the majority of people in the entire culture. Over time these beliefs and values evolve and change. Because of the human tendency to engage in unconscious projection, we "find" our dominant story outside ourselves, in this case in the starry heavens.

Significantly, neither the image of Christ nor of the Anti-Christ includes the body, instinctuality, intuitive knowing, or the spirit in nature, but the belief systems they both represent specifically exclude them. In these systems instinctuality, particularly sexuality, is to be restricted or overcome. Consequently these now repressed hallmarks of the ancient reverence for nature are projected, in this case on to women and Satan. Therefore, both symbols, the Christ and the Anti-Christ, lack wholeness.

By contrast, it is easy to find evidence that our ancestors located the divine in the natural world and saw cyclic paradox and contradiction at the heart of matter. Evidence of their observation of cyclic process is first apparent in the Paleolithic people's recordings of the phases of the moon. These first moon-watchers documented the progression of the moon with carved markings on horns and bones (Marschack 1972). The moon became the first timepiece. Surely the correspondence of women's menstrual cycles to the 29.5-day phase of the moon was noted at this early time. The moon displayed waxing and waning, three days of darkness, then swelling light. We surmise that the paradigm of opposites, dark and light, scarcity and plenty, death and life, formed a backdrop of expectation that was the foundation of their worldview.

The three days of the dark moon took on an ominous character, portending disintegration and disaster. Ritual that sought to contain and regulate this three-day sojourn of the moon deity focused on women's careful tending of their menstrual periods. Woman is the only mammal whose period parallels the moon's phases, her 29.5-day cycle corresponding exactly with the moon's. The time of awesome bleeding must have carried a conviction of a connection to the moon deity.

Judith Grahn's visionary book *Blood, Bread, and Roses* (1993) describes this elementary ritual in which fragile consciousness moved dangerously close to the disintegrating power of the numinous dark moon and the sacred blood. In the menstrual hut the women enclosed themselves in darkness as a reminder of the dark time of chaos before world creation, i.e., before the little human group had secured consciousness of itself. Consciousness was held and protected there by ritual acts and taboos. Ultimately the world was created again, and the women returned to the light. According to Grahn, their sacred belief was that this monthly enactment protected the entire tribe, its history, its emerging cultural values, and its consciousness of itself. Naturally, it also influenced its politics.

I am using the material evidence of moon-tracking along with documentation of menstrual ritual to support a mythology based on paradox, on the containment of dark and light, death and life, scarcity and plenty, evil and goodness, violence and peace, a whole array of opposites. This mythology "taught" its believers to expect change and to develop forms to contain their vulnerability as subjects of their paradoxical goddesses and gods. Its wisdom lies in its ability to describe the legitimacy of opposing qualities, dark and light, as elements along a continuum. As an example, we know that worship of the moon god Nanna/Suen in Mesopotamia was widespread by the time of the first written evidence, suggesting "a well established cultic organization . . . probably of great antiquity" (Hall 1985: 224–225). Moon god worship in the ancient Near East may reach back to the beginning of the fourth millennium BCE, and continued almost into the Common Era; the cultic practice, the personnel, and the epithets of the moon god remained virtually constant over this 3000-year period. The qualities of change and rebirth were ingrained and frequently cited as characteristics of the moon god. It is possible that this mythology prevailed in the cultures of prehistory, and continued even after the final conquest of the lunar dragon goddess Tiamat by the Babylonian solar hero Marduk around 1600 BCE.

In contrast, the heroic mythology of nature-dominating monotheism tends to separate the opposites into disputing factions, fueling the psychological processes of splitting and projection. One may argue that splitting and projection serve ego development, and therefore individuality, providing the mechanism to renounce instinctual gratification and activate the powerful forces of desire for competition, achievement, and conquest. To be sure, the past 3600 years have witnessed enormous human achievement. Nevertheless, psychologists have learned over the past hundred years that the process of withdrawing unconscious projections fosters development into maturity. Understanding that the content of one's projections belongs to the shadowy unconscious reservoir of one's own psyche facilitates psychological growth and contributes to healthy self-knowledge.

On the brink of the millennium we are entering a new astrological age, the age of Aquarius. The image of Aquarius is the water bearer. Our eyes see in the starry constellation a figure holding a jar, pouring from it a stream of water. Immediately we grasp the difference between the warring brothers of Pisces and this gentle stream of water from the jar of Aquarius. Water in a creek or river collects substances from both banks. Water seeps through any crack. It dissolves sharp divisions. In a poem from 2300 BCE by the High Priestess Enheduanna, the Sumerian goddess Inanna says:

> A swollen, spilling water
> I have washed over the grasslands
> A rushing, risen water
> I have overrun the rope fence
> (Meador, forthcoming)

Jung believed that the Aquarian Age, the next 2000-year period, would constellate the problem of integration of the opposites in individuals and in the psychic forces of collective societies. In a logical movement of the psyche we would shift from the sharp splitting of opposites during the past 2000 years, into a time of wrestling with the difficult task of legitimizing and unifying these opposing ideas and forces.

If we follow Jung's paradigm of the mythological meaning in 2000-year astrological ages, the changing consciousness of the new millennium should be apparent by now in the real world. Such a sweeping transition will occur in fits and starts, will disrupt the status quo, will produce clashes of values, backlash, prophetic forecasts, and some significant change. If the hallmark of the past millennium was the projection of our dark inhumane motivations on to others, that trademark was most obviously apparent during the past decades in the west's view of the Soviet Union as the evil empire. The dangerous animosity between east and west took us more than once to the brink of disaster. In a surprising evolution the Communist hold on eastern Europe began to loosen, and their regimes toppled like dominoes. The Soviet Union lost its evil persona and revealed itself as a struggling, demoralized populace led by a power-grabbing elite. At the thrilling moment of the fall of the Berlin Wall, my husband and I were having dinner in a French village. Next to us sat a couple from Berlin. With little common language, the four of us acknowledged the event with warm looks, handshakes, and tears. With the collapse of the wall, the hatred that had separated east from west evaporated; the projections disappeared. The four of us in that small restaurant were four human beings greatly moved by the dissolution of the impenetrable barrier between the two sides of the wall. The crumbling of the Berlin Wall will remain an image of the resolution of the forces of entrenched enemies. Opposition reconciles.

Vaclav Havel is a political leader who lived through the Soviet domination of his country. Now President of the Czech Republic, he voiced his prediction of an era coming to an end in a speech at his receipt of the Liberty Medal in Philadelphia on 4 July 1994. Here is a prophet and a politician speaking:

> There are good reasons for suggesting that the modern age has ended. Many things indicate that we are going through a transitional period, when it seems that something is on the way out and something else is painfully being born. It is as if something were crumbling, decaying, and exhausting itself, while something else, still indistinct, were arising from the rubble.
>
> . . . something is being born, we are in a phase when one age is succeeding another, when everything is possible. Yes, everything is possible because our civilization does not have its own spirit, its own esthetic.
>
> (Havel 1994: A17)

In a time of great change we can expect voices of optimism, insight, and hope, as well as predictions of destruction and disaster. There will be those who cling ever more strongly to the values of the past, who fear the inevitable disruption which change brings. Havel's vision is on the side of hope.

> The artificial world order of the past decades has collapsed and a new more just order has not yet emerged. The central political task of the final years of this century, then, is the creation of a new model of co-existence among the various cultures, peoples, races and religious spheres within a single interconnected civilization.
>
> (Ibid.)

Before his audience of Americans celebrating Independence Day and democracy, Havel asserted that the fundamental ideas of modern democracy "are not enough. We must go farther and deeper" (ibid.).

> We are not at all just an accidental anomaly, the microscopic caprice of a tiny particle whirling in the endless universe. Instead, we are mysteriously connected to the universe, we are mirrored in it, just as the entire evolution of the universe is mirrored in us.
>
> (Ibid.)

Havel's large vision is that of a wise man. I imagine the deeply thoughtful Havel, hiding for years from the Communist regime, in jail, suffering, sacrificing, writing it all down. He came through his ordeal whole and real, with enough wise detachment to watch his beloved Czechoslovakia split in two, and still he remained the leader of the Czech Republic. Havel, the man and his vision, is a model for us of the wholeness and wisdom that is possible for one who transcends the deterioration of old forms and outworn mythologies. We do not know what the new myths will be, but we do recognize in Havel the wisdom and perception and openness to apprehend the new.

I recall seeing President Havel on TV in Washington, standing beside President Clinton, responding to reporters' questions concerning Clinton's then predicament, his possible impeachment. Havel replied that in this case he did not understand American culture. Had the reporters been able to grasp the mythological background of these political events, they might have explained the situation to Havel by quoting Representative Tom DeLay of Texas: "It was . . . a debate about relativism versus absolute truth"; or Representative J.C. Watts of Oklahoma: "What's popular isn't always right. . . . Polls would have rejected the Ten Commandments" (Clymer 1998: 26). These two voices invoke Christian biblical absolutism and the law of Moses to support impeachment, and in so doing they reveal an entire mythology.

In psychological terms biblical absolutism advocates the renunciation of instinctual gratification. Individuals bear the severe responsibility for their emotional and moral life: their rages, passions, lusts, greeds. The fear of eternal damnation shines a bright light on the treachery of the body's appetites.

In an interesting parallel, medieval alchemists described a similar situation of the human soul in its trek toward wholeness. In this, the initial process, the alchemists explain the necessity of luring the soul away from the desires of the body toward the moral stance of the spirit. They called this joining of soul and spirit the *Unio Mentalis*, i.e., being of one mind, having a singular morality based on spiritual principles (Jung 1963: 471). At this stage the alchemists are as one with the Christian right. Essayist David Denby, speaking of the Ten Commandments, says Moses' renunciation of instinctual gratification makes him a hero of civilization (1998: 187). Civilization survives by rules of law that restrict the acting out of bodily appetites. Christian interpretations of Mosaic law permeate the puritanical residue in American culture. It is the foundation of the "absolute truth," Representative DeLay invokes.

The upheaval of the 1960s was in many ways a reaction to the severity of a restrictive, unrealistic morality. The events of the 1960s exposed the cracks in the idealized hero and the virginal maiden. The flower children lived out the other side of the impossible standards of morality underwritten by certain Judeo–Christian teachings. These events were the first widespread cultural announcement of the end of an era and the beginning of a new underlying mythology. The spontaneous eruption of a worldview genuinely counter to the prevailing culture was fueled by an eruption from the unconscious of long repressed contents.

The morality of the 1960s was summoned in the impeachment debate. Clinton, a child of the 1960s, was suspect to sincere Republicans. He was said to have "avoided military service, smoked marijuana, and repeatedly cheated on his wife" (Bruni 1998: 6). Former Representative Robert F. Drinan of Massachusetts described the Republicans as having "a deep animosity to Clinton. . . . These people say that Clinton is responsible for abortion and homosexuality" (Nagourney 1998: 6). On the other side, Betty Friedan, speaking from the point of view of a dualistic mythology, called the impeachment leaders "a bunch of dirty old white men" (Bruni 1998: 6). Representative Maxine Waters of California concurs: "Republicans are the vehicles being used by the right-wing Christian Coalition to direct and control our culture" (ibid.).

The lines were clearly drawn. The impeachment debate swung between the adamant believers in a fierce morality and those who search for a new moral conviction that can embrace human frailty. The impossible standards of the Ten Commandments are self-defeating. Denby says:

> Moses, who asks us to worship what we can only imagine, and who is himself oddly unreachable, even hidden, represents the heroism of self-denial and a loathing of the commonplace. At the end of his life, his tormented fears reveal the contradictions in those demands. He holds others to standards that God has judged in him to have violated. He is not a hypocrite; he is a human failure like the rest of us, only far angrier about it than we are.
>
> (Denby 1998: 189)

House Majority Leader-elect Robert L. Livingston announced his withdrawal from the post before the House impeachment vote, presumably because of pressures brought about by his confession of marital infidelity. Minority Leader Richard A. Gephardt implored Livingston to reconsider, declaring that the founding fathers created "a government of men, not of angels" (Gephardt 1998: 32). He forecast that the standards "of an unobtainable morality" will empty the seats of Government. "We are on the brink of the abyss," he said, calling the process "this downward spiral which will culminate in the death of representative democracy" (ibid.). These strong words from a level-headed man reveal the persistence of a conflict of extremes. The outmoded morality of the past will die hard.

Change that questions the moral and religious values of a culture is bound to produce upheaval. The very splitting into extremes this change could resolve becomes the reaction on both sides to the turbulence. An example of the extreme is in the events of the 1960s with their excessive disregard for basic community values fueled by a naive idealism. The breaking of boundaries of the 1960s filtered into middle America. Being too old to revel in their hedonistic delights, I spent those years keeping my teenaged children alive and leading what seemed at the time to be a revolutionary invention called the basic encounter group. With naive and fervent zeal my humanistic organization carried the banner of salvation through self-revelation. Our largest conquest was an entire Catholic school system, grade school through college, and the order of nuns who ran it. In small groups of eight to fifteen people we sat through hours of intense, intimate, feelingful confession. Many of the sisters ultimately left the Order. I believe we counted these resignations as victories.

I am not saying what we did was wrong, only naive. The women who left the Order did so with thoughtful and intelligent consideration. However, I do not think that many of us as leaders had the maturity or experience to understand the complexity of individual psychology and the potential for psychological damage to one who in a weekend is encouraged to let go of a lifetime of defenses.

Now this confessional atmosphere has invaded the national government. To minimize its destructiveness, this atmosphere that pierces the veil of public political persona requires a mature tolerance for human nature and a new inclusive mythology. Neither of these is yet in place.

Havel's vision calls upon "a renewal of our certainty that we are rooted in the Earth and, at the same time, the cosmos" (Havel 1994). Our roots stretch down into the Earth, into the reality of the human condition, into limitation and mortality. At the same time we belong to the cosmos through some mysterious connection. In the foresight of the old alchemists, we must now rescue the soul/spirit union from its isolation and return it to the body from whence it came. The three, body, soul, and spirit, must learn to live together in paradoxical harmony. The only way this can happen, say the alchemists, is by the production of the *caelum*, an ethereal blue substance, "the azure quintessence," related to the divine spark hidden in the individual or "the God-image imprinted on the world" (Jung 1963: 494). Only when the *caelum* is in place can the soul resist the forceful desires of the body. Even then, the soul falls, and falls again.

British psychoanalyst Donald Meltzer describes three "states of mind" that have a striking parallel to the stages of the alchemists (Meltzer 1973: 151–156). First is the "rebellious state of mind" that would surely involve the alchemists' image of the soul yielding to the appetites of the body. With attention to moral and spiritual values, the soul wrests itself away from the desires of the body and aligns with the spirit, Meltzer's second stage, "the conservative state of mind." Finally, with the anchor of the large perspective of a sense of sacred meaning to life in the universe, the soul/spirit duo dares to re-enter the body and risk its potent desires. The parallel in Meltzer's scheme is the "revolutionary spirit," a spirit that can think and act creatively and independently, freed both from the body's demands and from the conformist claims.

Given the human predicament, we ask what we can expect of our political leaders. Havel's example reminds us that wisdom comes with age, experience, and, indeed, suffering. His vision, like that of the alchemists, includes the "certainty that we are rooted in the Earth and, at the same time, the cosmos." That certainty is born of an inner experience of a divine image and a conviction that "we are not . . . just an accidental anomaly but mysteriously connected to the universe." His conviction makes possible the ability to find a position, comparable to Meltzer's revolutionary spirit, above the opposites, one that includes the earth and the cosmos. He calls on us to honor the Earth Mother, saying,

> the dense network of mutual interactions between the organic and inorganic portions of the Earth's surface form a single system, a kind of mega-organism, a living planet, Gaia, named after an ancient goddess recognizable as an archetype of the Earth Mother in perhaps all religions.
>
> (Havel 1994: A17)

This "dense network" swells and recedes in unending natural process, in paradoxical cycles.

The wisdom of tolerating paradox surfaced long ago in the character of the Sumerian goddess Inanna. She seems to express the guiding belief of our ancestors that divine being surges through matter and legitimizes the paradoxical swings from one side to the other, of blessing and curse, scarcity and plenty, life and death. With its very female correspondence to the cycling of the moon, this system of belief belongs to the archetypal feminine. Compensating for thousands of years of subordination, the wisdom of the archetypal feminine now emerges to take its place in a newly forming mythology that includes the vicissitudes and imperfections of nature. As we search for the elements of the new myth, we can look to the writings of the first poet of record, Enheduanna, Sumerian high priestess to the moon god and goddess in Ur around 2300 BCE, and devotee of Inanna. Enheduanna's poems to Inanna teach us about paradox.

your hands seize the seven fixed powers
  my queen of fundamental forces
  guardian of essential cosmic sources
you lift up the elements
bind them to your hands
gather in powers
press them to your breast
vicious dragon you spew
  venom poisons the land
like the storm god you howl
  grain wilts on the ground
swollen flood rushing down the mountain
YOU ARE INANNA
SUPREME IN HEAVEN AND EARTH

In the wide steppe
the silent glare of noon
she turns to black and shrouded light
she blurs the eyes
so friend's face
changes shape to foe. . . .
Mistress Plow
the vacant wastelands
split beneath your tooth
before you
the high-flown proud
bend wily necks and
strain against your truth. . . .

She is Inanna
Bearer of Happiness
whose strapping command
hip-dagger in hand
spreads radiance over the land
fish dragged from the deep
in her stretched-out net
never will slip through
birds trapped in her nimble cast
thrash in the fine-eyed mesh . . .
The scent of fear stains her robe
she wears
the carved-out ground plan
of heaven and earth . . .
mercy compassion attention
returning your heart to someone
folded-hand prayer
are yours Inanna
your storm-shot torrents
drench the bare earth
moisten to life
moisture bearing light
floods the dark . . .

to run to steal away
to cool the heart to soothe
are yours Inanna
fitful wandering
speeding by
rising falling
reaching the fore
are yours Inanna
to destroy to build
to lift up to put down
are yours Inanna
to turn man into woman
woman into man
are yours Inanna

mistress of the scheme of order
great Queen of queens
babe of a holy womb
greater than the mother who bore you
you all knowing

you wise vision
lady of all lands
life giver for the many
faithful Goddess
worthy of powers
to sing your praise is exalted
You of the bountiful heart
You of the radiant heart
I will sing of your cosmic powers
(Meador, forthcoming)

The new millennium, the Aquarian Age, the new mythology, will evolve as we, as individual human beings, evolve. To be conscious of the inevitable clash of the forces of desire within us, to develop the ability to tolerate paradox, reality, human limitation, these are the demands that we face. More importantly, we are called on to bear the anguish, even humiliation, of a changing image of the divine. We wait for this new mythology. Fortunately, its evolution can take its time. We have 2000 years.

BIBLIOGRAPHY

Bruni, F. (1998) 'Week in Review', *New York Times*, 20 December.
Clymer, A. (1998) 'National', *New York Times*, 20 December.
Denby, D. (1998) 'No Exodus', *The New Yorker*, 7 and 14 December: 180–189.
Gephardt, R. A. (1998) 'National', *New York Times*, 20 December.
Gimbutas, M. (1982) *The Goddesses and Gods of Old Europe 7000–3000 B.C.*, Berkeley and Los Angeles: University of California Press.
—— (1989) *The Language of the Goddess*, San Francisco: HarperCollins.
Goff, B. L. (1963) *Symbols of Prehistoric Mesopotamia*, New Haven: Yale University Press.
Grahn, J. R. (1993) *Blood, Bread, and Roses*, Boston: Beacon Press.
Hall, M. G. (1985) 'A Study of the Sumerian Moon-God, Nanna/Suen', unpublished Ph.D. thesis, University of Pennsylvania.
Havel, V. (1994) *New York Times*, 8 July.
Jung, C. G. (1959) *Aion*, New York: Pantheon Books.
—— (1963) *Mysterium Coniunctionis*, New York: Pantheon Books.
Levy, G. R. (1948) *The Gate of Horn*, London: Faber and Faber.
Marschack, A. (1972) *The Roots of Civilization*, New York: McGraw-Hill.
Meador, B. D. (forthcoming) *Inanna: Lady of Largest Heart*, Austin: University of Texas Press.
Mellaart, J. (1967) *Catal Huyuk*, New York: McGraw-Hill.
Meltzer, D. (1973) *Sexual States of Mind*, Perthshire, Scotland: Clunie Press.
Nagourney, A. (1998) 'Week in Review', *New York Times*, 20 December.

Chapter 5

The Wizard of Oz

A vision of development in the American political psyche

John Beebe

The Wizard of Oz, the 1939 MGM color musical starring Judy Garland, Bert Lahr, and Ray Bolger, has been reissued so often that its presence within the American psyche has the quality of a recurrent dream. As nearly everyone knows, it is about a little farm girl, Dorothy, who, in what may or may not be a dream, is blown with her little dog Toto from Kansas by cyclone to the fairyland of Oz. With the help of a Scarecrow, a Tin Man, and a Cowardly Lion whom she meets along the Yellow Brick Road that leads to Oz's Capitol, she must persuade the country's ruling Wizard to develop a way for her to return home. In the course of these adventures, Dorothy kills two Wicked Witches and secures the invaluable protection of a Good Witch, who in the end turns out to be the mentor who guides her safely home.

This sentimental mythology is made to work because of the sure vaudevillian touch with which the transcendental meanings are delivered – as if Ralph Waldo Emerson were being pantomimed by Ed Wynn, right up to the end, when most of the actors gather for a final tableau. After years of simply enjoying its magic, I have thought to reflect on the film in these pages because it seems to address the American psyche directly. As the title of this chapter suggests, I think this movie about a journey across incommensurable realms offers a vision for bridging other opposites of the kind that divide the nation in its present crisis of value.

A recent analysis of the film by Salman Rushdie (1992) indicates the high estimation this seeming child's entertainment has achieved in its sixty years of repeated re-release. In the fall of 1998, a restored, color and sound corrected digital print won new respect not only for the high achievement of the film's various components – script, acting, cinematography, special effects, music, dance, costumes, and sets – but for their integration into a meaningful whole. As Rushdie notes, this integrity is all the more remarkable because "it's extremely difficult to say who the artist is" (Rushdie 1992: 13). *The Wizard of Oz* had a producer and associate producer with strongly creative personalities, four successive directors, at least two sublime stars and, by the bumpy filming's end, three charismatic supporting actors, as well as an exceptional team of expert scriptwriters and a remarkable lyricist and composer to shape the meaning of its story. A newspaperman and early specialist in marketing techniques, L. Frank Baum, had first told the story at the turn of the century to his own children (Traxel 1998: 140; 300–3).

He developed it into a best-selling children's book that quickly became the basis of a successful stage musical – the first of the major reconfigurings by other than the original author's hands (Gardner and Nye 1994: 26). Yet we will not be misled if we linger awhile with the problem of Baum's original intention in creating this profitable property.

Baum himself said in his April 1900 preface to the first Chicago edition of *The Wonderful Wizard of Oz* that it "was written solely to pleasure children of today" and that it "aspires to being a modernized fairy tale, in which the wonderment and joy are retained and the heart-aches and nightmares are left out" (Hearn 1983: 2). But it seems clear that he also took the occasion to limn the political reality of turn-of-the-century America. As Henry M. Littlefield first suggested in the similarly turbulent year of 1968, the cyclone that Baum envisages as hitting Kansas is likely to be his allegory for the Populist Movement. By the time Baum began to compose *The Wizard of Oz*, this movement had swept the entire Midwest into its vortex and had propelled the "silver-tongued orator," Nebraska Senator William Jennings Bryan, into his crusading 1896 run for the Presidency against the Eastern financiers' favorite (and eventual winner) William McKinley. Bryan's animus against the Republican Establishment "monometallists," who wanted America's paper currency to be backed up only by gold bullion, was enunciated in his famous "Cross of Gold" speech at the Chicago Democratic Convention ("You shall not crucify mankind upon a Cross of Gold"). His aim was to protect the farmers who preferred a loose, even inflationary monetary policy, since they had frequent need of credit. The Populist solution that he had appropriated for the Democratic Party was to continue to use silver as well as gold to back the currency, a strategy that also appealed to silver mining interests in the West. Bryan won the nomination, and L. Frank Baum participated in his torchlit parades. Bryan's rhetoric must have moved Baum to allegorize the more conservative Republican approach to economics as a fairy-tale Yellow Brick Road leading to an impossibly affluent Emerald City, where McKinley would preside as humbug Wizard (Littlefield, in Hearn 1983: 221–233).[1]

Of the passionate, yet stubbornly abstruse twenty-five-year political debate over Free Silver versus the Gold Standard, historians Samuel Eliot Morison and Henry Steele Commager made a classic assessment:

> We can see now that the issue was both deeper and less dangerous than contemporaries realized. It was deeper because it involved a struggle for the ultimate control of government and of economy between the business interests of the East and the agrarian interests of the South and the West – a struggle in which gold and silver were mere symbols. It was less dangerous because, in all probability, none of the calamities so freely prophesied would have followed the adoption of either the gold or the silver standard at any time during these years. When the gold standard was finally adopted in 1900, the event made not a ripple on the placid seas of our economic life. When the gold standard was abandoned by Great Britain and the United States, a full generation later, the

> event led to no untoward results. Historical parallels and analogies are always dangerous, but we are safe in saying that in the light of the experience of the 1930's much of the high-flown discussion of the 1890's was fantastic.
> (Morison and Commager 1950: 249)

Today, with the tools of Jungian psychology, we might better recognize why the idea of a Gold Standard elicited such an angry response from the political unconscious at the end of the nineteenth century. As an image symbolic of the metal that in alchemy was the earthly counterpart of the sun (Sol), an exclusive privileging of gold suggested the predominance of solar masculine values within the ruling establishment. In the grip of religious fervor unaccounted for by his economic argument, Bryan was urging his party to balance the Gold Standard with that of Silver, a metal which we know from Jung's alchemical researches to be the terrestrial representative of Luna and thus a symbol of the Feminine Principle. Already, through the charismatic leadership of the "silver-tongued orator," the Democratic Party's twentieth-century matriarchal stance, with its Eros toward the economically less fortunate, was taking shape in opposition to the more traditionally patriarchal Republican position emphasizing self-reliance.[2] But although such an interpretation of Bryan's movement would be fully compatible with the pre-eminence which Baum gives to the feminine in the narrative structure of the Oz books as a whole, its full implications would not have been conscious for Baum at the time. Baum must have imagined he was writing a topical satire of the politics of his day that children, amused by the pretensions of their elders, might at least intuitively appreciate and adults enjoy, even as it let him express his own political views. Littlefield, who has shrewdly deciphered the ingenious allegory, believes that the Scarecrow, with his anxiety over his intelligence, reflects the lack of self-confidence among many Midwesterners still reeling from the accusation leveled against them by William Allen White in an 1896 article called "What's the Matter with Kansas?" White, asserting that Kansas' farmers were ignorant, irrational and generally muddle-headed (Hearn 1983: 227), had suggested they should be worried about their thinking. The Cowardly Lion, according to Littlefield, is Bryan himself, with his mighty oratorical roar, his underlying chronic insecurity, and his ultimate courage in taking on the East Coast establishment. The rusted Tin Woodman's unwilling immobility represents the fate of the unemployed workers in the East after the Depression of 1893. The pair of Wicked Witches might refer to the threats posed, on the one hand, by the environment (i.e., drought, the traditional witch "of the West" that can only be "put out" by water) and, on the other hand, by the market (traditionally under the negative control "of the East"). These adversaries, the allegory argues, can be defeated through the energy provided by the Populist cyclone if only farmers can learn to think for themselves, mobilize their potential allies among the politically rusty East Coast workforce, and muster their courage in standing up to the hypocrisy of central government. Otherwise, the soul of traditional agrarian America must remain, like Dorothy, lost and unable to find its way home.

Although this is a convincing political reading of the tale, we cannot reduce the meanings of this perennially popular story to these topical references of the year of its creation or even to the probable intentions of its creator. Rather, Littlefield's exposure of the political subtext better serves us if it enables us to grasp that *The Wizard of Oz*, like so many works that have captured the American imagination, derives a good deal of its energy from a primary concern for the political health of the nation.

In the case of *The Wonderful Wizard of Oz*, this concern survives in the later constructions that have been placed on the tale. When the story was made into a film forty years after Baum first wrote it out, for instance, the allegory's point of reference seemed to have shifted to Midwestern anxiety about America's turn to internationalism on the eve of the Second World War. Its 1938 script certainly trumpets the message so often sounded by the isolationists at that time: "There's no place like home." In the 1970s with the advent of women's liberation and the feminist and gay rethinking of the constrictions of traditional gender-roles for men and women, the film began (in Jungian terms) to signify a triumph of matriarchal values over the threatening patriarchal anima (Witch) and the pompous patriarchal animus (Wizard). A liberated gay man, for instance, might describe himself as a "friend of Dorothy" and locate his own individuation story in hers (Hopcke 1989). Today, after winning the Cold War, we watch *The Wizard of Oz* knowing that our young nation's fate, inevitable as Dorothy's in the face of the cyclone, has been to be swept onto the international stage in the uncomfortably prominent role of peacekeeper, the destroyer of all world wickedness. From that last perspective, the film can now seem like a warning dream coming from some prescience in the American psyche of 1939, urging us to stiffen our integrity lest we lose our national center in the inflation of becoming the world's leading power, one indeed "not in Kansas anymore."

The Wizard of Oz, however, is more than a warning, for it resolves the tensions it creates. The anxiety is beautifully brought to life by Judy Garland, who is an image less of Baum's little Dorothy, as captured by W. W. Denslow's original drawings, than of a growing, insecure nation on the verge of its debut as a mature world power. But the film moves its heroine, and our sense of ourselves as a nation, toward the mature integrity we feel at the end when Dorothy, in a closing set piece suggestive of wholeness, is back from the dream and nightmare of Oz, and finds herself safe in her own bed, surrounded by seven of the Kansas characters. This final scene is like the coda of a human symphony, making explicit an eight-fold structure of consciousness in the relation of these characters to each other and to Dorothy. With this tableau as a key to the structure of the film, it is possible to trace how Dorothy's individuation proceeds through her links to the other characters.

The interaction of eight characters is one way to visualize the differentiation of consciousness in an individuating psyche.[3] Within such a polyphonic arrangement, the distinct consciousnesses represented by the characters have, like so many voices in a democracy, a potential for harmony, but one that will be either undermined or achieved by the particular political process which the film records. I call that process *political* because it involves alliances, contending parties, and struggles for audience and power, all revealed by the way the characters in a film play out their psychological roles – their different consciousnesses – in relation to each other. In a film with particular resonance like *The Wizard of Oz*, these roles can be specifically metaphoric of the political developments taking place in the American psyche at the moment of the film's construction.

A natural starting point in elucidating this political structure within *The Wizard of Oz* is with Dorothy herself. In terms of the film's idiosyncratic politics of American consciousness, the little girl's standpoint is privileged. She emblematizes a form of what nowadays is called "emotional intelligence" (Goleman 1995). As played by Judy Garland, who is ever poised to react to the feelings of the other characters (including her little dog Toto) and make them her concern, this standpoint is what C. G. Jung has called *extraverted feeling*.[4] It is in relation to this standpoint that we can understand her special relationship to the Scarecrow, the first of the fantastic companions she picks up on the Yellow Brick Road. The Scarecrow, who famously starts their acquaintance by singing and dancing Harburg and Arlen's "If I Only Had a Brain," is a marvelous depiction of the insecurities captured by Jung's phrase "inferior introverted thinking." According to Jung's theory of psychological types – that is, types of psychological consciousness, or what present-day cognitive psychologists call "intelligences" (Gardner 1983; Thompson 1985) – introverted thinking is at the opposite end of a rational axis from extraverted feeling. There is also a power differential in these arrangements. If extraverted feeling is superior, introverted thinking must be inferior. And indeed, the Scarecrow has an inferiority complex and gives image, with his comical physical incoordination, to the inherent unreliability of any "inferior function." The character's movements are not entirely under his conscious control, due to the flimsy quality of his embodiment as a cloth man stuffed with straw. But his connection with Dorothy gives him a "spine" to replace the beanpole she helps him down from. We can visualize the two characters together as the backbone of the movie itself. Their relationship is central to the integrity of the film. Figure 5.1 illustrates what I mean.

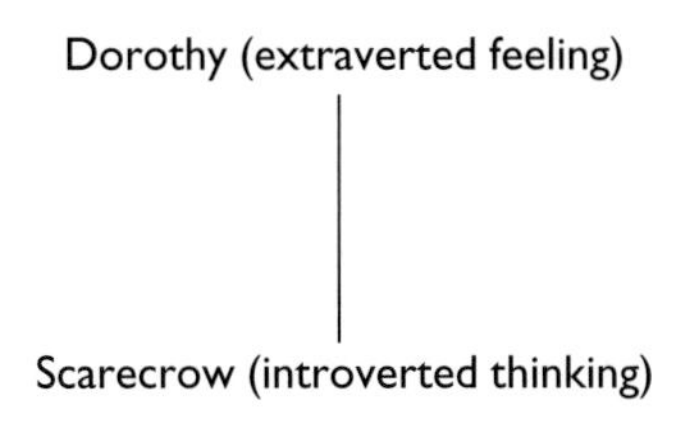

Figure 5.1 The relationship between Dorothy and the Scarecrow

In parenthesis, I have defined each character in Jungian terms according to the typical form of consciousness which that character displays throughout the film. The *position* of the characters in relationship to the other is also important if we want to understand the consciousness politics of the film. In relation to the Scarecrow on the spine or axis of integrity of the film, Dorothy is in the superior position. We have already suggested as much by saying that throughout the film her kind of intelligence is privileged. Although Dorothy describes herself as "the Small and Meek" when introducing herself to the Wizard (who with characteristic puffery has described himself as "Oz, the Great and Terrible"), there is little doubt that she trusts her feeling responses more than does any other character. In the end, it is just an uncensored spontaneous feeling reaction that allows her to accomplish the heroic deed of melting the witch by throwing a bucket of water over her. Dorothy is related to as a superior person, not only by the Munchkins whose Mayor and officials greet her as a visiting dignitary, but also by all the other characters. She is thus a perfect image of Jung's "superior function" of consciousness, a political designation that I have elsewhere described as the locus of the hero archetype in any psyche (see Harris 1996). Similarly, the Scarecrow – a marginally adapted even if magical figure with whom most people would not want to be seen in public – is a good personification of the way the animus (in relation to a woman's superior function) is forced to carry the "inferior function."[5] We could therefore draw our diagram again with new labels that emphasize the political relationship of archetypes in this arrangement of consciousness (Figure 5.2).

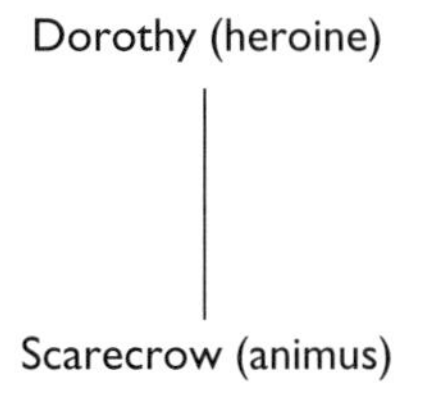

Figure 5.2 The political relationship between Dorothy and the Scarecrow

Putting the two kinds of construction – hierarchical status and archetype – together, the political diagram of these relationships would resemble Figure 5.3.

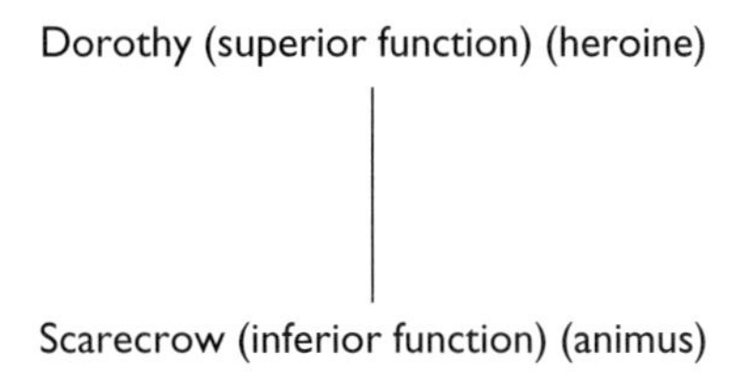

Figure 5.3 The relationship according to hierarchical status and archetype

When we start to introduce the other characters around this "spine" that defines the politics of consciousness within *The Wizard of Oz*, we can also identify an axis of "auxiliary" functions that set out to assist Dorothy in mature and less mature ways. This much more "irrational" axis is defined by Glinda the Good and the Cowardly Lion. Glinda represents a very motherly, and I would say introverted, intuition, which "knows" the right magic to protect Dorothy but largely keeps her knowledge of its workings to herself, until the time seems right to share it. The

Yellow Brick Road that she asks Dorothy to follow is itself an image of intuition, which Jung notes is frequently symbolized in fantasy by the color yellow (Jung 1959: 335, 379). On the other hand, the Cowardly Lion, in his physical size, his bullying swagger, and his need to impose his body on others ("Put 'em up, put 'em up!" he demands, as he thrusts forth his clenched fists and swings his tail) is defined in terms of *extraverted sensation*. This type of consciousness, according to Jung, can be a formidable intelligence, too, the inverse of introverted intuition in its immediate attention to present realities, but here it is in a primitive level of development. In contrast to Glinda's implied parental position within the story as Great Mother, he has the status of the Great Baby, whom the other characters must chide or reassure. He oscillates between boastful omnipotence ("I'll be King of the Forest") and cowering terror ("Why'd you have to do that?" he blubbers, when Dorothy slaps him across the nose for growling at Toto). Indeed, part of the comedy of the Lion, as played by Bert Lahr, is that his intuition is so inferior that, for all his fearfulness, he never seems to anticipate the real danger he invites by the physical (extraverted sensation) abandon with which he wades into each new situation. It is not so much that he lacks courage as that his courage is of the *puer aeternus* type. Bert Lahr's Lion displays an inflated sense of what he can pull off that is easily punctured by reality, at which point he falls into despair over his own cowardice. The *puer aeternus*, like the Great Mother, is an archetype that Jungian psychology has reintroduced to Western culture. Although the Latin (from Ovid) means "eternal boy," the phrase is perhaps best translated as a patient of mine once rendered it: endless boy. This certainly seems to define the Cowardly Lion. And so we can draw an auxiliary character axis for these two opposed consciousnesses that bring their strength to Dorothy (Figure 5.4).

Figure 5.4 An auxiliary character axis

Locating these characters now around Dorothy and the Scarecrow, we get a basic quaternity of figures that defines the particular pattern of consciousness which emanates from the story itself (Figure 5.5).

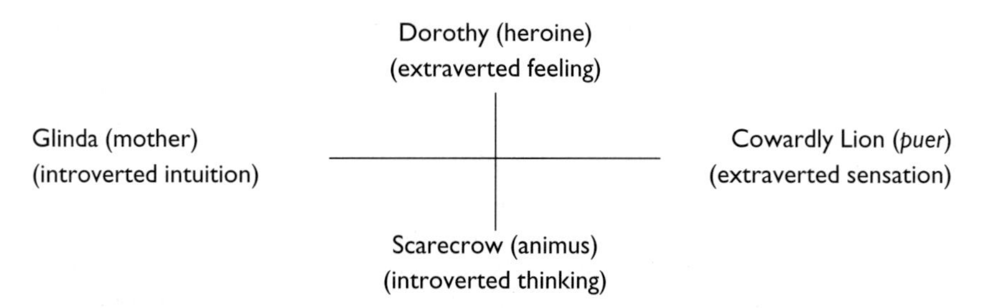

Figure 5.5 The pattern of consciousness emanating from the story

If, however, we replace the particular character names and the archetypal roles they occupy in the story by names for the consciousnesses they represent and add a political designation to suggest their relative *power* within the story, our diagram would resemble Figure 5.6.

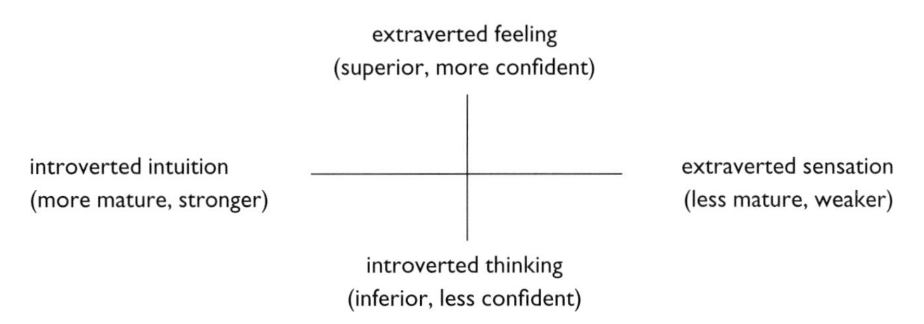

Figure 5.6 Consciousnesses and their political designations

Figure 5.6, as *aficionados* of Jungian type theory will recognize, defines the consciousness of the extraverted feeling type with auxiliary introverted intuition, or what the Myers-Briggs Type Indicator (a standard test of the pattern of consciousness preferences in individuals) scores as ENFJ. A recent description of ENFJ in the type literature is as follows:

> On the great highway of life, ENFJs are car poolers, making sure that everyone has a ride, wears a seat belt, and gets where they're going, safe and sound. . . . They have a psychological turn of mind, an interest in the journeys people take and how they're negotiated.
>
> (Thomson 1998: 357)

This description sounds like the sensibility of *The Wizard of Oz* taken as a whole. The consciousnesses of the characters and their relative positions combine to give the film itself a definite consciousness – that is, a certain set of concerns which define it not only as a psychological, but also as a political space. By establishing the positions of the characters in relation to each other in terms of the way they feel about themselves, how the other characters relate to them, and the degree of emotional development they display, we can understand the consciousness politics of the film.

Movies, of course, do not depend only upon functions of consciousness to get their effects. They also, notoriously, depict forms of unconsciousness that challenge the more conscious characters with life's threats, dangers, and complications, as well as their own defenses against moving forward. Unconsciousness itself is a political force in *The Wizard of Oz*, as we see in the remarkable scene where the enchanted poppies put the flesh-and-blood characters to sleep and threaten to stop this particular "road movie" in its tracks. And of course the entire film (unlike Baum's novel) is cast as a dream experienced by Dorothy in a coma, after a blow on the head by a window loosened in the cyclone. That the unconscious presents itself to Dorothy and her conscious helpers in the form of various personalities who represent a system of threats and defenses suggests that the film expresses a reaction to trauma itself. As Donald Kalsched has demonstrated, such shadow figures play a major role in the psyche's response to being traumatized, and they are both ambivalent sources of further complication as well as unexpected sources of help from within. What Kalsched (1996: 62) has written about therapeutic work is also true for our struggle to make sense of the psyche in art and politics:

> We encounter here a supreme irony in our work with the psyche. The self-same powers that seemed so set on undermining our . . . efforts – so ostensibly devoted to death, dismemberment, and annihilation of consciousness – are the very reservoir from which new life, fuller integration, and true enlightenment derive.

From the standpoint of Baum's allegory, the trauma from which Dorothy is seeking to recover is the split in the American political psyche itself, its historic, tragic tension between populist and plutocratic interests. It is from this "basic fault" in the American political psyche that the characters in the Oz story first drew life, and their tensions survive the later retellings of the tale.

We will now examine figures in both the novel and the film that are truly shadowy, in that neither their potential for good nor for evil is entirely clear, even when it seems to be. Rather, they participate in the murky ambivalence of the unconscious itself, as something not just to be overcome but to be faced and learned from. The most obvious of these characters is the Wizard. When he is unmasked at last by Toto, who pulls aside the curtain concealing the humbug, as the Scarecrow correctly names him, Dorothy is moved to offer one of her spontaneous, forceful feeling evaluations: " Oh, you're a very bad man!" The Wizard replies, "Oh no, my dear, I – I'm a very good man. I'm just a very bad wizard" (Langley *et al.* 1994: 62). Yet the same man, who with callous opportunism sent Dorothy and her friends to bring back the broomstick of the Wicked Witch of the West (a politically "smart" move, since the Witch had already sky-written with that broom her command to him to "surrender Dorothy"), proceeds to use his rhetoric to show them how best to think about themselves. In other words, he serves initially to undermine the consciousness of the ultimately prevailing characters, but ends up extending it. He is an image of the power of the unconscious to be used in both cruel and kind ways. Such ambivalence is characteristic of a psychological intelligence used demonically, and the Wizard as described by Baum in the novel resembles a demon in the way he assumes different shapes. To Dorothy he appears as a great Head, to the Scarecrow, a lovely Lady, and to her other, more sensitive, companion, the Tin Woodman, as a "most terrible Beast." (This last demonic avatar reminds us that the remarkable ability of a demonic figure to be "cruel and kind at the same time" was perhaps first remarked upon, as Joseph Henderson has noted (Jung *et al.* 1964:138), by Beauty's father in the quintessentially psychological fairy-tale *Beauty and the Beast*.)

In the film, however, it is the Scarecrow who is in the best position to stand up to the Wizard's impressive iconography and rhetoric by saying, "You humbug," a choice of words Frank Morgan's extraverted thinking Wizard for once does not correct and subvert. ("Yes, that's exactly so, I'm a humbug."[6]) This is a crucial moment in the politics of the film when the integrity of the Scarecrow's incisive introverted thinking succeeds in standing up to the obfuscations of the Wizard's demonic extraverted thinking. This confrontation near the end of the film is reminiscent of the moment before the cyclone trip to Oz when Dorothy rebukes Almira Gulch (who is trying to have the biting and cat-chasing Toto destroyed) by exclaiming "You wicked old witch!" In that earlier confrontation, our extraverted feeling heroine is standing up to a strongly opposing will symbolized by another feeling standpoint, the *introverted feeling*[7] Miss Gulch, who is solely concerned with protecting her own interests and doesn't care about the feelings of others.

We are now in the politics of confrontation, when consciousnesses encounter opposing attitudes, with respect to introversion and extraversion, in the form of figures they experience as shadowy. The characters that give the film its spine of integrity can be diagrammed in relation to their antagonists, naming the psychological types associated with each character. We should understand that even a figure of the unconscious can exhibit a characteristic type, implying that there is intelligence in the unconscious, although it is typically used in an unconscious and frequently unethical way, hence the description of such functions of potential but problematic consciousness as "in shadow" (Figure 5.7).

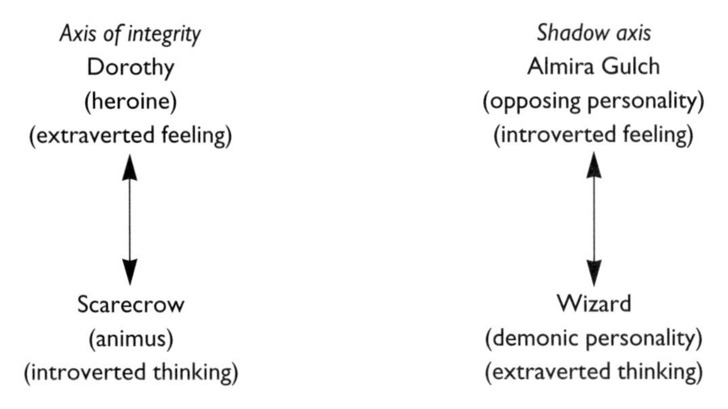

Figure 5.7 The characters in relation to their antagonists

In this scheme, we can see that Dorothy's heroic extraverted feeling is opposed by the introverted feeling of Almira Gulch, and that the Scarecrow's righteous indignation, expressing an animus demand for a higher standard of integrity, is directed against the pompous obfuscations of the Wizard. But these diagrams, emphasizing that similar psychological functions when deployed in ways that diverge with respect to extraversion and introversion seem to produce characters who are opposed in other ways, delineate the political stance of the characters whose relationship constructs the spine of the film. The connection of the extraverted feeling Dorothy to the introverted thinking Scarecrow is defined by their love for each other. By contrast, the introverted feeling Almira Gulch and, at least initially, the Wizard, are mere deployers of power, tyrants in their respective realms. We should look more closely at these shadow characters who together define a challenge to the spine of the film.

Although played by the same actress, Almira Gulch does *not* correspond in every psychological detail to the Witch she becomes in Dorothy's dream. Margaret Hamilton's extraordinary performance is in fact a dual role no less than the twin sisters played a few years later by Bette Davis in *A Stolen Life* and Olivia de Havilland in *The Dark Mirror*, films which define this Hollywood convention. The challenge to the actress to play two sharply contrasting characters in the same picture is traditionally posed in an American film by one character being (in the language of psychological type) extraverted and irrational, and the other introverted and rational. The political preference within the traditional American psyche for women who are introverted and rational, usually introverted feeling, can readily be noticed here. In terms of traditional American values, this has the psychological implication of asking women to take up the position of anima figures supporting and granting the legitimation of their approval to the heroic extraverted thinking of its ruling men.

In the world of *The Wizard of Oz*, everything is topsy-turvy. The extraverted thinking "ruling man" is the humbug Wizard in Oz, and the introverted feeling Almira Gulch owns "half the county" in Kansas in which Aunt Em's farm is located. Far from being represented as an anima figure supporting the integrity of the power structure, she is presented as an opposing personality threatening the rule of care in governing human relationships. Yet even though her "better" character is already shadowy, Margaret Hamilton runs true to the dual role genre in which her performance falls, in being asked to play an even more wicked character who is extraverted and irrational. Her magnificently menacing Witch, who is constantly threatening Dorothy with what she is *going* to do to her, is a marvelous example of the shadowy (indeed witchy) use of the psychological consciousness which Jung calls *extraverted intuition*, the function which concerns itself, in any situation, with future possibilities. She discloses this promise of bad things to come not just with specific frightening suggestions but with the anticipatory delight of her evil cackle.

And, unlike Hamilton's Almira Gulch, Margaret Hamilton's Witch finds her typological opposite in the film not in Dorothy, but Glinda. Glinda, the Good Witch (who almost never discloses her designs) and the Wicked Witch of the West (who always does), take opposite attitudes toward the irrational intuitive power (the ability to perceive and conjure by way of the unconscious) that is traditionally the province of any witch. Again in the language of Jung's typology of character, Glinda the Good's attitude is that of the introverted intuitive, and the Wicked Witch of the West's attitude is that of the extraverted intuitive. The Wicked Witch's winged monkeys rather perfectly embody an intuition used to terrify others with its unexpected ability to get to them, just as the Witch is always inserting herself into Dorothy's private spaces and thoughts – for instance, in the crystal ball sequence when she elicits and then mocks Dorothy's anxieties about Aunt Em. This is just the opposite of Glinda's reassuring use of her self-contained, bubble-enclosed intuition to solace and focus Dorothy without intruding on the latter's autonomy.

We find a similar pair of opposed attitudes in the two animal characters in the film, who together occupy the other pole – sensation – of the irrational axis. Toto and the Cowardly Lion are opposed from the moment when the Cowardly Lion first makes his appearance. When the Lion growls and threatens Dorothy, the Scarecrow, and the Tin Man, Toto barks. The Lion goes after Toto, but Dorothy slaps the larger beast, reducing him, as we have seen, to a sort of whimpering baby. Toto's role here is to facilitate in the exposing of the reality behind the bluster. That is precisely what the little dog again does when the Wizard of Oz tries to put off keeping his promise to reward Dorothy, the Scarecrow, the Tin Man, and the Lion after they succeed in bringing him the broomstick of the Wicked Witch of the West. This time it is the Wizard who roars, "Do not arouse the wrath of the Great and Powerful Oz!" At this point, Toto runs to the background of the big screening room on which Oz's propaganda image surmounts the throne and pulls aside a curtain hanging to one side. That is when the human Wizard is finally revealed, talking into a microphone.

Toto, who is normally rather still and never charismatic, is really the character to expose what Rushdie calls the Great Humbug. Rushdie confesses that he "cannot stand" Toto, finding even the purposive bit with the curtain "an irritating piece of mischief-making" (Rushdie 1992: 17–18). Toto, who works behind the scenes, is personally unprepossessing, does not usually call attention to himself, and makes few wasted movements, is a marvelous image of introverted sensation, a consciousness close to intelligent animal sense which concerns itself with identifying what is real. In the final scene of *The Wizard of Oz*, when Aunt Em's rational solution to Dorothy's account of the journey to Oz is to tell the girl "we dream lots of silly things," Dorothy cries exasperatedly to the Kansans assembled around her bed, "Doesn't anybody believe me?" and Toto jumps up beside her, as if to say he can vouch for the reality of her experience. Introverted sensation is an irrational function, which can appreciate the reality of the psyche even against rational considerations, because it trusts the evidence of its own senses.

But Toto is also a trickster, who consistently moves the plot forward by creating some kind of mischief that breaks with an established order of things (biting Almira Gulch, growling at the Lion, jumping out of the hot-air balloon just as the Wizard is about to take Dorothy back to America). The effect is usually to subvert an inflated use of power and force Dorothy, out of her feeling for Toto, to take a stronger position in defense of caring generally. In other words, Toto galvanizes Dorothy's instinctive courage, the very quality which the Cowardly Lion lacks. The puerile Lion therefore reflects something immature in Dorothy's character that Toto is helping her to grow beyond.

By adding the shadow functions carried by the (Wicked) Witch and trickster, we can now more fully illustrate the interplay of consciousnesses that give energy to the auxiliary axis between intuition and sensation which drives the irrational plot of the film, forcing Dorothy through their cross-fire to develop her integrity as a character (Figure 5.8).

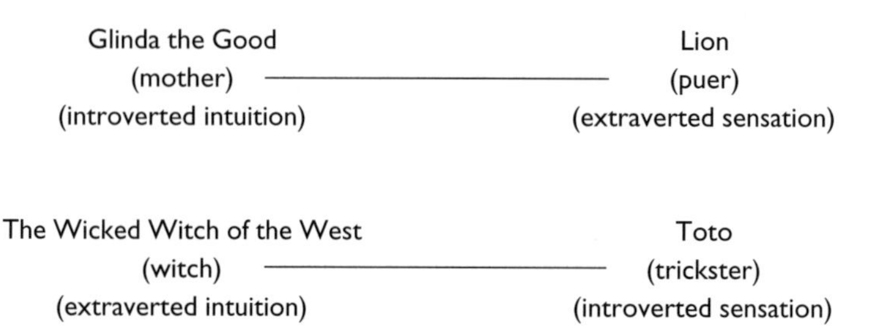

Figure 5.8 The interplay of auxiliary consciousnesses

The Witch's role in bringing out Dorothy's courage is obvious; that portion of the tale is a nineteenth-century hero story, with an obvious nod to Dumas. Dorothy becomes, perhaps, D'Artagnan (although she has to split this role with Toto), and the Lion, the Scarecrow, and the Tin Man become the Three Musketeers. This is the side of political effectiveness that is celebrated by successful revolutions, holy wars, and being on the "right" side in elections. It leaves out the deeper power of the shadow to catalyze political individuation, a development that can only take place when the shadow is included and appreciated as part of one's own political consciousness, rather than simply defeated or repressed as belonging to an Other who is "wrong." Heroic victories generally result in inflating the winner's standpoint beyond its true value. Here it really is up to the trickster to take the story of one's political development beyond simply "putting out the Witch." Anyone studying what Samuels has called "the political development of the person" (Samuels 1993: 53–61) should take heed of the way Toto forces even the victorious Dorothy to rethink her own values.

Nowhere in the film is Toto's shadowy role in linking Dorothy to her own need to think and feel made more evident than in the final scene of the technicolor (Oz) portion of the film, when, as a consequence of Toto's jumping out of the balloon basket, Dorothy is forced to turn to Glinda for help getting back home. When Glinda in her introverted way finally discloses to Dorothy the secret of the ruby slippers by leading Dorothy to articulate what she has learned in Oz about her "heart's desire," Dorothy is able to say with full heart, "There's no place like home." This is introverted feeling at last from the extraverted feeling heroine, and it is this expression of it that directs the slippers to grant her wish.

The deep red of the slippers would alone have justified the producers' decision to film *The Wizard of Oz* in color, for the hue imparts a value, and a psychological meaning, that Baum's Bryan-allegory "Silver Shoes" cannot convey. The power in the slippers is not just the power of the feminine, but the power of introverted feeling to deepen and ground love. This explains the role of two important characters in the film whom I have left until now to discuss: Aunt Em and the Tin Man. They are linked in Dorothy's fantasy by her shared concern for their hearts. In the Tin Man's case, the problem is simply his feeling that he lacks one, a problem that Dorothy takes on as if it were her own. In Aunt Em's case, real heart trouble is at issue. Or so Dorothy believes, for in the crystal ball vision related to Dorothy by Professor Marvel shortly after she runs away with Toto to escape Miss Gulch, the fortune-teller has seen Aunt Em putting her hand on her heart and falling onto a bed. Both Aunt Em and the Tin Man induce Dorothy to approach the problem within her own feeling, one that is not evident in the abundant empathy she shows for all the other characters and the appreciation they bestow on her for it. Dorothy's feeling, despite its privileged status in the film, is too unthinkingly, and too one-sidedly, extraverted.

It is not just Almira Gulch who is annoyed by Dorothy in Kansas. Aunt Em, that kindly, reserved keeper of order on the farm, whose caring for everyone is always held in reserve, is finally driven to ask Dorothy to "just help us out today and find yourself a place where you won't get into any trouble!" That place, of course, is "Over the Rainbow" – in Oz, where Dorothy is put magically in touch with the deeper value of harmony with her surroundings that Aunt Em is trying to convey to her.

One of the nicest touches in the film is that the quietly kind Aunt Em and the noisily mean Almira Gulch are psychologically actually quite similar. Both are concerned with property, and with proper order, and both, I think, are of the same psychological type. Miss Gulch defends her feeling with an extraverted thinking animus, personified by the Sheriff, whose order to have Toto seized she brandishes. Aunt Em shows the vulnerability of their type more openly when she says, "Almira Gulch . . . just because you own half the county doesn't mean you have the power to run the rest of us! For twenty-three years I've been dying to tell you what I thought of you . . . and now . . . well – being a Christian woman – I can't say it!" Interestingly, Almira Gulch can't respond openly either. The inability to articulate emotion that is nonetheless strongly felt is a particular hallmark of introverted feeling. But both women, with their different styles, oppose Dorothy's heedless willfulness with strong wills of their own coming from another direction.

> Introverted feeling, as Jung was the first to get us to see, is a valuation function which works at the archetypal (not the personal) level, taking the deepest possible sounding of a situation. It not only enables but compels us to feel the rightness and wrongness of images, arrogating from its very closeness to the archetypal a bench of judgment that grants it the power to decide what is appropriate and what is not.
>
> (Beebe 1992: 135)

This theme is carried forward in the Oz section of the film, when Dorothy happily starts to pick apples off an inviting-looking tree. The tree (an introverted feeling type) turns out to have other feelings than the extraverted generosity Dorothy instinctively expects. It asks, "How would you like to have someone come along and pick something off of you?" At this point in the film, Dorothy is no match for this attitude; she simply fails to understand it. The feeling value concealed in this standpoint is conveyed by the deep red of the apples on the tree, which "rhymes" visually with the ruby slippers. The overtones of the Garden of Eden in the forbidden apples suggest a Knowledge of which Dorothy is psychologically innocent. And this, of course, is the political issue at the heart of the film: the tension between extraverted feeling and introverted feeling. The value of introverted feeling is unavailable to the extraverted feeling because of the latter's blindness toward it. The tree is thus a marvelous symbol of the consciousness (and political problem) that I have already identified as the opposing personality challenging the heroine. It actually starts to throw its apples at Dorothy when manipulated to do so by the clever Scarecrow, who sees a way to get Dorothy her snack. But this comedic interlude, which culminates in Dorothy happily scrambling to pick up the apples, turns suddenly serious when her hand (that is, her extraverted feeling) presses into the hard, still foot of the Tin Man. The figure is rusty and immobile, and even after she oils him, so that he can talk, he quickly opposes her cheerful assurance that he's "perfect now" with a sarcastic retort: "Oh, bang on my chest if you think I'm perfect." Then the Tin Man explains that his chest is hollow because he hasn't got a heart.

In the ensuing song sequence, part of which is a duet, Jack Haley's Tin Man seems almost effeminately competitive with Garland's Dorothy. Like Almira Gulch, Aunt Em, and the Grouchy Apple Tree, the Tin Man embodies a feeling attitude that is opposed to Dorothy's. His appearance on the scene creates within the vaudeville show business leitmotiv of the film a political complication between the actors (upstaging) that was absent from Garland's previous duet with Bolger. From his sentimentality, moreover, it is obvious that the Tin Man doesn't exactly lack a heart; what he lacks (as the Wizard shrewdly figures out) is a testimonial, that is, an extraverted attestation of his feeling (which the Wizard gives him in the form of a heart-shaped watch). That the Tin Man is, moreover, all armor suggests that his introverted feeling is somehow rigid. By now, the audience will already have noted that stiffening up is one of Dorothy's own most characteristic defenses, conveyed perfectly by Judy Garland's self-referential double takes. The narcissistic side of this defense does in a way lack "heart," because it cuts the character off from appreciating the introverted feeling of others. For all Dorothy's vaunted empathy, where is her feeling for Miss Gulch's concern over cat and garden, and for Aunt Em's desire for order on the farm?

One can trace a whole chain of figures and images representing the opposing personality type which Dorothy is gradually coming to terms with in the film – from Almira Gulch and Aunt Em, through the Grouchy Apple Tree and the Tin Man, and on to the Witch's Cossack-like guard. The series is punctuated by, and culminates in, the most mysterious of all these images of introverted feeling: the ruby slippers.

These slippers, which originally belonged to the "sister" of the Wicked Witch of the West, that is, to the Wicked Witch of the East, are, I think, meant to represent the concealed introverted feeling standpoint of Almira Gulch, which is the more obvious standpoint of Aunt Em as well. In running away from both of these women, and then being swept up by the cyclone – the objectified force of her own instinctive repudiation of their standpoint – Dorothy has in effect "killed" introverted feeling. Herein lies a political complication that Jung understood better than any other psychologist, and very few contemporary politicians are subtle enough to grasp. Jung tells us that when someone succeeds in killing, that is overcoming, the *mana* of another person (Jung defines this Polynesian word for charisma as the "bewitching quality of a person"), the conqueror then automatically acquires that mana (Jung 1966: 227–228). This, Jung tells us, is in accord "with the primitive belief that when a man kills the mana-person he assimilates the mana into his own body." Our extraverted feeling heroine must therefore accept the mana of what she has defeated, which is the introverted feeling standpoint of Almira Gulch (and, implicitly, of Aunt Em as well). That is why the ruby slippers appear on her own feet and seem almost to be attached to them, so that the Wicked Witch of the West realizes she will have to kill her to get them back. Dorothy does not learn how to use the slippers' power, however, until the end of the film.

Again we can illustrate these stations in Dorothy's political development, which gradually transform her character from someone who is merely a partisan of her own standpoint to someone who is truly able to appreciate the value of a standpoint that is completely opposed to her own (Figure 5.9).

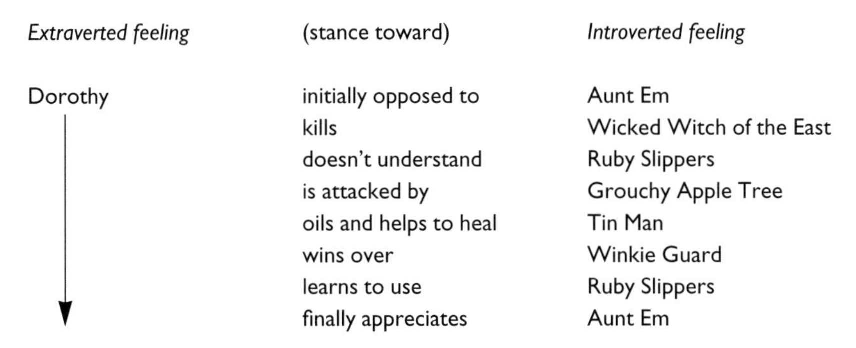

Figure 5.9 Stations in Dorothy's political development

It is an appreciation for the *introverted* side of feeling that Glinda the Good is able at last to bring out in Dorothy, when she gets her to articulate the value that the film calls "There's no place like home." This is the part of the script which many dismiss as sentimental or cynical, including Rushdie, who calls it a "conservative little homily," and Zipes, who says it "is all a lie" since the point of Baum's Oz stories is that "home cannot be found in America" (Zipes 1998: ix). What Zipes calls this "Home Sweet Home" ending can easily seem to lock into the isolationist Republican discourse of the America Firsters who were opposing Franklin Roosevelt's increasing interest in the problems of Europe at the time the film was made. Indeed, its introverted feeling was not at all a popular message by the time the film was released. Several re-releases were needed before the film made a profit, and only a series of annual television showings secured its status as a classic. America, after

1939, moved on to its manifest destiny to make the world safe for democracy, and extraverted feeling values were to predominate – that is, the values associated with selling and promoting "the American way of life."

We watch the film today in an age that has almost forgotten what introverted feeling is (could Gary Cooper be a star today?), and the return home to Aunt Em seems anticlimactic to many. At best the movie seems to record a return to traditional values which many politically sophisticated people are unwilling to make. Yet if one lets the magic of Judy Garland's performance work on one's political sensibilities, one can see how extraordinary it can be for a liberal extraverted feeling to make a gesture toward the other, more conservative, feeling standpoint. (It could be in the misunderstanding of introverted feeling's conservatism with regard to the fitness of things that liberal attempts to handle issues like abortion or homosexuality solely in terms of the feelings of unwed mothers or of gay people seeking legitimation for their relationships tend to fail. For progress to occur in the acceptance of these non-traditional contingencies of modern sexual life, some sense of feeling order apart from the sentiments of individuals must be addressed by the reformers, who would have to demonstrate a positive potential at that level to convince traditionalists to re-examine their positions.) It is much more common, in American films, for a cold, introverted feeling to warm up and make a concession to extraverted feeling. Garland's Dorothy, realizing as her own the power implied by the ruby slippers, really reaches out to Aunt Em, and we want to embrace her for it. On the part of the character, this is a step beyond maintaining the consistency of her own attitude, and also beyond the way she sharpened her integrity in Oz with the support of her magical helpers. Her final gesture, without disavowing her Oz experiences, is a stunning acknowledgment of a value beyond the heroic. Her political achievement in the film is finally not about justifying her own standpoint, but about finding common ground for the continuity of value.

Dorothy's ability, back in Kansas, to move herself into the territory originally pre-empted by Almira Gulch is paralleled by the Scarecrow's ascendance to the rulership of Oz when the Wizard abdicates in his favor. Together, Dorothy and the Scarecrow seem to represent a new, more conscious order with the integrity to supplant the patriarchal anima (Miss Gulch) and animus (the Wizard), who simply disappear from the story, like the totalitarian Wicked Witch of the West who melts away. This is of course the wishful level of Baum's fairy-tale, carried forward by the film. The Scarecrow, with his newly legitimized introverted thinking, promises to be a truly loving philosopher king, but this is in Oz, and ironic, because empathic introverted thinking has rarely prevailed in American politics. Even more rarely does the extraverted thinking that dominates America's discourse yield the power it wields by having control of the nation's image of itself. That power is satirized here in the portrait of the media-manipulating Wizard, who bears the same name as the country he rules. He is at best a well-intentioned purveyor of persona, at worst a propagandist, and his gracious surrender of power is exactly what we don't observe in this aspect of the American political character.

And just as ironic, in its distance beyond what we usually see, is the development of Dorothy's feeling. In an America whose dominant consciousness is extraverted thinking, extraverted feeling is in fact the function least likely to individuate. It is the one most likely to remain ambivalently in shadow, and thus to operate through rigid polarities of gratuitous charm and simplistic condemnation of what it does not understand. (John Travolta's character Vincent Vega in *Pulp Fiction* is a far truer depiction of this side of the American character than Judy Garland's unusual Dorothy.) And what is America's extraverted feeling, finally, but its political feeling, our feeling for each other within the contemporary fragmented *polis* that is our nation? It isn't hard to see in America today that political feeling is woefully undeveloped, and far more likely to be cynical, like Vincent's, than capable of seeing beyond its own self-interest, as Dorothy's does. Dorothy's colorfully visioned path of initiation, in which extraverted feeling sees through the overattachment to persona manipulations that the Wizard represents, and finds new value in a home that provides continuity and purpose, remains, for the political feeling of the country, a hopeful irony in a bleak political landscape.

Ever since Ronald Reagan's presidency, extraverted feeling has been making a comeback in America, but within a cynical culture and with disastrous consequences for the political health of the nation. Clinton's vaunted empathy, for instance, has all too evidently been unaccompanied by a respect for his own, and the country's, integrity. The problem has been mirrored in numerous films. For instance, in *As Good As It Gets* (1998) Jack Nicholson plays a man with demonic extraverted feeling who is ironically led to reconstitute himself as a lover considerate enough to finally win the introverted feeling waitress played by Helen Hunt. Throughout, their courtship is shadowed by the title's sense of limitation in what they can expect to accomplish together.

At the very end of 1998, a century after Baum began to bring *The Wizard of Oz* into being, Woody Allen released *Celebrity*, in which the hysterically floppy, Scarecrow-like introverted thinking type (played by Judy Davis) reinvents herself as a substantial contemporary success. She gets over her neurotic protests against the failures of value in contemporary life and accepts the guidance of a complacent, quietly shadowy producer of contemporary talk shows (Joe Mantegna), whose smoothly reassuring extraverted feeling propels her to a new career as one of his on-camera hosts. They end up marrying, in what feels like a compromise of her integrity. Her celebrity, like that of so many successful outcomes in the media politics of our day, is secured at the expense of value.

The final sequence of *Celebrity* occurs in a screening room to which the film's impotent Wizard (Kenneth Branagh as an extraverted thinking type entertainment writer) is taken. The image is from a new movie which begins with a plane slowly sky-writing the message, "Help." I think this is meant subliminally to make us recall that chilling moment in *The Wizard of Oz* when the Witch sky-writes her command to "surrender Dorothy." This time, however, it's as if the sky-writing is coming from Dorothy herself. I have not seen a more disturbing image in the past year. Imagine Dorothy, having succumbed to a greedy ambition, wandering lost in Oz.

APPENDIX

Archetypal complexes carrying the eight functions of consciousness in *The Wizard of Oz*

Dorothy
Extraverted feeling
heroine (superior function)

Uncle Henry, Glinda, Yellow Brick Road
Introverted intuition
father/mother
(auxiliary function)

Zeke, Lion, Citizens of Emerald City
Extraverted sensation
puer/puella

Hunk, Scarecrow
Introverted thinking
animus (inferior function)

Aunt Em, Almira Gulch
Grouchy Tree, Tin Man
Ruby Slippers, Witch's Guard
Introverted feeling
opposing personality (shadow of heroine)

Hickory, Wicked Witch
Winged Monkeys
Extraverted intuition
senex/witch
(shadow of mother)

Toto
Introverted sensation
trickster
(shadow of puer)

Professor Marvel, Wizard of Oz
Munchkins
Extraverted thinking
demonic personality (shadow of animus)

NOTES

1 See also Hearn (1973: 69) for a critique of these ideas, including the suggestion that, since the grandiloquent Wizard is originally from Omaha, Bryan may really have served as the inspiration for the character.

2 James Hillman, in his magisterial essay on the alchemical, archetypal meanings of silver (Hillman 1980, 1981), has noted that "the total collapse of the values of silver came during the heyday of western materialism, between 1870 and 1930, a debasement of silver that cannot be accounted for wholly in terms of new mines and mining methods." This was a time during which fact became divorced from value in many other areas of life. See especially Hillman 1980: 35–37.

3 For a discussion of my work on the differentiation of consciousness, see Harris (1996: chapters 4 and 5). In *The Wizard of Oz*, eight individual functions of consciousness are depicted: extraverted feeling (Dorothy), introverted feeling (Aunt Em, Almira Gulch, the Tin Man, the ruby slippers, the Grouchy Apple Tree, the Witch's Guard), extraverted thinking (Professor Marvel, the Munchkins, the Wizard of Oz), introverted thinking (Hunk, the Scarecrow), extraverted intuition (Hickory, the Wicked Witch of the West, the Winged Monkeys), introverted intuition (Uncle Henry, Glinda, the Yellow Brick Road), extraverted sensation (Zeke, the Cowardly Lion, the Citizens of the Emerald City), and introverted sensation (Toto). Note that two of the actors (Margaret Hamilton and Jack Haley) exchange psychological type when they move between the Kansas and Oz sections of the film. Although particular characters are left behind in Oz, in the last scene the eight *consciousnesses* come together in a final tableau. The archetypal complexes, i.e., subpersonalities, that I think structure this particular arrangement of functions and attitudes are shown in the Appendix to this chapter, where the relationship of the types to each other in *The Wizard of Oz* is illustrated.

4

> The extraverted feeling function concerns itself with other people's emotions – especially those that lie on or near the surface and are easy to sympathize with. Placing a value on people's feelings, extraverted feeling relates to them with discrimination, empathy, and tact. . . . In its shadow aspect, extraverted feeling tends to discriminate against feelings that are less easy to identify with, and therefore less socially acceptable.
>
> (Beebe 1992: 135)

5 Ann Ulanov has interpreted Dorothy's story "as a paradigm of a young girl's series of encounters with the animus function and with her ego's integration of the contents that the animus brings to it" (Ulanov 1971: 277–285). The animus, in Jungian psychology, refers to the support the unconscious gives to a woman's authority and is usually symbolized by contrasexual, i.e., male, figures. (The corresponding supportive and tutelary figure in the male unconscious is the anima.) From this standpoint, the Tin Man, the Cowardly Lion, the Wizard, and even Toto would be animus figures for Dorothy. I prefer, however, to reserve the term 'animus' for the figure most closely associated with the inferior function, who, when brought into relationship with the standpoint of the superior function, creates a plumb line of sufficient depth to allow the ego access to the ground of being (Jung's deep Self). This ego-Self axis associated with the animus is symbolized, in *The Wizard of Oz*, by the beanpole from which the Scarecrow attempts to give Dorothy directions when she has lost her way. Their ensuing contact succeeds in replacing this rigid, archetypal delineation of his potential to guide and ground her, with a living, human relationship that suggests the integrity Dorothy achieves through her connection with this "other." She later confesses that he is the one she thinks she'll "miss most of all" when she leaves the transformative Land of Oz.

6 The dialogue quoted from *The Wizard of Oz* is as given in the movie script published on the fifty-fifth anniversary of the film's release (Langley *et al.* 1994).

7

> The introverted feeling function concerns itself with the values expressed in the archetypal aspects of situations, often relating to the actual situation by measuring it against an ideal. When the actual is found wanting, introverted feeling can become intensely disappointed. Although it often finds it hard to articulate its judgments, or simply prefers to keep them to itself, introverted feeling also tends to ignore social limits regarding the communication of critical responses, to the point of appearing to depreciate others. It may withhold positive feeling as insincere and fail to offer healing gestures to smooth over difficult situations. In its shadow aspect, introverted feeling becomes rageful, anxious, and sullen. It may withdraw all support for attitudes it has decided are simply wrong, even at the risk of rupturing relationship and agreed-upon standards of fellow-feeling.
>
> (Beebe 1992: 135)

BIBLIOGRAPHY

Beebe, J. (1992) "Identifying the American Shadow: Typological Reflections on the Los Angeles Riots," *Psychological Perspectives* 27: 135–139.

Gardner, H. (1983) *Frames of Mind: The Theory of Multiple Intelligences*, New York: Basic Books.

Gardner, M. and Nye, R. B. (1994) *The Wizard of Oz and Who He Was*, East Lansing: Michigan State University Press.

Goleman, D. (1995) *Emotional Intelligence*, New York: Bantam.

Harris, A. S. (1996) *Living with Paradox; An Introduction to Jungian Psychology*, Pacific Grove, CA: Brooks/Cole Publishing Co.

Hearn, M. P. (ed.) (1973) *The Annotated Wizard of Oz*, New York: Clarkson N. Potter.

—— (1983) *The Wizard of Oz by L. Frank Baum*, New York: Schocken Books.

Harmetz, A. (1998) *The Making of The Wizard of Oz*, New York: Hyperion (paperback).

Hillman, J. (1980) "Silver and the White Earth (Part One)," *Spring*: 21–48.

—— (1981) "Silver and the White Earth (Part Two)," *Spring*: 21–66.

Hopcke, R. (1989) "Dorothy and Her Friends: Symbols of Gay Male Individuation in the Wizard of Oz," *Quadrant* 22(2): 65–77.

Jung, C. G. (1959) *The Archetypes and the Collective Unconscious* Princeton: Princeton University Press.

—— (1966) *Two Essays on Analytical Psychology* (2nd edn), Princeton: Princeton University Press.

Jung, C. G., von Franz, M. L., Henderson, J., Jacobi, J. and Jaffé, A. (1964) *Man and His Symbols*, Garden City, NJ: Doubleday & Company, Inc.

Kalsched, D. (1996) *The Inner World of Trauma: Archetypal Defenses of the Personal Spirit*, London and New York: Routledge.

Langley, N., Ryerson, F. and Woolf, E. A. (1994) *The Wizard of Oz*, Monterey Park, CA: The Movie Script Library, O.S.P. Publishing, Inc.

Morison, S. E. and Commager, H. S. (1950) *The Growth of the American Republic*, Volume Two, New York: Oxford University Press.

Rushdie, S. (1992) *The Wizard of Oz*, London: British Film Institute.

Samuels, A. (1993) *The Political Psyche*, London and New York: Routledge.

Thompson, K. (1985) “Cognitive and Analytical Psychology” (Review of Howard Gardner’s *Frames of Mind*), *The San Francisco Jung Institute Library Journal* 5(4): 40–64.

Thomson, L. (1998) *Personality Type: An Owner’s Manual*, Boston and London: Shambhala.

Traxel, D. (1998) *1898: The Birth of the American Century*, New York: Knopf.

Ulanov, A. B. (1971) *The Feminine in Jungian Psychology and in Christian Theology*, Evanston: Northwestern University Press.

Zipes, J. (ed.) (1998) “Introduction” to L.F. Baum, *The Wonderful World of Oz*, New York: Penguin.

Chapter 6

The politics of transformation: the transformation of politics

Andrew Samuels

Few would disagree that politics in many Western countries is fragmented and in a mess. We urgently need new ideas and approaches. In this chapter I suggest that we explore what psychology and the psychotherapies can offer as part of a general transformation of politics. In countries like the United States, Britain and Germany, politics is at a crossroads. Analysts and psychotherapists might ignore this and continue to focus on personal transformation, leaving politics to the professionals. Or we could try to transform self-concern into social and political concern, thereby transforming politics as we know it.

In the past ten years there has been a veritable explosion of interest in exploring the interface between Jungian psychology and politics.[1] Actually, it might be better to call it "post-Jungian psychology" to indicate both a connection to Jung's work and a critical distance from it. Analytical psychology has certainly not stood still since Jung's death in 1961 – but, as the psychoanalyst D.W. Winnicott put it, "there is no such thing as originality except on the basis of a tradition."

It seems to me that self-expression and self-development – the whole interior thing that analysis and therapy does reasonably well – and political activity are part of the same process. There is no need to abandon either analysis and therapy or politics. In the United States, Bill Clinton won the 1992 election partly by intuiting that, for many millions of people in the United States, political choices, as expressed in the crudity of voting, had become matters of self-exploration and self-expression. The Republican mid-term gains in 1994 traded off the same trend: when people look at their lives from the point of view of political ideas and commitments, what they see is an unfolding of their personalities in political terms. I call the figure of a new kind of citizen who walks in this space that is neither external and public, nor internal and private, "the politician within."

POLITICAL ENERGY

Jung noted that psychic energy was not confined in its expression to sexuality alone. He considered that energy flowed down "channels," citing biological, psychological, spiritual and moral channels. If there were also to be a political channel for energy, what would this involve? Political energy refers to the capacity to bring creativity, imagination and effort to bear on seemingly intractable problems and to try to solve them in ways that reflect concern for social justice. Hence there are usually spiritual and moral aspects to political energy as well. Imagine a computer graphic designed to show the location and quality of *political energy* in a modern country. The screen glows red in those places where political energy is to be found and pulsates in step with its intensity. Where would we find bright, flashing red lights? In the formal political institutions, in local and national capitals, in the military, in banks and factories? I doubt it. True, all of these are the traditional repositories of political *power*, and, true, they still control the economic and other resources – such as information – that make a complex modern society tick. But political energy has left these places and gone elsewhere. Politics has left its home base and gone out into the world to redefine itself and find other and new places to settle.

I see no need for me to *advocate* removing political energy from its moribund institutions. It is happening anyway. All one can do is to chronicle and struggle to comprehend one of the most significant sociocultural and psychological shifts to take place in the Western countries since the end of the Second World War. A striking feature in modern societies over the past twenty years has been the spontaneous growth of new social and cultural networks. More and more people are now involved in such networks – increasingly aware that what they are doing may be regarded as political. The elasticity in our idea of politics is not something done to politics by intellectuals. It is rather something which the very idea of politics seems actively to embrace. These new social movements operate in isolation from each other, seeming to have quite different agendas and programs. Because there is no alliance or coalition between them, they can only show up on our computer graphic as little scarlet pimpernels, scattered across the country. Yet their collective illumination, if we could garner it, measure it – and do this without damaging what might be going on – may be just what Western societies, starved of creativity and imagination in their politics, crave and need as we stumble into the next millennium.

These disparate social movements do have something in common, something psychological in common. They share in an emotional rejection of big politics, its pomposity and self-interest, its mendacity and complacency. They share a *Weltanschauung* and set of values based on ideas of living an intelligible and purposeful life in spite of the massive social forces that mitigate against intelligibility and purpose. They share a commitment to a *transformation of politics*, something I call the "resacralization" of politics. "Sacral" means holy, and the idea is to pick up on the attempt to get a sense of purpose, decency, aspiration and meaning back into political culture. As Jung put it, "we are so accustomed to regard meaning as a psychic process or content that it never enters our heads to suppose that it could also exist outside the psyche" (Jung 1952: 915). Even if such a state of political affairs never really existed, we behave and think as though it did – hence resacralization. Political reformers and resacralizers share a disgust with present politics and politicians – sometimes it is literal disgust, the gagging reflex, an ancient part of the nervous system, absolutely necessary for survival in a world full of toxins.

Such movements include environmentalism, demands for the rights of ethnic and sexual minorities, animal liberation, complementary medicine including therapy and counseling, spiritual and religious groups including paganism and neo-paganism, rock and other kinds of music and art, finding God in the new physics, sports, organic farming, and the pursuit of alternative lifestyles generally. The membership of these movements runs into millions, far more than are actively involved with the great political parties. In fact, every now and then a political party (the Democrats in the United States, the Liberals in Britain) will try to harness the rainbow energy in these resacralizing movements and turn it into votes. But something usually goes wrong when the parties try to assimilate the resacralizers.

Let me be the first to say that a transformation of politics at the end of the millennium is not going to happen in a simple and speedy way. It may not happen at all, given the uncontrollability of the social realm of existence! Many would dispute that the cumulative public significance of these developments is positive. Is not the proliferation of new networks and cultural practices merely a symptom of social malaise – a selfish retreat into personal, individual preoccupations, reflecting an abandonment of the aspiration to truly political values? Moreover – and it is a good argument – reactionary fundamentalist religious movements can also be seen as resacralizing. I admit it, there's always a down side. But what gets highlighted when religious fundamentalism is brought into the picture is the vastness of the energy pool available for the political reforms that are urgently needed. I remember discussing this topic with the director of a university center for the study of cultural values and environmental change. He asked me bluntly how my ideas differed from such concepts as pop singer Michael Jackson's "Heal the World" concert. For a moment I was flummoxed and could do no more than concede that Michael Jackson and I were undoubtedly responding to the same things "out there." Then inspiration came and I told the director that, without this self-same pool of energy, his own center would not have come into existence and achieved its remarkable success. He took the point, I am happy to say.

It often seems amazing to me how little progressive political people have managed to learn from the religious Right. I am not saying it would be desirable to share the moralistic and simplistic approaches of the religious Right. But it would be worthwhile trying to figure out what it is that such politicians have heard in the yearning of so many people in the Western world. It would be tragic if the most psychologically minded politicians were to turn out to be the leaders of the religious Right.

Words like "spirituality" are politically neutral. The harnessing of spiritual passion and energy for politics is not in itself bound to lead to conservative outcomes. In fact, history tells us how radical religions have been over time, whether in promoting the rise of capitalism and the bourgeoisie, or as a source of socialist ideas, or important principles, such as passive resistance and non-violence.

When I refer to psychology and to the psychotherapies in connection with politics, I have in mind modes of being as much as professional activities. I seek to encourage deep reflection on the great political issues of the day and on politics itself so that a recognition can emerge that there really is no divide between the spiritual and the social, between the private and the public, between the inner life and the world of politics.

Hence I believe we should read resacralization positively – as a healthy complement to the rapid decline in public identification with orthodox political institutions. In fact, if there is a future for formal politics, it may be on the back of resacralization. My further idea is that the resacralizing movements carry the seeds of new forms of politics that, going beyond formal politics, chime with modern, culturally diverse societies, forms which would indeed imply a transformation of politics or at least of what constitutes political activity. This is the kind of politics that feminism prepared us for but, for whatever reasons, did not take far enough, beyond the level of what is known (personal), to the level of what is not yet known (the unconscious), where the radical imagination sleeps, waiting to be tapped for political projects.

A POLITICAL PSYCHE

It is more important than ever to renegotiate what can be meant by politics so that we can engage with issues of empowerment and disempowerment in a more psychological way. In the late modern or postmodern Western world, politics and questions of psychological identity are linked as never before. This is because of myriad other interminglings: ethnic, socioeconomic, national. The whole picture is made more dense by the exciting and rapid course of events in the realms of gender, sexuality and sexual orientation. Because gender sits on the threshold between inner and outer worlds (part of personal identity; part of social reality), it is not surprising how central gender issues are in any discussion of the transformation of politics.

As I mentioned, it was feminism which introduced us to this new kind of politics. It is a *feeling level* politics, a subjective politics that encompasses a crucial interplay between the public and the private dimensions of power. For political power is also manifested in family organization, gender and race relations, in connections between wealth and health, in control of processes of information and representation, and in religious and artistic assumptions.

What might the role of psychology and the psychotherapies be in a transformed politics based on a search for intelligibility and purpose in social life, a search that is implicitly and sometimes explicitly spiritual and transpersonal in tone? We must acknowledge the limitations of a psychological approach to politics. Freud, Jung and the founders of humanistic psychology like Maslow had ambitions to be of use in the political world. But that world never really showed up for its first therapy session with them! I do not think this reluctance by twentieth-century politics to undergo psychological treatment of itself can all be put down to resistance to therapists. There is something offensive and ridiculous about the mechanical psychological reductionism that has been produced from time to time. I recall an article by a psychoanalyst in a newspaper during the Gulf War about the phallic symbolism of cruise missiles going down ventilator shafts in Baghdad, or a statement by another analyst that students protesting in Paris in 1968 were functioning as a "regressive" group. Jungians are just as bad: it doesn't help to be told that the military-industrial complex is all due to the Greek God Hephaestus. So-called archetypal themes and images can get used just as reductively as any Freudian ideas that childhood is decisive. Both are equally problematic in politics as the failure of both psychoanalysis and analytical psychology to comprehend what was happening in the 1930s show. Of whom was Jung writing in 1931 when he commented that, where civilization is the topic of discussion, "the speaker finds himself caught in the same presuppositions and is blinded by the same prejudices as those he wishes to view from a superior standpoint" (Jung 1931: 104)? (I have written at length in my book *The Political Psyche* (1993) about Jung's activities and writings in the 1930s. I believe that everyone's interests – Jungians and non-Jungians alike – are served by the most extensive research possible together with whatever concomitant changes in theory and practice might seem desirable.)

A multi-disciplinary approach is crucial as we face up to the possibility that we might lose the political altogether if we do not ourselves reclaim it from the media and the pundits. It is not that the media and their star columnists or presenters ignore psychology altogether. They certainly use a form of psychology. My concern is that a false dialogue has been started between psychology and the politicians in which we all join in a wild analysis of our politicians in a desperate search for the one with personal stability and integrity. It is a search that usually ends up with the provision of a single-strand nostrum for political ills – "integrity" gets misused like this. The professional psychologists are often little better. In the 1920s it was "genitality;" in the 1950s "identity;" in the 1990s "soul" or "meaning" or "virtue."

As far as the political psyche is concerned, I am not very interested in the psychological motivations of politicians. I am much more interested in considering what could happen to the political system were *citizens* to work on their political self-awareness. Then there would be a different and more self-referential basis from which to interrogate the motivations of the politicians.

It is not easy to make a psychological analysis of politics, because every element in our culture is undergoing fragmentation and Balkanization. Still, people have risen to the challenge. Our sense of fragmentation and complexity seems to be *healing* as well as wounding the possibilities of political and social empowerment. For, in the midst of the tragic anomie and baffling atomization, the dreadful conformism of "international" architecture, telecommunications and cuisine, the sense of oppression and fear of a horrific future, in the midst of war itself, there is this strange, equally complex attempt at transformation of politics going on.

Therapists are aware of this from what their clients tell them. Alongside the expected problems – relationship difficulties, early traumas, feelings of emptiness – we see the ecological and other crises presented as sources of symptoms and of unhappiness in individuals. From a psychological point of view, the world is making people unwell, and it follows that, for people to feel better, the world's situation needs to change. Perhaps this is too passive: for people to feel better, perhaps they have to recognize that the human psyche is a political psyche and hence consider doing something about the state of the world.

I recently sent a questionnaire to 2000 analysts and therapists of many schools worldwide, in which I asked them what political issues their clients mentioned in therapy, how they reacted, and what their own political views were. Aside from the revelation that the therapy profession is far more politically sensitive than one would think and that politics is a welcome theme in quite a few clinical offices, it was clear that clients are bringing economic, environmental, and gender-political issues to their therapy sessions much more so than in the past. I think this development in the therapy world justifies my wider claim that, in our age, we are witnessing the emergence of a new kind of politics.

One role for psychology and the psychotherapies would be to mount a challenge to accepted ideas of what constitutes "human nature." At the moment, when idealistic or even utopian political thinking gets a bit threatening to the old order and to established ways of doing things, someone usually says, "but what you are proposing goes against human nature!" What the speaker largely means is that human nature is violent, greedy, involves hostility to other people, and inevitably leads to a pecking order and social hierarchy. If such speakers are psychotherapists, it is usually (and understandably) assumed that they are experts in human nature.

However, I am not sure that there really are objective experts in human nature. Most statements about human nature reflect the social circumstances, ideological prejudices and even the personality of the writer – not to mention his or her purpose in writing. As Jung said, "every psychology is a personal confession." Here the tag "his or her" is very relevant, because males and females are usually portrayed differently by writers on human nature. What they say varies over time. For example, according to novels and letters of the period, men in Europe stopped crying at the end of the eighteenth century. Up to then, it was perfectly manly to cry. Similarly, some ancient Greek philosophers said that women do not have souls.

In spite of these arguments, many people continue to assert conservatively that human nature is one thing which does not change over time. However, the fact that people may always have had similar emotional and physical experiences does not mean that they experienced these experiences in the same way. For the means they have to tell us about it are totally embedded in the worlds in which they lived. This means that it is very difficult to say that something is politically impossible because of human nature. What analysts and psychotherapists can contribute is an explanation of why more positive aspects of human nature have such a struggle to emerge. Psychotherapists can point out that the depressing definitions of human nature that are around are not neutral – someone benefits from them: big business, conventional politicians, reactionary males, anyone with a stake in the system has an interest in preserving the system's conception of human nature. For example, ask yourself who benefits when we are told that environmentalism and all kinds of new ideas for economic policy are unrealistic or too idealistic because of human nature being so greedy and selfish.

Some might wonder if mine is a New Age point of view. Well, Oscar Wilde was not exactly New Age, and he said, "the only thing we know about human nature is that it changes. Change is the one quality we can predict of it. . . . The systems that fail are those that rely on the permanency of human nature, and not on its growth and development" (1978: 1010).

The question that arises from all of this concerns what kind of political player or citizen needs to emerge to make the vision of a transformation of politics into something more tangible. I will therefore offer some ideas about new models or paradigms of the citizen under the general heading or image of *the politician within*.

INDIVIDUATION OF THE POLITICIAN WITHIN

The politician within each of us needs to be approached with respect and affection for his or her diversity. I want to avoid creating another monolith, a "we" that does not exist in politics today. Who is the "we" that so often creeps into books and speeches on both politics and psychology? Sometimes, and uncontroversially, this "we" refers to those reading or listening to these words in the here-and-now. But at other times my use of the "W" word might seem to reflect the usual tendency of a white, Western, Jewish, middle-class, heterosexual male to see himself as representative of everyone. I have tried not to fall into this inflation, making it clear who I mean or could mean when I speak of "we."

Nowhere is this carefulness more necessary than in discussing what I call "political self-awareness." Indeed, it is because I have become so cautious about the possibility of anyone giving an objective account of how they got their political attitudes and commitments that I suggest we speak about the "political myth of the person."

The psychological thrust into politics has usually focused either on the psychology of the politician(s), their character and likely behavior in stressful situations and crises. Or there have been studies of the citizens, the voters, designed to help politicians appeal to or manipulate them. There has not been very much self-reflexive psychological work done in relation to politics, and this is where the experience garnered in clinical therapy practice becomes invaluable. For the resacralizing movements to be effective, we have to start to believe in the possibility of a "psychological citizen" whose individuation – in Jung's term, the process of becoming him- or herself, distinct from but related to others – has a political aspect to it.

In my view, unless ideas like those of the politician within and a more psychological citizen are embraced, there will be no transformation of politics. It will just have been another fad, a low-key reprise in the 1990s of the 1960s. Resacralization is at risk, not only because of the reactionary and cynical moves of patriarchal capitalists, but also because of something lacking in the kind of personalities who are typically involved in resacralization. All too often, the resacralizer is characterized psychologically by an attempt to construct a shadow-free politics, thereby not having to sacrifice self-respect by getting dirty hands. Leave that to the politicians, meaning the real politicians, not deep and profound people like us! The "shadow" is a term coined by Jung to refer to those aspects of ourselves that we would like to disown – but cannot, because to have a shadow is part of being human. Shadow-free politics are often achieved by locating the problem elsewhere – in men, in whites, in the free market and so forth. Then the beliefs which so many people have of an apocalyptic end, whether by the greenhouse effect, AIDS, pandemic or nuclear conflagrations, can be understood as attempts to shift a sense of self-blame on to other people and institutions.

Many of us are so full of self-punishing contempt for ourselves, so full of disgust for the culture in whose making we have participated, that we opt for a thin, purist, over-clean style of making politics. We are so anxious not to be contaminated by the shadow that on one level we do not really want to see our cherished ideals translated into pragmatic politics. We fear that being effective means sacrificing self-respect. Even when resacralizers do get involved in politics, it is often a half-hearted or incomplete involvement, psychologically speaking, characterized by the fear of dirty hands, and hence not a truly creative engagement with the world and its problems. Hence the collapse of so many of the Green parties and groups, torn between their idealism and more pragmatic notions of feasibility.

There is certainly a problem in bringing transformative politics into contact with official politics. This is a problem that anyone who has ever had a political ideal will know about. The closer you get to the "real world," with all its pressures, diversions and temptations, the more risk there is of the ideal getting sullied, of it losing its purity, shape and impetus. Anyone active in environmentalism or the women's movement will tell you the same thing. One role for a psychological commentator is to explore whether this is an inevitable process, or whether there might be anything of a psychological kind that we might do to achieve a better blend of idealism and realism.

Those who want to resacralize politics are often searching for something, some kind of self-fulfillment or self-actualization, that the political alone is never going to supply in perfect terms. Anyone who was active in the New Left or student politics, as I was in the late 1960s, will know about these issues. There was an incredible denial of the human needs that were also being met (or not met) as we sat around and spent hours discussing what to paint on banners with which to stand outside automobile plants. But were the human needs ever talked about? Absolutely not. In fact it was regarded as apolitical and highly problematic to ask about personal motivations – you could get booted out for it. I suspect it is still like this in much community politics today. The New Left of the 1960s failed its own people by outlawing subjectivity, and this may be one psychological reason why progressive politics in the West is so lackluster just now. When feminism took the opposite tack, encouraging people to say at length what their personal reasons were for turning up at the meeting, a gulf of style and ethos arose between feminism and other progressive political movements in the community that has still not been healed.

If we could work out ways of increasing political self-awareness, based on therapy work, then the fears of getting dirty hands and cooperating with people one does not exactly love might be addressed. Returning to our imaginary computer graphic, we want to see if those little red dots could coagulate and eventually color the screen red.

The various politically transformative groups do not communicate, let alone coagulate. Nor have they formed themselves into any kind of coalition. I think there is great value in trying to get members of the various groups to meet regularly, and I have had many experiences of trying to achieve this. Often members of different groups have not realized the degree of psychological similarity in their projects, and this comes out when, for example, a "women and poverty" person meets and talks with a "Christian ecology" person. People who are involved in human rights organizations do not always see what they have in common with ecofeminists. The psychological task is to generate a conversation and to try to bring out the similarities of aim, often in emotional terms or image terms, between the various enterprises. What I want to do is to point out affinities, possibilities for alliances, saying, in realistic vein, that each group does not have to love the other groups; all that is necessary is to make a temporary and partial alliance. Why should the capitalists and the patriarchs be so good at this kind of deal-making and the resacralizers so bad at it? Perhaps it is precisely because the various groups of capitalists and patriarchs have sensed what they have in common behind surface differences that they have been so effective.

One difficulty with these ideas concerns our profound reluctance in the West to connect the outer, public levels of life with the inner, private levels. It is the inner, private levels on which connections can be made. In a way, this reluctance is surprising, because people have always spoken about politics and politicians in emotional terms such as "character." In this regard, I think of the outpouring of books on Richard Nixon. Similarly, a good deal of political debate boils down to disagreement about what is human nature (what, if anything, lies beyond self-interest, to give an example).

If these new connections between outer and inner worlds could be made, we will become more accustomed to talking a mixed language of psychology and politics. In this new, hybrid language for politics, we will want to know not only what is being said, but who is saying it – and then exactly who is taking action. Therapists know that everyone teems with inner people ("subpersonalities") and this is always a difficult thing for clients to acknowledge. In the same way, we need to develop an approach to politics which understands that no society provides a single, unified psychological identity for all its members.

An awareness that politics is psychological is one theme which links all those engaged in discussions about the loss of meaning, purpose and certainty in communal and personal life. Yet such is the Western fear of the inner world that its implications are barely recognized, let alone discussed or made use of. It is tragic how little discussion there has been about the socialized, transpersonal psychology that will be needed to make current visions of community and communitarian politics viable. But there *are* psychological theories in existence that focus on the transpersonal ways in which people are already linked and attuned to one another, living in connection in a social ether. In this vision of humanity, it is possible to recognize that we were never as separate from each other as so-called free market, neo-liberal politics – which had its own tame psychological theory in there somewhere – claimed us to be. Politicians and citizens urgently need to explore, expound and cultivate the kinds of pre-existing connections between people that Jung called the collective unconscious. Such connections may be largely non-verbal, working on a psyche-to-psyche level. We are stalks growing, feeding and flowering from the same rhizome.

THE POLITICAL MYTH OF THE PERSON

How does the politician within grow and develop? An individual person lives not only her or his life but also the life of the times. Jung is always quoted as telling his students that "when you treat the individual you treat the culture." People cannot be seen in isolation from the society and culture that has played a part in forming them.

Once we see that there is a political person who has developed over time, we can start to track the political history of that person – the way the political events of her or his lifetime have impacted on the forming of their political myth. In my clinical practice I have come to see that it is possible to analyze the politics which a person has, so to speak, inherited from their family, class, ethnic, religious, national background – not forgetting the crucial questions of their sex and sexual orientation. Sometimes people take on their parents' politics; equally often, people reject what their parents stood for.

As far as socioeconomic background is concerned, I have become interested in the relationship of class and the inner world. Many of my clients over the years have achieved a higher socioeconomic status than that of their parents. And yet, when working with such clients, I have found that, in the inner world, the social class wherein they function is often the social class into which they were born. There is a staggering psychological tension that exists within the socially and economically mobile citizen between what he or she is and what he or she was. To the extent that the typical move has been from working class to middle class, and to the extent that passion and need for social and economic justice exist for good reasons in the working class, it is possible to see in the middle-class person concerns for economic and social justice appropriate to their inner-world version of themselves as working class.

But even this account of how a person's political myth develops is perhaps a bit too rational. If there is something inherently political about humans – and Jungian theory suggests that there is – then perhaps the politics a person has cannot be explained only by social inheritance. Perhaps there is an accidental, constitutional, fateful and inexplicable element to think about. Perhaps people are just born with different amounts and types of political energy in them.

If that is so, then there would be major implications both for individuals and for our approach to politics. What will happen if a person with a high level of political energy is born to parents with a low level (or vice versa)? What if the two parents have vastly different levels from each other? What is the fate of a person with a high level of political energy born into an age and a culture which does not value such a high level, preferring to reward lower levels of political energy? The answers to such questions form not only the political person but the shape and flavor of the political scene in their times.

The question can get much more intimate. Did your parents foster or hinder the flowering of your political energy and your political potential? How did you develop the politics you have at this moment? In which direction are your politics moving, and why? I do not think these questions are currently on either a mainstream or an alternative political agenda.

My interest is not in what might be called political maturity. No such universal exists, as evaluations by different commentators of the same groups as "terrorists" or "freedom fighters" show! My interest is in how people got to where they are politically and, above all, in how they themselves think, feel, explain and communicate about how they got to where they are politically – hence the political *myth* of the person. From a psychological angle, it often turns out that people are not actually where they thought they were politically, or that they got there by a route they did not know about. There is a political "narrative truth" to consider as well as a political "historical truth" (to use the terms of the American psychoanalyst Donald Spence).

People are becoming much more aware of and concerned by the gap between their private political histories, passions, dreams, ideas, feelings, bodily reactions to politics on the one hand, and how policy is made and what actually happens in the political world on the other. This gap is disturbing and painful for all of us, but where things are disturbing and painful is also a place where something creative can happen. Let us hope that citizens do not "repress" their needs to be political because of these problems.

Across the globe, people are indeed disgusted by the nature of today's mainstream politics. In the rich countries in the West, in eastern Europe and the former Soviet Union, in the Third World, people have risen to the challenge, and a search is on for a new kind of politics. Clearly I think psychology and psychotherapy can contribute to this search, but I believe this requires a two-way street to be opened up between inner reality and the world of politics. If we cannot manage a true dialogue between these two realms we could end up only with either (1) an inward politics of self-righteous ineffectiveness, full of rhetoric about soul and meaning, but lacking any weight with the electorate or in the corridors of power, or (2) fundamentalist, moralistic control of people's lives. An over-psychological politics might ignore the outer world and not be politically realistic at all, while the certitudes of religious fundamentalism show it to be as scared of the imagination and its irrepressible uninhibitedness as are mainstream political institutions.

We thus need a psychological perspective on pressing political problems in the real world such as leadership, the market economy, Third World development, environmentalism, nationalism, racism and anti-Semitism. But we also need to lay bare the hidden politics of all those experiences and images in life that used to be comfortingly regarded as private.

I will conclude this chapter by suggesting that there is something else which needs to be addressed, that we could call "political type." (My model here is Jung's typology: extraversion, introversion, thinking, feeling, sensation, intuition.) For a variety of reasons, some to do with their personal backgrounds, some to do with their inborn political constitutions, people will live out the political aspects of themselves in different ways. Some will be violent terrorists; some pacifists. Some will want empirical back-up for their ideas; others will fly by the seat of their pants. Some will definitely enjoy cooperative activity; others will suffer the nightmares of trying to do things in a group only because they believe in the ends. As we begin to make a start on a psychologically driven transformation of politics, let us not make the mistake of insisting that everyone do it in precisely the same way. There is probably something desirable and creative in a diversity of political styles being equally valued and honored, and we can think of ways of protecting and privileging such diversity.

NOTE

1 I am thinking of the writings of Jungian analysts and thinkers such as Theodor Abt, Louis Anschuler, John Beebe, Jean Bolen, Robert Bosnak, Gustav Bovensiepen, Carlos Byington, Hannes Dieckmann, Clarissa Pinkola Estés, Martin Gallard, Wolfgang Giegerich, Adolf Guggenbühl-Craig, James Hillman, Verena Kast, Thomas Kirsch, Mary Ann Mattoon, Peter Mudd, Walter Odajnyk, Renos Papadopoulos, John Van Eenwyk, Eli Weisstub, Polly Young-Eisendrath, and others who may have been accidentally omitted from this list.

BIBLIOGRAPHY

Jung, C.G. (1931) "Archaic Man," in *Collected Works*, Vol. 10.

—— (1952) "Synchronicity: An Acausal Connecting Principle," in *Collected Works*, Vol. 8.

Samuels, A. (1993) *The Political Psyche*, London and New York: Routledge.

Wilde, O. (1978) "The Soul of Man Under Socialism," in *Complete Works of Oscar Wilde*, London: Book Club Associates.

Part II

The one and the many in myth and politics

Foreword

Martin Krasney

Each of us is many and all of us are one. That is the essential and fundamental reality and paradox of being human. Recognition of these dualities – unity and multiplicity, disintegration and integrity – has been intensified in the twentieth century, both by an extraordinary array of "public" occurrences and by new insights into the instincts, inclinations and aspirations of the now nearly seven billion "private" individuals who share this small planet. Former Ambassador Paul Nitze, after whom the School of Advanced International Affairs at Johns Hopkins University was renamed, has proposed that the central task of this era "is the accommodation and protection of diversity within a framework of order," the validation of the many in the one.

We are the first generation to have seen the Earth whole from space, and the first to be engaged in mapping the full genetic structure of the human species, chronicling both our vulnerable interdependence and our robust individuality. The twentieth century bore witness to the creation of unprecedentedly powerful weapons of mass destruction and also the incipient recognition that extensive environmental and human devastation can often be an unintended consequence of what, until recently, we had considered unqualified industrial progress. During the twentieth century we have acknowledged the death of God, yet murdered tens of millions of each other in His name and, while perpetrating that carnage, have invented a dizzying array of new gods – from racial purification to national soccer teams, cheap gasoline to "the right to live" – for which we have also been willing to kill each other.

Among the twentieth century's innumerable, harshly divisive armed conflicts, two were denominated "world wars" and, in the aftermath of the second, The United Nations was established with a mandate for international peacekeeping and now with close to 200 member nations, many of them still in their turbulent infancies as sovereign countries. UN Peacekeeping Forces have been deployed in more than thirty of the nations of the world. The demise of the British Empire on the Indian subcontinent has resulted fifty years later in Hindu and Muslim nuclear adversaries, and the fall of the Communist regime in Russia and eastern Europe has almost instantaneously liberated vicious ethnic animosities that have been seething for generations. In Londonderry, neighbors and co-workers who attend different churches murder each others' sons, and in Los Angeles, boys and girls from the same schools and housing projects, chancing to join either the Crips or the Bloods, kill each other for sport.

Television has helped to crystallize our similarities as human beings and to clarify our differences, enabling "the whole world" to watch everything from the nightly body count of fatalities in Vietnam to the record daily closings of the Dow Jones Industrial Average, from student protesters in 1968 Paris, Berkeley or Mexico City to state repression in 1989 Beijing and 1999 Kosovo, from the assassination of a presidential assassin in Dallas to the perfect, ten-point Olympic performance of a state-trained child gymnast from Rumania.

The world is in thrall of the American entertainment industry, the first universal language since the destruction of the Tower of Babel, making Roseanne Barr and Bart Simpson celebrities of near mythic dimension in the remote villages of developing nations, and the NFL Super Bowl headline news in Taiwan, Madagascar and Easter Island. The cultural critic Guy Davenport has observed that "in our century, the great event has been the destruction of the city, and therefore of public life, by the automobile . . . and the next, the obliteration of the family by television" (Davenport 1996). George W.S. Trow (1980, 1997) has brilliantly described our preoccupation with the media, often to the detriment of social cohesion and personal empathy, as placing us "within the context of no context."

The internet takes up where television leaves off, further expanding our horizons and isolating our humanity, promising to link everyone with everyone, while deepening the perception that each of us is the center of our own universe, the spider in our own web, increasingly each able to develop a personal website. While we exult that we can communicate in nanoseconds by e-mail with strangers on distant continents, growing numbers of us are unable to name our city council person, our greengrocer or the new family next door.

Some urban male teenagers in the United States even swagger about their inability to identify their own children. And among the rest of us, although our sons and daughters might not be strangers to us, the average American parent spends less than fifteen minutes each day in genuine conversation with his or her children, more than an hour commuting to and from work and upwards of four watching television. The children watch a similarly numbing amount of television, but not with their parents.

In the increasingly monocultural global marketplace, which television has helped to establish, diversity is constantly being downsized, and products, services and employees are becoming more and more homogeneous. Japanese automotive plants in Tennessee employ Vietnamese immigrants alongside the men and women who attacked their nation in its "American War," while the company's shareholders in Osaka Prefecture douse their rice with soy sauce from Tennessee beans. Political and currency fluctuations in Djakarta can destabilize governments in Europe and turn speculators into millionaires in New York. Pseudo-choices proliferate while authentic ones dwindle. Small American cities now offer dozens of variations on coffee with which to wash down one's chocolate-chip bagel, and Starbucks has invaded tea-drinking Great Britain and China. Henry Ford's comment that consumers could have any color they wanted as long as it was black reverberates in the hegemony of the Microsoft operating system. Dee Hock, the inventor of the Visa card, has coined the term "chaordic" to describe the mix of chaos and order that typifies contemporary institutions. Perhaps one day soon there will be one bank. With very long lines. Or no lines at all.

Boundaries are disappearing. We are transfused with each other's blood and transplanted with each other's organs, perhaps purchased on the black market or, sometimes even, allegedly, "harvested" from kidnapped children. Unwanted baby girls from Asia are adopted by Latino lesbian couples in Houston. There are more Buddhists than Baptists in the United States and the Pope is Polish. Intermarriage is creating categories of ethnicity which the US Census is hard-pressed to track and tabulate. After apartheid, South Africa chose as its leader a black man with half a lifetime of imprisonment by the government he was elected to head and the buoyantly popular though widely despised President of the United States – a man whom Nobel Laureate Toni Morrison (1998: 32) has characterized as psychologically the nation's "first Black President" – quibbles about what "is" is. So must we all.

It is a quibble in which we all have a stake, a quest we must all share. Ironically, in his calculated legalistic opportunism, President Clinton has articulated the central moral dilemma of our historic moment. How can we know with confidence what actually exists, what has meaning, what to pursue, what to defend, what to value? Existentialism can easily slip into solipsism, with nihilism just a small step beyond.

The defining intellectual metaphor of the twentieth century is relativity. This was Einstein's century if it was anyone's. His theory of general relativity, said fifty years ago to be comprehensible to "only eight people in the world," is now in our blood. Elementary school students understand that the position of the observer can alter the perception of cause and effect (with Werner Heisenberg adding that the act of observation itself changes the outcome). Children today recognize from computer play that anything can be morphed into anything else. They intuit from the "celebracracy" that has become our Olympus how little it matters where anyone actually stands or whether they stand for anything. Individually and societally, we now "know" immeasurably more than our parents did, but perhaps we understand less and honor or love even less. It has long been accepted that it is necessary to kill a cat in order to dissect it. A newer idea is having to "destroy the village to save it." How far we are willing to take this line of thought is not a rhetorical question in a world where our carbon-based life-style has generated global warming and the chemical dependency of our society might be mutating the endocrine systems of posterity. Late in his life, Einstein himself summarized the world that we have evolved: "The distinctive characteristic of our age is perfection of means and confusion of ends."

Five hundred years ago, Shakespeare famously wrote that "one man in his time plays many parts, passes through seven ages" and, close to three hundred years later, Wordsworth declared that the child is father to the man, suggesting a through line of determinism and an assumption that there is an individual destiny, unique for each of us. In the twentieth century, Freud hypothesized about the life-defining ramifications from the minutiae of infant experience, and Jung, while acknowledging that "each of us carries his own life form," posited the existence of a collective unconscious that precedes, supersedes and unifies individuals.

In the words of the eminent public executive John Gardner, "the play of conflicting interests in a framework of shared purposes is the drama of a free society." But what happens when the conflicting interests overwhelm or undermine the shared purpose? What happens when the concept of shared purpose is forgotten, forsaken or foreclosed? Intellectual historian and contemporary Celtic Bard William Irwin Thompson has been probing such questions for decades. Invoking Gregory Bateson's philosophy, Thompson (1986: 129–30) proposes that:

> . . . in the battles between good and evil "the difference that makes a difference" is difference itself. Evil is the destruction of differences; good is the creation of ever new differences. The good emphasizes diversity, individuation . . . and the participation in the universal through the unique. This is the difference that makes a difference, the difference between isomorphic groups: between the followers of Rudolph Steiner and those of Adolph Hitler, between the communities of Findhorn and Rajneeshpuram, between a tall grass prairie and the animal concentration camp of a Kansas feed lot.

Between integrity and disintegration. Between the many able to embrace and enhance each "one" and the many that subvert each one.

As we move into a new millennium, the challenge that faces humanity is to construct the necessary myths and the necessary politics to respond effectively to the rapid and accelerating changes we are experiencing in what it means to be many, and what it means to be one. It seems appropriate to let Albert Einstein have the last word: "We cannot solve the problems that we have created with the same thinking that created them."

BIBLIOGRAPHY

Davenport, Guy (1996) *The Hunter Gracchus and Other Papers On Literature and Art*, Washington: Counterpoint.

Morrison, Toni (1998) "Talk of the Town," *The New Yorker*, 5 October 74: 32.

Thompson, William Irwin (1986) *Pacific Shift*, San Francisco: Sierra Club.

Trow, George W.S. (1980 and 1997) *Within the Context of No Context*, New York: Atlantic Monthly Press.

The many

Chapter 7

Arresting Orestes

Mythic events and the law

Craig San Roque

"Justice shall be taken directly on all who act above the law."
Orestes, in Sophocles' *Electra*

THE FIRE BY THE ROAD

There are four men in the pick-up truck driving north from Alice Springs. Two white men, both silent, expecting something but not knowing what. Two black men, big men, big in body, big in intent. They are heading for a dry sandy creek, fifteen miles out of town. The vehicle lifts away from the valley hidden among the serpentine contortion of mountain ranges which cradle the small isolated town. The truck crosses the Charles River gorge, skimming through clumps of arid, ochre rock hill, then out into unbounded, uncluttered brilliant blue sky. The bundle of Whiteman civilisation left behind, there is a shift of mood in the cab, a small smile of relief and excitement as a foretaste of Warlpiri tribal country comes into view. Out to the left, the ranges again, crawling in long lines from the Western Desert. Blues, purples, delicate greys, tawny ochre, red. Close up: bleached yellow, glistening grasses. Bare rusted red earth. They pass the junction to the Tanami Desert, a narrow road strip heading for the north-west. The road sign is spattered with bullet holes.

To speak about certain things, undisturbed, the black men – indigenous, Aboriginal, tribal – habitually go outside the boundaries of settlement. The exact identity of these four men does not matter, or rather, it is better if their identity is obscured a little. The four men are heading for a quiet conference. The matter they have in mind is a matter of law. The two Aboriginal men represent the law, they are negotiators of justice, they negotiate Aboriginal law. They negotiate and mediate on matters when the white Australian law is brought into play to deal with their own people. This is a chronic perpetual condition. There are many Western Desert Aboriginal people being brought in to face the magistrates and judges of the European legal system. This system is perceived by many Aboriginal people as an invention that came from another country with no explanation and no "instruction booklet." A glance at the statistics will show you that 90 per cent of the people in the nice new gaol in Alice Springs are Aboriginal black. Eighty per cent of these people, mostly men, are there for offences kicked off by alcohol. Drunkenness and the law and the lore. These are the matters in mind.

The two white men in the truck are not policemen or lawyers.

You may not be familiar with the way business is done in this unique part of the world. Sometimes "role" or "identity" is not very firm or fixed. Sometimes the most unlikely people are engaged in matters which are apparently "not their business"; and those whose job it may officially appear to be are unaware of what is really happening. It is worth noting that the realities of Aboriginal country are veiled by a kind of membrane which renders most of what goes on invisible to those whose eyes have not been trained by Aboriginal experience. Much goes on "behind the veil."

The two white men in the truck are doctors. One, myself; the other, a psychiatrist. Both of us are known to the Warlpiri as having a special facility in Aboriginal matters. We frequently deal with offenders and with Aboriginal folk who suffer derangements. Psychic casualties of the undeclared combat. We are assuming, perhaps, that someone is in trouble. All we know is that these two men, almost family, have picked us up, requesting a meeting; and thus it happens. So far, the business of the meeting to which we have been invited has not been declared.

We settle ourselves into the dry, washed sand of the creek bed. Hidden from the road. No human being within ten miles on any side. The silence wafting in, a small fire drifts smoke.

One man, Kumanjai Japaljarri[1], shifts his bulk and begins drawing in the sand with a slender stick. He is not wearing his police uniform. He is an Aboriginal Community Policeman, perhaps similar in function to a Navaho Tribal Police Officer, but the system here in the Northern Territory of Australia is also significantly different to that of the Native American Reservations. When Kumanjai is in white man's police uniform he does not speak much about the philosophical problems of Warlpiri law, of *Yappa* "our people's" law. When he is in uniform he takes on the persona of the Australian law. He speaks Australian police language, except when he is specifically asked to mediate with his own people in their own language. When he takes off the ceremonial dressage of Aboriginal Community Policeman he becomes free to speak as a Warlpiri man, an exponent of Warlpiri culture, lore and law. The Warlpiri are a vigorous tribal group, with a specific language and specific tribal country which covers an area about the size of the state of Utah. And the Warlpiri are only one tribe among the twelve or so in this region whose lands stretch in time and space from horizon to shifting horizon. A territory held in custodianship by the "original dwellers" in an uneasy climate of resistance to the anxious and dominating demands of Australian "industry."

The other black man, bigger in size than the other three, is known affectionately as Perentie, the Big Lizard. His appetite for consuming vast quantities of desert game is legendary. This good-natured man drives all over the country, north of Alice, as a law negotiator. Administrators of the Correctional Services Department for whom he works are often in despair about him. He takes a departmental vehicle and disappears, they say. He might be 200 miles away helping negotiate the consequences of a murder or a jealous fight; but he will not tell his boss that story. He will smile, saying something in a monosyllabic, mixed-up language, part English, part Warlpiri, and the boss has to guess where he has gone and what he is up to. The truth cannot be declared, for reasons of discretion. Fortunately, his current boss does have the necessary discretion and can guess, because he understands the way the Aboriginal law negotiations work and how valuable it is to have one of his own men present at such proceedings. Attending negotiations inside Warlpiri country is not Perentie's paid job. He is supposed to identify and chase up Aboriginal men, mostly youths, who are on parole or community service sentences, or otherwise sought by the guardians of white Australian law and order. Perentie seeks them out, mainly to ensure that they do not get into deeper trouble.

Perentie does not have a philosophical turn of mind; this is left to Kumanjai Japaljarri, but when Perentie is present at a Warlpiri negotiation over a crime, defined as such according to Warlpiri law, he is always fair, balanced and commands respect. One day this inestimably valuable man will get into trouble from the Justice Department. There will be a review, for instance, and some new Minister or Departmental Secretary will want to know what Mr Perentie Japananka is up to. No one will tell the truth; some officer will shrug and say we don't know what he's up to, "maybe he's got a woman somewhere. . . ." Or perhaps Perentie's knowledgeable boss will get into trouble for permitting his employee to operate outside the system and the job specification. When Mr Perentie Japananka is "let go," as the administrators so blandly say, the Department will lose one of its most potent, secret, trouble-shooters. Regrettably, no one in the office of the Territory's Attorney General or the Ministry of Justice will realize the mistake they have made. It will be the same for Officer Kumanjai. One day, he will become sick of the tension between the stability of Aboriginal custom and the fickle mysteries of white man's law enforcement. He will become sick of wearing, for too long, his white man's police persona. He will be brought down by the constraints on his ability to operate freely in the air of his own culture. He will be brought down by the clash between the mythology of the white world and the mythology of the black world.

TWO LAWS

Kumanjai hunches over the fire and makes his point to the two white men. There is very little preamble. The preamble was the time in the vehicle driving, sitting silently, letting thoughts settle and come into alignment.

He quickly sketches a diagram in the sand. A concentric circle and small marks indicating figures sitting in a circle in meeting. He sketches another figure off to the side, flanked by two others. "This man here," he says, "this one is in trouble, he has broken our law – *Yappa* law." Kumanjai Japaljarri uses the Warlpiri word which identifies his own people. *Yappa* means "us – our people." The alternative word, used to denote the White people, is *Kardia*, meaning "your mob . . . you others . . . not us."

I prefer this term over the crude color distinctions of "Blackfella/ Whitefella." There is little dignity in those terms and an undertone of contempt which it is not necessary to perpetuate.

"This man, here, is in trouble and these men sitting round the circle, are discussing what to do about him in *Yappa* law. We are making arrangements that will satisfy all the families because of the crime. When we do these things properly everything is settled and payback (revenge) killing is stopped."

Kumanjai draws another series of circles on the sand and connects them with lines. He is drawing something to represent a dreaming story. "Now this here is Jukurrpa that backs up our law. When we are making these arrangements we don't just do it out of nothing, out of empty minds. We have the Jukurrpa behind us. Jukurrpa backs us up. It backs up our decisions. All the *Yappa* know that and respect the decision, even the family of the murderer here."

We listen, attentive, making no comment, careful not to interrupt his flow with irresolute questions.

Kumanjai sketches again, this time a large framing rectangular design, then another rectangle inside that one, with figures sitting on all four sides. Then little rectangles inside the big rectangle. A portrait of a meeting table, with paper documents on the table. In Kumanjai's mind, this is an icon of the white man's system. Chairs, table, papers, enclosed in walls. A pattern of concentric rectangles and straight lines.

"This is *Kardia* meeting. They have all their law books on the table. They try to work out what to do with this man too. They use *Kardia* law. No one is coming over to talk about *Yappa* law. See, the walls are all around them. They ignore the *Yappa* law, like we had no law and no Jukurrpa to handle this business. The *Yappa* law is invisible to these judges. That is a big problem for us. Do they teach *Yappa* law to these judges and lawyers? They don't. Do they send them to us for training?"

There is a long silence. The smoke continues to drift. A large, shiny black ant struggles across the sand through the diagrams. A crow settles itself on the bare greying branch of a eucalyptus. A bright, watchful eye.

"This is the problem we have to ask you. What backs up your *Kardia* law? What is there behind you? See. When these men sit here around the table, the lawyers, judges, prosecutor and defence, tell me this, what backs them up? What dreaming do they lean back on? What keeps them steady?"

Perentie nods, repeating the concern, "*Uwai*, your people's law. You *Kardia* got a Jukurrpa for this?"

Now the two white men know where they are. They have been through this kind of conversation before. The last time it was about drunkenness and alcohol use.

A couple of years before (1991) Kumanjai wanted to know if the Europeans, those who made alcohol in the beginning, were responsible enough to know the "dreaming story" that controlled alcohol and drunkenness. That is to say, the mythological creation story for intoxication. Did the Europeans, the *Kardia*, still use the ceremony which managed its use or were matters out of the control of the

Figure 7.1 Aborigines sandpainting
Source: from the ARAS collection of the C.G. Jung Institute of San Francisco

white people also? Had drunkenness raged, unrestrained, through the families of the white man, always?

Kumanjai's subtle point, which he repeated in many ways until the reality of it sank into the minds of the two doctors, was this: with a "story" to go with the substance, the management of the substance would have a place in *Yappa* law. Why? Because if it had a place in *Yappa* law it would have a place in *Yappa* mind. Thus the responsibility for management of the character of alcohol could have a place in the culture.

No story . . . result . . . mindless drinking.

Kumanjai's thinking process went something like this. "A story gives a mental image. A mental image gives a concept. Concepts linked together give thought systems. Thought systems help generate ways of managing behavior. What trust are *Yappa* to have in laws which seem to come from nowhere? Why should *Yappa* believe laws of managing behavior which have no visible thought behind them, no concept behind them, no image behind them, no story behind them? Of course, the police can enforce these laws and try to make *Yappa* behave, but there can be no respect for a law which has no origin image to carry it and no visible history."

In traditional Aboriginal culture every land form, major and minor, every animal, reptile, bird and insect, every substance, water, liquid and food, and every family relationship and cultural or ceremonial action has a precedent in cultural history and in a creation story, a dreaming story, a Jukurrpa, as it is known in the Warlpiri language.

Kumanjai Japalajarri, through his questions, helped start off a project of exploration and research into European, Middle Eastern and Asian history. It became a cross-cultural revelation of the mythology of intoxication. The legends of the ancient world were turned over like so many stones, looking for signs underneath the debris of history. Finally, we settled on the Dionysos legends (known most vividly through Euripides' play *The Bacchae*) because Dionysos' ancestry, birth, life, adventures, trials and tribulations contained stark, primal imagery about the drunken states of men and women. We were to shake these old mythological dramas inside out. The answer to Kumanjai's inquiry would eventually become a display of paintings and a sequence of theatre works, designed as the basis for "instruction" in the Lore and Law of Intoxication.

The four men sitting in the sand by the delicately smoking fire all had their hand in the resurrection of this strangely disturbing but illuminating European mystery. But at the point at which we are telling this story the future performances were yet to occur. Some local white people hearing about work being done on old Greek myths were intrigued and inspired, offering to help; others were appalled by this "misguided attempt to tell to the blacks" about Greek mythology, as some put it. There was a wave of scepticism and contempt. "What do you want to shovel that old shit around for?" And because of the scepticism we had gone very quietly. The irony is that Christians rely upon a 4000-year-old lineage of myth and legend, re-covenanted. It is the basis of much of the Western world's law and ceremony. A modest Passover meal of bread and wine and bitter herbs, shared in an upper room in Jerusalem, has been converted into a pivotal ceremonial liturgy: the Communion. In Alice Springs, the very people who base their moral and spiritual lives upon a sequence of mythological creation stories were shaking their heads when they heard rumours of a request from some Aboriginal people to be instructed in the European's foundation myths. There is a blind spot about it somewhere. It took an insightful Aboriginal man to point out to white Australians that their own cultural history might hold a way of dealing with the present social problems.

Here we go again. Kumanjai Japaljarri and Perentie are opening another layer of the problem by asking for some kind of explanation of the philosophical and mythological background to European law.

How did the *Kardia* develop the ideas that killing was a crime, that incest was a crime, that stealing, breaking and entering, assault, were all crimes? How did the *Kardia* sort out the punishments to fit the crimes and who was to decide and who was to carry out the sentence? How did the special ceremonials of the court room develop? What does it all mean and where does the *Kardia* law come from?

THE ORIGINS OF JUSTICE

The two white men knew why this question was coming up now. There had just been (yet another) very disturbing fight between two Warlpiri men. One had been killed. The family members of both the murderer and the dead man were in turmoil. There were arrangements in place for a ritual settlement of the killing and a ritualized payback according to customary law. It is a method familiar to Sicilians perhaps. If conducted properly, the two families' sense of justice is satisfied; if not, the fight would spawn into a dangerous feud. The Territory Government, at that time, was moving cautiously toward a process of considering whether to accept the existence of the Aboriginal system of handling offences. This could involve punishment by controlled infliction of spear wounds, a method with which the Australian courts had difficulty. The matter at issue was the recognition of Aboriginal customary law. It was a challenge to both cultures to find an adjustment to each other. It would be called the "Two Laws Debate."

The two white men sigh, exchanging glances, anticipating the trouble this is going to bring them if they get involved. Looking at Perentie's beaming dark face, it has to be admitted that there is also a thrust of excitement at the creative possibilities. Maybe a collaborative ceremony on the Two Laws could take shape.

"Yeah Japaljarri," the psychiatrist says, "We have dreamings that back up our law. But I don't know how you mean this." Being cautious: "have your mob got a dreaming that backs up your law?"

"Yeah, we got him," Japaljarri says, and Perentie nods and they speak rapidly to each other in Warlpiri and reach an agreement. "We'll tell you two . . . but its secret, you know, you can't walk around telling everyone this; it's only for you two here."

"OK , let's have it."

So Perentie launches into a succinct tale of how a mythological being from the creation time committed a crime and what it was and how he was detected and how he was punished and by whom and what the consequences were and how this story sets the precedent for punishments in traditional custom.

The story is pitched at a poetic level; there is not a direct one-for-one relationship between myth event and sentencing event. Like the acts of the prophets and those of Jesus, the numinous doings of remarkable Aboriginal beings set patterns for their cultural group. The Jukurrpa creates an emotional attitude and a framework from which are derived specific actions. Sometimes the Jukurrpa is adapted or re-interpreted according to the needs of contemporary circumstances. The Warlpiri recognize that Christian dreaming is an authentic Jukurrpa.

In a Christian-based country, like America or Australia, when a police force or the judicial system becomes out of touch with the compassionate preceding shape of the Christian myth, the common people get anxious. They complain about the law; they take the law into their own hands; they mistrust their police; they express contempt for the lawyers who exploit the law. The ordinary people get upset and the High Court judges, who act on behalf of the original intent and spirit of the law, are called in to restore the balance. Kumanjai and Perentie are witness to these very events in Australia. Then and now, legal battles unfold about the rights of Aboriginal people, about the rights to possession of their own land. In Australia, the Mabo Case and the Wik Case are two landmark Land Rights cases. They hold a place in the heart of national justice. The Warlpiri men know all about this. It is their business.

I say, "The Christian story backs up white man's law. The Jewish story backs up the Christians, you know . . . Adam and Eve and getting thrown out of the garden . . . and Moses and the ten laws on stone and Jesus coming and sorting things out again and making new laws. . . ."

"We know that story," acknowledge the two men, "is that all you have?"

This is a serious question, I know that. Kumanjai Japaljarri and Perentie have a lot of respect for the Christian Tjukurrpa. They are Baptists, and Perentie plays Christian country and Western hymns on the tape player in his vehicle on the long drives through Aboriginal country.

"No," I say, "there is a lot more." Now, my companion is a psychiatrist of Jewish family origins, Russian/Polish; kicked out of home by the Nazis; his family living in fear on the cold barren roads of eastern Europe, then western Europe and then "rescued" as refugees to Australia and condemned to sterile suburbia. For years his family had been trying to keep ahead of the injustice of a "pure white European civilization." I invite him to speak about justice. He declines. He says, "That war and the German delusion hasn't reached the status of Jukurrpa for the Warlpiri. Let's go back in time a bit more. Try Orestes and Oedipus."

"Yeah," I say, "you men want to know about European law; you have got to go back along another track too, different to the Jesus track. . . ."

Oedipus

"One Jukurrpa from our old people's time is about a man called Oedipus. His name means 'swollen foot.' He used to have a limp, but there might be another secret meaning to his name too. . . . This story tells us a lot about family law and about investigations. It is about finding out the truth." And so I launch into a brief version of the Theban legend, known to us best through Sophocles' tragedy, *Oedipus Rex*. We clear the sand of Kumanjai's drawings and lay out the scene of Oedipus.

Sketching the city with its seven gates, the road, the junction where three roads meet, the cave at Delphi . . . and so on.

". . . So the people in the city were sick . . . a big dog woman had them all by the throat . . . she sits outside the place and kills men who can't answer her questions. The king's brother-in-law was so worried that he went to a sacred cave and talked to the spirit snake there. The spirit voice (we call it the Oracle of Delphi) said: 'The trouble with your place is that the old king before Oedipus was murdered; and the murderer is still in the city. The proper payback has not been carried out. Fix that and you will fix the city's problem.

"So Oedipus got everyone together and carried out an investigation and the truth came out. The trouble was that Oedipus had been sent away by his father, as a baby, to be killed. They tied wire through his feet, that's why he limps. The father of Oedipus was frightened of him; the spirits had said that the father would be killed by his own son one day. The daddy didn't want his boy to grow up. The man was told to take the baby out on to a mountain and leave him to die, poor thing, but the man was sorry for the little feller and gave Oedipus away, instead of killing him. Oedipus was brought up by another family, a long way away. When he became a man he ran away. You know why? Because people said that when he became a man he would kill his own father and sleep with his own mother, his father's wife. He didn't want that so he ran away. Poor thing, he didn't know he had another father and another mother, somewhere else, back in Thebes. He was heading this way (showing the path taken on the sand diagram) and came to a road crossing . . . and he ran into an old man there and they ended up having a fight . . . Oedipus killed the old man . . . (there was a witness) . . . and Oedipus limped toward the town but he ran into that dog woman sitting up on the cliff outside of town, making trouble for everyone.

"Now, Oedipus is really smart and he sorted out that dog woman's problem. Everyone thought he was a clever man so they asked him to be the new king because the old king had gone away and died, someone had murdered him, and they needed a king to run the city. So Oedipus became the new king and married the old king's wife. You see the trick, eh Kumanjai?"

"Yeah, I see it."

"They had three children and then the sickness and trouble started . . . which is why the brother-in-law went to see the snake and came back saying they had to find out who really killed the old king. So Oedipus calls everyone together and starts an investigation.

'We've got to find out the truth,' he says.

"Trouble is it turns out, after they have this big enquiry, that the one to blame was himself. He was to blame, not somebody else. Oedipus was the murderer."

"This is a big story for us," says the psychiatrist, throwing a meditative stick into the fire, "we use it to explain about running away from the truth, and finding out who is responsible for serious problems . . . it's about taking responsibility for yourself . . . among other things."

The two Warlpiri men sit in silence for a long time.

This is probably the first time in the history of the Warlpiri nation that the tale of Oedipus has been told. "We never heard that story," says Kumanjai.

I say, "There are stories the Christian missionaries did not tell you."

The psychiatrist says, "You see that, Kumanjai? There is one story-line comes in with Christians, another lot come in through the Greeks and Romans. Another line (tradition) comes straight from England, it came with Captain Cook."

There is a long pause and a bit more wood goes on the fire.

"Anymore stories?" asks Kumanjai.

"Yeah, but this is not our business, you should talk to the judges, it's their business to know all this."

"We're asking you," says Perentie.

"Well," says the psychiatrist, "there is the story about Orestes and the jury court. It's about white feller payback, I guess." He nods to me. "Let's tell it."

Orestes

My hand smoothes Oedipus from the sand and draws a map of ancient Greece, locating the main sites and the sea road to Troy. With twigs and leaves I set out ships and characters upon a miniature arena. Now the smoothed sand has become an almost magic and potent theatre space, marking a halfway overlap between the cultures; European mythology and the Warlpiri, meeting in the creek bed. The two Aboriginal men watch the drama unfold with rapt attention.

"This big mob went off to war. You heard about Troy and the trick with the wooden horse? No . . . ? OK. . . . Well, this is the guts of the story. These two families were fighting about a woman, Helen. She ran away from her husband (Menelaus). She ran off with another man (Paris) and went back to his country with him. Everybody got upset. Wife-stealing was a big problem in those days." The Warlpiri men smile and nod with understanding appreciation.

"The husband got all his brothers and relatives together and chased after them. They sailed over the sea, this way, and landed on the beach. They pulled up their ships, here on the sand, like in this creek . . . only there is a lot more water than we get here. . . . They camped and got ready for a fight. They fought for a long time. Ten years. Too many people got killed. After ten years they went home. No one really won. They were all sick of it. The husband didn't get his wife back. Now, Menelaus has a brother (this one here). He had come on the war too, to support his brother. His name is Agamemnon, he's the main one for this side of the story . . . watch what happens."

The Warlpiri men nod again, approving the brother's supportive action.

"This one, Agamemnon, had left his wife at home, for the full ten years. She must have got sick of him being away and started sleeping with another man. When the army came home Agamemnon's wife came out smiling and telling him to come in and sit down and eat. But first she took him into the bath house to give him a good wash down. While he was lying naked in the bath with no spears around him she came in and killed him. She and her lover came and stabbed him to death. The bath water was red with blood."

"Now, she had two daughters and one son. One daughter, Electra, went a bit mad because of this. The other daughter sucked up to the murderers and kept quiet. The young son became frightened and ran away. But he knew that one day he would have to come back and do the payback for what had happened to his father. He did. We call him Orestes."

The Warlpiri men are gazing at the scene, their eyes quiet and open, savouring the complexity of the problem.

"Now Orestes, he came back quietly and talked to the mad sister. She was really mad with sorrow and anger. When she saw Orestes back and grown up to be a man she got well again. Her mind cleared. Together they worked out how to kill the mother and the mother's lover. They did it just how they planned. They stabbed them both. Then they ran away. But there was trouble. The 'old time' women spirits came out of their cave. We call them The Furies or 'Erinys.' Their job is to keep an eye on the woman's law. They also track down people and punish them for crimes. Sometimes you can't see them, but they are there anyway in the dark. Sometimes they carry snakes."

"Uwai," nods Perentie, "we have that too."

"Well, these mothers chased the brother, and the sister too I guess, but they really chased poor Orestes for years. He had bad dreams; it nearly made him go mad. They chased him so much that he had to return and give himself up to the women. The mothers got everyone together for a big court case. They got a council of twelve people. Maybe this was the first time the *Kardia* had a jury, I don't know. Maybe that's how we started up the jury system."

"Anyhow, in the morning all the judges sat down and said, 'We got to punish you for something, but what? What's the worst thing? Is the worst thing for a son to kill his mother or is it worse for a wife to cheat on her husband and kill her husband? Should Orestes be killed for murdering his mother or should he walk free because he was doing payback for his father?'"

"After a long talk, maybe days went by while people worried about the right decision, the people voted. . . . The twelve council members had to put a black stone in a pot if they thought Orestes was to blame and should die for killing his mother or a white stone for him to walk free. It was half and half. Six black and six white."

"'What happened?' asked Perentie, looking down at the row of twelve stones which had been placed on the sand, six on one side, six on the other."

"The people didn't know what to do; then a strange thing happened. A woman came down out of somewhere . . . maybe the sky. It was like she stepped out of a dreaming. Her father is the one we call Zeus, same as in the Dionysos story. He's Dionysos' father too, but this woman, Zeus' daughter, is a different one. Her name is Athene. She is very clever and has power over the law, not only woman's law. Her father is boss for the spiritual law of that country, but she talks for him."

"She said to all the people that this case was a really important one. It would sort out what was to happen in the future. She settled all the women down and she settled all the men down. She worked out an arrangement. She said that from now on revenge justice (what you *Yappa* call 'payback') would have to be different. She said that Orestes should be allowed to walk free because of 'compassion.' He killed his mother, that was true, but he carried out the payback for his father, he had to do that. You couldn't say one was worse than the other, people had to find another way of solving these conflicting problems. The old way couldn't show the way out. They had to learn about 'mercy.'"

The two Warlpiri men sit very still. We all realize that we are touching on a current problem, that it is being spoken about sideways, as it were. None of us are ready to engage in direct open debate about the present conflict between deeply held positions on Aboriginal law and European-based law.

I continue: "But she made a deal with the mothers. The men had to promise that the women's ceremonies would have to be respected by the men and protected. The mothers would have a special place of their own, in a cave that no men could come into and that it would always have to be so. . . . Maybe that cave was like the one where the 'Seven Sisters' dreaming is, down south in Pitjanjatjara country," I added, feeling a bit cautious about mentioning things that bordered on the secret and sacred. After all, according to the ancient Greek tradition I knew, I was edging close to the Mysteries, much of which was forbidden to speak of, publicly. On the other hand, Euripides, Aeschylus and Sophocles had all written plays about these events, so I was on fairly safe ground. I pointed out this dilemma to the men.

"Our women have got that too," Kumanjai speaks quietly, looking as though he is satisfied with the way this story is turning out. I look across at my friend, the psychiatrist, for some guidance. He has shrugged himself into a shape almost like a granite rock, very still and contemplative. He has nothing more to add.

"Well, that is the story," I say, slowly dismantling the scene and wiping the sand clear.

After that Japaljarri doesn't say much. We stand up and get into the truck and drive south, back to town. I am thinking, "Shit, where is all this going to lead?"

REQUIEM

This scene happened late in 1993.

After that a lot of things happened around Alice Springs to do with the uneasy, abrasive confusion of one law rubbing up against the other. The "Two Laws Debate" . . . except that it has never really been a debate. More like a dissociated conversation between groups of people who sit muttering to each other in consternation. It has reminded me of a mental ward in a hospital. Small groups of deranged people, clustered around beds, smoking tobacco, busily ignoring each other's painful inner reality and illusion. Meanwhile it seems that a whole world is falling apart, a kind of "Twilight of the Gods," indigenous Australian style. These days, in Alice Springs, it seems that the singing we catch on the night wind is a requiem for a lost nation.

I have known those two Warlpiri men for ten years now; at least we try to converse directly with each other. They know they are living through the disintegration of their families and their culture. They feel it and they make me feel it.

But this culture has lived continuously in Australia for how many thousands of years? Fifty thousand maybe; certainly twenty thousand. They and their ancestral line have never experienced the kind of catastrophe which is occurring now, ever. There is no comparable precedent. The Warlpiri take the advice of lawyers, of course, and government trouble-shooters, and appear to politely listen to the well-meant advice that will "save the Aboriginal health" and the families and culture. I see and hear all this rational activity, but behind the scenes, in the camp at night, a different interpretation of reality seems to emerge. I don't pretend to understand it. People like Kumanjai and Perentie keep telling me that a catastrophe is happening. But they tell it in a very strange way; they don't view it in the same way as the European habit of mind would expect. But I think they do keep expecting me to do something about it, perhaps because they know I am some kind of doctor who deals with madness and they know that the things that are happening have a madness about them. The way they communicate about the "state of the nation" is perhaps rather oblique. They keep making me feel strange states of mind. They keep trying to change me temporarily into a Warlpiri. They keep passing on fragments of the dreaming stories that deal with dismemberment and ruined relationships and sometimes healing. They keep inviting me to visit dreaming sites of significance and urging me to appreciate the significance. They keep pushing me to talk about Aboriginal lore and aspects of the law to judges and lawyers and even the Queen. This kind of thing happens to many other *Kardia* (white people) who live on the borderline of the indigenous people's world. They project feelings and images and expectations on to us and into us and expect actions from us that are mostly beyond our authority and powers. I do a bit, of course, and so does my psychiatric colleague. We do our best and we do communicate with judges and police and various transitory departmental directors who assiduously ignore most of what we manage to convey. I've even become quite clever at slipping covert communications through to these higher levels of authority. But I am not a political operator, and have reeled despondently, time and again, from these encounters. Then, one day, I started to apply to the intercultural situation the techniques I have learned from psychotherapeutic work. In particular I applied the techniques we use in therapy about "transference" and "countertransference" and came up with a different way of thinking about the strange and sometimes frustrating cross-cultural transactions. I call it "cultural transference."

I reflected upon the imagery of the story bits which Aboriginal contacts wanted me to hear. I analyzed the strange states of mind I fell into during and especially after my contacts. I noted the almost unconscious responses I made to Aboriginal people and Aboriginal situations. I noted the moods I fell into, the actions I was compelled to make, the despair, the grief, the despondency and the Messianic hopes and hopelessness. In short, I began to analyze my personal reactions for an indication of the intercultural transference and countertransference. I became sensitized to streams of consciousness within Alice Springs.

Slowly I began to see that a communication system had sprung up between us whereby messages about the Aboriginal condition and the European condition were somehow passing at a subliminal level between us. The key to establishing and maintaining the communication system seems to lie in a "foundation process." The communication foundation seems to involve the skill of being able to exchange authentic myth-like stories at certain crucial moments of relationship. This, I think, is why I engaged in the quixotic activity of the Sugarman/Dionysos Project, bringing to performance an epic drama from Greek mythological history. In the star-filled desert, at night, by the light of fires, we revealed the origins of European thought, the stations of the European dream marked out in the suppression of Rhea, the killing of Uranos, the subjugation of Kronos, the revolt of Zeus' siblings, the conflagration of Semele, and the birth of Dionysos. We depicted the destruction of civilized cities by delusional intoxicated violence. Through the performance of mythology we revealed to our Aboriginal associates the backdrop of modern Western civilization. Just as they had revealed the background of their thinking when, on occasion, I had been invited to witness the performance of Aboriginal ceremony and performance. It was a way that we could start to make sense of each other.

We said, through the medium of the "Bacchae" performance, for instance: "This is us. Disintegration and dismay has been the successive fate of our cultures. Now that we are among you, be warned. Accept our goods and you accept our fate. We dismember and we delude."

We pitched our warnings in the containing forms of archetypal drama because such doings are the closest equivalent we have to Aboriginal dreaming stories.

"Look," we said, "our people have been through these (such and such) experiences, we have this kind of history, we have these stories to show it. You observe our tracks, this is our nature."

"We never knew about all that," said the Warlpiri men. "No," I said, "some things the missionaries didn't have time to tell you."

THE USEFULNESS OF MYTH

From the point of view of psychotherapy, the mythic stories which were enacted through the Sugarman Project, in the politicized climate of Central Australian racial consternation, were psychoanalytic cultural interpretations of the situation. Or perhaps by referring to an intense cultural epic we had a means by which Aboriginal people, stuck in the problem with us, could see a way of mentally managing the states of mind which our Western civilization had been inflicting upon them. Our myths reveal the progression of our European struggles with creation, destruction and preservation. We must learn to tell our traditional stories simply and honestly to each other and we must be patient in giving the story/myth the time needed to reveal its relevance. In a tense situation, one cannot expect the deeper meaning of a myth to be immediately appreciated and usable as an instrument of reconciliation. People involved in a conflict may be so emotionally stirred up that clear thinking is impossible. But a culturally valued myth may have the potential to aid in reconciliatory thinking if its symbolic meaning is given time to unfold in the context of an intercultural situation or conflict.

Exchange of stories is not the whole story of negotiating across racial and cultural chasms, but it does seem to help. Not long ago, in the company of a small group of desert tribal men, with the aid of a painting and a mixed language translation, I recounted the epic coming into being of Uranos, Kronos, and his six children, the Olympian siblings and their descendants. The Olympian siblings, Jukurrpa beings, really. The men followed every image intently, saying again, "No one has ever shown us this before."

"No," I said, "that would be true. The white men you mostly meet don't even know these stories themselves. They don't know where their lore comes from. They only show you the surface story, the latest things; they never show you what is underneath, what is behind. They do not treat you with that high degree of respect."

"And that's why we blindly kill you," I think, sitting quietly back on the stones, in the shade of the river eucalypus, watching the Western Desert men touching the painting that we made depicting the history of the western world. They touch it, stroking it, absorbing its images. I continue to think, "We came to your country blindly, unconsciously, acting out our own mythic tragedies and unaware of the consequences to ourselves and to you. We project our culture into you like an injection and watch you die perplexed, pouring millions of dollars into sewerage programs and health programs and wagging our heads when you do not survive the psychic onslaught. We never told you the true story of where we came from, as a warning to you. We told you lies. We tried to make you into lost souls so as to save you with 'Jesus.' We made you the recipients of our own psychological projection system. And is it only the *Kardia* – the white people – who project their culture on to others? Surely we are all victims of one another's desires and fears. You, the *Yappa* – the Aboriginal people – also convert us into victims of your projections. We are all doing things with one another. Hunting and gathering left-over bits and pieces from each other's civilizations. The detritus of white civilization makes you sick, it seems. Relationship with us does not enhance you, but who knows, perhaps you will survive. Perhaps there will be no need for a requiem, old men."

CONCLUSION: SOME THOUGHTS ON CULTURAL TRANSFERENCE

Part of the skill of decoding cultural transference projections involves attending to the stories and myths which a cultural group uses as a reference point. These myths, in some disguised form, may be spontaneously projected in any intercultural transaction. Every cultural group has, as it were, an internally known structure of "taken-for-granted" myth – a skeleton of the mythologic – which like a bone structure, supports and directs the movements of that cultural group.

The intelligent use of cultural myth, as a carrier for communication between peoples, is one element in the equation of intercultural knowledge transfer and intercultural political and spiritual negotiation.

The anxiety of experiencing cultural disintegration seems to throw up attempts to reiterate one's primary belief systems, which are usually expressed in myth and/or cultural law. Culturally specific myths may be covertly or subliminally exchanged in political and therapeutic relationships as a subtext, because the myths which express or sanction one's identity help to contain and defend an individual or group, especially when their identity is under threat.

Two main categories of "myth" may be in operation simultaneously. One category is collective cultural fantasies, possibly recently invented; for example, that the USA has a destiny as the peacemaker of the world. The other category of myth might be those deeply embedded and probably ancient "stories" which hold in the collective mind, the origins, adventures and cultural laws of a specific group.

A clash of cultures may be seen as a clash of myths, of either category. Basic assumption myths seem to intensify feelings and also help to direct political manoeuvres and commercial purposes. Chaotic emotion and confused thoughts arising between cultural groups can be perplexing and destructive. Perhaps, however, useful communication may be established by considerate exchange of those culturally sanctioned myths which a people hold close to their heart. Perhaps recognition of these deeply held myths may serve as a diplomatic preliminary to political negotiations. Intercultural negotiations may be helped by intelligent recognition of the guiding mythologies which underpin a cultural group's existential understanding of itself.

Intelligent use of myth is not simply a matter of taking a crash course in local language and culture. Such a facile approach is naive because many cultural assumptions are deeply embedded in the psychic structure of a given group. It may not be explicit. The real psycho-mythology may emerge only slowly, by a process of empathetic identification with the other. This can be expensive and time consuming.

It is possible, however, that the experience of negotiating transference relationships as developed in the practice of psychotherapy may save time and money for those engaged in cross-cultural negotiations. The intelligent use of cross-cultural transference process implies the development of skill in attending to and decoding images and states of sensation, as well as perplexing feelings and thoughts, which may be being projected as communications. Pre-conscious projections seem to be evoked when people of differing races and cultural histories meet and engage intensely. This must be apparent to anyone working in intercultural turmoils. Understanding those projections is not easy, but rationalist insistence upon remaining blind to intercultural transference process is not recommended because it is wasteful of cultural knowledge and lives. This fact is demonstrated in Central Australia where the waste of lives and the insane derangement of knowledge is occurring daily.

The psychological health of nations requires as much attention as the health of individuals. In a multicultural society the custodianship of that health is surely a joint enterprise. We can rely upon our ancestral mythologies as a guide and reference. This I have learned from the Warlpiri. I have learned most from quiet conversations in the dry sand of secluded river beds and on the back roads on long journeys. This story, I hope, gives a sense of learning from such experiences.

NOTE

1 The order of the names here is not relevant. Japaljarri is what we call a "skin name", think of it as a totemic clan name. Kumanjai is a word used to obscure a person's real name, mostly used when a person of the same name has passed away. If someone of the same name has died in their family circle then the word is used as a replacement since the actual name cannot be spoken out loud for a period of a year or so. The word Kumanjai is used in *Arresting Orestes* to obscure the real name of the person involved.

Chapter 8

Factionalism and interethnic conflict

Narratives in myth and politics

Renos K. Papadopoulos

In this chapter I would like to reflect on some aspects of factionalism and conflict in political contexts. However, it is important to state at the outset that I am not a politician, and hence I am approaching the subject matter from the perspective of a mental health professional and more specifically that of a Jungian analyst. Moreover, I feel the need to clarify that my reflections are based on my therapeutic and consultation work in this field and are not a product of armchair theorizing. In addition to my conventional clinical and analytical work (in the context of both private practice and in a British National Health Service specialist psychotherapy clinic) as well as my academic duties at a university, I have been acting as a consultant to various relief organizations and have been directly involved in therapeutic work with refugees and survivors of political violence.

The Jungian approach is mainly known for its applicability to traditional analytical contexts with individuals within the confines of a consulting room or in well-defined mental health settings, and it is not particularly known for its applicability to working in these kinds of difficult situations. Although Jung himself (e.g. Jung 1928, 1945, 1946a, 1946b, 1946c) and others after him (e.g. Adams 1996; Bernstein 1989, 1992; Lopez-Pedraza 1990; Odajnyk 1976; Samuels 1993; Stevens 1989; Tacey 1997) used theoretical concepts derived from analytical psychology to discuss issues of political nature, it seems that not many actual therapeutic interventions in this area have been explicitly informed by a Jungian approach. Apart from the work of Harry Wilmer who worked with Vietnam veterans (Wilmer 1986, 1996, 1999; Woodruff and Wilmer 1988), I am not aware of other Jungians engaged in this type of work.

When confronted with the distressing effects of the manifestations of factionalism and armed conflict, we tend to experience a mixture of emotional reactions which, however, are often covered up quickly by attempts at rational understanding and explanation. These attempts usually consist of combinations of various modes of explaining which include several semi-identifiable facets – historical, political, sociological, moral, military, psychological, religious, economic, etc. These explanations tend to be of limited value for at least two reasons: first, the nature of the phenomena is fairly complex and multifaceted, and second, the explanations are likely to be impulsive attempts at covering up or reducing our own distress; as such,

their predominant defensive motivation does not allow for a compr
of the various constituent components of the situation (including
and personal dimensions), and therefore they tend to overcomper
to be clear and rational. In this way, the predominantly defensi
attempts will adversely affect their validity. Yet the nature of tl
that we cannot ignore them; the media keep bombarding us with a multiplicity
images connected with them which create a demand in us that we develop some kind of order and understanding. Thus the pressure is both from the outer and from the inner world to arrive at some working understanding of these destructive conflicts. The difficulty is that, as rational human beings, we need to understand these disturbing phenomena and yet the type of understanding that emerges in these circumstances appears to be of the wrong kind.

According to the Jungian approach, images play an important role in these kinds of highly charged situations. They provide a containing function which prevents dangerous over-rationalization and acting out; their appeal to a domain beyond the intellect enables irrational elements to be included in the wider picture, and thus images may facilitate our entrance into the spirit of the events. Images have the ability to move us into realms beyond rational deadlocks and to expand our perspectives. It is for these reasons that I would like to introduce some poetic images to assist us in our exploration of these distressing phenomena. These images come from a poem ("Helen") which refers to the Trojan War, the archetypal confrontation between two factions of the ancient world. The poet, George Seferis, based his poem on a play by Euripides (also called *Helen*), where the idea is put forward that Helen perhaps never went to Troy, and therefore the whole Trojan War was fought in vain. Here are some excerpts from the poem:

> . . .
> Lyric nightingale,
> on a night like this, by the shore of Proteus,
> the Spartan slave-girls heard you and began their lament,
> and among them – who would have believed it? – Helen!
> She whom we hunted so many years by the banks of the
> Scamander.
> She was there, at the desert's lip; I touched her; she spoke
> to me:
> "It isn't true, it isn't true," she cried.
> "I didn't board the blue-bowed ship.
> I never went to valiant Troy."
>
> Breasts girded high, the sun in her hair, and that stature
> shadows and smiles everywhere,
> on shoulders, thighs and knees;
> the skin alive, and her eyes
> with the large eyelids,

she was there, on the banks of a Delta.
And at Troy?
At Troy, nothing: just a phantom image.
That's how the gods wanted it.
And Paris, Paris lay with a shadow as though it were a
solid being;
and for ten whole years we slaughtered ourselves for Helen.

Great suffering had desolated Greece.
So many bodies thrown
into the jaws of the sea, the jaws of the earth
so many souls
fed to the millstones like grain.
And the rivers swelling, blood in their silt,
all for a linen undulation, a filmy cloud,
a butterfly's flicker, a wisp of swan's down,
an empty tunic – all for a Helen.

. . .

I moored alone with this fable,
if it's true that it is a fable,
if it's true that mortals will not again take up
the old deceit of the gods;
if it's true
that in future years some other Teucer,
or some Ajax or Priam or Hecuba,
or someone unknown and nameless who nevertheless saw
a Scamander overflow with corpses,
isn't fated to hear
messengers coming to tell him
that so much suffering, so much life,
went into the abyss
all for an empty tunic, all for a Helen.

(Seferis 1982: 357–361)

This powerful poem captures the tragedy of the incomprehensibility of factional conflicts. Although we need to undertake rational (historico-political) investigations in a meticulous and systematic way in order to arrive at satisfactory explanations as to why such hostilities break out, it is useful to remember that there is also another relevant dimension to these conflicts. The unspeakable horrors of this kind of strife make any rational explanations lack real and credible significance – regardless of the actual external realities (which, I emphasize, need to be identified and respected in their own right). These phenomena shift us on to another perspective which introduces the unanswerable questions about the meaning of destructiveness and aggression, and which exposes the mysterious nature of the human condition and the ungraspable reality of good and evil.

"THE OLD DECEIT"

In "Helen", these questions are addressed poetically when it is claimed "that's how the gods wanted it": gods make mortals "take up the old deceit"; they provide them with illusory reasons, the flimsiness of which the poem exposes as being like that of a "phantom image," "a linen undulation, a filmy cloud, a butterfly's flicker, a wisp of swan's down, an empty tunic." The tragedy is that these elusive and beautiful images can become "the cause" of enormous devastation. The poem dares to question the motives for such wars: even Helen herself, a very real human being, may not, after all, be so real. Many unshakeable certainties about "rational reasons" for wars were later proved to be either wilful fabrications or mistaken impressions. For example, in a recent BBC documentary, convincing evidence was provided to argue that the Six Day War started from a wrong piece of information based on incorrect intelligence; both Arabs and Israelis did not wish to embark on an armed conflict, but once that mistaken information entered the system, the wheels began moving inexorably in the direction of war and all human efforts were unable to prevent it. In order to facilitate the Holocaust, the Nazi propaganda machine had to call the Jews "vermin" that needed to be exterminated. Tragically, such an image, which under ordinary circumstances would have been dismissed by any thinking human being as laughable, became a central image that led to the actual extermination of people. So, what is this "old deceit of the gods?" What allows images to have such power?

Helen is an apt and complex mythic image because she combines beauty and seduction along with bigotry and destruction. Potentially, she could have been the symbol of bringing together the Greeks and Trojans. Like Romeo and Juliet, Paris and Helen could have provided an opportunity for their respective factions to come together; they dared to bridge the gap between their group differences, and they challenged the validity of these differences. However, they did this not after strategic planning or logical calculations but because their love forced them to; they were driven to it by forces outside their own individual and collective conscious identities. It was the charm of elusive Eros that enticed them into their fateful attraction and not any cerebral design. It was the "old deceit of the gods" that wove the intricate scenario according to which a loving attraction ended up becoming the cause for destruction. Their transgression of boundaries went a little too far, it crossed that invisible line which separates the loving and uniting attraction from the hateful and dividing repulsion. It was due to the "phantom image," to "a linen undulation, a filmy cloud, a butterfly's flicker, a wisp of swan's down, an empty tunic" that the motive which was supposed to bring people together was pushed over the line and became the torch to light up the conflagration. The "old deceit of the gods" recast the spirit of love between Paris and Helen into a war cry that led to a catastrophic confrontation of epic dimensions; indeed, the genre itself, the epic, was first introduced to narrate this horrendous conflict between Trojans and Greeks.

Such richness of imagery is lost when we attempt to analyze the dynamics of concrete conflicts in the world around us today. We look only for the cerebral designs which, nevertheless, do exist and which we must study; however, we remain focused there and we leave out the fateful undulations, we forget about the evasive Helen. Although history keeps repeating itself with conflicts flaring up all the time in different parts of the world, we keep insisting on looking for answers exclusively in the rational realm. How do we introduce the imagistic dimension into these matters? In what way can we begin to conceptualize non-conceptual perspectives? What epics are enacted during these conflicts within which our role is that of actors and not that of script writers or directors?

Fundamentalist nationalism and consequent armed conflicts are not psychological phenomena as such, but they need to be comprehended from an angle that acknowledges both their external reality as well as their psychological and imagistic dimensions. In a sense, we may need to allow ourselves to be overwhelmed by the incomprehensibility of these phenomena, however frightening this may be, so that we may open up to layers of deeper understanding, beyond rational comprehension.

DIFFERING DIFFERENCES

As human beings, we are joined by similarities and differences with our fellow humans: in certain respects all of us are the same and in other respects we are different. It is a truism that some differences matter more than others, and that some differences are welcome whilst others are potentially disrupting. In the course of our everyday life, we interact with people who are both similar to and different from us; they are similar in relation to some characteristics and dissimilar in relation to other characteristics. Some of these characteristics are more changeable than others with regard to time and context; physical differences and some cultural differences may be less changeable than differences in taste and ideology. What is puzzling is that under certain circumstances, some differences which did not matter all of a sudden acquire different meaning and become crucial in our lives in ways that may lead to conflict. Some dormant similarities may also change and become responsible for developing a new closeness among people. "Life is full of these fluctuations and ordinarily they pass almost unnoticed. Yet, under certain circumstances, the different meaning of similarities and differences may become instrumental in flaring up wider conflicts" (Papadopoulos, in press).

In his seminal book on ethnic war, Michael Ignatieff (1999: 50) discusses this process as follows:

> Gender and racial difference are certainly minor relative to the overwhelming genetic commonality that unites men and women and persons of different races,

> but they become major when used as markers of power and status. No human difference matters much until it becomes a privilege, until it becomes the basis for oppression. Power is the vector that turns minor into major.

Ignatieff argues that the sequence which leads to interethnic war begins with the "collapse of the overarching state" which creates fear in people, which leads to "nationalist paranoia" (1999: 45), which then results in actual warfare. According to him, it all begins when the "equilibrium of forces" in an interethnic state becomes unstable; then, ethnic minorities no longer trust that the ethnic majority will "not use its preponderance to turn the institutions of the state into an instrument of ethnic favouritism or ethnic justice" and begin to feel unsafe. Subsequently, what Ignatieff calls the "fiction" of nationalism is created when individuals have the feeling "I can't trust my neighbours, and come to think of it, we've always been different" (1999: 44). It is then that "nationalism creates communities of fear, groups held together by the conviction that their security depends on sticking together. People become 'nationalistic' when they are afraid; when the only answer to the question 'Who will protect me now?' becomes 'my own people'" (1999: 45). In this way, it is not only power which is the vector that changes minor differences to major ones but also fear. In addition, Ignatieff mentions guilt as another vector. Guilt, because "if you have shared a common life with another group and then suddenly begin to fear them, because they suddenly have power over you, you have to overcome the weight of happy memory; you have to project on to *them* the blame for destroying a common life" (1999: 56).

Ignatieff's thesis provides one of the best accounts of this puzzling transformation of differences from minimal, inconsequential and even imperceptible to major and decisive in creating and escalating conflict among ethnic groups. Crucial to his argument is that nationalism is not an expression of "some primordial essence, formed by history and tradition," but essentially is a "relational" construct: "A Serb is someone who is not a Croat. A Croat is someone who is not a Serb" (p. 37). Such a claim is not only in accordance with current theories of social constructivism (e.g. Burr 1995; Gergen 1999; McNamee and Gergen 1992; Parker 1998) but is also born out of experience in the field.

An example of this relational identity is a Bosnian Muslim man in his sixties who was brought to the UK as part of the first group of medical evacuees the Red Cross freed from a Serb camp in Bosnia in 1992. I have been working therapeutically with most individuals of this group over a period of time (Papadopoulos 1996, 1997, 1998b, 1999a; Papadopoulos and Hildebrand 1997). This man had lived peacefully next to Serbs for all his life and was shaken to the core when he was arrested by Serbs during the war in Bosnia and taken to a camp because of his Muslim identity, of which he was hardly aware. In Tito's Yugoslavia, his life did not highlight differences between him and his Serb neighbors but, all of a sudden for him, the war created his own separate Muslim identity as well as the Serb identity of his new enemies. At the beginning of his stay in the UK, he was acutely aware of the differences between himself and the Serbs whom, understandably, he hated.

However, he could not find many similarities or affinity with his Muslim brethren from Pakistan and India who welcomed him in London. Instead, what were more apparent to him were the differences between them; the fact that they were both Muslims meant little to him next to their other cultural and linguistic differences. Gradually, he met other ex-Yugoslavs in London (including Serbs) of his own age and together they re-created a mini-multiethnic group of friends which has become, for him, a source of great joy in his otherwise miserable life in this inhospitable city. However, he keeps this connection with this group secret from most of his fellow Muslim Bosnians.

Evidently, his national identity is indeed relational and dependent on what is usually referred to as "the circumstances." In Bosnia, the polarization of war bestowed upon him a distinct Muslim identity which remained with him until the fear of power of others over him began to loosen up. In London, as he began feeling safer, he re-created a composite identity based on both similarities and differences with members of other ethnic groups from the former Yugoslavia; moreover, he found a creative way of selectively activating the different aspects of this identity appropriate to the time, place and context. Although he will no longer ignore his new-found Muslim identity, this identity does not now seem to prevent him from mixing with non-Muslim ex-Yugoslavs. Moreover, he told me, characteristically, that had he continued to hate Serbs, he would have allowed them to "win," insofar as it was "them" who imposed on him the rule of distinction and difference among people.

Thus this man has managed, with the help of therapeutic intervention, to free himself from the clutches of paranoid nationalism and to develop a flexible way of accessing his identities. He has succeeded, as an individual, in connecting and identifying with different collectives at different times in ways that are enriching rather than being defensive and restrictive.

COLLECTIVE NARRATIVES AND VIOLENCE

In another paper, I introduced the term "storied community" (Papadopoulos 1999b) to refer to a community which is created around a certain story. "We know that communities create stories but the reverse also happens: stories create communities when people form various types of associations (from informal personal networks to institutional organisations) because they all share a certain story" (Papadopoulos, in press). Ignatieff mentions the formation of "communities of fear" (1999: 45), but these are not the only communities that are formed. Many types of communities are created around different stories all the time, but such communities are particularly powerful during times of ethnic upheaval.

> Collective stories locate individuals within them and reciprocally (with individuals) co-construct reality. For as much as individuals construct stories, stories also construct individual identities. Moreover, stories form communities

> around them that share the same meaning and belief systems which they convey. Thus, stories of defiance against oppressive regimes create a community of opponents who share the same abhorrence of stifling authoritarianism. In this sense, one may speak of a "storied community" which is the group of people who are joined together by certain shared narratives. A storied community provides the coherent narratives which are essential ingredients of resilience.
>
> (Papadopoulos 1999b)

During the turbulent times of destabilized state structures, collective narratives acquire a specifically pertinent status. Indeed, they provide a containing and holding function for individuals by giving shape to their chaotic feelings, thoughts and even their sense of identity, and by channeling them in certain (seemingly intelligible) directions. The structure of these collective narratives is usually fairly simple and their message tends to be simplistic. They account for most key elements and players at a given historical time in a rather basic way. Perhaps the most important element in their structure is the inclusion of powerful mythic imagery which gels all other loose elements together in some magnetic-like attraction. By mythic imagery, I do not mean that they employ identifiable characters from specific ethnic mythologies. If anything, the imagery is more universal and more basic, referring to heroic and tragic characters and situations. Collective narratives in times of interethnic conflict are usually based on variations of themes of heroic saviours, of persecuted special people, of barbaric neighbors, of outstanding individuals, of saintly devotion, of selfless acts, etc. It is not unusual that both embattled ethnic groups have almost identical collective narratives which shape almost two isomorphic storied communities. In other words, what they think of themselves and of each other is almost alike.

Many social scientists have criticized the illusory notion of *we*. For example, Esther Wiesenfeld challenges the "concept of *we* as a totality of people" who are "clearly set apart from *them* who are conceived as a *not us*" (1996: 338). She argues that our "identity with a community" is only "one of multiple collective identities" (p. 340) and explains that "in the process of constructing the *we*, a dimension is created that we call *macrobelonging*, which is not disturbed by the vicissitudes of everyday life" (p. 341). In addition, she distinguishes a "*microbelonging*, which has to do with the multiple collective identities which call for the redemption of diversity and privacy" (p. 342). Thus although the *we* may be illusory, the collective stories strengthen the "reality" of this illusion by addressing what Wiesenfeld refers to as "macrobelonging." Moreover, it could be said that it is the mythic images, with their fascination and strong impact, that organize the storied communities and give form to the "macrobelonging."

Other authors who address the "psychological sense of community," such as Hill (1996), McMillan and Chavis (1986) and Sarason (1994), have emphasized the need for accounting for a "sense of transcendence" in community. Hill maintained that "a complete understanding of a psychological sense of community can only be obtained within the context of understanding a sense of transcendence" (Hill 1996:

436–437). Again, one could argue that it is the mythic images that can provide as well as be the carriers of this sense of transcendence which clearly elevates the community to a different level of group, above the collection of all its individuals and above the locus of shared activities and exchange.

However, all collective narratives, regardless of their mythical dimensions, have their own cracks, insofar as they cannot possibly account for the variety of experiences and diversity of differences among members of a storied community. The final element that makes a storied community solid and compact is violence. As long as factional antagonism does not erupt into violence, there may be openness to produce alternative stories with relative flexibility. It is the combination of a mythic image and violence that creates a deadly mixture which becomes impenetrable to any alternative views. Once violence and mythic images of a storied community connect, we move on to another level where polarization rules supreme and the possibility of bringing together opposites in any way becomes remote if not impossible.

The state, like the home, has the ability to connect and indeed contain various opposites such as joy and sorrow, proximity and distance, harmony and discord, love and hatred, success and failure, and many other archetypal polarities. Referring to the refugee experience, Papadopoulos and Hildebrand argued that home is a "key construct which interconnects three overlapping realms – the intrapsychic, the interpersonal and the socio-political." They likened

> the destruction of homes, as in the refugee experience, to nuclear explosion when all the contained forces erupt creating widespread devastation. So, what the refugees yearn for may not be just the specific [houses and other property] . . . which they left behind but the restoration of the holding functions which the home symbolised and actually performed.
>
> (1997: 213)

Thus the state, like the home, has a certain protective membrane which enables opposites to coexist. In these circumstances, differences are tolerated and even provide enriching possibilities. However, once that membrane is damaged by violence then, according to the colloquial expression, "all hell breaks loose." This expression conveys in an apt way what happens when the alchemical vessel of a pluralistic state becomes incapable of containing differences and interethnic conflicts; then, diversity no longer promotes enhancing development, but instead solidifies into rigid polarities, the sparks from which ignite conflagration. Moreover, in a similar way, the international community has the capacity to act in a containing way in relation to factionalism and interethnic conflicts which occur either within one state or between states. The alchemical vessel of the international community has the potential ability to prevent escalation of local clashes; however, when the containing membrane of this community is damaged (by rifts or inappropriate siding with one combatant group), more disastrous consequences of wider proportion follow.

Once violence erupts the polarization becomes complete and ultimate. As Ignatieff puts it, "violence . . . keeps things simple" (1999: 37). It resolves painful contradictions, and awkward internal conflicts at an individual as well as a state level. As I quoted in another paper (Papadopoulos 1998b), Louis de Bernières offered an astute description of when soldiers, after a period of anxious inactivity, experience action:

> We found that there is a wild excitement when the tension of waiting is done with, and that sometimes it transforms itself into a kind of demented sadism once an action is commenced. You cannot always blame the soldiers for their atrocities, because I can tell you from experience that they are the natural consequences of the inferno of relief that comes from not having to think any more. Atrocities are sometimes nothing less than the vengeance of the tormented.
>
> (de Bernières 1995: 61)

Indeed, once violence begins, other priorities are activated and thinking tends to seize up. This offers enormous relief, because all conflictual considerations and dilemmas are then set aside and what becomes imperative is "action without thought." It should not be forgotten that the mental state of action without thought is a fairly complex phenomenon. Although much has been written about it, there is one important facet that has not received its deserved attention (Papadopoulos 1998b). This refers to the fact that "action without thought" constitutes the basis of two diametrically opposite phenomena: the one is the much sought-after goal of many spiritual disciplines (e.g. the Zen doctrine of "pure action"), and the other is the ordinary psychopathic "acting out." In this way, good police and community planning, psychological theorizing and moral abhorrence may all prove ineffective in curbing violence in our society, unless we are fully aware of the complexity of this phenomenon along with some of its "dark benefits."

FURTHER JUNGIAN REFLECTIONS

When we encounter atrocities like the ones we have experienced recently in El Salvador, Bosnia, Rwanda, and Kosovo, we seem to reach the limit of our own usual understanding of human destructiveness. We think we know all about human destructiveness, being aware of our own aggressive impulses; sometimes we become aware of what we term "animal destructiveness" in ourselves or others. This occurs when we feel that one is almost possessed by a violent impulse and is "beside himself." However, this kind of violence reminds us of another kind of destructiveness which can only be described as the result of "pure evil." There is an unmistakable feeling that these deeds are an act of evil in its absolute pure form. I am aware that evil is not a psychological term and I am particularly pleased that we do not attempt to psychologize evil. By naming these phenomena as evil we move into the realm of incomprehensibility which I outlined above.

Once we begin to examine more deeply this pure evil we are surprised by the far-reaching consequences. This surprise comes from the fact that this purity exerts a remarkable fascination and it is very disturbing to catch ourselves being fascinated by evil (Guggenbühl 1996); it challenges the understanding of our human nature. As Jung (1945) put it, "the sight of evil kindles evil in the soul – there is no getting away from this fact" (*CW* 10, par. 410). In Jungian terms, this pure evil is a pure unipolar archetype; an archetype completely devoid of any personal content, and it exists in its uncontaminated collective nature. Thus the fascination and attraction have an almost numinous character.

It is difficult to discuss these phenomena because we do not encounter them every day. Anybody can terrorize anybody else fairly easily; it does not take much to frighten someone. Yet in some of these trouble spots we have recently witnessed acts by people who have gone to endless trouble to devise "ingeniously" evil ways of inflicting pain on others without any personal feeling; with excessive zeal the torturer devises atrocities as part of a routine everyday duty. This comes close to what Hannah Arendt (1999) spoke about as the "banality of evil;" indeed there is "nothing personal" in these acts – they are acts of archetypal possession where no personal dimensions interfere; hence the impersonal, inhuman feel about them. Something awful seems to happen once the situation crosses a certain line of human decency (cf. Krog 1998; Pauw 1997). Evil begins to take over completely, and keeps perpetuating itself. Evil acts for its own sake. It is then that there is some coldness, purity and fascination – a Luciferian light with its immense attraction. Jung (1936), in his essay on Wotan, quoted a passage where he described the "piercing icy frost arrows" of the hunter-god (*CW* 10, par. 381).

Although we think that these are extreme phenomena, we may be surprised if we turn to the culture of violence in our society today (Stanko 1994). Our cinemas, novels, paintings, art, and even fashion are deeply rooted in archetypal violence which exerts a deep but almost imperceptible fascination. There is no doubt that violence "sells" in our culture. Yet there are some interesting twists if we examine these phenomena further.

That very impersonal nature of these experiences may, paradoxically, have a liberating effect. Foucault, admittedly in a completely different context, welcomes the loss of personal identity as a positive deconstruction. Writing about the gay bath houses on the American East and West coast, he says, "you meet men there who are to you as you are to them. Nothing but a body with which combinations and productions of pleasure are possible. You cease to be imprisoned in your own face, in your own past, in your own identity" (cited in Miller 1993, p. 107). For him, the loss of self has a liberating effect because one loses the imposed sense of self which society constructs for us. Thus, under certain circumstances, the loss of individuality is a most welcome goal. After all, is it not the aim of ecstatic practices within religious contexts to liberate the person from a false sense of individuality by immersing them into a collective identity? The tragic paradox is that, under certain conditions, brutalized practices may inadvertently have a similar result.

In Jungian terms, the loosening of a rigid ego identity may allow the deeper sense of self to emerge. Another implication of this encounter with pure evil is that one also usually tends to experience its diametrically opposite polarity: distilled and pure love and goodness. Invariably, in our encounters with these phenomena, both polarities may become available to us if we are open to them. In practical terms, in conditions of extreme depravity one also encounters acts of unbelievable generosity, self-sacrifice and pure love.

One way of describing my own therapeutic work with survivors of such atrocities (Papadopoulos 1997, 1998b, 1999a) would be to say that I have been endeavouring to humanize this unipolar archetype of pure evil and thus create the conditions for experiencing its direct opposite – the good. Another paradox concerns the method of breaking the unipolar archetype. In a sense one has to introduce conflict and begin to shake that firmness in its unipolar position. This is not easy, since the last thing a therapist wishes to do is to introduce additional conflicts in people who have been so severely traumatized already.

Ultimately, factionalism is based on unipolarity and purity. No conflict or integration is tolerated by factionalism. The division is imposed automatically and no individual seems to have the power to oppose it. Jung, characteristically, wrote that under certain circumstances of rising national sentiment, "willy-nilly we identify ourselves with the nation, chalking up its supposed good qualities to our own account, and attributing our own bad qualities to others" (1928 *CW* 10, par. 910). It is indeed a "willy-nilly" condition where the collective nature of the impulse overshadows all personal values.

These are difficult and highly complex dynamic mechanisms – under the intense "archetypal radiation" (Papadopoulos 1998a, 1998b) of pure evil, the potential capacity that containers have for holding together opposites is shattered; under such conditions, potential containers such as individual personalities, the home, the family, the state and the international community split up violently and project parts of the polarities everywhere, in an indiscriminate way. Disabled in this way, these containers cannot tolerate differences, opposites, contradictions, variety, plurality, diversity; instead they glow under the illusory brightness of purity. It is then that factionalism becomes fanatical nationalism. Images of purity and cleanness predominate and evil perpetuates itself sustained by self-righteousness. Ethnic cleansing then becomes a natural consequence of this damaged state. Factionalism increases its power by its fascinating purity which expresses itself in ethnic cleansing. The fascination, attraction, seductiveness and power that the worshipped purity has on people enables the continuation of evil and the blindness to any human (i.e. bipolar) qualities. People, in this state, are not troubled but are possessed by this radiating and evil purity. Thus the virtues of ambiguity, the richness of diversity, the containing nature of plurality, are all lost. Inevitably, "willy-nilly" people get caught up in this archetypal unipolarity. However, not all people remain possessed all the time by this Luciferian purity. These frightful circumstances may also push individuals to a point where they sense the inhumanity of this trap, and they may break out of it with immense gains. It is possible that, whereas the majority of people get overwhelmed and keep becoming further enslaved by a brutal collective, some individuals, if they have sufficiently conducive inner and outer conditions, may gain unique insights and become liberated.

One of these conducive conditions is the provision of an appropriate therapeutic space. However, therapists may also inevitably get caught up in this archetypal whirlpool of unipolarity, because of the wider rhetoric and media imposition at the time. The therapists" unipolarity will not, of course, be that of pure evil but some variation of a reaction to it. This means that therapists are likely to become victims of another, equally powerful archetypal radiation, that of the saviour: they will become possessed by the sanctity of their calling and are likely to become crusaders against the evil of the opposite side. This is a most difficult condition because, objectively, the survivors are indeed victims of brutality and evil. However, if the therapists fall into the trap of the opposite polarity of rescuer, the danger is that, by implication, the survivors are likely to be pinned down in the role of victims forever. The more the therapists glow in the self-righteousness of "good," the more the survivors will glow in the complementary position of victims, without the prospect of breaking out of it and developing their lives further.

Under these conditions, the therapeutic space between therapist and client will be infected and will lose its capacity to create the protective membrane to contain good and evil. In this way, imperceptibly, both therapists and survivors will fall prey to the "willy-nilly" condition and they will become "collective." This collectivization amounts to dehumanization. We dehumanize nations, we dehumanize individuals and then, unwittingly, we perpetuate the purity of the supposed "good" and of evil. This is a great tragedy because in this way, blinded by the archetypal radiation of the purity from unipolarity, we keep perpetuating the very problem we had set out to solve.

Yet opening up to wider collective narratives can have a most healing effect. Jung repeatedly emphasized that the collective realm of archetypal images provides a healing correction for an individual. Characteristically, he wrote: "The great psychic systems of healing, the religions . . . consist of universal myth motifs whose origin and content are collective and not personal" (1954 *CW* 13, par. 478). When an individual reaches an impasse within the confines of his or her own psyche, opening up to wider realms of collective narratives can be most rejuvenating and, indeed, healing. There are many such collective realms in societies that can provide this restorative function: they include religious, cultural, aesthetic, sporting and other narrative systems. If therapists, in their work with survivors of interethnic violence, acknowledge (at least to themselves) their "infected" position by the archetypal radiation of unipolarity, and with humility and genuine respect connect with healing collectives, not relying entirely on their own individual therapeutic prowess, they have a chance of maintaining the containing therapeutic membrane; they can enhance the resilience of the therapeutic container by locating the therapeutic activity in the context of wider narratives in the community at large. In this way, by re-storying the survivors" and their own narratives (in the light of healing collectives), they have the opportunity of restoring their vital connection with their own nourishing archetypal roots. One difficulty in such attempts is when therapists, in their eagerness to appear politically correct or culturally minded, attempt to incorporate in their own therapeutic work elements of the cultural and religious rituals from the survivors' background. Needless to say, such empty mimicry is not only a mockery of the dignity of these rituals but it is also ineffective and even dangerous.

Jung, in a poignant passage, echoes some of the dark dynamics discussed above:

> When evil breaks at any point into the order of things, our whole circle of psychic protection is disrupted. Action inevitably calls up reaction, and, in the matter of destructiveness, this turns out to be just as bad as the crime, and possibly even worse, because the evil must be exterminated root and branch.
>
> (1945 *CW* 10, par. 411)

THE EX-GUERRILLA'S PLEA

During a meeting I had in El Salvador with a group of ex-guerrillas and ex-government troops as part of a project run by the United Nations Development Programme, an ex-guerrilla said from the bottom of his heart: "Until recently, I strongly believed that what was going on in our country was a struggle between good and evil and, of course, I was on the side of the good. Now, I do not know any more. . . ." He was unable to complete his sentence but his anguish was obvious to all, who were very moved. What he was trying to express was that the collective narratives that gave meaning to his life and to his will to fight until death were no longer sufficiently strong and had lost their meaning, leaving a painful gap which was filled by a disturbing lack of clarity. What he was crying out for was a new story that gave meaning to his identity, his history as a guerrilla, his new observations after the end of hostilities in his country and his sense of the future. In other words, he was desperate for new collective narratives that would contain and nourish him. In a trusting way he demonstrated how open he was to belong to another storied community that would protect and nurture him.

He was a brave and trusting man who dared to stay out of quick and easy polarizing stories and, with his plea he was in a sense inviting others who were both similar to and different from him to join him in co-constructing new and more appropriate narratives for his country where the polarities would be held.

Unfortunately, there are not many brave people like him today; it seems that most of us tend to grasp any collective narrative which could offer some relief from the pain of incomprehensibility. Moreover, the media play a pivotal role in being only too eager to supply us with ready-made and pre-packaged stories. Politicians endlessly trade on mythic images, desperately weaving them into various narratives (consciously or unconsciously) in an anxious attempt to invent a new and fitting yarn.

Aid workers are particularly vulnerable to the need to find narratives within which to locate themselves. Shortly after the beginning of the devastating war in Kosovo and Yugoslavia, UNICEF asked me to prepare a set of guidelines for their workers. I thought it would be useful to include here what I prepared for them as an illustration of how some of the above issues can actually take shape in practice.

I will not discuss each item and the reasons why it is formulated as it is. This, I trust, will be evident from the overall context of this chapter. What needs to be clarified is that these workers have been working across the entire territory of Yugoslavia, i.e. in Serbia, Kosovo, and Montenegro, and that therefore they have been suffering from the violence and destruction perpetrated by all sides: NATO, the Serbs, and the various Kosovar factions. They are people with varying degrees of psychological sophistication, involved in all kinds of jobs from managerial to menial, all connected with the psycho-social welfare of child victims of the war. Here are the guidelines.

Caring for the carers

Do not forget that the tragedy in your country is at many different levels, ranging from losses of material property to losses in human lives; from destruction of social networks to damage of the psychological sense of safety. Your work focuses only on a tiny spectrum of the wide devastation but this does not mean that what you are doing is not important.

The people you are attending to have a multiplicity of needs and it is impossible for you or any one single service or agency to address all of them.

Do not forget that this tragedy will bring about changes in a way that many things will never be the same again.

Expect that at times you will feel inadequate; so do not despair, look around you – it is likely that you are the best person to do what you are doing.

Yet, at the same time, do not think that you are indispensable or that you are the saviour of the world.

The enormity of the task is likely to push you to expect heroic achievements from yourself. Limit your expectations and set small and tangible tasks.

Focus on your small achievements, appreciate them and build on them. Marvel at the resilience of human nature.

Make it a priority to create a support group for yourself. This should be a group of people you trust and where you all can have the space to simply talk freely about whatever comes to your mind – thoughts and ideas as well as about the cluster of mixed feelings and reactions.

Do not forget that your mood and feelings are likely to be confused and fluctuating. It may be a good idea to develop some kind of reflecting position within yourself to monitor and digest these confusions and fluctuations. You may wish to keep some record of them and you may also wish to share some of this with your support group.

It will be most useful to keep some record of your actual work as well. Do not allow yourself to get flooded by the enormity of the work. The moment you are lost the people who depend on you will also be lost.

Watch out for "somatic signals of distress," for example, insomnia, indigestion, changes in your bowel movements, excessive perspiration, headaches. Monitor them, discuss them with your support group, take a break and, if needed, see a specialist.

Watch out for psychological signals of distress: recurring and intrusive recollections of traumatic experiences, nightmares, excessive and protracted apathy or other avoidance behaviour, persistent irritability, lack of concentration, hyper-vigilance, exaggerated startle response. Monitor them, discuss them with your support group, take a break and, if needed, see a specialist.

Do not forget that the monitoring and digestion of all this is not a luxury but one of the most important ingredients of your work. Therefore, plan your actual work schedule in a way that it includes these activities. Do not fill up your time with only what you offer to others.

Your work deals not only with unbearable human suffering but also with violence, hatred, and evil. Do not forget that these negative feelings are likely to activate similar emotions in you; unless you are vigilant, they will overwhelm you, with unpredictable consequences.

Do not forget that there are many powerful systems of meaning in society, for example, religious, cultural, political, etc. Endeavour to make use of them in an appropriate way with those you work with. Respect human values and belief systems because they can provide meaning to many situations that appear meaningless.

Finally, do not neglect yourself. Do not forget to enjoy things in life and to have fun.

CELEBRATION OF INCOMPREHENSION

To end this chapter, I wish to employ another set of poetic images. One colleague with whom I collaborated on refugee programs in Yugoslavia wrote to me that the first phase of the original war which led to the breakup of Yugoslavia produced a shock; she felt helpless and did not know how to speak and conceptualize the tragedy. Then she identified a second phase, which she called a phase of naive optimism or optimism from despair. She believed in the power of rational knowledge. She did not give a name to the third phase but instead she sent me a poem. In fact, it is not an actual poem; it is part of a short story by the Russian author Danil Harms (1993). I call this phase that of deep pain. For me, this is the most moving celebration of the sharing of the anguish resulting from our incomprehension. There is time for answers and there is time for silence; there is time for logic and there is time for deeper contemplation. Yet the human togetherness and unique contact that can be achieved through the help of mythic imagery can create most precious effects:

"Is there anything in the world which would make sense
and moreover would change the course of events
not only on earth but also in other worlds?"
I asked my teacher.
"There is", answers my teacher.
"What is it?", I ask.
"It is", begins my teacher, and suddenly goes silent.
I stood silent and stretched expecting his reply
but he was silent.
I stood and he was silent.
And he was silent.
And I stood in our silence.
And he was silent.
Both of us stand and are silent.
"Hoy La La".
Both of us stand and are silent.
"Hoy Le, Le".

REFERENCES

Adams, M.V. (1996) *The Multicultural Imagination. "Race", Color, and the Unconscious*. London: Routledge.

Arendt, H. (1999) *The Human Condition*. Chicago: Chicago University Press (2nd edn).

Bernstein, J.S. (1989) *Power and Politics: the Psychology of Soviet – America Partnership*. Boston: Shambhala.

Bernstein, J.S. (1992) Beyond the personal: analytical psychology applied to groups and nations. In Renos K. Papadopoulos (ed.), *C.G. Jung: Critical Assessments*, Vol. IV, pp. 22–37. London and New York: Routledge.

Burr, V. (1995) *An Introduction to Social Constructionism*. London: Routledge.

de Bernières, L. (1994) *Captain Corelli's Mandolin*. London: Random House, Minerva (1995).

Gergen, K.J. (1999) *An Invitation to Social Constructionism*. London: Sage.

Guggenbühl, A. (1996) *The Incredible Fascination of Violence*. Woodstock, CT: Spring Publications.

Harms, D.I. (1993) *'They Call Me Capuchin'; Selections from the writings of Danil Ivanovitch Harms*.(in Russian). Moscow.

Hill, J. L. (1996). 'Psychological sense of community: suggestions for future research'. *Journal of Community Psychology*, 24(4): 431–438.

Ignatieff, M. (1999) *The Warrior's Honor. Ethnic War and the Modern Conscience*. London: Vintage.

Jung, C.G. (1928) The Swiss line in the European spectrum. *Collected Works*, Vol 10.

Jung, C.G. (1936) Wotan. *Collected Works*,Vol 10.

Jung, C.G. (1945) After the catastrophe. *Collected Works*,Vol 10.

Jung, C.G. (1946a) Preface to essays on contemporary events. *Collected Works*, Vol 10.

Jung, C.G. (1946b) The fight with the shadow. *Collected Works*, Vol 10.
Jung, C.G. (1946c) Epilogue to essays on contemporary events. *Collected Works*, Vol 10.
Jung, C.G. (1954) The philosophical tree. *Collected Works*, Vol 13.
Krog, A. (1998) *Country of my Skull*. Johannesburg: Random House.
Lopez-Pedraza, R. (1990) *Cultural Anxiety*. Zurich: Daimon Verlag.
McMillan, D. and Chavis, D. (1986) Sense of community: a definition and theory. *American Journal of Community Psychology*, 14, 6–23.
McNamee, S. and Gergen, K.J. (eds) (1992) *Therapy as Social Construction*. London: Sage.
Miller, J. (1993) *The Passion of Michel Foucault*. New York: HarperCollins.
Odajnyk, V.W. (1976) *Jung and Politics. The Political and Social Ideas of C.G. Jung*. New York: Harper & Row.
Papadopoulos, R.K. (1996) 'Therapeutic presence and witnessing'. *The Tavistock Gazette* (Autumn): 61–65.
Papadopoulos, R.K. (1997) 'Individual identity and collective narratives of conflict'. *Harvest: Journal for Jungian Studies*, 43(2): 7–26.
Papadopoulos, R.K. (1998a) 'Jungian perspectives in new contexts'. In Ann Casement (ed.) *The Post-Jungians Today*. London: Routledge.
Papadopoulos, R.K. (1998b) 'Destructiveness, atrocities and healing: epistemological and clinical reflections'. *The Journal of Analytical Psychology*, 43(4): 455–477.
Papadopoulos, R.K. (1999a) 'Working with families of Bosnian medical evacuees: therapeutic dilemmas'. *Clinical Child Psychology and Psychiatry*, 4(1): 107–120.
Papadopoulos, R.K. (1999b) 'Storied community as secure base'. *The British Journal of Psychotherapy*, 15(3): 322–332.
Papadopoulos, R.K. (in press) 'Narratives of translating – interpreting with refugees; the subjugation of individual discourses'. In R. Tribe and H. Raval (eds) *Working with Interpreters in Mental Health*. London: Routledge.
Papadopoulos, R.K. and Hildebrand, J. (1997) Is home where the heart is? Narratives of oppositional discourses in refugee families. In Renos K. Papadopoulos and John Byng-Hall (eds) *Multiple Voices; Narrative in Systemic Family Psychotherapy*. London: Duckworth.
Parker, I. (ed.) (1998) *Social Constructionism, Discourse and Realism*. London: Sage.
Pauw, J. (1997) *Into the Heart of Darkness. Confessions of Apartheid's Assassins*. Johannesburg: Jonathan Ball.
Samuels, A. (1993) *The Political Psyche*. London and New York: Routledge.
Sarason, S. (1994) *Psychoanalysis, General Custer, and the Verdicts of History, and Other Essays on Psychology in Social Sciences*. San Francisco: Jossey-Bass.
Seferis, G. (1982) *Collected Poems*. Translated, edited and introduced by Edmund Keeley and Philip Sherrard. London: Anvil Press.
Stanko, E. A. (ed.) (1994) *Perspectives on Violence*. London: Quartet Books.
Stevens, A. (1989) *The Roots of War. A Jungian Perspective*. New York: Paragon House.
Tacey, D. (1997) *Remaking Men. Jung, Spirituality and Social Change*. London: Routledge.
Wiesenfeld, E. (1996) 'The concept of "we": a community social psychology myth'. *Journal of Community Psychology*, 24(4): 337–345.
Wilmer, H.A. (1986) 'The healing nightmare: a study of the war dreams of Vietnam veterans'. *Quadrant*, Spring: 47–62.

Wilmer, H.A. (1996) 'The healing nightmare: war dreams of Vietnam veterans'. In Dierdre Barrett (ed.) *Trauma and Dreams*. Cambridge, MA: Harvard University Press.
Wilmer, H.A. (1999) *How Dreams Help*. Einsiedeln: Daimon.
Woodruff, P. and Wilmer, H.A. (eds) (1988) *Facing Evil: Light at the Core of Darkness*. La Salle, IL: Open Court.

Chapter 9

Reflections from the back side of a dollar

Myth and the origins of diversity

Eli B. Weisstub

The biblical myth of the Tower of Babel begins:

> "Throughout the earth men spoke the same language," with the same words. The people united to build a city and a tower with its top reaching to heaven, "to make a name" for themselves. God saw this unity, "one people with one language," had resulted in a drive for power and decided that man would stop at nothing to achieve his ends. He confused their language so that they could not understand one another. He scattered them over the face of the whole earth and they stopped building their city. It was named Babel because there God confused the language of the earth. Inflated power resulted in a disintegration of the original union. This led to the formation of diverse languages and nations.
>
> Quoted extracts from *The Jerusalem Bible* 1968: Genesis 11. 1–9

A Greek legend tells of a time that lasted for many ages, when men lived at peace without cities and without laws, speaking one language and ruled by Zeus alone. "At last Hermes introduced diversities of speech and divided mankind into separate nations. So discord arose among mortals, and Zeus offended at their quarrels, resigned the sovereignty and committed it to the hands of the Argive hero Phoroneus, the first king of men" (Hyginus, fable 143, cited in Gaster 1969, p. 136). Diversity led to discord and the relationship with the original unity and the supreme God governing this unity weakened. In the biblical myth, diversity occurs as a result of hubris, whereas in the Greek version it originates from a god, reflecting an archetypal need for change.

In our present time, ambition and technological advance have made possible rapid global communication. The world is "speaking one language." Humans have reached into the heavens with skyscrapers, satellites and space shuttles. The power that accompanies these achievements has given rise to a god-like hubris; the importance of a transpersonal God has correspondingly diminished. Concurrently, we are also witnessing difficulties in communication and cooperation. Former political unities have broken apart, and others are encountering inner disintegration due to problems of inequality, poverty, violence and a lack of meaning. Many are finding answers to the uncertainty in religious fundamentalism. This is especially

Figure 9.1 The Tower of Babel
Source: Pieter Bruegel. Reproduced with permission by Kunsthistorisches Museum, Vienna

true in Islamic countries, in the former USSR and, to a lesser extent, in the United States. The search for political and economic solutions is inextricably linked to a religious and spiritual quest.

HISTORICAL RELATION BETWEEN RELIGION AND THE POLITICAL

Armstrong (1993: 36–37) describes a period of transformation in the *Oikumene* (civilized world) occurring in the Axial Age, between 800–200 BCE, a time which culturally has certain parallels to the present age:

> There was a new prosperity that led to the rise of a merchant class. Power was shifting from king and priest, temple and palace, to the market place. The new wealth led to intellectual and cultural florescence and also to the development of the individual conscience. Inequality and exploitation became more apparent as the pace of change accelerated in the cities and people began to realize that their own behavior could affect the fate of future generations. Each region developed a distinctive ideology to address these problems and concerns:

> Taoism and Confucianism in China, Hinduism and Buddhism in India and philosophical rationalism in Europe. The Middle East did not produce a uniform solution, but in Iran and Israel Zoroaster and the Hebrew prophets respectively evolved different versions of monotheism. Strange as it may seem, the idea of "God," like the other great religious insights of the period, developed in a market economy in a spirit of aggressive capitalism.

Religious reform may also occur in response to political oppression. The need for spiritual and religious renewal often underlies social and political change. Historically, major religious movements have evolved out of difficult political circumstances. Although there is little information about the political context of the origins of Judaism (estimated to be between the twentieth and nineteenth centuries BCE) it is known that the birth of Jesus and hence of Christianity occurred during a period of political turmoil. Israel was then under the domination of the Romans, who had taken over power in 63 BCE. In 4 BCE Jews revolted in Jerusalem and in many other parts of the country. The rebels entreated the commander of the Roman troops "to depart and not stand in the way of men who after such a lapse of time were on the road to recovering their national independence" (Josephus 1961: War II, 75). After the insurrection was suppressed, the Romans inflicted harsh punishment on the insurgents: two thousand Jews were crucified around the walls of Jerusalem. The populace was asked to render homage to Caesar as a divine ruler. The situation was causing division among the Jews with the formation of religious factions and sects. According to Bishop James Pike, former Episcopal Bishop of California (Pike and Kennedy 1972) and others (Brandon 1967), the historical Jesus was part of a political revolutionary movement to deliver Israel from the oppression of Rome and to establish a Kingdom of God on Earth. Of the disciples, at least one (Simon) had been a revolutionary "zealot." When Jesus and his followers became overtly political, they not only sought to cleanse the Temple of materialism by overturning the tables and chairs of vendors and money changers, but they were actively striking against the Temple authorities and provoking insurrection against the more powerful Roman oppressors. The origin and creation of a world religion and the mythology associated with Jesus' Messianic mission were deeply rooted in an historical context, which was ripe for political revolt and religious transformation.

The search for unity was a motivating force in Islam:

> When Muhammad began to preach the Word in Mecca, the whole of Arabia was in a state of chronic disunity. Each of the numerous Bedouin tribes of the peninsula was a law unto itself and in a state of constant warfare with other tribal groups. It seemed impossible for the Arabs to unite and that meant that they were unable to found a civilization and polity that would allow them to take their place in the world.
>
> (Armstrong 1992: 46)

> Muhammad had been an Arab merchant, member of a formerly nomadic tribe which had become extremely successful in trade and made Mecca the most important center in Arabia. They had become very wealthy. Yet their drastically altered lifestyle meant that the old tribal values had been superseded by a rampant and ruthless capitalism. People felt obscurely disoriented and lost. Muhammad knew that the Quraysh [his tribe] were on a dangerous course and needed to find an ideology that would help them to adjust to their new conditions.
>
> (Armstrong 1993: 155)

Previously, the tribe had come first and the members depended on each other for their survival. They had a duty to take care of the poorer and weaker members. "Now individualism had replaced the communal ideal and competition had become the norm." There was fighting between the less successful clans and those who were wealthier. (Muhammad came from a less successful clan.) "Muhammad was convinced that unless the Quraysh learned to put another transcendent value at the center of their lives and overcome their egotism and greed, his tribe would tear itself apart morally and politically" (Armstrong 1993: 156). There was a need for spiritual renewal and unity. As with Jesus, Muhammad's religious solutions cannot be separated from the economic and political context of his time.

> Muhammad had political gifts of a very high order: he had entirely transformed the conditions of his people, rescued them from fruitless violence and disintegration and given them a proud new identity. They were now ready to found their own unique culture and Muhammad's teaching had unlocked such reserves of power that within 100 years, the Arabs' empire stretched from Gibraltar to the Himalayas. . . . His success depended on the religious vision that he communicated to the Arabs and which was adopted with alacrity by the subject people of the empire, clearly fulfilling a deep spiritual need.
>
> (Armstrong 1992: 46)

Power and wealth are not sufficient in providing for a deeper sense of security and well-being. Political change is inevitably tied to spiritual need.

The connection between the spiritual and the political was recognized in ancient Greece. Heraclitus' (late sixth to early fifth century BC) "logos" refers to something universal, eternal and divine, "common" or "shared" by all" which manifests itself in discourse. The logos provides the common bond between all men. "For Heraclitus there will be no conflict between self interest and the social conception of '*arete*' [human excellence, generally translated as 'virtue,'] since the deepest structure of the self will be recognized as co-extensive with the universe in general and the political community in particular" (Kahn 1979:14). Political philosophy from its earliest origins unites the social-political with the spiritual dimension. Heraclitus discovered in what is shared or "common to all" a universal connecting principle. This principle is at the origin of religious and political movements. It can be regarded as the unifying factor of the self extended to the collective.

THE INDIVIDUAL SELF AND SELF IN RELATION TO OTHERS

In Jungian theory the self is constituted by the God-image, the spiritual core of one's being. Buber's *I and Thou* (Buber 1958) complements Jung's inner psychological orientation. In Buber's philosophy, the inner core of one's being relates to the core of others in an "I–Thou" union which transcends the individual self, resulting in a collective unification. The individual self is part of an ever-expanding greater self, which encompasses all of humankind and the natural universe. Buber's conception is based on Heraclitus' "logos." All selves are united through the spiritual core of each individual self.

Within the field of depth psychology there is the beginning of a trend to move the focus from the individual and the intrapsychic to a greater concern with our relation to the external world, encompassing the social and political communities of which we are a part (Samuels 1993: Castoriadis 1994; Hillman 1994). This is not merely using the outer world as a backdrop for one's narcissistic self-preoccupation but implies the development of a self, which in recognizing its involvement in an inner community is capable of developing a real relationship to the world and a concern for the other. The goal of individuation is not only achieving an inner unity with what Jung has called the "One that dwells within" (Jung 1952); it is the realization of oneness through uniting with the many.

When the inner God connection becomes manifest in the "I–Thou" relationship between self and others, there is no interiority which does not take into consideration its exteriority. The *anima mundi*, the world soul, is not a metaphysical abstraction but a reality which can be experienced in the encounter with an other, be it in the human sphere or in relation to other parts of the natural world in which we live.

Jung tended to regard relationship primarily as serving the goal of individuation. When the outside world was considered, it was usually seen in terms of its significance for one's self. "Individuation does not shut one out from the world, but gathers the world to oneself" (Jung 1946: 432). In contrast to Jung, Buber emphasizes relationship:

> For the inmost growth of the self is not accomplished, as people like to suppose today, in man's relationship to himself, but in the relation between the one and the other, between man, that is, pre-eminently in the mutuality of the making present – in the making present of another self and in the knowledge that one is made present in his own self by the other – together with the mutuality of affirmation and confirmation.
>
> (Buber 1966: 71)

For Buber, relationship and community are central. The Center is that which manifests in a living mutual relationship. "The community is built up out of living mutual relation, but the builder is the living effective Center" (Buber 1958: 45):

> The communal life of men can no more than man himself dispense with the world of It, over which the presence of the Thou moves like the spirit upon the face of the waters. Man's will to profit and to be powerful have their natural and proper effect so long as they are linked with, and upheld by, his will to enter into relation. There is no evil impulse till the impulse has been separated from the being; the impulse which is bound up with, and defined by, the being is the living stuff of communal life, that which is detached is its disintegration. Economics, the abode of the will to profit, and State, the abode of the will to be powerful, share in life as long as they share in the spirit. If they abjure spirit they abjure life.
>
> (Ibid.: 48–49)

When Buber speaks of the individual's participation in communal life he is referring to the essence of spirit, a spiritual element in the service of relation. It is important to Buber that there be a freer political organization of the state and that economics should be more equitable, but he argues that for true and significant change to occur, it has to occur in a reality where communal life is imbued with the spirit which relates to the Thou (ibid.: 50).

Jung sees the future development in man as the "Christification of the Many," the incarnation of God in empirical man. He foresees potential clashes. "Such a transformation would lead to insufferable collisions between them, to say nothing of the unavoidable inflation to which the ordinary mortal, who is not freed from original sin would instantly succumb" (Jung 1952: par. 758). The realization of God incarnate in humans may be the next step in individual and collective evolution. Along with this development comes a god-like responsibility to our fellow man and to nature (Weisstub 1993). The danger of potential "collisions" could be lessened by centering on the "I–Thou" relation, which would preclude an inflated self-centeredness. "The spirit is truly in its own 'realm' if it can confront the world that is unlocked to it, give itself to this world, and in its relation with it save both itself and the world" (Buber 1958: 50–51). We cannot be part of the one without being related to the many. In the twentieth century, some 2500 years after Heraclitus, we are coming into the consciousness that "The world of the waking is one and shared" (Plutarch. *De Superstitione* 166 CE quoting Heraclitus) (Kahn 1979: 31).

THE REDEEMING FEMININE PRINCIPLE OF EROS

The world of human beings is constantly undergoing diversification and fragmentation. Fragmentation may be at the source of creation. This idea has been expressed in *Kabbalah* as the fragmentation of the world vessel. In modern scientific theory it appears as the "big bang" origin of the universe. *In Lurianic Kabbalah* (sixteenth-century *Kabbalist* Rabbi Isaac Luria), the main work in restoration (*Tikkun*) of the fragmented world is the bringing together of the isolated points

(*Nekudim*). The feminine principle is essential to the process of restoration. "The rebuilding of the *Nekudim* by God and man together is, in its profound sense, their common shared effort to unfold the constructive aspect of the merciful and compassionate feminine" (Jacobson 1993: 250). Human relationship and the togetherness aspect of community can be considered to be representative of the feminine principle. In the *Kabbalah*, the feminine aspect of God is referred to as the *Shekinah*. The created world and community [in *Kabbalah*, the community of Israel] are earthly manifestations of the lower spheres of the *Shekinah*. "The idea is that God has, in fact, a feminine receptive part of Him, a kind of consort as the Higher *Shekinah* or the Mother, who has an earthly representative in the lower spheres, Rachel, the Community of Israel, or the daughter and, just as the lower *Shekinah* fares in the material realms, so fares the Higher Feminine in transcendence. The whole reason for creation is that, through the efforts of the daughter in the world of substance, God should be reunited with His *Shekinah*" (Gottlieb 1994: 66).

The myth of a redeeming and redeemed feminine principle may be particularly relevant to the problems of fragmentation and disintegration. Through the feminine principle the many can be integrated into a cooperating world community. Individuation in the fullest sense is enacted socially in relation to the larger community as well as within our inner self. In the Judaic tradition the *Tsaddik* (Saint or good person) "is only capable of bringing redemption to Israel and to man because he contains an image of the fragmentary souls of all men" (Gottlieb 1994: 69).

Knowing that we contain within ourselves the many, linked through the common archetypal heritage of the collective unconscious, enables us to connect with the many in our external reality. Accepting and loving those aspects which we share and have in common with others unites us with other human beings.

This is a modern variation of the biblical "Love thy neighbor as thyself." "Eros is a *kosmogonos*, a creator and father-mother of all higher consciousness" (Jung 1965: 353).

EROS AND THE POLITICAL

Freud's pessimistic political views expressed in "The future of an illusion" (Freud 1927) and "Civilization and its discontents" (Freud 1930) were based on the conviction that civilization is a thin veneer overlying more powerful primitive and destructive instinctual forces. *Thanatos* inevitably predominates over *Eros*. In one of his last papers, "Analysis terminable and interminable" (Freud 1937), he points to several factors that could explain failure in analysis. The "bedrock" of the failure is the repudiation of the feminine, "which takes the form of penis envy in women and refusal of the passive or feminine attitude towards another male in men. He also mentions the aggressive-destructive drive and the death wish" (Castoriadis 1994: 10). Psychoanalytic theory does not sufficiently value *Eros* and the feminine principle. Feeling and relatedness are not emphasized in analytic practice.

"Repudiation of the feminine" may also contribute to failures and shortcomings in political systems.

Power and *logos* dominate in politics. When there is a sincere readiness for relatedness and the willingness to take the needs, feelings and concerns of the other seriously, resolution of conflicts becomes possible. This was evident when the Egyptian–Israeli, Jordanian–Israeli and the Oslo (Palestinian–Israeli) peace accords were signed. To enable this to happen, opposing sides have to sacrifice and give up the tendency to control and dominate. Peace, economic considerations and the concern for the welfare of one's children become more significant than national pride and conquest. If the feminine principle is to be truly incorporated and represented in the political, as well as on the personal level, a more balanced and mature political attitude can develop.

Acknowledging masculine and feminine principles as being equally important may constitute the coming spiritual and political myth. The present preoccupation with gender issues, especially in the United States, may be a more superficial expression of a deeper trend towards internalization and integration of feminine and masculine principles in all persons, regardless of gender orientation.

When we accept, as part of ourselves, those ethnic, gender, racial and religious characteristics which we considered alien or inferior, we can become more tolerant of others. Non-acceptance, fear, rejection and hatred of the other are often based on negative projections. If we withdraw these negative "shadow" projections and (in Jungian terms) "integrate the shadow," we are more capable of relating fairly to others. Integration of the shadow is necessary for mature social, political and ethical development (Neumann 1969).

Empathic relating and caring, usually associated with the feminine principle, are crucial elements in human relationships. In the political realm, sincerity and true feeling are often missing. Relatedness has still to gain acceptance and respect as a political mode of being and communication, and furthermore, as a uniting force among peoples and nations. Politically and legally instituted legislation are not adequate in solving issues of inequality and unfairness. The movement towards genuine relatedness, respect and valuing of diversity in the other requires a shift from a power and wealth politics to one where concern for human values becomes an equally important priority (Lasswell and Kaplan 1950: xxiv).

ACCEPTANCE AND TOLERANCE OF DIVERSITY

Healthy ego development and deep appreciation of the all-encompassing nature of the self enable tolerance of diverse and even opposing positions without the fear of disintegration. "It is only when man learns to experience himself as the creature of a creator who made light and darkness, good and evil, that he becomes aware of his own Self as a paradoxical totality in which the opposites are linked together" (Neumann 1969:147). A less integrated person is more prone to adopt mass/ collective solutions which provide unequivocal and simplistic answers. The consciously individuating person still represents a small and lonely minority in the midst of the largely undifferentiated collective.

THE ONE AND THE MANY SELVES

The self in depth psychology represents a unifying concept. Conceiving of the self, and by extension the collective self, as one, encourages a belief in absolutes. Extending the concept of the one to the political level raises certain difficulties. The unitary collective self is encountered in its most pure form, when there is a consensus of almost all members of a group, party or nation that they are represented by one person or one belief uniting all of them. This usually occurs where there is domination by one leader, one party or one religion. A total consensus by its nature may become totalitarian. In Jung's conception, at its core, the self is represented by a God-image. The God-image is rarely the same in a mass of individuals. If it becomes the same, there is the danger of a possession by one dominant archetypal image. One-sided "truths" spoken in the name of God or a God-principle are often evoked to give the political movement a needed sense of power and righteousness. In contrast, the democratic state is a reflection of many selves. It is constituted by as many critical egos as there are selves. The diversification which democracy provides is a safeguard against totalitarianism.

To avoid an over-emphasis on the one "self," the self of an individual may be represented by its component sub-selves. The idea of a many-faceted self may have its origin in William James (1890). He delineated a self which was composed of a material or body self, a social self, a spiritual self and what he termed "the pure Ego" (p. 292). The social self of an individual is constituted by "as many different social selves as there are distinct groups of persons about whose opinion he cares. He generally shows a different side of himself to each of these different groups" (p. 294). Lasswell (1950) took the concept of the social self further, introducing a more explicit interpersonal dimension. The self became the set of these "different sides" in their inter-relatedness (Lasswell and Kaplan 1950: 12).

The archetypal self expressed through a God-image gives the sense, sometimes illusory, of absolute truth. Reliance on the one, the central image of the self tends to favor elitist rule. At the extreme, a central God-image may be evoked in a nation and utilized by a dictator. Such was the case in Nazi Germany when the nature god Wotan, god of wind and storm, became the inspiring archetypal force (Jung 1939). "The democratization of the omnipotent divine self" (Redfearn 1993) within the individual psyche is no less formidable a task than humanizing and democratizing the archetypal in the political realm. There is a strong tendency to submit and be governed by a dominant God-image, versus relating to the diverse sub-selves which represent various facets of the personality and, collectively, diverse facets of society. By extension, if we relate to the various "sub-selves" of society we would have to accept many "Gods" (albeit referring to the same "God"), represented by a multiplicity of god-images.

The reliance on the one rather than on the many tends towards dictatorial rule rather than democracy. While this may guard against disintegration, the price is repression of democratic and pluralistic free expression. In his work *A Pluralistic Universe*, James (1909) considers the one and the many to be complementary perspectives. Samuels (1989) takes the pluralistic position a step further. "The paradox is that pluralism becomes the absolute! And the only unity to be found will be in diversity" (p. 8).

DIVERSITY AND THE RETURN TO ABSOLUTISM

The drive to diversity may arise as a response to an oppressive authority or authoritarian regime. This has been true of the republics which have established independence after years of an imposed "union" in the former USSR. The creation of diverse nations may signify freedom, but diversity does not necessarily result in tolerance. Diversity is not solely an outcome of oppression, but may stem from a belief in one's special identity and superior way. Some of the diverse developments are characterized by a return to old forms of absolutism. The "new" true believers soon become the oppressors in their own right. In Iran, the fundamentalists who were oppressed under a previous political regime are intolerant of pluralism and the beliefs of others. Radical Muslims deeply believe in the moral and spiritual superiority and "rightness" of fundamentalist Islam. Their striving for diversity takes the form of revolutionary movements, whose goal it is to establish a new and strengthened identity through a return to religious and nationalistic roots. Although the turning to radical Islam is in part a reaction to feeling humiliated and degraded by the power of the West, and feeling "disoriented and lost because their own traditions seem to be swamped by the dominant Western culture" (Armstrong 1992: 264), there is also an inflated aggressive aspect. They are committed to the military struggle of *jihad* or "holy war," in the absolute conviction that Muslims are fighting for the only "true" way in which God intended man to live.

THE UNIVERSALITY OF DIVERSITY AND CONFLICT

Diversity serves the function of differentiating the totality. Aristotle (Eudemian Ethics vii.1) quotes Heraclitus as saying: "Homer was wrong when he said, 'Would that Conflict might vanish from among gods and men!' (Iliad xviii.107). For there would be no attunement without high and low notes nor any animals without male and female, both of which are opposites" (Kahn 1979: 67).

Another saying taken from Aristotle (Nicomachean Ethic viii, 1) is also attributed to Heraclitus: "The counter-thrust brings together, and from tones at variance comes perfect attunement, and all things come to pass through conflict." One of Heraclitus' more provocative sayings is: "War is father of all and king of all" (Kahn 1979:

LXXXIII, 67). Heraclitus not only refers to war as a father of gods and men, like Zeus, but "of all things that come to pass," implying a universal principle of opposition that goes beyond the personification of a god.

Conflict is associated with the masculine principle. Jung referred to the ego's function of consciousness as representing the masculine principle. In the individual psyche, the ego can be regarded as that which differentiates and recognizes the reality of opposing elements. On the collective political level, the need to develop separate identities, national and otherwise, makes dealing with opposing forces inevitable. A conscious collective ego is necessary to deal with these conflicts, an ego which can contain the movement towards diversity without it resulting in disintegration. Ongoing conflict and opposition are integral to a vital political process.

POLITICAL CHANGE AND FEAR OF THE FEMININE

Diversity of belief and opinion threaten those who believe in an absolute truth, whether it be religious, political or theoretical. Those who politically represent the old order, king or god are threatened by change. They tend to be orthodox in their beliefs, precluding open, creative dialogue. They are unable to listen and be receptive to the opinions of others. At the core of their reactionary position may be a fear of the "feminine." The feminine has often been associated with evil and the sinister.

In biblical legend Lilith was the first woman. She was rejected because of her unwillingness to adopt the "inferior" position, to be beneath Adam in the sexual act. She is the seductive, instinctual and dark feminine who does not submit. In the *Zohar*, the main *Kabbalistic* text, she is identified with unchastity, the mother of the diverse, the "mixed multitude" (*Zohar* 1949: I 27b). The "second" woman, Eve, was guilty of encouraging Adam to disobey God and to eat of the fruit of the Tree of Knowledge. The independent quest for knowledge, which gives rise to diversity, can be interpreted as a revolt against the original one; parental, national or divine authority. The primary state of unity, the at-oneness with the authority is maintained through unconsciousness. Coming into consciousness, becoming separate and independent is a threat to the authority and to the original unity.

Recognition of the opposites, the evil as well as the good brings into consciousness the limitations of the prevailing order and of the creators of that order. God punishes Adam and Eve for coming into the forbidden knowledge of the reality of opposites (good and evil) and, thus, the knowledge that all is not perfect and good in the creation. In a patriarchal culture, change and the development of diversity are often attributed to the negative feminine or some symbolic representation of it. This is manifest in hostile reactions to peace and civil rights movements, as was the case in the anti-war movement in the United States and against the "Peace Now" movement in Israel. Peace activists are often regarded by the Right as weak, unpatriotic and unmasculine.

TOWARDS THE EVOLUTION OF A NEW MYTH

The modern "myth" of capitalism and the free market economy is almost universally accepted. It is considered positive and relevant for most peoples of the world at this time. The limitations of the system are increasingly evident, especially in those areas where capitalism has "worked." There are many who are not successfully competing, with the resultant problems associated with poverty and the humiliation of failure. Among the successful, many experience a lack of meaning which is not answered by the political and economic myth nor by conventional religion.

For some individuals, depth psychology provides an answer but its influence in the social and political realm has been limited. It has tended to encourage a withdrawal from the world, rather than an active involvement with it. Samuels (1993) has proposed an integration of depth psychology and the political. He has utilized the myth of Hermes or the trickster as relevant to the political. Although the myth of Hermes emphasizes competition, diversity and change, it does not adequately represent a related and caring aspect, which is vital to a mature and differentiated political process (Weisstub 1994). A myth relevant to our time would have to incorporate *Eros* and the feminine principle as an equal partner in the social and political process.

INTEGRATION OF THE OPPOSITES

In the liberal and democratic tradition of the United States, diversity is tolerated if it can ultimately be assimilated into a homogenized American identity, "the melting-pot" phenomenon. In many ways this "worked" with immigrants of European origin. It has been more problematic with Americans of African, Hispanic and Asian backgrounds. There is still a strong tendency not to accept and be tolerant of diverse identities; racial, ethnic and gender.

Intolerance of differences which are based on religious belief makes peace difficult to achieve in the Palestinian–Israeli conflict. Irreconcilable positions are taken when Israeli Jewish settlers regard the West Bank as their legitimate biblical heritage and the Palestinian Islamic extremists (*Hamas*) see the existence of a Jewish nation in the predominantly Islamic Middle East as cause for a Holy War. In Russia and the former Yugoslavia the Islamic breakaway states, Chechnya and Bosnia, were attacked for wanting to establish their own separate national entities. On the other hand, diversity, when carried to the extreme, can cause disintegration of an existing unity. This is evident in Canada, where unity based on an ethnic mosaic is threatened by the Quebec separatist movement.

Opposing principles are at work on the global political scene. There is a drive towards global unity which emphasizes peace, economic cooperation and ecological concern. Distinct from this movement and often opposing it is the drive to establish national entities based on religious beliefs and ethnic origin. Their striving for recognition and a separate identity often results in armed conflict and destruction of the established order.

Conflict, although not necessarily war, may be essential in the establishment of a separate identity. In the Palestinian–Israeli conflict, previous enemies are attempting to unite efforts in achieving peace and economic cooperation, while respecting rights to autonomy and nationhood. Those who are moving towards peace are opposed by religious fundamentalists and political extremists who cannot tolerate diversity and are ready to wage war, engage in terrorism and die for their beliefs. The task of accepting the need for separate identities, and enduring differences and conflict while striving for peaceful cooperation, is very trying. The conflict of opposites which exists both externally (between Palestinians and Israelis) and internally (between moderate and extremist elements) threatens to undermine the overall peace process. The principles of opposition and cooperation coexist in a relative peace marked by the tension of opposites. The situation requires a dual political attitude; a collective ego which can consciously contain the diversity of differing or conflicting positions and a collective self which serves to unify opposing parts.

The following fragment taken from Heraclitus summarizes the dynamics of political process and illuminates some of its archetypal essence: "Graspings [*holding together, bringing things together or comprehending*]: wholes and not wholes, convergent divergent, consonant dissonant, from all things one and from one thing all" (Kahn 1979: CXXIV).

Kahn's (1979) paraphrase helps clarify Heraclitus' thought on the paradoxical nature of social and political structure and process as follows:

> Graspings, that is to say groups holding together, apprehensions bringing things together: these are wholes and not wholes; they characterize a system which is convergent, divergent, structured by cooperation and by conflict; this system is consonant, dissonant, held together by harmony and discord alike; from all its components a unity emerges, and from this unity all things emerge.
>
> (Ibid.: 286)

> The notion of the plural "wholes" indicates a subordinate diversity of parts and thus a greater richness of structure, a more organic unity, than the contrast of one and many alone. We might say that the notion of "whole" expresses the concept of unity as dynamic rather than static: each unit is built up out of an internal plurality.
>
> (p. 283)

These conceptual antitheses help in understanding the paradoxical nature of the whole and not whole political units of which we are a part. This gives us a perspective on how political bodies ranging from the smallest groupings to the larger global political unity are interconnected.

"Convergent, divergent" is "the movement of plurality together in the direction of unity, balanced by the movement apart to diversity. The spatial imagery may be taken as a figure for the dynamic tension between totality and partiality, unity and diversity that runs through all cases of opposition." . . . What is depicted is "an actual process of alternating motion towards unity and diversity" (Kahn 1979: 285).

"Consonant, dissonant," literally "singing together" and "singing apart," suggests being in harmony or in discord. "From all things one and from one thing all"; the theme of unity and plurality. The plurality does not simply refer to the many, but is total and all-inclusive; "all things." It is not the numerical contrast between the one and the many that is the focus of concern, but the "world-constituting antithesis between unity and totality: the one and the all" (ibid.).

The reality of diversity and opposition is as central as that of unity. When the centrality of opposition is accepted, one grasps that while unity serves to hold diversity together, diversity is essential to the vitality and creative development of any political system.

THINKING WITH THE HEART

In contrast to the predominating drive towards acquisition and competition, which characterizes the present world situation, I will refer to a dialogue which took place in the 1920s between Jung and Ochwiay Biano (Mountain Lake), the chief of the Taos pueblo. The chief was speaking of the white man:

> "they are always seeking something. What are they seeking? The whites always want something; they are always uneasy and restless. We do not know what they want. We do not understand them. We think they are mad." I [Jung] asked him why he thought the whites were all mad. "They say that they think with their heads," he replied. "Why of course. What do you think with?" I asked him in surprise. "We think here," he said, indicating his heart.
>
> (Jung 1965:248)

Whereupon Jung went into a deep meditation, contemplating the conquering Roman legions, the violent transmission of the Christian creed to the Britons, the forced conversion of the heathens, the murdering Crusaders, the Conquistadors, the illnesses that accompanied colonization and the spread of civilization. Jung envisioned the other face of the white man's progress as "the face of a bird of prey seeking with cruel intentness for distant quarry – a face worthy of pirates and highwaymen. All the eagles and other predatory creatures that adorn our coat of arms seem to me apt psychological representations of our true nature" (ibid.: 248–249).

THE BACK SIDE OF THE DOLLAR

The eagle serves as a symbol of the United States. As well as being a higher power which can swiftly dominate and destroy those below, the eagle symbolizes height, lofty ideals and the spiritual principle. The eagle appears on the American dollar, carrying in its beak a message of unity, "*E Pluribus Unum*" (Out of the Many, One).

In its claws it holds the opposites: the olive branch in one, a sheath of arrows in the other.[1] The dollar has become a universal currency of exchange and the common reference point of the world's free market economy. Unnoticed, on the back side of the dollar bill are the symbols of a spiritual vision which goes beyond the mundane political and economic reality. Thus, on the right side, the eagle holds both a message of social and political unity and the symbols of diversity, the opposites of peace and war. These stand in contrast to the more mystical symbolism on the left side of the bill. Here the pyramid symbolizing strength and endurance is watched over by the Eye of Divine Providence. Above is inscribed: *Annuit Coeptis*: "He has approved of what has begun." Below the pyramid, *Novus Ordo Seclorum*: "The New Era." The two sides are linked by a boldly inscribed ONE. Above the ONE is "In God We Trust." Faith, religious belief, unity, the opposites are all unified in the theme of the one, which symbolically underlies the economic reality of the dollar. Were we to include the missing element, *Eros* – "thinking with the heart" – a new democratic unity could be created, where relatedness in diversity is equally valued.

Being there for one's self, being there for others and the importance of actualizing oneself, is formulated in one of the sayings of Rabbi Hillel the Elder (first century BCE to first century CE):

> If I am not for myself, who will be for me?
> And when I am (only) for myself, what am I?
> And if not now, when?
> [From Pirkei Avot, The Sayings of the Fathers II, 4]
>
> (Toperoff 1997: 57)

NOTE

1 Senator Bradley pointed out to me in a personal communication that President Harry Truman ordered the mint to change the image of the eagle on the back side of the dollar bill so that the head of the eagle now turns toward the olive branch rather than toward the sheath of arrows as it had prior to Truman's administration. In my mind, this reflects a conscious shift in attitude from a power orientation to an *Eros* orientation.

BIBLIOGRAPHY

Armstrong, K. (1992) *Muhammad*, London: Victor Gollancz Ltd.

—— (1993) *A History of God*, London: Heinemann.

Brandon, S.G.F. (1967) *Jesus and the Zealots*, New York: Charles Scribner's Sons.

Buber, M. (1958) *I and Thou*, New York: Charles Scribner's Sons.

—— (1966) *The Knowledge of Man*, New York: Harper & Row.

Castoriadis, C. (1994) "Psychoanalysis and politics" in S. Shamdasani and M. Munchow (eds) *Speculations after Freud*, London and New York: Routledge.

Freud, S. (1927) "The future of an illusion" in *The Standard Edition of the Complete Psychological Works of Sigmund Freud* (hereafter *SE*), ed. James Strachey, London: Hogarth Press, 1953–1974, 21.
—— (1930) "Civilization and its discontents" in *SE*, 21.
—— (1937) "Analysis terminable and interminable" in *SE*, 23.
Gaster, T.H. (1969) *Myth, Legend and Custom in the Old Testament*, New York and Evanston: Harper & Row.
Gottlieb, F. (1994) "The Kabbala, Jung and the feminine image" in J. Ryce-Menuhin (ed.) *Jung and the Monotheisms*, London and New York: Routledge.
Hillman, J. (1994) "'Man is by nature a political animal' or patient as citizen" in S. Shamdasani and M. Munchow (eds) *Speculations after Freud*, London and New York: Routledge.
Jacobson, Y. (1993) "The aspect of the feminine in Lurianic Kabbalah" in P. Schafer and J. Dan (eds) Gershom Scholem's *"Major Trends in Jewish Mysticism" 50 Years After*, Tublingen: J.C.B. Mohr (Paul Siebeck).
James, W. (1890) *The Principles of Psychology*, New York: Henry Holt.
—— (1909) *A Pluralistic Universe*, London: Longmans, Green; Cambridge, MA: Harvard University Press (1977).
The Jerusalem Bible (1968) General Editor, Jones Alexander. Garden City, NY: Doubleday.
Josephus (1961) *The Jewish War*, Cambridge: Harvard University Press, The Loeb Classical Library Edition.
Jung, C.G. (1939) "Diagnosing the dictators" in W. McGuire and R.F.C. Hull (eds) *C.G. Jung Speaking*, Princeton: Princeton University Press (1977).
—— (1946) "On the nature of the psyche" in *C.G. Jung Collected Works*, Vol. 8, Princeton: Princeton University Press (2nd edn).
—— (1952) "Answer to Job" in *C.G. Jung Collected Works*, Vol. 11.
—— (1965) *Memories, Dreams, Reflections*, New York: Vintage Books.
Kahn, C.H. (1979) *The Art and Thought of Heraclitus*, Cambridge: Cambridge University Press.
Lasswell, H.D. and Kaplan, A. (1950) *Power and Society*, New Haven and London: Yale University Press.
Neumann, E. (1969) *Depth Psychology and a New Ethic*, New York: Harper & Row.
Pike, D.K. and Kennedy, R.S. (eds) (1972) *The Wilderness Revolt*, New York: Doubleday.
Redfearn, J. (1993) *The Exploding Self*, London and New York: Routledge.
Samuels, A. (1989) *The Plural Psyche*, London and New York: Routledge.
—— (1993) *The Political Psyche*, London and New York: Routledge.
Toperoff, S.P. (1997) *Avot*, Northvale, NJ, and Jerusalem: Jason Aronson.
Weisstub, E.B. (1993) "Questions to Jung on answer to Job," *Journal of Analytical Psychology* 38(4): 397–418.
—— (1994) Journal Review of A. Samuels' "The mirror and the hammer:
depth psychology and political transformation", *Journal of Analytical Psychology* 39(3): 406–409.
The *Zohar* (1949) Trans. Harry Sperling and Maurice Simon, London: Soncino Press.

Chapter 10

The cultural complex and the myth of invisibility

Samuel L. Kimbles

> A dark invisible craftsmanship that reconciles discordant elements and makes them move in one society.
>
> William Wordsworth

INTRODUCTION

The major conflicts in the world today are essentially conflicts around ethnic, racial, class, religious, and gender differences. These conflicts are manifested in a variety of economic, social, and political situations. They occur within culturally homogeneous groups, for example, in Bosnia among the Serbs and Croats; in Rwanda through the conflict between Hutus and Tutsis. They reflect long-standing class differences and struggles in Latin and Central America, for instance, Peru and Guatemala; religious and ethnic differences in the Middle East (Israelis and Palestinians), or between Irish Catholics and Irish Protestants in Northern Ireland. Race is the polarizing issue in South Africa and the United States.

Whatever the cause of religious, social, racial, and ethnic conflicts, they are often bloody and violent, tending toward genocidal rage. They involve rigidly polarized "us/them" categories and are governed by stereotypes which harden mutual negative projections. Victimization and revenge dynamics operate in a kind of lock step tandem, and many of the consequences of these psychosocial traumas stretch over many generations. Often, the theologies of righteousness turn some of these struggles and conflicts into Holy Wars (for example, Islam in the Middle East). As members of collective bodies, humans have yet to learn how to deal less destructively with the implications of these powerful intragroup shadow processes.

As I think about cultural dynamics, I am struck by the apparent intractability over time of these ethnic/racial/class/religious conflicts even though many political and social solutions have been tried through the generations. As a psychologist and Jungian analyst I am equally surprised at the dearth of psychological approaches to these problems in the literature. In this chapter, however, I will focus on race as a way to introduce the concept of cultural complex. The concept itself applies equally to religious, ethnic, gender, and social identities. My approach to social and collective issues grows out of my experience as an African American man and my clinical work as a psychologist and analyst. The chapter reflects my attempt to think from an analytical point of view about these horrendous transgenerational conflicts.

THE SOCIAL ATTITUDE TO THE CULTURAL COMPLEX

A number of years ago while still in my analytical training, I had the following dream:

> I had been called to be a consultant in a large prison system whose population was composed of a majority of young black men. I met with three other black psychologists: one was the first president of the American Association of Black Psychologists. Another was a psychology professor who taught humanistic and existential psychology at a local university, and the third was a psychologist who was unknown to me but whose personality was composed of a combination of my father and the Supreme Court Justice Clarence Thomas. Apparently the three of them, as consultants, had been unsuccessful in identifying and working with the factors that produce the large black prison population. Something was missing for them.

I had been called in to consult to them because of my Jungian orientation. By way of shaping my initial reflections on the above dream, I can say that the three psychologists already on the case operated from a "social attitude" that takes into account the adverse effects of racism as a significant factor in the histories of the prison population. According to Henderson (1984: 17):

> The social attitude is concerned with maintaining the ethical code of the culture, whether of the established culture or any specific counterculture deviation from it. I have often found this attitude provides a particular resistance to analysis, since the patient may assume that if the social problems of our time were solved, all conflict would vanish and psychotherapy would be unnecessary.

The stories that flow from this social perspective would include pointing out the huge disparity in the percentage of blacks versus other groups in the prison system and that the number of young black men between the ages of 18 and 30 in the criminal justice system is equal to or exceeds the number of black men in college. The collective expressions of racism in employment, housing discrimination and education are considered as basic contributors to this disparity by those with a social attitude.

Personal difficulties that this prison population have had in combating collective racial factors through internalization of racist attitudes toward themselves would be noted along with institutional obstacles expressed through discrimination. Taking into account these factors, those responding to racism with a social attitude advocate the following solutions: job training, education, better housing, broader economic opportunities, and racial pride. Although I am well aware that these intractable social problems tend to swallow up all well-intentioned approaches, I took this dream to mean among other things that analytical psychology might have something to offer not only to clinical populations but to the world at large. My dream seems to suggest that something else needs to be considered in understanding these problems. I harbor no illusion that I had a magical insight which would "cure" the problem. But for a long time I have wondered if I might bring a fresh understanding to the situation.

Over the years, I have frequently noticed in clinical situations that when deep feelings about ethnicity, race, and gender are touched they often change how the patient and I experience each other. We both seem caught in something sticky, emotional, organized within a pattern of in group/out group (or us/them) feelings. These feelings connect each of us through an intergenerational, social narrative to our different reference groups. This can precipitate projection, blame, and misunderstanding that must be analyzed. Reflecting on my clinical experience in the light of my dream I began to wonder if there were not group-based collective dynamics that organize themselves in the unconscious of the group member. Could these be group complexes that function beyond individual dynamics?

CULTURAL COMPLEXES

In Jungian psychology we use the theory of complexes to describe patterns of interlocking associations grouped around emotionally toned themes and ideas. Complexes express themselves in powerful moods and repetitive behaviors. Complexes are basic, naturally occurring elements in human beings that structure the individual responses to biological givens such as the body, aging, death, and to interpersonal relations within family, tribal and broader communal systems. We tend to be unconscious of our complexes until suffering makes us aware of their existence and organizing power in our daily life. This is the consciousness which psychotherapy fosters. Without psychological work complexes function compulsively and autonomously through our reactions to others and to the world, i.e., through projections. Caught in such automatic modes of acting and reacting, we feel moved or carried by the force of a powerful energy over which we have little control. Psychologically, this can lead to an inflated sense of one's own righteousness or a deflated sense of one's own inferiority in relation to others.

Complexes also operate through the group's expectations, its definition of itself, its destiny, and sense of its uniqueness. We can find complexes operating in and through the group's fears, enemies and its attitudes toward other groups. In our group life as in our individual life, at first we tend to be in identification with our complexes, i.e., we take our group's attitudes, feelings, and points of view as absolutely true. As a result, we respond to other groups in a compulsive way through our projections. Although in analytical psychology we think of complexes all the time when considering individual dynamics, we have not yet learned to adapt the concept to the group level of functioning.

Cultural complexes may be thought of as expressions of a dynamic system of relations that serve the basic individual need for belonging and identity through linking personal experiences and group expectations as these are mediated by race, ethnicity, religion, and gender processes. Jung's idea of the psyche as a spectrum is applicable here: "psychic process . . . behaves like a scale along which consciousness slides" (Jung 1947, par. 408). Hence, consciousness may manifest itself or be pulled in the direction of identification with the most collective cultural expressions of behavior, i.e., black Muslim, Hasidic Jew, to the most individual expressions, i.e., Buddhist black man, pagan Jew.

Cultural complexes impose constraints on the perception of differences or accentuate them; emphasize identification with the group or differentiation from the group; and allow for feelings of belonging to or being alienated from the group. Cultural and individual factors function in a quasi-psychological manner that organizes group and individual thinking, behavior, and feelings, particularly in terms of us/them dynamics.

Cultural complexes allow us to relate psychologically to cultural factors that operate beyond the individual but intersect with the individual's sense of self. From the point of view of a cultural complex, religious, ethnic, racial, and gender expressions do not pertain only to politics, sociology, anthropology, or mythology. Rather, I should say, they belong to all of the above and archetypally, to the psyche's mode of narrating its relationship to the group. Cultural complexes are truly part of the collective psyche and can surface in the individual or in the group.

In trying to understand the "prison dream" I mentioned above, I thought about the black slave quarters in an earlier America. Such quarters were prisons to be sure, but they were also a sequestering of people from very different African tribes into a foreign land that destroyed the possibility of individual cultural continuity. Somehow, as a response to this imprisonment and fragmentation, pieces of different cultures and tribes – including European and Native American groups – had to be constructed into viable cultural forms by the black slaves. They needed to create religions and rituals to help them recognize and deal with the dehumanizing effects of racism. The creation of a cultural complex – not by willful construction – but by the slow accretion of events, feelings, memories, and traumas into an unconscious collective structure allowed for survival by fostering identity and a sense of belonging to and with the racial group. In my prison dream, for instance, my psyche utilized the prison image to point to an identity between the most denigrated, neglected group, and the educated helpers and mentors. Imprisoned young black males are joined with older black male psychologists. My racial identity is there too, but I bring something different from outside the cultural racial frame – an archetypal analytical attitude. From this attitude I ask, "Is this situation a cry for an initiatory attitude toward a social problem? If so, what would that look like? Also what part of my psyche is in prison and in need of an analytical attitude?" Concretely identified as a black person and crucified by the collective assumptions of racism, a part of me must indeed feel stuck.

By asking such questions I am putting forth a hypothesis that the psyche operates autonomously at both the individual and collective levels to generate group level processes that are not reducible to individual dynamics. Yet I have found this idea to be a difficult one to grasp even among psychologists.

ANTI-POLITICAL BIASES IN TRADITIONAL PSYCHOLOGICAL THINKING

The difficulty in grasping the idea of the cultural complex has been hampered chiefly, I feel, by three biases that operate in the collective life and in our psychological thinking:

1 opposition between inner and outer
2 opposition between psyche and the political
3 a tendency to understand the "outer" collective in terms of individual (psycho)dynamics.

As regards the first opposition, we have consistently chosen to put the psyche "inside" and have relegated outer to politics, sociology, economics, and anthropology. The psyche is then known personalistically by what we want, need, desire, think, etc. To quote Jung (1964: 660):

> A rapprochement between the two standpoints is nowhere in sight, unless we can acknowledge the peculiar nature of the self, which embraces the individual as well as society . . . the archetypes . . . can sometimes manifest themselves . . . such . . . that they seem to belong as much to society as to the individual.

Andrew Samuels (1993), in his book *The Political Psyche*, speaks to the second opposition when he states:

> Involvement in the mess and confusion of the external world and passionate political commitment to that world are as psychologically valuable as an interior perspective or an intimate I–Thou relationship. Political involvement can certainly be a means of avoiding personal conflicts or acting out such conflicts, leaving others to do the changing. But political involvement can also surely be a means of expressing what is best in humans, acknowledging the fact of our social being, that we are not the isolated solipsistic monads that some psychological theories might lead us to believe we are.

In considering the third opposition that biases us to see the outer collective in terms of individual psychodynamics, I refer back to Jung's idea that the psyche is primarily collective (common, shared) and social. Our individual psyches emerge out of the deeper levels of the unconscious and are derived from the collective, communal, and social experiences of humankind. These collective experiences provide at least part of the containers and forms of our individual psychological experiences. They extend backwards into archaic history and forwards into the unknown. None of us are free to step completely outside this river of collective experience. The foundation for, and the context of, our individual identity is grounded in the symbols, rituals, language, and shared historical memories of our families, countries, and nations. At a deep psychological level it is not easy to draw a distinction between individual and cultural dynamics. It is a common conception that history and individual identity may be understood as social constructions, but even our most intimate self-relations (our subjectivity) has everything to do with the kinds of choices and freedoms we have in our society.

Erikson (1980: 22) was the first to locate identity in "the core of the individual and also in the core of his/her communal culture – a process that establishes at bottom the identity of these two identities." In archetypal language, the individual and group poles of identity are different manifestations of one underlying process. At the level of this underlying process of collective and individual, a psychological attitude allows us to ask what the psyche is doing with the fact of differences and similarities, both individually and culturally. Such a psychological attitude implies that each individual has to be approached polyvalently; that is, with an understanding that group and individual processes simultaneously make their contribution to subjective experience.

An example of a psychological attitude toward cultural dynamics can be seen in Jung's 1936 essay "Wotan." Impressed by the spirit of National Socialism in Germany, Jung was concerned about the power of collective forces to swallow up individuals by making them vulnerable to mass possessions. He described the reappearance of an archaic northern European mythological figure, Wotan, who was taking over German consciousness during the development of Hitler's Germany. Nazism was a cultural complex that expressed itself through a specific kind of relationship between the individual and the group. It was largely mediated by a belief in an Aryan ideal, but it was structured symbolically by an archetypal figure – Wotan.

The calamitous events of the Holocaust have become part of the West's collective spiritual history. The Jewish community in particular has had to incorporate this historical nightmare as part of remaking its own identity within the wider community. It has had to continuously come to grips with its role as collective victim and the horrific trauma inflicted on the Jewish people. Since remembering is a way of healing, the very processes that Jung spoke to in "Wotan" that can obliterate individual and group identity must be related to in order to heal wounds suffered at both the individual and group level. That is, traumatic events and suffering must be reconciled with hopefulness, or belief in a loving God or a sane universe if life is to go on. From the point of view of analysis, the soul is healed "by insisting that it experience its afflictions within the discrete proportions of the images in which those afflictions reside" (Mogenson 1989). Collective memory, the good, the bad, and the traumas must be worked with in order to sustain and give grounding to culture and individual identity. Such a process solidifies shared historical experiences that are basic to forming group identity and belonging. We see presently that black Americans' complicated history of slavery, racism, and discrimination must be remembered and reconstructed if blacks are to participate fully in the process of identity making which is so characteristically American.

INVISIBILITY AS A CULTURAL COMPLEX

Ralph Ellison (1956) in his book *The Invisible Man* speaks through his narrator to the problem of social invisibility generated by racism. One night the narrator recalls that he bumped into a blond man who proceeded to insult him.

> I sprang at him, seized his coat lapels and demanded that he apologize. He was a tall blond man, and as my face came close to his he looked insolently out of his blue eyes and cursed me. . . . I pulled his chin down sharp upon the crown of my head, butting him . . . I felt his flesh tear and the blood gush out, and I yelled, "Apologize! Apologize!" I kicked him repeatedly . . . and in my outrage I got out my knife and prepared to slit his throat, right there beneath the lamplight . . . when it occurred to me that the man had not seen me, actually; that he, as far as he knew was in the midst of a walking nightmare! And I stopped the blade, slicing the air as I pushed him away.
>
> (p. 8)

In this passage Ellison is addressing the feeling that whites neither see blacks nor do they differentiate between them. He realized he was invisible to the white man. "The next day I saw his picture in the Daily News, beneath a caption stating that he had been mugged. Poor fool, poor blind fool, I thought with sincere compassion, mugged by an invisible man!" Psychologically, Ellison is describing an invisibility that can occur at the intersection of individuality with cultural consciousness. This is the awesome power of the cultural complex operating in such a way as to obscure and swallow up individuality.

To know another is to have an empathetic sense of them, a grasp of their lived situation. Stereotypes and racism have had profoundly deleterious effects in the deformation of the self-esteem and spirit of black people. Prejudice, however, has also unleashed from its victims a compensatory effort to redeem, define, and construct a collective and individual identity that can deal effectively with the destructive forces of racism. Legitimizing their social identity has become part of the collective work of American blacks. This contemporary construction of social identity should be viewed against the backdrop so vividly painted by Ellison. Ellison eloquently painted the picture of group-level process with his depiction of a modern myth of the invisibility of citizens of color. His depiction of this myth of invisibility describes precisely how a group level process annihilates identity. The novel is a compelling example of how destructive the cultural complex can be.

The cultural complex does not just wreak havoc between different groups by invalidating the humanity of people. Intra-group dynamics, fueled by the cultural complex, can generate invisibility-making processes within the group as well, creating a powerful way of shunning a member who has deviated too far from group norms. Shelby Steele (1998) in his book *A Dream Deferred* speaks about his own being shunned as he took the stance of a neo-conservative within the black community. Shelby, a self-labeled black conservative, has challenged the victim-focused racial identity that he feels has defined many of the social programs designed to help blacks. He states:

> The problem for the black conservative is more his separation from the authority of his racial group than from the actual group. He stands outside a group authority so sharply defined and monolithic. . . . This authority is very often based on a strategic explanation of a group's fate, a narrative that explains why the group is in a given situation and therefore why it is justified in pursuing a certain kind of power. This explanation is all-important because it establishes the group as a collective being with a history, a present, and a future – a life, as it were, that entitles it to all the considerations of sovereignty.
>
> (p. 6)

At the collective level, the group demands loyalty in ideology and behavior as a condition to be recognized by the group. Invisibility making through shaming and exorcism is a powerful dynamic that keeps group members loyal; it acts as an inhibition against the individual developing a consciousness separate from the group.

As confused and conflicted as his motives may have been, black Muslim leader Louis Farrakhan in his Million Man March was attempting to awaken blacks to their own power through confronting the "invisibility making" processes within the black community. Overtly, "The Men" had gone to a revival meeting in Washington to renew black pride through a day of atonement and reconciliation. The march reminded me of another dream which I had on the night before my interview for admission to an analytical training community.

> In the dream I am sitting in a mosque with other black Muslim men. Someone comes to let me know that it is time for my interview with the training committee. As I get up to leave, the door is barred by several black Muslim men who will not let me pass until I demonstrate to them that I remember the secret handshake. This handshake will demonstrate that I remember their mission and maintain a continued connection to them.

Originally, the black Muslim organization attracted ex-convicts among others. The members became clean, well-dressed, quiet, self-composed, racial separatists. In the Million Man March a key point made by the Farrakhan supporters was that they had gone to Washington to challenge themselves morally and to look at what they had done with the problem of white supremacy in their lives. Through the Million Man March, Farrakhan, in his own way, addresses the problem of my prison dream cited at the beginning of this chapter. For the men were marching to recognize themselves symbolically, to affirm their individual and group identity, and to assert their power in the face of racist disempowerment. This is a far cry from the dismemberment of identity experienced in the slave quarters or by all the young black men in prison today. Even as I join a mostly white organization, my dream reminds me as an individual to remember racial struggles and affirm my group identity as a black man through the secret handshake. The dream underlines the importance of affirming group identity in the individual psyche. The same can be said of the Million Man March. Like the handshake in my dream it makes clear that the antidote to cultural invisibility is group remembering. A message contained in the Million Man March is that blacks have to recognize themselves and their power in the face of their own self-disempowerment (that is, believing the myth of white supremacy and black invisibility).

FROM ETHNOS TO POLIS TO SOCIAL IDENTITIES

In the analytic literature a distinction is sometimes made between "*ethnos*" and "*polis*" (Hersh 1985). "*Polis*" values of the city/state are expressed through written agreements and contracts, i.e., marriages, constitutions, mortgages, etc. "*Polis*" is carried by the word, which when given is binding. On the other hand "*ethnos*" values refer to nonverbal contracts sealed in terms of blood relations and expressed through loyalty and respect to the group. The more primal level of feelings and thoughts that originate at the *ethnos* level of being have deep roots, and operate according to "old laws" of the psyche. These "old laws" (i.e., "an eye for an eye") constitute the archetypal foundation that structures social-psychological processes. They provide a blood basis for relating to those who are part of one's group and those who are not. The destructive side of this *ethnos*/racial "logic" we see expressed everyday as collective evil all over the world – in ethnic cleansing, apartheid, slavery, fascism. These *ethnos* processes are the ones responsible for most of the world's profound nonrational suffering and misery.

However, the positive side of these same *ethnos* processes also provides the archetypal foundation for a sense of belonging and identity. Our need to belong and to have an identity grounded in a reference group seems to be an archetypal given of being human. In the American landscape, *ethnos* needs tend to be subordinated to civic identity governed by the "new laws" of the *polis*. A perfect example of the *polis*' "new laws" is embodied in the democratic ideal of equality even though actual equality does not exist. As an American collective we tend to relate to differences among people in a profoundly ambivalent way. "Political correctness" reflects this ambivalence through its mixed message that we must all be the same in affirming differences among people. And we are all equal in our differences. We are asked by this *polis* doctrine to treat each other with civic and civil equality. The *ethnos* level of being is supposed to vanish under the "new laws" of the *polis*. These observations are not meant to denigrate the democratic ideal and the new laws of *polis*. Indeed, the problem of equality in public spaces has been addressed largely through the civil rights movement and its emphasis on the new laws of *polis*.

In America, our social identities rather than ethnic identities have come to be primary references for belonging to groups. *Ethnos* needs are pushed to the background, i.e., the unconscious. Some have labeled this movement as "identity politics." This is another way of expressing the psychological fact that we are shaped by the group to which we belong; we draw strength and self-authority from this belonging (see Steele 1998). Our membership in a group is central to our sense of who we are. Our reference group then goes on to pursue the politics of recognition. Sooner or later each group seeks recognition and power for its specific group identity.

SOCIAL PROCESSES GOVERNED BY THE CULTURAL COMPLEX

There are several implications that follow from the concept of the cultural complex:

1. The cultural complex is organized toward the end of generating "in-group" feelings of belonging and identity. It is formed through the conscious and unconscious accumulation of negative and positive group feelings and experiences over many generations. Through projection it further develops attitudes towards groups that are different from its own. I conceive of this movement as unitary; that is, a single process with multiple phases. This unitary movement is composed of a number of powerful emotions and psychological processes: guilt, pity, avoidance, denial, mistrust, suspicion, hostility, ambivalence, identification with the in group; and projection on to the out group through collective shadow processes. These processes cannot simply be engaged from the point of view of the right social attitude. Advocating equal justice for all without addressing the archetypal dynamics involved in group splitting and group projection will not work.
2. The cultural complex is organized around specific images and affects, roles and rituals, and a worldview that has historical continuity and is recognized within the body politic. Although cultural complexes are rooted in ethnic (Jewish, Italian), racial (black/white), religious (Protestant/Catholic), gendered (male/female) group identities, they may manifest in a variety of social identities as well (gay, physically challenged), each reaching for its own political and historical continuity.
3. Cultural complexes shape the individual's psyche through highly charged group memories of specific traumas and historical assumptions that operate

within the individual's connection to present conditions, i.e., blacks and slavery, Native American and genocide, Jews and the Holocaust, etc.

4 The collective shadow processes related to "otherness," i.e., the denigrated other (disowned parts of one's group) are perpetuated within the cultural complex. In-group/out-group dynamics, us/them differences, are long-standing categories along with images, and affective responses for comprehending stereotypes, racism, genocide, and all manner of deformations of others based on differences.

DEALING WITH ETHNOS LOGIC: TWO EXAMPLES

Taken together, the four processes listed above function to generate invisibility from one group to another. People literally cannot see one another for who they really are when they are in the grips of a cultural complex. These complexes incorporate bits of mythology, politics, psychology, sociology, and they operate as a whole beyond individuality. They swallow up individuals (Jung's "Wotan," my prison dream, Jewish Holocaust, etc.). They become too big to be taken on and dealt with individually. They require a collective response. It is not entirely clear what a more effective response would look like, but a recent example of an attempt to respond to the *ethnos* logic of revenge and retaliation through a *polis* logic may be seen in South Africa. In the aftermath of generations of apartheid violence, the South African Truth and Reconciliation Commission (TRC) was established. The purpose of this commission was both political and psychological. The stated aim was to reconcile South Africans with the brutality of the past by dealing with the thousands of traumas inflicted on millions of people by the apartheid system. The psychological intent was to allow a place where citizens would both relive and come to terms with their past, since these traumas have emotional consequences for both individuals and society. The political side of the process (which I believe may have been its primary intent) was to limit future racial and ethnic retaliation. Part of the reconciliatory function of the Truth and Reconciliation Commission was to grant amnesty. Perpetrators of gross violations of human rights who applied for and met the Truth and Reconciliation Commission criteria for amnesty were to be freed from prosecution and all criminal and civil liability. The Truth and Reconciliation Commission took over 20,000 statements. I think this approach, though noble, has had only limited success.

For one thing, the opening up of a traumatic past in a public way is only a first step toward connecting with ongoing individual and social processes of healing. I don't think that they succeeded in building institutional processes and structures that would allow an ongoing confrontation with these forces over time. The focus on perpetrators was limited. The large group of mostly silent white South Africans who clearly benefited from the system of apartheid were not included in the process. To begin creating a truly healing social narrative they too should have been part of the processes.

A second, more important reason that the impact of the Commission's work to date will be limited is that a psychological model of individual catharsis has been asked to carry the burden of a reparative effort for the entire collective. Although each individual in each system must find a separate connection to these social/psychological traumas, individual awareness is not enough to transform them. Real healing of a cultural complex requires a collective effort which should include addressing the perpetrators and silent beneficiaries as well as the victims, i.e., addressing the underlying *ethnos* logic. Furthermore, truly bringing a cultural complex to consciousness requires a real inquiry into what each group means to one another and how they have functioned within the us/them dynamic to carry each other's shadows.

Let me take another contemporary example. In America, the debate over affirmative action programs can be seen from an archetypal perspective to be an *ethnos–polis* conflict. From the *polis* side of the conflict, affirmative action programs are misguided government policies that have generated a welfare mentality, lowered group standards of achievement, and fostered feelings of dependency. Inclusion of minorities has been pushed at the expense of our American ideal of a color-blind constitution. The reality, though, is that there has never been a color-blind constitution. From the perspective of *ethnos* logic, affirmative action programs are a responsible collective response to the legacy of slavery, discrimination, and institutional racism. These programs are an attempt to redress the fact of a disparity in opportunity that has been created by these historical and collective forces. But cultural complexes can blind us to the reality of cultural complexes. Hence well-intentioned men like Steele can end up minimizing the importance of *ethnos* processes in shaping a healing collective response.

CONCLUSION

Intergroup conflicts, expressed through us/them dynamics, projection and righteousness, are the expression of normal group processes. The pathological miscarriage of these processes that leads to genocidal violence or more insidious injustices seems to reflect a mismanagement of dynamics created at the group psychological level. I have introduced the concept of cultural complex to recognize the organized intentionality of these dynamics and to add a psychological dimension to our discourse about it. Typically, such issues have been responded to at the political, sociological, or economic level. The psychological level of these dynamics, however, has a life of its own and requires a reorientation of our thinking. We need a concept like the cultural complex to engage forces that constellate themselves in such a way as to function beyond our individual control and creation.

BIBLIOGRAPHY

Ellison, Ralph (1956) *The Invisible Man*, New York: The New American Library, Signet Books.
Erikson, Erik H. (1980) *Identity and The Life Cycle*, New York: W.W. Norton.
Henderson, J. (1984) *Cultural Attitudes in Psychological Perspective*, Toronto: Inner City Books.
Hersh, James (1985) *From Ethnos to Polis: The Furies and Apollo*, Dallas, TX: Spring Publications.
Jung, C. (1936) "Wotan," *Collected Works*, Vol. 10, Part III, Princeton, NJ: Princeton University Press.
—— (1947) "On the nature of The psyche," *Collected Works*, Vol. 8, Princeton, NJ: Princeton University Press.
—— (1964) "Civilization in transition," *Collected Works*, Vol. 10, Princeton, NJ: Princeton University Press.
Mogenson, Greg (1989) *God is a Trauma*, Dallas, TX: Spring Publications.
Samuels, A. (1993) *The Political Psyche*, London and New York: Routledge.
Steele, Shelby (1998) *A Dream Deferred*, New York: HarperCollins.

Chapter 11

Under the shade of Pol Pot's umbrella

Mandala, myth, and politics in the Cambodian genocide

Alexander Laban Hinton

On 17 April 1975, the Khmer Rouge – a group of Maoist-inspired communist rebels headed by Pol Pot – victoriously entered Cambodia's capital, Phnom Penh, thus ending a bloody civil war in which perhaps 600,000 Cambodians had died. They immediately ordered the inhabitants of the capital to leave the city "for a few days," usually on the pretext that the departure was for their own safety since the United States was supposedly about to bomb the capital. The city dwellers were not allowed to return. Instead, they were dispersed into the countryside to participate in Cambodia's agrarian revolution. The inhabitants of the cities were referred to as "new people" and generally had fewer rights and were treated worse than the "old people" who had lived in Khmer Rouge controlled zones during the war.

This rustication program was part of a Khmer Rouge plan to totally transform Cambodian society. Borrowing a phrase from Maoist discourse, the Khmer Rouge initiated a number of structural changes designed to help the country attain a "great leap forward" (*moha lot phloah*) into communism.[1] Economic production and consumption were collectivized. Buddhism and other forms of religious worship were banned. Money, markets, and trade were eliminated. Family structure was undermined. Freedom of choice, movement, and speech were severely curtailed. In addition, people were frequently forced to work extremely long hours each day while receiving meager rations. Not surprisingly, many Cambodians still refer to Democratic Kampuchea (DK), the period of Khmer Rouge rule, as the "prison without walls" (*kuk et chonhcheang*).

By the time the Vietnamese army invaded Cambodia in January 1979, over one and a half million of Cambodia's eight million inhabitants had died of starvation, disease, overwork, or outright execution. Many of the dead came from the ranks of "new people," who were suspect from the start of DK because of their "counter-revolutionary" class and/or political backgrounds and their implicit support of the US-backed Lon Nol regime, the hated enemy whom the Khmer Rouge had defeated in the civil war. Still other victims, however, came from the ranks of the Khmer Rouge themselves as bloody purges, reminiscent of Stalinism, were carried out. Higher-ranking cadre were incarcerated at Tuol Sleng, a former Phnom Penh high school that the Khmer Rouge converted into an interrogation center. Such prisoners were coerced, often after enduring days of excruciating torture, into giving

"confessions" that detailed their "treasonous" behaviors and listed their
of accomplices. Afterward, the prisoners were executed at a nearby "kil

Thus Koy Thuon, an intellectual and long-time revolutionary wh
leadership positions in the Khmer Rouge hierarchy, was arrested in January 1977
and eventually killed. What is particularly striking about Thuon's demise is not just that a seemingly committed revolutionary could fall from power so quickly, but the fact that thousands of his subordinates in Northern Cambodia and the Commerce Ministry were also subsequently purged. This chapter explores the roots of such virulent purges during the Cambodian genocide.

Specifically, I argue that, in order to understand why the purges took place, one must understand Cambodian notions of patronage and power, which hold that power comes to be invested in certain "centers" around which social networks, or a "periphery" of followers, develop. This conception of the political "center," in turn, mirrors Hindu-Buddhist ideas about the mandala, or symbolic circle, which are manifest in Cambodian myth, history, and cosmology. The sunshade constitutes a key mandala metaphor that links these various domains, moving us from the realm of Hindu-Buddhist myth to the mandala-like dynamics of Cambodian political processes. In the final section of this chapter, I illustrate how these notions of patronage and power structured part of the violence that took place during DK – the purges.[2]

MANDALA MYTHS: CAMBODIAN NOTIONS OF PATRONAGE AND POWER

Mandala myths

The mandala, or symbolic circle/center, is a multivalent symbol that has cosmological, spatial, topographical, social, psychological, and political dimensions in Hindu and Buddhist thought. In Khmer, a mandala (*mondol*) means a "circle/center; a place having a round shape . . . the disk of the sun or moon."[3] This term is etymologically derived from Sanskrit and Pali, where *mandala* refers not just to a circle, but to an encompassing center circumscribing a field of symbolic space, one that may have such diverse referents as the universe itself, social relations, the political order, psychic integration, the cardinal directions, and Enlightenment. I explore many of these dimensions of mandala symbolism below, often through the metaphor of the mandala-shaped sunshade that links myth and politics. Eventually, I argue that in Cambodia, as in other southeast Asian societies, sociopolitical relations may be conceptualized as a pulsating mandala that shrinks and expands. The core–periphery image of the mandala signifies the key importance of a raised political center of power that dominates a surrounding space of followers.

My analysis of the political dimensions of mandala symbolism in Theravada Buddhist societies such as Cambodia is framed around several culturally salient myths and themes.[4] In Cambodia, for example, many sculptures depict the Buddha

Figure 11.1 Buddha seated in meditation on the coils of a *naga*
Source: Illustration by Jim McManus, based on Ka 1680, National Museum of Cambodia

seated in meditation on the coils of a *naga*, or serpent, whose raised hood forms a protective covering over him (see Figure 11.1). This image references an episode that occurs in the Buddha's life after he rebuffs the temptations and assaults of Mara, the Lord of the Realm of Desire, and attains Enlightenment under the Bodhi tree.

Soon thereafter, the Buddha goes to a lake and begins meditating under a Muchalinda tree. A torrential rainstorm breaks out, one with such force and duration that it threatens to inundate the Buddha. The area, however, is the home of a *naga*-king named Muchalinda. Muchalinda comes forth and coils his body around the Buddha seven times, spreading "his large hood over the Blessed One's head, thinking to himself: 'May no cold (come to) the Blessed One; May no heat (come to) the Blessed One; May no touch of gadflies and nats, storms and sunheat and reptiles (come to) the Blessed One'" (Brewster 1926: 51–52). The *naga*-king remains in this position for seven days until the inclement weather passes. After unwinding his coils from the Buddha, Muchalinda takes the form of a youth and pays homage to the Buddha, raising his hands in reverence. The story ends with the Buddha giving the following sermon:

> Happy the solitude of him who is content, who has heard the Truth, who sees. Happy is non-malice in this world, [self] restraint toward all beings that have life. Happy is passionlessness in this world, the getting beyond all sense-desires. The suppression of that 'I am' conceit, this truly is the highest happiness.
>
> (Ibid.: 52)

The Cambodian/Buddhist sculptures that celebrate this event are imbued with multivalent symbolism.[5] As illustrated by Figure 11.1, the Buddha is often portrayed as sitting in meditation on three coils of the *naga*, which gives the effect of creating a raised throne for him. Besides signifying the *naga*, the number of coils – three – is symbolically loaded in Buddhist cosmology. For example, the coils likely denote the "Three Gems" of Buddhism – the Buddha, the *Dhamma* (i.e., the "truth" preached by the Buddha), and the *Sangha* (i.e., the monastic order that the Buddha founded). During religious ceremonies, Cambodians usually declare their faith in the "Three Gems" and burn three sticks of incense before an image of the Buddha. There are three realms in Buddhist cosmology (i.e., the realms of desire, form, and formlessness), three "baskets" of Buddhist doctrine (i.e., the basket of discourses, of discipline, and of metaphysics), and three cardinal vices (i.e., desire, passion, and ignorance) and virtues (i.e., compassion, equanimity, and wisdom) in Buddhist morality. Moreover, in attaining enlightenment, the Buddha gains the superordinate "threefold knowledge" of his past lives, the nature of rebirth, and the origins and elimination of suffering.

While there are many other levels of symbolism in the Muchalinda–Buddha sculptures, I would like to focus on the one most relevant to my analysis – the *naga* hood that forms a protective canopy over the Buddha. Many of these hoods contain six minor serpent heads looking upward to the topmost major head. The number seven may represent the seven directions or the seven concentric landmasses and oceans in Buddhist cosmology. Alternatively, there are seven *cakras*, or energy centers, in the human body, the highest of which are located in the head and throat, where Enlightenment occurs (Jessup and Zephir 1997: 273). The Buddha also took seven steps upon his birth and spent seven days at a time meditating under the Bodhi tree, the Banyan tree, and the Muchalinda tree after attaining Enlightenment. In fact, the *naga*-heads and the hood itself resemble lotus buds and the heart-shaped leaves of the Bodhi tree, thereby symbolizing Creation and Enlightenment.

The hood of the *naga* may also be seen as forming a protective umbrella over the Buddha.[6] As anyone who has traveled through southeast Asia will recall, ornate sunshades are omnipresent, particularly in association with royalty and Buddhist shrines and ceremonies. In Khmer, the Cambodian language, the word for an umbrella, *chât*, refers to a "halo, circle around the sun or moon; parasol, umbrella" (Headley 1977: 210) and is derived from the Pali root *chatta*, meaning "a sunshade . . . a canopy . . . the royal canopy" (Rhys Davids and Stede 1992: 274). The *chatta*, or sunshade, is a symbolically loaded mandala image in Hindu-Buddhist cosmology, with its raised center and circular shape. As the Khmer definition suggests, the sunshade may be seen to represent the sun, the moon, or the sky itself, with the ribs of the umbrella signifying rays of light. When a king or the Buddha are covered by an umbrella, they are thus being associated with the power and enormity of the sky, including the sun and the moon it contains. At the same time, the sunshade provides protection from the elements that come from the sky. The king and the Buddha are thus also associated with the ability to protect others from danger and harm.

Still other dimensions of the symbolism of the umbrella are illustrated by the sunshades which adorn Buddhist stupas, or reliquary/memorial shrines. The dome-shaped stupas themselves are elaborate mandala symbols that express such Hindu-Buddhist themes as the creation and shape of the universe, the pathway to liberation, the generative "egg" or womb of life, the pure space of dhamma from which the disordering demonic forces have been expelled, and the cosmic mountain, pillar, and navel of the universe (Snodgrass 1985; Swearer 1995). The spires that emerge from the dome of stupas are often crowned by, or take the shape of, sunshades. In this context, the sunshade has an array of referents. For example, the sunshade forms an image of the cosmos. Its canopy, often multi-layered, represents the heavens in Buddhist cosmology, which ascend from the six realms of desire through the eighteen realms of form to the four realms of formlessness in which Enlightenment is attained.

The pole of the sunshade, in turn, may be viewed as standing for the *axis mundi*, or cosmic axis, while the dome surface from which the pole rises represents the earth. In Hindu-Buddhist cosmology, the heavens and earth are connected by Mount Meru, which stands at the exact center of the world and at whose summit Indra and his attendant gods reside. Mount Meru is surrounded by seven concentric mountain ranges separated by seven oceans, the last of which contains the four continents, located at the four cardinal directions, including Jambudvipa, the southernmost one where human beings reside. The outermost sea is enclosed by the Iron Mountain, which divides the cosmos from the void. As the *axis mundi*, Mount Meru plays an important role in much Hindu-Buddhist mythology.

The Hindu myth of the Churning of the Milky Ocean, for example, recounts an epic struggle between the gods (*devas*) and the titans (*asuras*), who dwell under Mount Meru:

> The legend starts at the beginning of the world, when the *devas* and the *asuras*, fought bitterly between themselves for 1,000 years in an effort to produce the *amrita*, an elixir that would render them immortal.
>
> After some time, when they were tired and unable to achieve their goal, they asked the help of Vishnu. He appeared and ordered them to work together, not against each other. They agreed and organised themselves, the *asuras* to the left headed by the three generals, with Bali holding the snake's head, and the *devas* to the right commanded by a general with an unusual head-dress, Lord Shiva (with five faces), and, at the end, holding the tail of the *naga*, the mighty monkey king Sugriva.
>
> They started then to churn the Ocean of Milk by using Mount [Meru] as the pivot. However, this suddenly started to sink. Vishnu intervened in his incarnation as the tortoise Kurma, and offered the back of his shell as a support for the mountain. The divine serpent Vasuki, with five heads, offered himself as the rope and curled himself around the pivot, which many gods, including Indra, helped to keep in position. The spinning of Mount [Meru] created such a violent whirlpool that the mythological creatures and fish around it were torn to pieces in great numbers.
>
> The Ocean of Milk was churned for another 1,000 years before producing the much-desired elixir and other treasures including the goddess Lakshmi (Sri Devi), the elephant Airavata, the horse Uccaishrava, a wishing tree, and the *apsaras*. A bitter confrontation took place between the *devas* and the *asuras* as to who would have the *amrita*, and another great battle took place. Vishnu had to intervene again, and with the help of the *devas*, won the battle and gained possession of the *amrita* which he kept out of harm's way. Once peace was established, Indra was reinstalled as the king of the gods. In Khmer mythology this act was very significant, since it could be related to the peaceful installation of the king of the Khmers.
>
> (Roveda 1998: 54)

This event is celebrated in a magnificent bas-relief at Angkor Wat, the renowned Cambodian temple built by an ancient Khmer king, Suryavarman II. By analogy, the bas-relief may have been invoking the epic battles which the ancient Cambodians (as *devas*) had fought against their nemesis, the Chams (as *asuras*). However, it is crucial to note the key role played by Mount Meru in this myth. As the *axis mundi*, Mount Meru is the cosmic pillar that both centers the earth and is a source of creation and vitality – in this instance, it produces magical objects and the elixir of vitality. The Muchilinda myth, in which the Buddha, like Mount Meru, is encircled by the coils of a *naga* (the seven coils paralleling the seven mountains and oceans surrounding Mount Meru), seems to have been indirectly referencing the Myth of the Churning of the Milky Ocean. The enlightened Buddha is analogically portrayed as a cosmic axis insofar as he is the creator and "center" of Buddhism who revitalizes the world through his sermons on *dhamma*. By signifying the *axis mundi*, then, the pole of the sunshade has an array of connotations including the pillar of the world, the Buddha himself, creativity and vitality, *dhamma*, and the link between microcosm and macrocosm.

Alternatively, the sunshade is also often interchangeable with and/or may connote the cosmic wheel, tree, or lotus.[7] For example, the sunshade, which is sometimes adorned with small petals hanging from the rim of its canopy, may reference the lotus. A powerful and multivalent symbol in Hindu-Buddhist cosmology, the lotus is linked to the very creation of the universe. Just as a lotus opens to reveal a mandala-shaped flower, so too does the universe expand outward from the cosmic center. This generative association is widely developed in Hindu lore, as the lotus is likened to a womb and is said to have given birth to the god Brahma. Moreover, the lotus, which rises from watery depths, is linked to the foundational, fertile, and life-sustaining qualities of water. Because the lotus rises unsullied out of the mud, it also connotes purity. These associations have been incorporated into Buddhist iconography, which frequently groups the Buddha with the lotus; the Buddha may be seen holding a lotus or lotus bud, sitting under a parasol adorned with lotus petals, or meditating on a lotus "throne." Thus, in some Muchalinda-Buddha sculptures, the Buddha sits on a lotus that is supported by (or supports) the *naga* coils. In such Buddhist contexts, then, the lotus may symbolize the Buddha's re-creation of the universe with *dhamma*, the Buddha's revitalizing presence in the world, and the purity of *dhamma* and Enlightenment.

Relatedly, the world tree is another vegetal symbol linked to the sunshade in several ways. Both have a similar mandala shape and common referents. Thus the branches of the tree represent the heavens and higher stages of consciousness, while the tree trunk forms an *axis mundi* that connects the heavens to the earth and underworld. The cosmic tree symbolizes the cycles of existence and the center of the universe. As such, it may stand for Mount Meru in some contexts and for the Buddha himself in others. In fact, almost all of the key life-events of the Buddha – his birth, first meditation, attainment of Enlightenment, and death – take place under trees, the most famous of which is the Bodhi tree underneath which the Buddha fends off the temptations of Mara and attains Enlightenment. Through this connection to and identification with the cosmic tree, the Buddha indexes the *axis mundi*, the center of the universe, the nexus between the earthly and heavenly realms, the conduit for the spread of *dhamma*, and an exemplar for reaching a higher spiritual state.

It is interesting to note that the image of the Buddha sitting underneath the Bodhi tree bears great similarity to the Muchalinda–Buddha sculpture. Some scholars have speculated that the design of the multi-headed *naga* hood was modeled after the branches and/or leaves of the cosmic tree, in which case the *naga*'s body would signify the cosmic tree, among other things (see Bosch 1960: 202). This similarity between the *naga* and the cosmic tree provides another way of linking the Muchalinda hood to the sunshade, since the cosmic tree is one of the sunshade's referents. In fact, the tradition of using multi-layered sunshades to indicate rank and royalty may have originated with an attempt to imitate the branches and shade of the cosmic tree.[8]

The wheel, like the canopy of a sunshade, constitutes yet another mandala in which spokes radiate out from a central point toward a circular periphery. In Hindu-Buddhist thought, the cosmic wheel may signify cosmogony (the universe spreading out from a primordial center), the revolving sun, the psyche, cyclic time, and space (the expanse emanating from the cosmic center). Within Buddhism itself, the wheel figures prominently in a variety of contexts. Thus the seven steps which the Buddha takes upon birth may be seen as his metaphorically mapping out the six directions of the cosmos and establishing himself as their center, the seventh point. The Buddha's post-Enlightenment perambulations parallel this event (Snodgrass 1985: 40f.). Moreover, the Buddha's first sermon after attaining Enlightenment, in which he expounds The Four Noble Truths and The Noble Eightfold Path to Enlightenment,[9] is known as "The Setting in Motion of the Wheel of *Dhamma*." Like the hub of a wheel, the Buddha becomes the center/*axis mundi* from which *dhamma* spreads throughout the cosmos. After the Buddha's death, the religious order (*sangha*) that lives by and preaches about the laws of *dhamma* and the righteous Buddhist ruler (*dhammaraja*) who orders his kingdom in accordance with *dhamma* came to be known as "the two wheels of *dhamma*."

Through his association with the wheel and other symbols of royalty, the Buddha is also linked to kingship. In Hindu-Buddhist thought, select kings were viewed as *cakravartin*, or "wheel-turning" rulers who became the center of the universe by conquering the four quarters of the earth.[10] As we shall see, Cambodian kings often made claim to being *cakravartin* by building magnificent palaces that replicated the cosmos and located them at Mount Meru, the center of the world. Interestingly, upon the Buddha's birth it was prophesied that he would become either a *cakravartin* or a Buddha. While he takes the path of renunciation, the Buddha's actions parallel those of a universal monarch. If a *cakravartin* rolls the wheel of conquest to gain dominion over the world, the Buddha rolls the wheel of *dhamma* to conquer ignorance throughout the cosmos. His dual status as Buddha and *cakravartin* is indicated in numerous ways. The Buddha sits upon a *naga* or lotus throne, has the distinguishing marks of a *cakravartin*, is placed as an *axis mundi* at the center of the cosmos, is associated with the royal insignias and symbols (for example, the wheel, sunshade, turban), is described with royal terms and metaphors, and is buried in royal fashion.

As illustrated by the Muchalinda–Buddha sculpture, we can see that the Buddha, like Hindu-Buddhist kings, is connected to the *naga*. Long before Indian traders and travelers began frequenting what is now Cambodia (perhaps as early as 300 BC), the inhabitants of the area are thought to have worshipped spirits and beings who dwelt in the forests, mountains, waters, and lands in which people worked and lived (Mabbett and Chandler 1995). These beliefs were quite compatible with Hindu-Buddhist myths about creatures like the *naga*, thus perhaps partially explaining why these beings were incorporated into and continue to play such a prominent role in the Cambodian religious cosmos. As deities that reside in the waters and the earth, *nagas* are regarded as extremely powerful and dangerous.[11] They are believed to have control over rain and thus the fertility of the lands. This association with fertility is evident in a Hindu myth that depicts Vishnu, the creator of the universe, as sleeping in between cosmic eras on the back of the cosmic serpent, Ananta, who floats on the life-giving Ocean of Milk. *Nagas* are also linked to both local territories, which they are thought to protect, and the riches of the earth, which might lead them to bestow wealth upon someone who finds their favor. Like a poisonous snake, however, *nagas* can be destructive if angered or not properly worshipped; they may destroy those who betray them and bring famine and disease to those who are in their disfavor.

Given the *nagas*' crucial role in producing abundant harvests, it is not surprising that rulers made claim to having a special relationship with these serpent deities. Indian notions of kingship, which were largely assimilated into Cambodian cosmology, held that there was a correspondence between the earthly and divine realms. The king who properly ordered his kingdom established a special link to the gods, who would respond by bringing prosperity to him and his people (Bloss 1973). If he faltered, however, chaos and blight would ensue. To positively channel the forces of nature, then, kings needed the authorization of deities such as the *naga*. Several southeast Asian countries have legends in which a dynastic line is given authority over the land by a *naga*. In many cases, the mortal founder of the kingdom marries a *nagi* princess, thereby symbolically ensuring the fertility of the crops and the prosperity of the kingdom that is established. As illustrated by the examples below, Cambodia has several of these origins myths, which often center on the legendary characters Kaundinya and Preah Thong and their *nagi* brides.

> According to one version of the myth, a brahman named Kaundinya, armed with a magical bow, appeared one day off the shore of Cambodia; a dragon-princess paddled out to meet him. Kaundinya shot an arrow into her boat; this action frightened the princess into marrying him. Before the marriage, Kaundinya gave her clothes to wear, and in exchange, her father, the dragon-king, "enlarged the possessions of his son-in-law by drinking up the water that covered the country. He later built them a capital, and changed the name of the country to 'Kambuja.'"
>
> (Chandler 1992: 13)

> This legend of the Hindu Prince and the Serpent-Woman, the Nagi, is related in modern chronicles and is so much alive that certain present-day marriage rituals still recall it. A son of the King of Delhi, Preah Thong, became the sovereign of the Khmer country. "One night he was caught by the tide on a

> sand-bank and forced to spend the night there. A young Nagi rose from the waves and came to join him. Smitten with her fabulous beauty the King united himself to her and thus a powerful dynasty was formed which long ruled the country."
>
> (Porée and Maspero 1938: 69)

As late as the end of the thirteenth century, a Chinese traveler reported that this mythological relationship was still believed to be ritually renewed by the Cambodian king and his *nagi* bride each night.

> Out of the palace rises a golden tower, to the top of which the ruler ascends nightly to sleep. It is common belief that in the tower dwells a [spirit], formed like a serpent with nine heads, which is Lord of the entire kingdom. Every night this [spirit] appears in the shape of a woman, with whom the sovereign couples. Not even the wives of the King may enter here. At the second watch the King comes forth and is then free to sleep with his wives and his concubines. Should the [spirit] fail to appear for a single night, it is a sign that the King's death is at hand. If, on the other hand, the King should fail to keep his tryst, disaster is sure to follow.
>
> (Chou Ta-Kuan 1987: 2)

Such legends provide a warrant for kingship, symbolically ensuring that, through the proper dynastic relationship to these water and earth deities, the realm will prosper from abundant rainfall and bountiful harvests.

Buddhist myths depict the Buddha as also having a special tie to the *naga* (Bloss 1973). If a king gains the favor of the *naga* by properly ordering his kingdom, the Buddha subdues these deities through the force of virtue and *dhamma*. Thus Muchalinda is transformed from a fierce, powerful, and potentially destructive deity into one who protects, serves, and pays homage to the Buddha. By extension, the Buddha, who sits on the *naga* throne, is portrayed as a conduit who can bring prosperity to all those who come into contact with the power of *dhamma*.[12] His ability to control the forces of nature – and, by implication, to channel rain to the fields – is illustrated by the fact that he brings a *naga*, the source of rain, to protect him from a violent storm. Like a king, the Buddha's right to spread *dhamma* throughout the earth is symbolically acknowledged by his taming of such territorial deities. Ultimately, the *naga* becomes a guardian of the Buddha and his relics. Just as Muchalinda is brought to shelter the Buddha from the elements, so too can the Buddha protect those who follow the laws of *dhamma* that he spreads.

Besides establishing a connection to the *naga*, Cambodian kings attempted to demonstrate that they were "wheel-turning" rulers in other ways. During the Angkorean period, for example, kings built enormous Hindu-Buddhist monuments that replicated the cosmos and placed themselves at its center – just like the gods who resided at the summit of Mount Meru. Thus the most renowned Angkorean temple, Angkor Wat, which was built by the powerful ruler Suryavarman II (AD

1113–1150) and dedicated to the Hindu god Vishnu, is a mirror image of the universe (see Figure 11.2). At its center stand five raised towers (the highest one is in the center and enclosed by the four others that form a quincunx, or the corners of a square) that correspond to the peaks of Mount Meru. These towers are enclosed by a wall and a moat that represent the rings of land and the oceans that encircle the cosmic mountain. As a representation of the *axis mundi*, the central tower is constructed to seem as if it both burrows into the earth and reaches into the heavens, thus linking Suryavarman II to the earthly and celestial deities who could help bring success and prosperity to his realm. This connection between the micro- and macrocosmic realms is further signified by a long causeway, adorned with *naga*-shaped balustrades that symbolize both fertility and the rainbow which forms a path from the earth to the heavens, that leads across the moat and into the central temple complex. The architectural complexity of Angkor Wat is staggering, as it geometrically references not just Mount Meru, Vishnu, and Suryavarman II, but the cycles of time and space, the movements of the sun and moon, and the creation of the universe.[13]

Cambodian kings were portrayed as the center of the cosmos in many other ways, particularly during royal rituals.[14] In 1906, for example, King Sisowath was crowned in a ceremony that lasted for several days and symbolically portrayed him as taking control of his kingdom and, after being established as its center, linking it to the heavens and earth. On the coronation day itself, Sisowath was anointed with water representing the waters of the earth in general and each of the Cambodian provinces in particular. He therefore symbolically incorporated the kingdom and its source of fertility – water – into his own body. The king's possession of the realm was further indexed by a ritual circumambulation of the capital, in which he stopped at each of the cardinal directions and changed his attire, thus establishing himself as the regent of all points of the earth. In addition, all of the provincial lords attended the occasion and pledged their lands to the king. Throughout this process, the king was ritually identified as Mount Meru, with "his right eye representing the sun, his left eye the moon, his arms and legs the four cardinal points, the six-tiered umbrella above his head the six lower heavens, his pointed crown the spire of Indra's palace on the summit of the Meru and his slippers the earth" (Heine-Geldern 1942: 22). Interestingly, a protective spirit was thought to reside in the royal umbrella and to assist the Cambodian king during times of crisis. As noted above, the umbrella would also have had an array of other referents, associating the king with the cosmic tree, the lotus, the *axis mundi*, and, as I will now discuss, patronage and power.

Mandala politics: patronage and power

In Cambodia, as in other southeast Asian societies, power is viewed as continuously in flux and as unequally distributed throughout the cosmos; it becomes concentrated to greater and lesser degrees in various objects, places, and persons.[15] One scholar has likened such a conception of power to a field of energy:

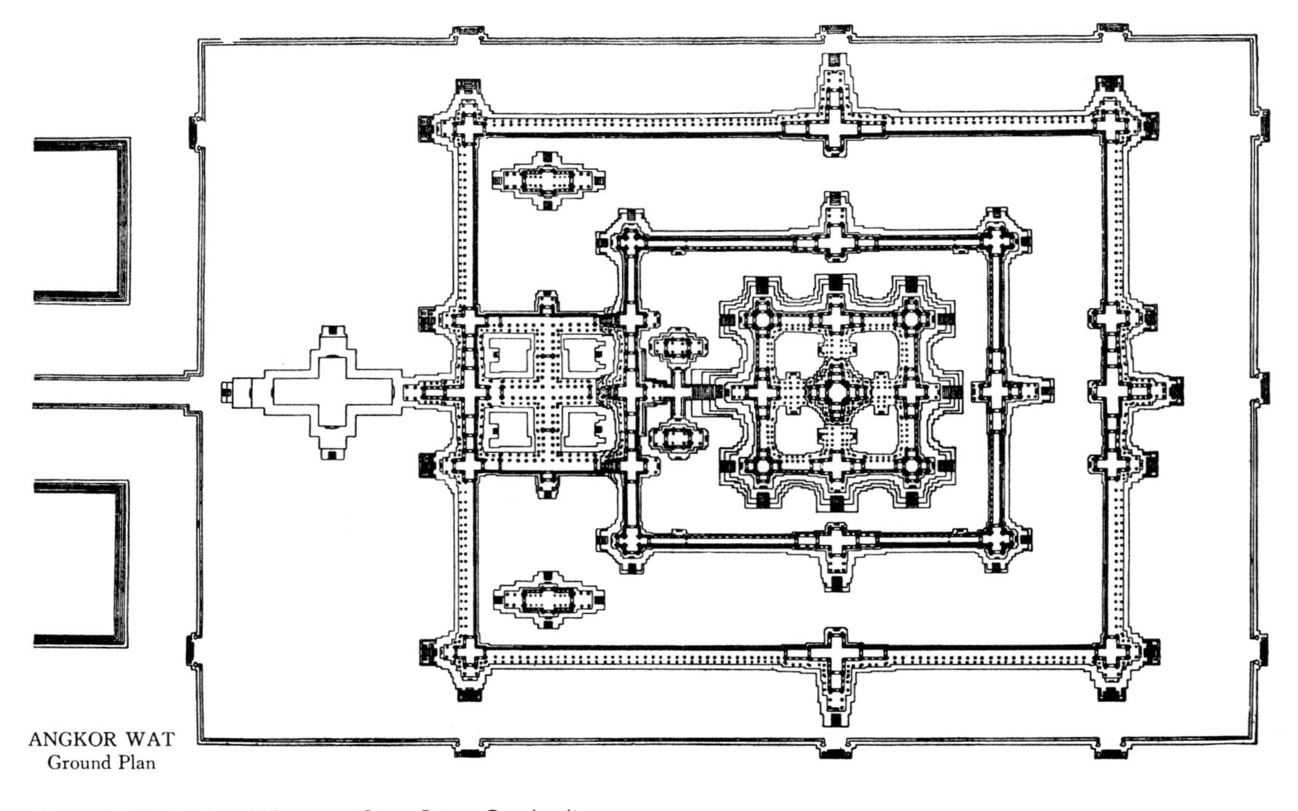

Figure 11.2 Angkor Wat near Siem Riep, Cambodia.
Source: Reproduced from George Coedes, *Angkor: An Introduction*, Singapore: Oxford University Press (1986).

> The energy exists everywhere in the field, but it is unevenly distributed: in some places it is quite thin; in others, densely concentrated. The energy is continuous – there are no boundaries and no empty spaces, but only thinner and thicker concentrations. . . . It is continuously moving, waxing and waning from particular locations. Its flux is usually, though not always, gradual. In addition to currents of energy, numerous visible objects occupy this field. One of the differences between the objects and the currents of energy is that the objects are discrete: they have boundaries and surfaces. . . . The objects provide locations and nodal points at which the energy collects, though in differing degrees of concentration.
>
> (Errington 1989: 58)

From this perspective, every being is differentially ranked in terms of power. Thus the Buddha and the gods have more power than humans, while humans have more power than those who reside in the hells. Likewise, within the human realm, each person will have more or less power than other individuals. This power may be derived from a number of sources, including experience, knowledge, the possession of wealth, and special objects (for example, amulets, tattoos, magical strings), authority (*amnach*), strength/influence (*khlang*), and skill/effectiveness (*poukae*). A person in whom such power is concentrated is said to have "potency" (*etthipol*).

These forms of power are, in themselves, morally neutral – beings choose to use them in good or bad ways.[16] However, there is a second source of potency that comes from the religious merit (*bon*) a person has accumulated in past lives and that rises or declines depending on how one acts in the present life. This moral power is a key determinant of the station into which one is born, though one's rank may change over time as one's store of merit fluctuates. In contrast to a Western conception of power as an abstract formulation about observed patterns of social behavior (for example, coercion, control, influence, disciplinary technologies, authority, freedom), then, the animating energy that constitutes "power" in much Cambodian thought is viewed as concrete, homogeneous, and, with the exception of religious merit, amoral (see Anderson 1990: 21–23). Moreover, the key Cambodian political concern is more about the accumulation and preservation of power than the exercise of power, which is the central issue in much Western political discourse (ibid.: 23).

Because power is an amoral force that may be (un)domesticated and used for good or evil purposes, Cambodians often view the world as a potentially dangerous place, one in which people need protection. One way to protect oneself is to increase one's own potency. However, this is difficult to do, since there is only a limited amount of power distributed throughout the universe. Cambodians may therefore attempt to gain the protection of more powerful beings, often by entering into patronage relationships with them. While there is great variation in the form, intensity, and duration of such ties, clients almost always provide some type of support, loyalty, and/or resources to their patrons in return for their protection and nurturance (see Hanks 1962, 1975). Patrons, in turn, incrementally increase their own power base by controlling clients.[17]

Although his role has changed in the past century, the king has traditionally been a prototypic patron in Cambodia. On the one hand, he protects and ensures the prosperity of the realm; his subjects, in turn, owe him loyalty and support. On the other hand, the king provides his ministers, generals, and officials with protection and key resources – the right to distribute land, titles, prestigious court appointments and ceremonial roles, war booty, and lucrative government positions – that ensure their loyalty and support. His clients then use these resources to build their own patronage networks. The personal nature of these patronage ties stands in strong contrast to the impersonal, generalized interests around which groups in Western societies frequently form: a Cambodian client owes allegiance to his or her patron, not to the other members of the patron's "circle" of clients.

In Cambodia and elsewhere in southeast Asia, the sunshade is often used as a metaphor for such patronage relationships. This metaphor references the mandala-like structure of the patronage system, as powerful patrons (i.e., the centers/poles of the sunshade) are linked (i.e., the connecting ribs) to a peripheral circle of clients (i.e., the perimeter). As a traditional signifier of rank, the umbrella is also an emblem of power. Just as the sunshade provides refuge from the sun and the elements, so too is a powerful patron able to offer protection from the dangerous world. (Ironically, some people who gain the protection of a powerful patron may rely on this "backing" to do as they please, thus making the world an even more dangerous place.) Such protection is likened to the cool "shade" of an umbrella (or one of its interlinked symbols, the tree), which is an extremely evocative image in the hot climate of southeast Asia. Thus a mother, who defends, helps, and cares for her children, is said to provide them with comforting "shade" (see Ledgerwood 1996). Similarly, various ancient Cambodian inscriptions and chronicles speak of how the realm prospered under the "shade" of the king's parasol (e.g., Chandler 1992: 59, 75).

The Buddha's power is sometimes described in similar terms. One Shan Buddhist man stated that the Buddha's power was so great that it created a protective sphere into which spirits could not enter: "It is this protection which allows people who respect the Buddha to be healthy. . . . It is like having an umbrella when it is hot and sunny. [The umbrella] keeps people from getting a cold. Without it you would be sick" (Tannenbaum 1995: 82). Likewise, during the Buddhist *kâthen* festival in Cambodia, lay sponsors are sometimes ceremonially escorted into the pagoda underneath a sunshade that represents the Buddha's patronage (see Sokundara and Chaumeau 1998: 16). The Buddha–Muchalinda myth and iconography may also be interpreted in similar terms, as Muchalinda pays reverence to his new-found patron. The Buddha's power and protective capacity are signified by the umbrella-hood under which he meditates, by his ability to subdue even a *naga*-king, and by his associations with the cosmic tree, wheel, lotus, and *axis mundi*, all of which place him at the center of the universe.

While the ideal patronage bond is one in which a person lives comfortably under the "shade" created by a powerful patron's "umbrella," the reality is more unstable. Like energy, power is thought to ebb and flow, accumulating for a time in one location before scattering to the winds. This potential flux means that powerful beings may lose their "potency" over time and weaker beings may increase theirs. For clients, particularly in high-level political patronage networks, this precarious state of affairs means that their benefactor may suffer a "fall" from power, thus (1) enabling the client – if their own store of power has increased – to usurp their patron's place at the center of the sunshade, or (2) necessitating that the client be ready to suddenly switch allegiances to a new patron so that they are not left in the open without protective shade. The instability of such relations is further reinforced by the Buddhist view that a person's store of merit may suddenly "kick in" or expire, thereby resulting in a sharp rise or decline in standing. Moreover, prior to Democratic Kampuchea, few extra-familial institutional links existed between the peasant and the state, thus making patronage relations both more significant and less enduring, since they were often not directly predicated on state-level authority (Ebihara 1968).

While there are mechanisms that provide stability to patronage relations (for example, genuine affection and respect, feelings of moral debt, the difficulty of finding new patrons, the fear of retribution, kinship ties), these relationships are nevertheless sometimes characterized by uncertainty and, in the extreme, chronic mistrust. In an essay entitled "Suspicion," one Cambodian described the extreme situation as follows:

> From ancient times onward, Cambodian leaders have been constantly suspicious of one another. This doubt has led to there being merciless killings between them. Those who are in the process of holding power (*amnach*) never trust those who work with them, always fearing: "that person is inclined to quietly try to seize my authority! That person will try to secretly kill me in order to take over my position!" . . . When a person thinks in this panicked manner and stops trusting a person, if one of his subordinates inflames his suspicions a little bit, telling the leader that a colleague or long-time friend has in fact betrayed him, the leader will believe him at once. Immediately after this, the leader will find a pretext to accuse this colleague or friend of doing something bad so that the person can be killed and discarded.
>
> (Bun 1973: 213–214)

In varying forms, this type of distrust has periodically plagued Cambodian politics as far back as the Angkorean era and perhaps beyond.[18] Angkorean history is replete with episodes of revolt, betrayal, and usurpation, as various princes, lords, and rulers vied for the right of succession and power. Some inscriptions and chronicles describe this state of flux as one in which the realm suffers under the chaotic shade of "many umbrellas" as opposed to the orderly and comforting shade of just one umbrella (Chandler 1992). Such mistrust continues into the present. In July 1994, for example, Second Prime Minister Hun Sen arrested several members of his party whom he claimed were attempting a *coup* (see Hinton 1997: 114f.). All of the officials implicated in the coup had links to a rival faction within Hun Sen's party. Since then, Cambodian politics has continued to be plagued by troop maneuvers, political violence, arrests, and party splits that illustrate how suspicious leaders frequently fear being overthrown by both rivals and power-seeking clients to whom they have delegated authority.

Obviously, major changes have occurred in Cambodia from the Angkorean era to the present. With French colonial rule came a new system of more centralized administration and taxation that was superimposed on traditional forms of rule. Similarly, after Cambodia achieved its independence in 1953, the political landscape was transformed by increasing nationalism, the introduction of a parliamentary democracy, the emergence of a small middle class, and Prince Sihanouk's program of social and educational development in the name of "Buddhist socialism." Nevertheless, the mandala-like structure of patronage was never fully displaced and continued to co-evolve with new sociopolitical circumstances (Thion 1993; see also Tambiah 1976).

Thus, with regard to patronage, there are strong parallels – though not exact correspondences – between past and present political processes in Cambodia. One way to conceptualize these similarities is through the image of a *pulsating mandala* or sunshade (Tambiah 1976). To summarize, Cambodians believe that power is concentrated in certain individuals. Upon seeing signs of the power of these raised "centers," other people often seek their patronage and become their subordinates, or part of the graded "periphery" of the patron's mandala. Because anyone might become invested with the power or merit that legitimizes a rise in rank, this periphery may be unstable and changing. The center, in turn, must suspiciously guard against betrayal. This situation often generates a social dynamic I have elsewhere called the "mandala principle" (Hinton 1997), characterized by two countervailing tendencies that mirror the graded center–periphery shape of the sunshade.

On the one hand, a centripetal or "centering" force arises from some people's desire to accumulate power, to raise their status, and to become the political center. When successful, such individuals are able to maintain control over their peripheral subordinates through benevolence, nurturance, or fear, and to ensure prosperity for all those standing under the shade of their umbrella. On the other hand, the cohesion of the polity is constantly subject to a centrifugal or "decentering" tendency that, ironically, arises from the desire of other people standing in the periphery to increase their own power and status and, ideally, to become the political center themselves. Leaders, in turn, will be wary of such threatening subordinates and often use all of the means at their disposal to undercut their power, to absorb them through patronage, or to destroy them outright after deciding they are "enemies." In times of chaos, a number of peripheral centers may unsuccessfully vie to establish themselves as the pre-eminent center. The pulsating mandala will shrink or expand according to the extent to which the aforementioned centrifugal or centripetal tendencies predominate. In the next section, I will argue that Democratic Kampuchea provides a clear illustration of this dynamic, though in an extreme and lethal form.

UNDER THE SHADE OF POL POT'S UMBRELLA

In genocide and other forms of political violence, perpetrators often find it difficult to distinguish between themselves and the "enemy," thereby inserting a fundamental condition of uncertainty into the murderous process (Appadurai 1998). For it is frequently hard to differentiate between Hutus and Tutsis, Bosnian Serbs and Muslims, Irish Protestants and Catholics, Nazi Germans and Jews, and Soviet and Maoist revolutionaries and counter-revolutionaries; moreover, even when differences are ostensibly found, they may not seem to affirm the dehumanized stereotypes which murderous ideologies assert. As a result, genocides are often characterized by a process of "manufacturing difference," whereby perpetrators transform their victims into caricatures of the dehumanizing images by which they are being portrayed.

The most infamous instance of this lethal process, of course, occurred in the Nazi concentration camps, where Jews were stripped of the last vestiges of their humanity (clothing, hair, names, free will), treated like animals (being beaten, verbally abused, and made to perform dehumanizing acts), and forced to live in horrendous conditions that led to starvation, disease, stealing to survive, and death. By subjecting Jews to such circumstances, the Nazis attempted to turn them into beings who were, as Nazi anti-Semitic propaganda proclaimed, a "disease," "bacilli," "thieves," "lice," "subhumans," "parasites," "alien bodies," and so on (Hinton 1998: 14). And, once such difference had been manufactured, genocide was made to seem like a justifiable "purification" process necessary for the protection of the health of the German national body.

An analogous process of manufacturing difference may be seen in almost all genocides, including the one that took place in Cambodia.[19] Consider the following message that was broadcast by Phnom Penh domestic radio in April 1978, as Khmer Rouge purges were in full swing and border tensions with Vietnam were escalating, thus setting the stage for the invasion of Cambodia and collapse of the DK regime in January 1979:

> It is necessary to draw a clear line between us and the enemy and stand on our side to make the revolution. First of all, let us determine who we are. "We" means our nation, people, worker-peasant class, revolution, collective system of the proletariat, cooperatives, trade unions, Revolutionary Army and KCP. The "enemy" includes imperialist aggressors and lackeys of all stripes; the enemy has the intention of annexing and swallowing our territory; the enemy which is planted within our revolutionary ranks; the enemy in the for[m] of the feudal-capitalist and landowner classes and other oppressor classes; the enemy in the form of private and individualist system; and particularly, the expansionist, annexationist Vietnamese enemy.
>
> It is absolutely necessary to distinguish clearly between patriotism and treason, between love for the nation and people and betrayal of the nation and people, between worker-peasant class and the feudal-capitalist landowner

> and other oppressor classes, between revolution and counter revolution, between the collective system of the party's proletariat and the private system of the antiproletarian classes, and between the KCP and another antinational and counterrevolutionary sham party. It is essential that we draw a clear-cut line in terms of political, ideological, organizational, sentimental and traditional views and politics. This is the initial and fundamental stand necessary for conducting the revolution to the end.
>
> Why is it necessary for us to build up and strengthen the drawing of a clear line between us and the enemy? Each of us joined the revolution in order to fight against the enemy of our nation, people, class and revolution. This does not mean all of us clearly know the enemy and have drawn a clear distinction between ourselves and the enemy. Many joined the revolution at first and later switched to the enemy's side against the revolution. This is because of weakness in drawing a firm and clear line between us and the enemy. To know the enemy is to have a resolute political, ideological and organizational stand geared for the fight against the enemy to the end. Knowing the enemy without having the determination to fight to the end is useless.
>
> (FBIS 1978: H3)

This passage is revealing about DK in several respects. For example, it illustrates some of the major goals of the Khmer Rouge and the social transformation they undertook to achieve them. Upon taking power, they set out to create a "pure," egalitarian, revolutionary society in which the "worker-peasant class" would no longer be exploited by the "feudal-capitalist landowner and other oppressor classes." To this end, the Khmer Rouge collectivized property and established numerous agrarian cooperatives in which everyone worked in teams for long hours on communally owned lands. Such labor, and revolutionary activity in general, had to be performed with the proper spirit. As a later portion of the above radio broadcast stated, everyone was supposed "to feel a constantly seething hatred for the enemy; a profound revolutionary sentiment toward the oppressed classes; [and] a powerful love for the nation, revolution, collective system and party." The "private and individualist" system of capitalism – including private property, free trade, markets – was banned, as were its invidious legacy, the "private" sentiments, leanings, and thoughts that could potentially subvert the revolution. Of course, it is difficult to police a person's mind, a fact that increased dramatically the level of uncertainty about the "enemy" in DK, just as it had in the Stalinist and Maoist regimes after which much Khmer Rouge policy was modeled.

The radio broadcast also defines some of the many "enemies" of the DK regime. On the one hand, the Khmer Rouge had to fight external enemies such as the "expansionist, annexationist Vietnamese" against whom the DK army was skirmishing on the border and "imperialist aggressors" and neo-colonialists (i.e., US, French, and other foreign nationals/governments) who had traditionally exploited and oppressed the Cambodian people. On the other hand, the regime was opposed by a number of internal foes who were "planted within our revolutionary ranks," in particular, those individuals belonging to the "feudal-capitalist and landowner classes and other oppressor classes." While this category may seem somewhat general, the Khmer Rouge actually had conducted a detailed, if somewhat skewed, analysis of Cambodian class structure.[20] Thus the category of "feudalists" included both members of the royal family and former high-ranking government military and civilian officials; the "capitalist" class comprised Cambodians with foreign and domestic business concerns; "petty capitalists" referred to civil servants, intellectuals, teachers, small traders, craftspersons, monks and other religious figures, hairdressers, tailors, and so on; the "landowner" class comprised rich and upper-middle level peasants who hired others to work their lands; and "other oppressor classes" referred to former members of the Lon Nol military, police, civil service, among others. Counterposed to these "corrupt" groups were the workers and poor to middle-lower level peasants who had traditionally been oppressed and thus supposedly formed the core of the Khmer Rouge base of support for the revolution.[21]

Finally, the radio broadcast reveals the deep sense of uncertainty and paranoia that pervaded DK. While many factors contributed to this unease, at least three key sources can be discerned (Chandler 1991), though conditions varied across time and place (Vickery 1984). First, the Khmer Rouge's attempt to achieve a "great leap forward" into the new communist order was, in many ways, not successful. Plans to immediately and dramatically increase rice production could not be accomplished, leading many local officials to meet their quotas with current rice supplies that should have been set aside for later consumption. The result was often starvation, leading to disease, illness, death, and decreased productivity. Local and central authorities viewed the decreased productivity as an indication that "subversive" elements were at work. Thus, the broadcast continues:

> In the past, enemy running dogs of all colors planted within our cooperatives sabotaged the 3-ton-per-hectare target of our party and cooperatives. This was possible because some of our cadres and comrades did not pay enough attention to weeding out enemy elements. . . . In other words, the movement whipped up to wipe out the enemy planted within the cooperatives was not vigorous enough. This allowed saboteurs to carry out their activities. The explanation is that the stand of drawing a clear line between the cooperatives and the enemy planted within them is not firm and resolute.

Second, factional strife broke out as the Party Center attempted to strengthen its control over the country, a point I shall explore in more detail below. Real and imagined plots against Pol Pot and his inner circle convinced them of the need to purge the party ranks of "impure" elements. And, third, the military conflict with Vietnam escalated after 1977. When the Revolutionary Army was unable to resoundingly defeat the Vietnamese, questions arose over the loyalty of party members and East Zone inhabitants whose supposed Vietnamese sympathies seemed to be undermining the fight.

All of these factors contributed to the perception that the pure new DK social order-in-the-making was being corrupted by enemies that needed to be "weeded out." This process started as early as March 1976, when the DK central committee decided to authorize regional and military officials to "Smash (People) Inside and Outside the Ranks" (Chandler *et al.* 1988: 3). Later directives, speeches, and radio broadcasts spoke of the need to "wipe out" and destroy "enemies" who were "planted" or "burrowed within" the ranks of the new society. Because regional and local-level officials chose to interpret such pronouncements in different ways, spatial and temporal variation occurred in the pattern of killing. Nevertheless, in most places cadre and soldiers began to systematically annihilate suspect groups.

The first to come under suspicion were the "new people" (*brâcheachon tmey*) who had lived or taken refuge in the cities during the civil war, and thus indirectly supported the Lon Nol regime, the hated enemy of the Khmer Rouge. Moreover, from the perspective of the Khmer Rouge, the vast majority of "new people" came from suspect class backgrounds and/or had been corrupted by "imperialist" and "capitalist" influences that could threaten the "pure" new society-in-the-making. They were differentiated from the "old people" (*brâcheachon chas*) or "base people" (*brâcheachon moulâdthan*) who had lived in Khmer Rouge-controlled zones during the civil war. While both groups suffered during DK, "old people" tended to fare much better than "new people" because they were accustomed to agrarian life, frequently resided in their traditional homes and communities, often procured more food, enjoyed greater rights, held positions of power, and were generally favored because they embodied the "traditional peasant values" glorified by the Khmer Rouge. If a "new person" and an "old person" made a "mistake" (for example, lost a water buffalo, stole food, broke a tool, missed work), the Khmer Rouge were much more likely to severely punish or kill the "new person."

Suspect from the start of DK, "new people" were frequently the target of dehumanizing rhetoric and practices. After they had been relocated to a rural village, many "new people" found that they were despised by the locals. One former "new person" told me, "When we arrived in my grandparents' village, my entire family was looked down upon by the old people. We received less food than them and were told things like, 'The despicable new people, they lived happily in the capital, exploiting the peasants, while we had great difficulty. Now let them suffer.'"[22] Such devaluation was sometimes fueled by the perception that "new people" were "prisoners of war" (*neak chanh chloey soek*) or "parasites" (*bânhnhaoe kâ'aek*) who would impede social progress (Locard 1996: 148–149). Like war slaves, "new people" often had to work long hours on starvation rations, dwell in squalid conditions, and live in a state of fear and terror.

In some cases, the harsh treatment they received and the squalid conditions in which they lived were analogous to those of animals.[23] One "new person" who lived in a particularly difficult region of Cambodia recalled, "We were hungry, too tired to wash or clean our clothes, and we lost all sense of hygiene. We didn't care what we ate as long as we could put something in our stomachs. We didn't mind where we had a shit, or who saw us. Disease spread through the village – cholera, malaria, dysentery, diarrhoea and skin infections" (May 1986: 165). Such remarks highlight one of the devastating ways in which difference was manufactured during DK: "new people" were stigmatized as polluting the new "pure" society; because of this marginal position, they were treated badly; poor living conditions, in turn, led to decreased self-respect, hygiene, and health; the resulting dirt, filth, and physical decay reaffirmed and potentially increased the polluting status of the victims.

When local cadre received orders to "weed out" enemies who were "planted within" the cooperatives, they immediately suspected "new people" and other marginal groups (for example, Muslim Chams and ethnic Vietnamese and Chinese who did not act like "real Khmer") whose enemy status could be distinguished by their attitude, behavior, class/ethnic background, and "polluting" appearance. Tens of thousands of these helpless individuals were massacred during DK. One former cadre told me how, in 1977, local forces began to massacre people after his superior at the subdistrict office received a letter that "instructed us to smash enemies: Chams, Vietnamese, capitalists, former Lon Nol workers, intellectuals, and CIA agents" (see also Kiernan 1996: 190). The soldiers who participated in such killings often described their actions as "cleaning up" – a euphemism that was often seemingly affirmed when their victims looked and smelled disgusting. The victims were murdered in various ways. Sometimes they were taken into the nearby jungle or forest and executed with a blow to the back of the head; in other cases, they were driven to large extermination centers where they were killed *en masse*. While it is obviously impossible to describe the full range of experiences and suffering during DK, one survivor of a massacre, Ronnie Yimsut, has written about his horrifying ordeal:

> The thought of coming face to face with death terrified me . . . I thought about escape right then but after long consideration couldn't do it. I didn't have the heart to leave my family, especially my pregnant sister-in-law, who was already a week overdue. Besides, where would I go from here? I would eventually be recaptured and killed. If I was to die, I preferred to die among my loved ones. . . . We knowingly walked toward our death, just like cattle that were being herded to the slaughterhouse. Even the children seemed to know it. But I still had a little hope despite everything I had seen and heard. . . .
>
> We were no more than 300 yards off the main road when they asked us to sit down on the edge of a small shallow canal that ran east to west. Both of our legs were stretched forward, and we had to shut up or they would beat us. . . . People began to plead for their lives. . . . The soldiers screamed for all of us to shut up. They said they wished only to ask a few questions. They said they suspected that there were enemies among our group. They claimed there were Vietnamese agents in our group, which was a bogus claim. . . . It was a premeditated plan. . . . [The soldiers] quickly tied the rest of the people without any problem. By this time it was totally chaotic, and people continued to plead for their lives . . . I had tears in my eyes, not from the blood or the pain, but from the reality that was setting in. I became numb with fear.

> I was beyond horrified when I heard the clobbering begin. Oum's elderly father was next to me, and his upper torso contracted several times before it fell on me. At that moment I noticed a small boy whom I knew well get up and start to call for his mother. And then there was a warm splash on my face and body. I knew that it was definitely not mud. It was the little boy's blood and perhaps brain tissue that got splattered from the impact.
>
> The rest let out only a short but terrifying sound, I could hear their breathing stop. Everything seemed to happen in slow motion, and it was so unreal. I closed my eyes but the terrifying sounds continued to penetrate my ear canals and pierce my eardrums. The first blow to hit me came when I was lying face down on the ground. It hit me just below my right shoulder blade. The next one hit me just above the neck on the right side of my head. I heard fifteen more blows, and the victims landed everywhere on my skinny body.
>
> Fortunately, I didn't feel them until much later. I didn't even remember anything after that . . . I woke to the sound of mosquitoes, which were still buzzing like bees over my body. . . . My eyes were open, but my sight was blurry. I thought I was blind. I was disoriented. I couldn't remember where I was. . . . Suddenly reality set in at full blast and I broke into a heavy sweat. The memories of the event came rushing back and smacked me right in the head. . . . My eyesight came back, but after seeing the scattered bodies lying in every direction, I wished that I was blind. Some were beyond recognition. Some were stripped completely naked. Bloodstains that had already turned a dark color gave the area a new dimension . . . I was a survivor!
>
> (Yimsut 1997: 187–193)

Although most of the victims of the Khmer Rouge never had such a chance for survival, Yimsut's experience provides an illustration of the terror many of them must have felt as they were being killed.

This lethal process of "weeding out" the "enemy" encompassed not only groups marginalized during DK, but also the ranks of the Khmer Rouge themselves. The deep sense of uncertainty that pervaded DK and helped fuel the purges can be directly linked to the dynamics of the mandala principle. From the early 1970s until the Vietnamese invasion in January 1979, the internal political dynamics of the Khmer Rouge were strongly shaped by the party leadership's attempt to establish and maintain control over the country by eliminating potential rivals and regional interests (Kiernan 1996). In a manner that resembles the actions of powerful Angkorean kings, this Pol Pot-led faction repeatedly attempted to increase its power by rewarding loyal clients and undercutting the authority of individuals it regarded as a threat (i.e., by separating these "enemies" from their base of support and/or increasing the Party Center's own strength in suspect regions), usually prior to executing these rivals and their associates.

While political purges within the Communist Party occurred in the 1960s, not until the early 1970s did such killings began to take large numbers of lives (Chandler 1991; Kiernan 1996). After the Lon Nol *coup*, for example, over one thousand

Cambodians who had been receiving training in North Vietnam since the 1950s returned to help fight the Lon Nol regime. Pol Pot's faction distrusted these fellow communists because of their close ties to Vietnam and saw to it that most of them were killed over the next few years. Other Khmer Rouge cadre loyal to Sihanouk, sympathetic to the Vietnamese, or overly lenient on the people, were also eliminated during the pre-DK period. These early purges often foreshadowed the later Khmer Rouge practice of eliminating suspected "traitors" and their "networks."

Upon coming to power after the civil war, the Pol Pot-led central leadership of the Khmer Rouge took a number of steps to consolidate its power (Becker 1986; Chandler 1991; Kiernan 1996). The Party Center transferred three influential regional chiefs – Northern Zone Secretary Koy Thuon, Northeast Zone Secretary Ney Sarann, and Region 25 Secretary Non Suon – to Phnom Penh, thus separating them from their bases of power. (The Khmer Rouge revamped the administrative structure of Democratic Kampuchea, dividing the country into zones which, in turn, were composed of a number of Regions, as illustrated by Figure 11.3.) At the same time, the Party Center rewarded its most loyal regional clients by increasing their power (Kiernan 1996). On the one hand, Mok was given control over the most populated parts of the southwest, including Non Suon's Region 25. Continuing his past practices, Mok placed his relatives in leading positions throughout the Southwest Zone military and political administration and purged Region 25 of cadre loyal to Non Suon. On the other hand, Pauk, the Military Commander of the Northern Zone, was promoted, and replaced Koy Thuon as Zone Secretary, eventually becoming head of the newly formed Central Zone. Like Mok, Pauk appointed relatives to important administrative posts throughout the following year. Finally, the Party Center also established the Revolutionary Army of Kampuchea which, while not displacing regional troops, greatly enhanced the military might of Pol Pot's faction.

Despite such moves, the Party Center continued to perceive itself as threatened by dissent. Several rebellions are thought to have taken place from mid-1975 to mid-1976, though the details are difficult to confirm (Kiernan 1996). In addition to a possible failed *coup* attempt in September 1975, bombs were detonated in Siem Reap city in February 1976. Koy Thuon's subordinates may have been responsible for the bombing. Of even greater concern to the Party Center, however, were a series of explosions that occurred in Phnom Penh in April 1976. Chan Chakrei, a military officer who had ties to East Zone Secretary So Phim and was rumored to have tried to poison Pol Pot, was arrested after being implicated as the leader of the rebellion. After being tortured at Tuol Sleng for two months, Chakrei confessed that he was part of a larger espionage network. This event seems to have convinced the Party Center that they needed to purge their ranks. In his 1978 confession, Deputy Prime Minister Vorn Vet recounted that "After the Chakrei affair . . . the Party decided to arrest the contemptible Touch [Koy Thuon] and the string of intellectuals" (Chandler 1991: 292).

In the months that followed, several prominent Khmer Rouge figures – including Ney Saran, Keo Meas, Non Suon, Prum Nhiem, Keo Moni, Thouch Phoeun – and

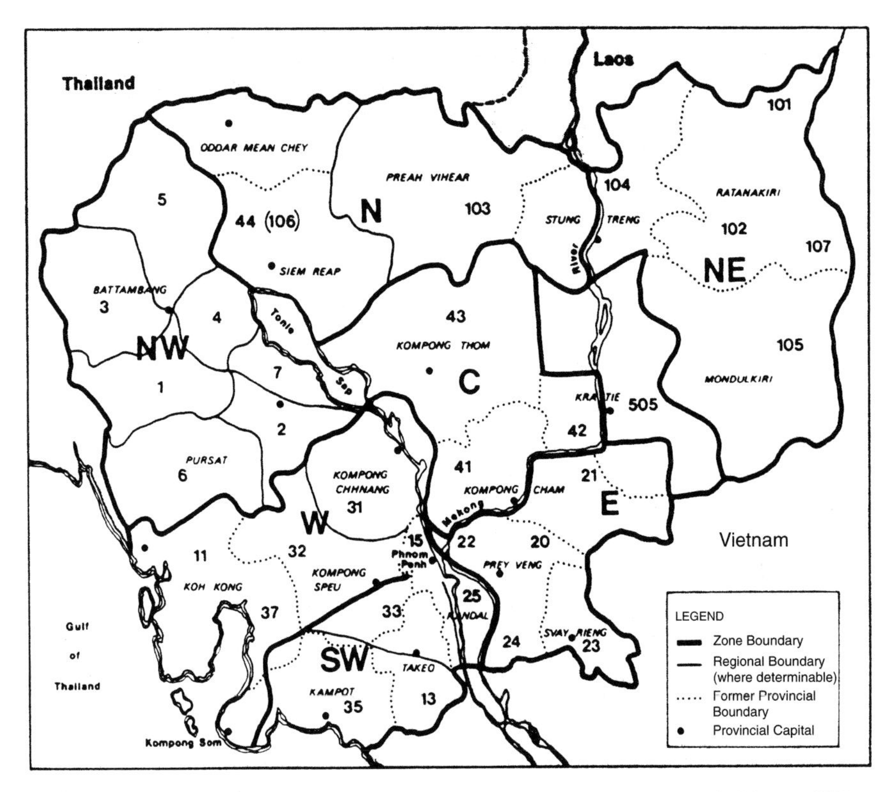

Figure 11.3 Administrative divisions of Democratic Kampuchea, 1975 to 1979.
Source: Map drawn by Margaret Pitt

their clienteles were arrested. These cadre were sent to Tuol Sleng – a former Phnom Penh high school that had been converted into a prison and interrogation center for important "criminals" – where they were interrogated under torture until they confessed their "crimes" and revealed the names of the other members of their "networks." Tuol Sleng became the engine of the Party Center's paranoia. Pol Pot's faction suspected treason and was provided with corroborating evidence by the confessions that were manufactured at Tuol Sleng. As the amount of "evidence" increased, the Party Center's paranoia grew accordingly. Thus, in December 1976, Pol Pot gave the following speech in which he stated that there was a "sickness" in the party that needed to be eradicated:

> In 1976, for example, speaking only of internal Party matters, while we are engaged in a socialist revolution, there is a sickness inside the Party. . . . We cannot locate it precisely. The illness must emerge to be examined. Because the heat of the people's revolution and the heat of the democratic revolution were insufficient at the level of people's struggle and at the level of class

> struggle among all layers of the national democratic revolution, we search for the microbes within the Party without success. . . . Contradictions exist. If we scratch the ground to bury them, they will rot us from within. They will rot society, rot the Party, rot the army. . . . We must expose them.
>
> – Report of Activities of the Party Center According to the General Political Tasks of 1976.
>
> (Chandler *et al.* 1988: 183–184)

Throughout the country, suspicion, mistrust, and purges increased dramatically. The behavior and background of party members were carefully scrutinized for signs of betrayal; in fact, all party members had to fill out an eleven-page biographical questionnaire that included detailed questions about the person's spouse, children, in-laws, siblings, and friends. Such information was used to help "distinguish between patriotism and treason," between friend and foe. Numerous arrests ensued. One woman living in Phnom Penh recalled, "Shocking news came from every unit, from every region, citing instances of schemes and plots. The wave of purges, which until a few months before were thought to be limited . . . swept through the whole country. Cambodia, it was said, was infested with international subversion" (Picq 1989: 100). The rise in paranoia was paralleled by an increase in the number of individuals who were sent to Tuol Sleng; from mid-February to mid-April 1977 alone, 1566 people were incarcerated at Tuol Sleng, a figure approximately equal to the number of arrests throughout 1976 (Kiernan 1996: 350).

This was the atmosphere in which Commerce Minister Koy Thuon was arrested in January 1977. In accordance with a Cambodian notion that it is necessary to "completely destroy" enemies to prevent them from retaliating at a later date, the Party Center attempted to annihilate the entire patronage networks of such suspected traitors. Thuon's clients in both the Commerce Ministry and the Northern Zone, guilty by association, were purged *en masse* after his arrest. Of the 1566 people who were imprisoned at Tuol Sleng between mid-February and mid-April 1977, 240 were commerce ministry officials, 112 civilians were cadre from the Northern Zone, and almost 400 were Northern Zone military personnel (Kiernan 1996: 339, 350). Such arrests were accompanied by the outright execution of tens of thousands of lower-level cadre, soldiers, and civilians from the Northern Zone whose allegiance to the Party Center was suspect. After a second real or staged rebellion broke out in Siem Reap's Region 106 in March 1977, for example, a massive purge took place in which up to 10,000 people may have been executed (Kiernan 1996; Vickery 1984).

As a result of such plots, real or imagined, the Party Center's paranoia rose, and it continued to consolidate power by cleansing its ranks of suspect dissidents and regional rivals. In addition to purging the Northern/Central Zone and executing many high-ranking officials (for example, Phouk Chhay, Phom, Hu Nim, Tiv Ol) and their factions during 1977, Pol Pot's group also increased their efforts to undermine the strength of the secretaries of the Northwest and Eastern Zones – Ros

Nhim and So Phim, respectively. When Ieng Thirith, the Minister for Social Affairs, visited the Northwest Zone in mid-1976, for example, she attributed the poor conditions of the inhabitants to internal enemies: "'Agents had got into our ranks,' she said, 'and they had got into the highest ranks. They had to behave with double faces in order to make as if they were following our line [policies]'" (quoted in Becker 1986: 247). By the end of 1976 and throughout 1977, Southwest cadre loyal to Mok and the Party Center arrived in the Northwest Zone, assumed positions of power, and carried out large purges of local cadre and suspect elements of the civilian population (Kiernan 1996). After having their power base eroded in this manner, Ros Nhim and the remaining members of his patronage circle were finally arrested in June 1978. Mok took over his position as Northwest Zone Secretary. Careful to check the power of even a seemingly loyal client like Mok, the Party Center had earlier sent thousands of Western Zone cadre to work in the Northwest Zone political administration.[24]

Nhim's arrest occurred just eight days after Eastern Zone Secretary So Phim committed suicide. Perhaps the most powerful of the regional chiefs at the beginning of DK, So Phim came under suspicion because of his zone's moderate policies, his long association with Vietnam, and Vietnamese military successes in an offensive beginning in October to November 1977. Moreover, Chan Chakrey, the man who was arrested for the April 1976 uprising in Phnom Penh, was a former subordinate of Phim. Based on the confession of Chakrey and other "traitors" who had been incarcerated, Deuch, the head of Tuol Sleng, informed Pol Pot that the East Zone contained an espionage network which he called "the rubber plantation network" (Kiernan 1996: 322). Pol Pot's faction began to undermine Phim's power. When Phim went to China to receive medical treatment in May 1976, several of his military and civilian officials were arrested. The Party Center also gathered evidence that implicated Phim's client and Secretary of Region 24, Chhouk, in a conspiracy. During the following months, the Southwest cadre began to take over Regions 23 and 24 of the East Zone.

However, not until Phim's power base had been sufficiently eroded and he went to receive medical treatment for a second time in March and April 1978 did the Party Center make its major assault on the East Zone (Kiernan 1996). Phim returned to find that hundreds of his officials had been arrested. During the first three weeks of May, Pauk summoned several high-ranking East Zone military officers to "meetings" and had them executed. Pauk then sent two divisions of Central Zone troops to attack the East Zone. Despite receiving additional support from Center and Southwest Zone forces, Pauk met stiff resistance. Phim, who had been summoned to Phnom Penh, committed suicide as he was about to be arrested. Thousands of his soldiers nevertheless continued to resist the Party Center for months before regrouping in Vietnam.

As the Party Center took control of the East Zone, it conducted a massive purge of local cadre and civilians in which perhaps 250,000 or more of these people having "Khmer bodies with Vietnamese minds" (*khluon khmaer khuor kbal yuon*) were executed (Kiernan 1996: 404). Bunhaeng Ung, for example, secretly witnessed the murder of hundreds of East Zone villagers who were supposedly being relocated. The victims

> were led to the pits where they were slaughtered like animals by striking the backs of their skulls with hoes or lengths of bamboo. Young children and babies were held by the legs, their heads smashed against palm trees and their broken bodies flung beside their dying mothers in the death pits. Some children were thrown in the air and bayoneted while music drowned their screams.
>
> (Stuart-Fox 1985: 142)

Many other inhabitants of the East Zone were sent to distant parts of Cambodia, where they were often singled out for harsh treatment and/or extermination.

One of the primary reasons for the massive purge of the East Zone populace was their perceived ties to Vietnam. The Party Center was extremely anti-Vietnamese and, ostensibly to regain the part of "lower Cambodia" (Kampuchea Krom) which had been annexed by Vietnam over the centuries, had been launching increasingly harsh attacks against Vietnam since early 1977. The DK army's military failures suggested domestic subversion, and the East Zone, which bordered Vietnam and was the site of most of the fighting, was the obvious scapegoat. Ultimately, however, the Party Center's assault upon the East Zone and Vietnam proved its undoing. Repeating a long-standing Cambodian tradition, So Phim's East Zone followers enlisted the patronage of the Vietnamese (who were fed up with Khmer Rouge military raids into their territory) to help them overthrow the DK regime. In just a few weeks, 150,000 Vietnamese troops and perhaps 15,000 Cambodian rebels launched a massive assault that was successful in routing the Khmer Rouge. Phnom Penh was captured on 7 January 1979. By this time, over one and a half million Cambodians had died.

CONCLUSION

In conclusion, I have argued that Cambodian political processes are often characterized by a pulsating center–periphery pattern that has both centripetal and centrifugal tendencies. This dynamic, which I earlier called "the Mandala Principle," emerges from the structure of sociopolitical relations, as individuals attempt to accumulate power and to develop or become part of patronage networks. These pulsating political networks schematically embody the mandala images – in particular, that of the sunshade – that are so prevalent in Cambodian myth, history, and cosmology, thereby providing a key link between myth and politics. Thus, during DK, the party constituted a mandala-like raised center in which an enormous amount of power had been concentrated. This power was distributed down through political patronage circles to the periphery, where cadre exercised immense control over the populace. However, the Party Center never totally trusted many of these clients and became increasingly paranoid over time. Consequently, DK came to manifest this pulsating mandala pattern.

At the beginning of DK, the Pol Pot-led Center took control of a state in which power was diffuse. As Ieng Thirith later commented, "We were not yet in full control in 1976. . . . The power was in the hands of the governors [zone secretaries]. . . . They controlled millions of people and we, the government, we controlled nothing but factories" (quoted in Becker 1986: 247). Like many of their predecessors, Pol Pot's faction responded to this situation by attempting to eliminate opposition and to accumulate more and more power. This centripetal tendency was manifest in several political domains. First, the Khmer Rouge consolidated their control by initiating a number of sociocultural transformations that undermined the primary bonds in the old regime – for example, the Lon Nol military and political apparatus, urban patronage networks, village solidarity, Buddhism, and the family. In the new communist society, loyalty and attachment would ideally be directed first and foremost toward the parent-like state. Second, the Party Center revamped the government's military and political structure to increase its influence. Third, Pol Pot's faction reduced the strength of its rivals by undermining their power and/or through massive purges. Fourth, the Party Center rewarded clients like Mok and Pauk for their loyalty by gradually increasing their authority, although not to the point that these regional chiefs could take over the government.

Despite the overall success of such measures, the Party Center was nevertheless threatened by other leaders who wished to increase their own power. This centrifugal tendency led to attempted rebellion, extreme paranoia, and a great loss of human life. One of the primary institutions that made DK so lethal was the state security apparatus which greatly increased the Party Center's paranoia by finding treasonous plots, real and imagined, both in Phnom Penh and in the Zones. In order to crush dissent, the Party Center destroyed the patronage networks of such rivals as Non Suon, Keo Moni, Koy Thuon, Hu Nim, Chou Chet, So Phim, and Nhim Ros. The Party Center's elimination of such "microbes" often led to the execution not only of incriminated cadre, but also of suspect groups of civilians living under their jurisdiction (frequently "new people" and ethnic minorities). Ultimately, however, the Party Center made a huge miscalculation by antagonizing Vietnam. As the Party Center continued its attempt to take firm control of the zones, it was toppled by a dissident faction that was able to procure the support of this powerful external ally. Despite the extreme centripetal forces at work during DK, the centrifugal tendencies of the Mandala Principle eventually predominated and Pol Pot's umbrella collapsed. The legacy of its genocidal shade, however, continues to plague Cambodians, who have suffered through decades of war, international isolation, political upheaval, trauma, and loss.

ACKNOWLEDGEMENTS

This research was supported by funding from an NSF Graduate Fellowship, an NIH NRSA Fellowship, SEASSI FLAS scholarships, an AAS SEAC small grant, an NSF Doctoral Dissertation Improvement Grant, a scholarship from the Institute for the Study of World Politics, and a grant from the Joint Committee on Southeast Asia of the Social Science Research Council and the American Council of Learned Societies with funds provided by the Andrew W. Mellon Foundation, the Ford Foundation, and the Henry Luce Foundation. The support of these agencies is greatly appreciated. In addition to Tom Singer, I would like to thank Nicole Cooley, Bradd Shore, Robert Paul, Charles Nuckolls, David Chandler, Ben Kiernan, Jim McManus, Margaret Pitt, Judy Ledgerwood, Sophea Mouth, Toni Phim, Rob Borofsky, Fredrik Barth, Frank Reynolds, Kurt Bredenburg, Seng Vanna, May Ebihara, and Ladson Hinton for their helpful comments and suggestions. Of course, the ideas expressed remain my responsibility alone. This chapter is dedicated to the victims of the Khmer Rouge genocide.

NOTES

1 All transliterations are based on Franklin E. Huffman's Franco-Khmer transcription system as reproduced in Heder and Ledgerwood (1996: xvii).

2 I want briefly to address an issue that may arise since much of the following section deals with Buddhism. Cambodia has sometimes been characterized as a "gentle land" full of smiling, kind Buddhists. This stereotype is what led some people in Western countries, forgetful of the Crusades, the witch hunts, the Inquisition, and other atrocities committed in the name of their own religion, to wonder how these "smiling Buddhists" could participate in a brutal genocide. There are several responses to such a question. First, Buddhism was banned during DK, thus undermining traditional Buddhist prosocial norms. Second, while Buddhism certainly promotes an ethic of nonviolence in many contexts, it can also legitimate the use of force against "enemies" who threaten or subvert the socio-moral order. Thus Buddhist monks have sometimes supported violent protests in countries like Cambodia and Sri Lanka (see Chandler 1992; Kapferer 1988; Kiernan and Boua 1982; Tambiah 1992). Third, Buddhism constitutes just one (albeit important) of the many sources from which Cambodian cultural knowledge is derived. The Cambodian religious cosmos alone is a complex amalgam of Buddhist, animist, Hindu, and even Chinese conceptions (Ebihara 1968, 1987). Fourth, Cambodian behavior is informed by numerous non-religious cultural elements (Hinton 1996, 1997). To stereotype Cambodians as "smiling, nonviolent Buddhists" is thus an erroneous oversimplification that ignores the complexities of Buddhism, the Cambodian religious system, and Cambodian culture in general. In fact, it is just this sort of oversimplifying argumentation that led Daniel Goldhagen (1996) to characterize all Germans as zealous anti-Semites. While anti-Semitism clearly played a crucial role in the Holocaust, other factors were also of great importance (see Hinton 1998).

3 See the *Khmer Buddhist Dictionary* (1967: 871) and Headley (1977: 713). On the etymological origins and symbolic dimensions of the mandala, see Jung 1968; Rhys Davids and Stede 1992; Snodgrass 1985; Tambiah 1985; Tucci 1961.

4 As noted earlier, ancient kingdoms located in what is now Cambodia were exposed to and incorporated various elements of Indian religious and political cosmology, which had been brought to the area by Indian traders, travelers, Brahmins, and officials. During the first millennium, Hindu influence was particularly strong in the area. During the thirteenth century, the majority of Cambodians began converting to Theravada Buddhism (Chandler 1992). While Theravada Buddhism remained a dominant force through the twentieth century, Cambodian religion is a complex amalgam of Hindu, Chinese, and animistic beliefs, whose roots pre-date the period of Indian influence. Moreover, Buddhist and Hindu cosmology share many elements, though with slight variations – thus my use of "Hindu-Buddhist" in much of the text.

5 My analysis of the symbolism of the Muchalinda–Buddha sculpture has been greatly assisted by various plate descriptions from a catalogue of ancient Cambodian art (Jessup and Zephir 1997).
6 On the possible origins of the "serpent-umbrella" motif in Buddhist iconography, see Coomaraswamy (1972: 24–27). My analysis of the symbolism of the sunshade, in turn, has been strongly influenced by the work of Coomaraswamy (1938) and Snodgrass (1985). See also Vogel (1972) for variations in the Muchalinda myth and links between the *naga* and the sunshade.
7 The following analysis of the symbolism of the cosmic wheel and lotus draws heavily on Coomaraswamy (1935), Snodgrass (1985) and Zimmer (1946). See also Bosch (1960) and Govinda (1976) for some of the links between the parasol, the lotus, and the cosmic tree.
8 Govinda (1976: 79) explains:

> It must have been an old custom that the head of the community has his seat of honor under the sacred tree in the center of the settlement where public meetings used to take place on religious and other important occasions. Consequently the umbrella, which replaced the tree when the head of the community moved about or presided over similar functions in other places, later on became one of the insignia of royalty. In order to mark distinctions in rank the ceremonial umbrella was doubled or tripled or increased by even greater numbers of umbrellas which were fixed one above the other, thus transforming the umbrella back again into the original tree shape with its numerous layers of branches spreading about the stem and gradually getting shorter towards the top.

9 Briefly, the Four Noble Truths hold that (1) life is suffering, (2) desire is the source of suffering, (3) suffering can be overcome by freeing oneself of desire, and (4) the way to liberate oneself from desire and thus suffering is to follow The Noble Eightfold Path of Right Understanding, Right Thought, Right Speech, Right Action, Right Livelihood, Right Effort, Right Mindfulness, and Right Concentration (see Coomaraswamy 1964).
10 For descriptions of the notion of the *cakravartin* and the portrayal of the Buddha as royal, see Coomaraswamy (1972), Reynolds (1972), Snodgrass (1985), and Tambiah (1976).
11 On the symbolism of the *naga*, see Bloss (1973), Snodgrass (1985), Vogel (1972), and Zimmer (1946).
12 The prosperity that *dhamma* brings is illustrated by accounts of the Buddha's life. After the Buddha is born, for example, all the world benefits from the power of his *dhamma*: "at the moment of incarnation the heavens and the earth showed signs, the dumb spoke, the lame walked, all men began to speak kindly, musical instruments played of themselves, the earth was covered with lotus flowers, and lotuses descended from the sky, and every tree put forth its flowers" (Coomaraswamy 1964: 13–14). Likewise, as the Buddha attains Enlightenment under the Bodhi tree:

> Innumerable wonders were manifest at this supreme hour. The earth quaked six times, and the whole universe was illuminated by the supernatural splendour of the sixfold rays that proceeded from the body of the seated Buddha. Resentment faded from the hearts of all men, all lack was supplied, the sick were healed, the chains of hell were loosed, and every creature of whatsoever sort found peace and rest.
> (Coomaraswamy 1964: 35–36)

13 See Mannikka (1996) for an in-depth discussion of the geometric and symbolic dimensions of Angkor Wat. See also Heine-Geldern (1942) for an analysis of micro- and macrocosmic correspondence.

14 For descriptions of the Cambodian coronation ritual, see Chandler (1992), Heine-Geldern (1942), Porée and Maspero (1938), Snodgrass (1985), and Wales (1977).

15 My account of power and patronage in southeast Asia has, in part, been influenced by the following sources: Anderson (1990), Errington (1989), Hanks (1962), Mulder (1994), and Tannenbaum (1995). See Hinton (1997) for a more detailed description of power, patronage, and suspicion in Cambodian society.

16 This Cambodian conception of power as amoral and as manifest in the mandala structure of patronage relations (see below) resonates with Jung's (1968, 1969) notion that archetypal structures are, in themselves, morally neutral (Ladson Hinton, personal communication). Just as power is used in good or bad ways, so too do archetypal structures take on positive and negative valences as they are psychically expressed.

17 On royal and contemporary patronage in Cambodia, see Chandler 1992; Hinton 1997; Mabbett 1978; Marston 1997; Osborne 1966.

18 On factionalism in Angkorean history, see Chandler 1992; Cœdès 1968; Hall 1981; Wolters 1982.

19 Article II of the United Nations Genocide Convention defines genocide as "acts committed with intent to destroy, in whole or in part, a national, ethnic, racial or religious group, as such." Given the conceptual vagueness of this definition, there has been some debate about whether or not the violence which took place in Cambodia can be accurately classified as genocidal (Kiernan 1993). I believe that it is appropriate to use this term with reference to Cambodia because ethnic groups (Muslim Chams and ethnic Vietnamese, Chinese, and Thai) and religious groups (Buddhists and Christians) were subject to systematic elimination, through both outright execution and extremely harsh living conditions (see also Kiernan 1993, 1996). Moreover, people have noted that the original Genocide Convention definition excluded political groups and social classes because of pressure from countries like the Soviet Union that feared being indicted. To correct for this bias, many genocide scholars have redefined genocide in a more inclusive manner. Thus Fein defines genocide as: "sustained purposeful action by a perpetrator to physically destroy a collectivity directly or indirectly, through interdiction of the biological and social reproduction of group members, sustained regardless of the surrender or lack of threat offered by the victim" (1990: 24). Given the purges, the attack on "new people," and the execution of members of the Lon Nol military and government, DK clearly classifies as a genocide within such a broad definition. See Andreopoulos (1994) for an examination of the historical and conceptual issues surrounding the use of the term "genocide."

20 See Nuon Chea 1987; Pol Pot 1977; Summers 1987.

21 The Khmer Rouge seem to have dramatically mis-estimated the numbers in each of these groups in asserting that 70 per cent of the population could be classified as poor peasants. Scholars have suggested that the bulk of the peasantry were self-sufficient middle peasants and perhaps only 20 per cent poor peasants (Summers 1987). While many peasants did support the Khmer Rouge, others did not, particularly after work and living conditions began to deteriorate. This lack of popular support contributed to the downfall of the Khmer Rouge (Frieson 1993).

22 This statement was made to me while I was conducting ethnographic fieldwork on violence in Cambodia in 1992 and from 1994 to 1995.

23 One woman recalled how a soldier told her that it was better for her sick mother to die "than a cow. The cows are good. They help us a lot and do not eat rice. They are much better than you pigs!" (Moyer 1991: 123). Another time, the same woman heard soldiers shout the following at "new people": "Prisoners of war! You are pigs. We have suffered much. Now you are our prisoners and you must suffer" (Moyer 1991: 81). See also Criddle and Mam (1987: 70) and Ngor (1987: 202).

24 The Western Zone had been the site of an earlier purge, one that was foreshadowed

by Nuon Chea's mid-1977 comment that "enemies and various classes" were in control of some parts of the Zone (Carney 1989: 86; Kiernan 1996: 347). While some local cadre were purged in 1977, it was not until March 1978 that Zone Secretary Chou Chet and his faction were arrested after allegedly plotting to rebel against the Center. Chet's two rivals in the Zone, his deputy Pal and military commander Soeung, assumed control. During the next few months, Pal and Soeung, both of whom were loyal to the Center, trained thousands of new cadre. Many of these cadre were sent to work in the Northwest Zone.

BIBLIOGRAPHY

Anderson, B. (1990) *Language and Power: Exploring Political Cultures in Indonesia*, Ithaca: Cornell University Press.

Andreopoulos, G. J. (ed.) (1994) *Genocide: Conceptual and Historical Dimensions*, Philadelphia: University of Pennsylvania Press.

Appadurai, A. (1998) "Dead Certainty: Ethnic Violence in the Era of Globalization," *Public Culture* 10(2): 225–247.

Becker, E. (1986) *When The War Was Over: Cambodia's Revolution and the Voices of its People*, New York: Touchstone.

Bloss, L. W. (1973) "The Buddha and the Naga: A Study in Buddhist Folk Religiosity," *History of Religions* 13(1): 36–53.

Bosch, F. D. K. (1960) *The Golden Germ: An Introduction to Indian Symbolism*, The Netherlands: Mouton & Co.

Brewster, E. H. (1926) *The Life of Gotama The Buddha*, New York: E. P. Dutton.

Bun Chân Mol (1973) *Châret Khmaer [Cambodian Character]*, Phnom Penh: Nokor Thom.

Carney, T. (1989) "The Organization of Power," in K. J. Jackson (ed.) *Cambodia 1975–1978: Rendezvous with Death*, Princeton, NJ: Princeton University Press.

Chandler, D. P. (1991) *The Tragedy of Cambodian History: Politics, War, and Revolution since 1945*, New Haven, CT: Yale University Press.

—— (1992) *A History of Cambodia*, Boulder, CO: Westview.

Chandler, D. P., Kiernan, B. and Boua, C. (eds) (1988) *Pol Pot Plans the Future: Confidential Leadership Documents from Democratic Kampuchea, 1976–1977*. New Haven, CT: Yale Center for International and Area Studies.

Chandler, D. P., Kiernan, B., and Muy Hong Lim (1976) *The Early Phases of Liberation in Northwestern Cambodia: Conversations with Peang Sophi*, Melbourne: Monash University Centre of Southeast Asian Studies Working Papers.

Chou Ta-Kuan (1987) *The Customs of Cambodia*, Bangkok: The Siam Society.

Cœdès, G. (1968) *The Indianized States of Southeast Asia*, trans. S. Brown Cowing, Honolulu: University of Hawaii Press.

Coomaraswamy, A. K. (1935) *Elements of Buddhist Iconography*, Cambridge, MA: Harvard University Press.

—— (1938) "Usnisa and Chatra," *The Poona Orientalist* 3(1): 1–19.

—— (1964) *Buddha and the Gospel of Buddhism*, New York: Harper & Row.

—— (1972) *The Origin of the Buddha Image*, New Delhi: Munshiram Manoharlal.

Criddle, J. D. and Teeda Butt Mam (1987) *To Destroy You is no Loss: The Odyssey of a Cambodian Family*, New York: Anchor Books.

Ebihara, M. M. (1968) "Svay, A Khmer Village in Cambodia," unpublished Ph.D. dissertation, Columbia University.

—— (1987) "Khmer Religion," in M. Eliade (ed.) *The Encylopedia of Religion, 8*, New York: Macmillan.

Errington, S. (1989) *Meaning and Power in a Southeast Asian Realm*, Princeton, NJ: Princeton University Press.

FBIS (Foreign Broadcast Information Service) (1978) *Asia and Pacific Report*, Springfield, VA: US Department of Commerce, 14 April: H3.

Fein, H. (1990) "Genocide: A Sociological Perspective," *Current Sociology* 38(1): 1–126.

Frieson, K. (1993) "Revolution and Rural Response in Cambodia, 1970–1975," in B. Kiernan (ed.) *Genocide and Democracy in Cambodia: The Khmer Rouge, the United Nations and the International Community*, New Haven, CT: Yale University Southeast Asia Studies.

Goldhagen, D. J. (1996) *Hitler's Willing Executioners: Ordinary Germans and the Holocaust*, New York: Alfred A. Knopf.

Govinda, L. A. (1976) *Psycho-cosmic Symbolism of the Buddhist Stupa*, Emeryville, CA: Dharma Publishing.

Hall, D. G. E. (1981) *A History of South-East Asia*, London: Macmillan.

Hanks, L. M. (1962) "Merit and Power in the Thai Social Order," *American Anthropologist* 64(6): 1247–1261.

—— (1975) "The Thai Social Order as Entourage and Circle," in G. W. Skinner and A. T. Kirsch (eds) *Change and Persistence in Thai Society: Essays in Honor of Lauriston Sharp*, New York: Guilford Press.

Headley, R. K., Jr. (1977) *Cambodian–English Dictionary, Volume I and II*, Washington, DC: The Catholic University of America Press.

Heder, S. and Ledgerwood, J. (eds) (1996) *Propaganda, Politics, and Violence in Cambodia: Democratic Transition under United Nations Peace-Keeping*. Armonk, NY: M.E. Sharpe.

Heine-Geldern, R. (1942) "Conceptions of State and Kingship in Southeast Asia," *The Far Eastern Quarterly* 2(1): 15–30.

Hinton, A. L. (1996) "Agents of Death: Explaining the Cambodian Genocide in Terms of Psychosocial Dissonance," *American Anthropologist* 98: 818–831.

—— (1997) "Cambodia's Shadow: An Examination of the Cultural Origins of Genocide," unpublished Ph.D. dissertation, Emory University.

—— (1998) "Why Did the Nazis Kill? Anthropology, Genocide, and the Goldhagen Controversy," *Anthropology Today* 14(5): 9–15.

Jessup, H. I. and Zephir, T. (eds) (1997) *Sculpture of Angkor and Ancient Cambodia: Millennium of Glory*, Washington, DC: National Gallery of Art.

Jung, C. G. (1968) *Psychology and Alchemy, Volume 12 of the Collected Works of C. G. Jung* trans. R. F. C. Hull, Princeton, NJ: Princeton University Press.

—— (1969) *The Archetypes and the Collective Unconscious, Volume 9, Part 1 of the Collected Works of C. G. Jung*, trans. R. F. C. Hull, Princeton, NJ: Princeton University Press.

Kapferer, B. (1988) *Legends of People, Myths of State: Violence, Intolerance, and Political Culture in Sri Lanka and Australia*, Washington, DC: Smithsonian Institute Press.

Khmer Buddhist Dictionary (1967) *Vochânanukram Khmaer*, Phnom Penh: Buddhist Institute.

Kiernan, B. (ed.) (1993) *Genocide and Democracy in Cambodia: The Khmer Rouge, the United Nations, and the International Community*, Monograph Series 41, New Haven, CT: Yale University Southeast Asian Studies.

—— (1996) *The Pol Pot Regime: Race, Power, and Genocide in Cambodia under the Khmer Rouge, 1975–79*, New Haven, CT: Yale University Press.

Kiernan, B. and Chanthou Boua (1982) *Peasants and Politics in Kampuchea, 1942–1981*, Armonk, NY: M. E. Sharpe.
Ledgerwood, J. (1996) "Politics and Gender: Negotiating Conceptions of the Ideal Woman in Present Day Cambodia," *Asia Pacific Viewpoint* 37(2): 139–152.
Locard, H. (1996) *Le "Petit Livre Rouge" de Pol Pot ou Les Paroles de l'Angkar*, Paris: Editions L'Harmattan.
Mabett, I. (1978) "Kingship in Angkor," *Journal of the Siam Society* 66(2): 1–58.
Mabbett, I. and Chandler, D. (1995) *The Khmers*, Oxford: Blackwell.
Mannikka, E. (1996) *Angkor Wat: Time, Space, and Kingship*, Honolulu: University of Hawaii Press.
Marston, J. (1997) "Cambodia 1991–1994: Hierarchy, Neutrality and Etiquettes of Discourse," Ph.D. dissertation, University of Washington.
May, S. (1986) *Cambodian Witness: The Autobiography of Someth May*, New York: Random House.
Moyer, N. (1991) *Escape from the Killing Fields: One Girl Who Survived the Cambodian Holocaust*, Grand Rapids, MI: Zondervan.
Mulder, N. (1994) *Inside Thai Society: An Interpretation of Everyday Life*, Bangkok: Editions Duang Kamol.
Ngor, H. (1987) *A Cambodian Odyssey*, New York: Macmillan.
Nuon Chea (1987) "Statement of the Communist Party of Kampuchea to the Communist Workers' Party of Denmark, July 1978," *Journal of Communist Studies* March: 19–30.
Osborne, M. (1966) "Notes on Early Cambodian Provincial History: Isanapura & Sambhupura," *France-Asie* 186: 443–449.
Picq, L. (1989) *Beyond the Horizon: Five Years with the Khmer Rouge*, New York: St Martin's Press.
Pol Pot (1977) *Long Live the 17th Anniversary of the Communist Party of Kampuchea*, Phnom Penh: Ministry of Foreign Affairs.
Porée, G. and Maspero, E. (1938) *Traditions and Customs of the Khmer*, Paris: Payot.
Reynolds, Frank (1972) "The Two Wheels of Dhamma: A Study of Early Buddhism," in G. Obeyesekere, F. Reynolds, and B. Smith (eds) *The Two Wheels of Dhamma: Essays on the Theravada Tradition in India and Ceylon*, Chambersburg, PA: American Academy of Religion.
Rhys Davids, T. W. and Stede, W. (1992) *The Pali Text Society's Pali–English Dictionary*, London: Cohen & West.
Roveda, V. (1998) *Khmer Mythology: Secrets of Angkor*, New York: Weatherhill.
Snodgrass, A. (1985) *The Symbolism of the Stupa*, Ithaca, NY: Cornell University Southeast Asia Program.
Sokundara, P. and Chaumeau, C. (1998) "Pomp and Pageantry at Kathen Ceremony," *Phnom Penh Post*, 16 October: 16.
Stuart-Fox, M. (1985) *The Murderous Revolution: Life & Death in Pol Pot's Kampuchea Based on the Personal Experiences of Bunheang Ung*, Chippendale, Australia: Alternative Publishing Cooperative Limited.
Summers, L. (1987) "The CPK: Secret Vanguard of Pol Pot's Revolution: A Comment on Nuon Chea's Statement," *Journal of Communist Studies* March: 8–18.
Swearer, D. K. (1995) *The Buddhist World of Southeast Asia*, Albany: State University of New York Press.
Tambiah, S. J. (1976) *World Conqueror and World Renouncer: A Study of Buddhism and*

Polity in Thailand against a Historical Background, New York: Cambridge University Press.
—— (1985) *Culture, Thought, and Social Action: An Anthropological Perspective*, Cambridge, MA: Harvard University Press.
—— (1992) *Buddhism Betrayed?: Religion, Politics, and Violence in Sri Lanka*, Chicago, IL: University of Chicago Press.
Tannenbaum, N. (1995) *Who Can Compete Against the World? Power-protection and Buddhism in Shan Worldview*, Ann Arbor: Association for Asian Studies.
Thion, S. (1993) *Watching Cambodia: Ten Paths to Enter the Cambodian Tangle*, Bangkok: White Lotus.
Tucci, G. (1961) *The Theory and Practice of the Mandala: With Special Reference to the Modern Psychology of the Subconsious*, trans. A. Houghton, London: Rider & Company.
Vickery, M. (1984) *Cambodia 1975–1982*, Boston: South End.
Vogel, J. Ph. (1972) *Indian Serpent-Lore or The Nagas in Hindu Legend and Art*, Varanasi, Dehli: Indological Book House.
Wales, H. G. Q. (1977) *The Universe Around Them: Cosmology and Cosmic Renewal in Indianized South-east Asia*, London: Arthur Probsthain.
Wolters, O. W. (1982) *History, Culture, and Region in Southeast Asian Perspectives*, Singapore: Institute of Southeast Asian Studies.
Yimsut, R. (1997) "The Tonle Sap Lake Massacre," in Kim K. DePaul (ed.) and Dith Pran (compiler) *Children of Cambodia's Killing Fields: Memoirs by Survivors*, New Haven, CT: Yale University Press.
Zimmer, H. (1946) *Myths and Symbols in Indian Art and Civilization*, ed. J. Campbell, Princeton: Princeton University Press.

The one

Chapter 12

Practicing politics in the economic myth[1]

Betty Sue Flowers

One day, as President Thomas Jefferson was riding into Washington, he stopped to greet a stranger on the road. They fell into a conversation about politics, and the man began to criticize Jefferson, particularly in relation to his private life, about which stories were circulating. What's new?

> "Do you know the President personally?" Jefferson asked the man.
> "No, and I wouldn't want to," he answered.
> "Will you go to his house tomorrow at ten if I promise to be there?"
> After hesitating a minute, the man said, "Yes, I will."

Jefferson rode off, and the man soon guessed his identity. But he showed up, and when Jefferson appeared, he said, "I have called, Mr Jefferson, to apologize for having said to a stranger. . . ."

"Hard things," Jefferson interrupted, "of an imaginary being who is no relation of mine" (adapted from Hall 1981: 20–21).

For most of us, the President – any president – is an imaginary being, the main character of a story told by journalists. But I'm not bashing journalists, because most of us would tell the same kind of story they always tell. Why? Because of the economic myth in which we are embedded.

Four myths have shaped this society: the hero myth, the religious myth, the democratic (or Enlightenment) myth, and the economic myth. By myth, of course, I don't mean a story that is untrue, but a story that we accept uncritically, that we breathe in unconsciously, like air. That story now is an economic myth.

The economic myth may be true, or it may not be. What makes it powerful is that we use it to explain what reality is and what is valuable. We appeal to "the bottom line" to win arguments; we see the history of the world as an economic history, not as the march of great men across a stage or as the working out of the plan of God; in the US we win elections by offering not "a covenant" with America (a term coming from our religious myth) but a "contract" with America.

Whatever form the economic myth takes, it displays four central characteristics:

1 *Its medium is numbers and pictures.*
2 *It honors quantity over quality.* Unlike the democratic myth, in which truth

can arise from any quarter, in the economic myth, truth *does* arise from every quarter, through counting or polling. Power lies in the numbers.

3 *Its ideal is growth.* The economic myth has at its base the ideal of growth: bigger – or more – is better. In addition, we tend to think of this growth as necessarily involving competition. Implicit in much of our language about growth is a kind of early Darwinian notion of natural selection: the strong survive and grow, while the weak are inevitably, naturally (and therefore rightly) weeded out. There are stories within stories here. For example, woodcutting in Malaysia adds to GDP (Gross Domestic Product), making Malaysia eligible for international loans. Damage done to soil, which affects long-term economic viability, is not counted against the GDP. These so-called "externalities" are not taken into account in the GDP story. That is one reason economists say we are doing great and ordinary folk often feel we are not.

4 *Its motivating power is self-interest.* Within this economic myth, the story of the President – any President, or even a Presidential candidate – has a very simple plot. He goes up in the polls; he goes down in the polls. Even when the event being narrated is the signing of a complicated treaty or bill, the underlying story is simply this: "Does this event make his numbers go up or down?" When people ask, "How is the President doing?" they're not asking for a comment on his health or his record in passing legislation or furthering world peace. They're asking, "Are his numbers up or down?"

But this is a very dull plot. And television, especially, has to keep its viewers entertained in order to sell advertising. Television news is, after all, a business. So the story has to be spiced up with a little dash of hero myth thrown in: conflict, action. This poses a problem with politics because politics is, essentially, talking heads. It is the conflict of ideas, not of men. The archetypal conflict of men is war. But you can't *see* the conflict of ideas, so ideas have to be turned into personalities in order that we can have visible conflict. Put another way: ideas bore; war entertains. Entertainment sells.

Another difficulty of practicing politics within an economic myth is that most political stories cannot be told as news – only the outcome of politics can be seen as news. What went into the signing of the treaty or the passing of the bill – all the talks and deals and compromises – cannot be contained in a short summary.

News happens fast. News is "new" – the unusual. "Once again today, nobody in our neighborhood was bitten by a dog" is not news. But that's how you build community: by creating the structures and institutions that result in nobody being bitten, day after day. Politics in the best sense is like community: it is the building of relationships and trust over time. This is a slow story – it is slow news – not good sound byte material.

A third difficulty with the practice of politics in an economic myth is that it does not allow for noble self-sacrifice – or, more precisely, it does not allow for the *stories* of noble self-sacrifice. Why? Because the motivator in the economic myth is self-interest. "Self-sacrifice" belongs to the hero narrative or the religious narrative.

Every time someone does something that might look like self-sacrifice, journalists are bound by the economic myth through which we see reality to ask the question: "Where's the self-interest? What's the hidden agenda? What's in it for him?"

So here's the *necessary* plot for the story of presidential politics in an economic myth: the main character, motivated by self-interest, fights other characters, while onlookers, like Romans in the Coliseum, point their thumbs up or down. Meanwhile, real political business – the conversations and compromises that lead to the solution of problems – is deeply affected by the necessity to present this gladiatorial entertainment and by the necessity for the gladiators themselves to raise money to pay for it.

There is a further complication in this for us Americans. Our hero myth is deeply influenced by our religious narrative. That means that we are always tempted to turn any conflict into a fight of good and evil, or good guys and bad guys, white hats and black hats. The two greatest heroes of the *Iliad*, Hector and Achilles, are brave men, but they are both deeply flawed. Yet our version of the hero myth, shaped by the forces of our religious myth, makes it very difficult for us to tolerate personal flaws – sin – in our heroes. The virtues of perfection and purity, so important to the religious narrative, cripple the production of any real story in the political arena because our religious version of the hero story does not allow for compromise. Add together these three ingredients – our disdain for compromise, our insistence on purity, and our assumption that everyone's motives are always grounded in self-interest – and you end up with the familiar story: a hero myth of good guys and bad guys, both motivated by a quality our religious myth defines as bad: self-interest. So, underneath, the good guy is a bad guy too. The resulting plot is the political movie we see every day: two bad guys slinging eight-second sound bytes at each other's character. Who wins depends not on some objective criterion of truth, or the battle of the issues, but who scores loudest on the applause meter.

No wonder we give politics and the presidency such bad reviews. We complain a lot about lack of leadership. But I think sometimes our complaints are just an excuse. I am reminded of a friend of mine who was trying to get her two teenage daughters to clean up their room. After numerous admonitions and threats, one of her daughters looked up and said, "Mom, if you were a more charismatic leader, you could get us to clean up our room."

If only we had a more charismatic leader, we could clean up our act – or if only the journalists would behave, or the voters, or the lobbyists. But I think we are wasting precious time trying to fix the blame for the sorry state of politics on these various groups. The real question is: how can we create a better story about who we are and who we might become as a nation?

This better story is critically important – more important than a better choice of leader. It is interesting that whenever one myth breaks down, we look for a leader. Perhaps it's time we grew up and looked at our broken-down myth and consciously, for the first time in human history, worked together to create a better one.

How do we do this? First, we must learn to read the news mythologically. For example: in the summer of 1995, an international oil company attempted to dump a no-longer-functioning oil platform into the ocean and was prevented from doing so by a worldwide protest led by a prominent environmental group. Sales of the company's gasoline plummeted as dramatic footage of protesters occupying the platform was televised and as some of the company's service stations were attacked. Later, the environmental organization apologized, acknowledging that the solution which the oil company had devised for getting rid of the platform was actually the best one for the environment. All three of the parties involved – the oil company, the environmental group, and the media – wanted what was best for the environment. What happened, politically, to create a situation that was dangerously explosive, even though the facts were there for anyone to examine?

What happened, in part, is that the three participants in the drama were acting from within different mythological frameworks. The oil company leaders were speaking from within the Enlightenment myth – "Come let us reason together" – trotting out scientific facts and figures and making a logical argument for their best possible solution. The environmental group was operating within a religious myth, in which there are absolute values (such as not polluting the ocean) and where compromise is not tolerated. The television reporters were operating within the usual hero myth – in this case, using the particularly compelling model of David and Goliath to dramatize a situation in which it would be easy to tell who was the good guy and who was the bad. In such a situation, political solutions are impossible until one of the actors shifts mythological frameworks – or until the public sees that the impasse lies at a level other than the simple facts.

The second way we could work together to improve our politics is to realize that some conversations are impossible in the economic myth. We cannot expect the economic myth to foster the ideals of individual responsibility that the hero myth embodied; or to encourage the ideals of community the religious myth promoted; or to emphasize the pursuit of a common good that the democratic myth supported. Yet these ideals of responsibility, community, and the common good are absolutely necessary for the health of the civic spirit. But we cannot simply return to the old myths, no matter how many movements in their direction we try to beat the drums for. These myths don't hold up for us now. We don't want to look up to the chosen few as our heroes; we don't want to re-introduce the sense of division and intolerance that a ruling religious myth so often fosters; and we are rightly suspicious of the idea of one common good because we know how much suffering has been caused in our diverse society by insisting that our identity fit one mold. For example, we can no longer blindly tell our history from the point of view of Columbus. We don't have one story about who we are any more, so how can we articulate a common good?

The philosopher Herbert Spencer is credited with saying that civilization is a progress from an indefinite, incoherent homogeneity toward a definite, coherent heterogeneity. We need a new myth that takes into account our diversity but that makes it coherent – that allows us to stick together in the name of a higher ideal and to work for a common good, but at the same time to celebrate our individuality. We need a higher organization of our complexity. We need a new myth of who we are – and who we might be.

But how do we make a new myth? The first thing to understand about myths is that we cannot simply make them. They arise out of what is there. We cannot hold up a myth of community and wait for it to take hold. We have to work within the myth of our time, however impoverished it seems to us. We have to look at the opportunities offered by the economic myth within which we live.

Here are three of them:

Opportunity 1: The economic myth, because it operates through numbers and images rather than language, is the first truly global myth.

Opportunity 2: The economic myth supports a systems view of the world. When everyone's business becomes everyone else's business too, our interconnections have to be figured into our decision making. It is ironic that some of the downsizing in corporations that has resulted in the loss of jobs is the consequence of a call for tighter operations from big investors – often workers' pension funds. We increasingly see the need to look at the environment as an interconnected system, to look at our families in terms of systems theory, and to look at biological life itself as a complexity of interacting systems. We are all woven into the same net, and if we ever truly grasp the significance of this, our short-term them-versus-us habit of formulating problems will have to change. From an economic perspective, the task of building the future must take everything into account. This means that we work not simply for an ideal of purity or perfection, but for *wholeness*. We work not for control, but for coherence of parts – for what might be called "harmony." We have not yet begun to understand, even at the level of the individual, what an ideal of wholeness might mean.

In the case of the economic myth, the whole world is not the United States, but that blue pearl of the earth as seen from space – the first view of the whole we have ever seen, an image now so familiar all over the globe that it has profoundly influenced our story about who we are, especially in relation to the environment. Schoolchildren all over the globe take daily measurements of air and water quality and send their numbers to centralized computers for scientific analysis. This picture and these numbers suggest a story about self-interest, the driving force of the economic myth, that is more complex and interconnected than any story we have ever told before as human beings. How well we practice politics within this first truly global myth – the economic myth – will determine our future.

Opportunity 3: The economic myth – if seen as a myth – allows for the continual re-creation of possibility. The economic myth is a myth in the sense that it is a context for values organized around a supreme value, or "reality" – in this case, self-interest, whether "self" is defined as a solitary individual or a specific group. But unlike the hero myth with stories of representative individuals, or the religious myth with its many stories of fall and redemption, or the myth of Enlightenment, with its story of progress, the economic myth has no authoritative story. This means that instead of holding the story of who we are as a belief, we can hold it *self-consciously* as a fiction, as a myth, as an ideal. We don't have to defend it against change. We can let it evolve as we tell it and live in the present that is created by the future we tell.

The stories we tell ourselves about who we are and what is possible are extremely important. We need to tell better stories than we are telling now. For example, if we choose, we can declare this to be a time like that when our nation was founded – an amazing opportunity, right now, at this moment in history.

Tom Paine expressed the feeling of possibility in his time, and some would say that Paine's expression of possibility, in his pamphlet *Common Sense* (1776/1986), was what made coherent the ideas that resulted in the American Revolution. *Common Sense* helped to create the public consensus out of which came the possibility of a new basis for government, as expressed in the Declaration of Independence; the Declaration of Independence then led, ultimately, to a new form of government, as expressed in the Constitution. Perhaps, like Paine, we can declare, "We have it in our power to begin the world over again. A situation, similar to the present, hath not happened since the days of Noah until now. The birth-day of a new world is at hand." (Paine 1776/1986: 120).

NOTES

1 This chapter on politics and the economic myth grew from my earlier monograph on "The Economic Myth," Center for International Business Education and Research, University of Texas at Austin (1995), and from my work on myth represented in *Exploring Sustainable Development: World Business Council for Sustainable Development Global Scenarios 2000–2050* (Geneva, 1997).

BIBLIOGRAPHY

Hall, D. (1981) *The Oxford Book of American Literary Anecdotes*, New York and Oxford: Oxford University Press.

Paine, T. (1776/1986) *Common Sense*, London: Penguin.

Chapter 13

Cultural transition and spiritual transformation

From Alexander the Great to cyberspace

David Ulansey

> Let us suppose that in modern Europe the faithful had deserted the Christian churches to worship Allah or Brahma, to follow the precepts of Confucius or Buddha, or to adopt the maxims of the Shinto; let us imagine a great confusion of all the races of the world in which Arabian mullahs, Chinese scholars, Japanese bonzes, Tibetan lamas and Hindu pundits would be preaching fatalism and predestination . . . a confusion in which all those priests would erect temples of exotic architecture in our cities and celebrate their disparate rites therein. Such a dream, which the future may perhaps realize, would offer a pretty accurate picture of the religious chaos in which the ancient world was struggling before the reign of Constantine.
>
> Cumont 1906[1]

"Such a dream, which the future may perhaps realize. . . ." As I sit in front of my computer at the turn of the millennium, aware that in any large American or European city I can expect to find a Tibetan Buddhist temple, a Sufi retreat center, a Zen meditation hall, the office of a Chinese acupuncturist, a communal home of Hari Krishna devotees, and a store selling the visionary art of tribal shamans, it is surprising to realize that as recently as 1906 the great Belgian classicist Franz Cumont could only "dream" of such a future. More significant, though, is the fact that most of Cumont's contemporaries would not have been able even to dream of such a future. For Cumont was able to imagine the possibility of the global culture of our own time only because he was knowledgeable about a previous epoch when a remarkably similar situation existed.

The epoch to which I refer is that which is usually called the "Hellenistic" age: the period that began with the conquests of Alexander the Great in the late fourth century BCE. While the Hellenistic age as a strictly chronological division is often understood as coming to an end with the emergence of the Roman empire toward the end of the first century BCE, historians also recognize that the culture of the Roman empire was in many ways merely a continuation of Hellenistic cultural patterns. Thus the expression "Hellenistic culture" is often used to name the large cultural system encompassing the Mediterranean and Near East from the time of Alexander the Great until the Roman empire's conversion to Christianity: as it is often put, "from Alexander to Constantine."

In the discussion which follows, I will suggest that an understanding of the Hellenistic age can provide a crucial insight into the nature and dynamics of our own contemporary culture. While I will not be focusing on the immediate political implications that such insight might have for our present circumstances, what follows will, I hope, contribute to an understanding of politics in the larger sense as consisting in the evolution of the structures by which individuals are related to the societies of which they are members. Without such a larger understanding, I believe, any vision of enduring solutions to our current political problems must remain hopelessly myopic.

The defining quality of Hellenistic culture was the unification and intermingling of previously separate and autonomous political and cultural entities – city states, nations, tribes – in a single new imperial system. This unification was the result of the conquests of Alexander the Great, the outcome of which was that what had formerly been a vast collection of diverse societies in the Mediterranean and Near East were absorbed into a single Greek (and subsequently Roman) imperial order.

Living now in our own time of cultural and political unification and intermingling – this time on a planetary scale – it is extremely valuable to possess in Hellenistic culture a case study of a previous period in which a similar process took place; for in the Hellenistic age we are able to discern a variety of effects of cultural unification which seem to be emerging once again in our own world. Or perhaps it would be more precise to say "re-emerging," since of course the history of Hellenistic culture is not simply an isolated case study in cultural dynamics, but simultaneously an investigation of the very roots of our own modern society and worldview. Nowhere is this more clearly demonstrated than in the fact that the most enduring product of the Hellenistic age was the new religion of Christianity, a system of belief, symbol, and ritual that today still occupies a central role in our cultural life and psychological circumstances.

One of the most powerful effects of the Hellenistic political unification was the fundamental shift it produced in people's sense of personal identity. Up until the Hellenistic period, the structure of one's identity was centered in the group – tribe, polis, nation – of which one was a member. This does not mean, of course, that people were entirely unaware of their own individuality, but it is the case that the sense of belonging to a group was decisively more in the foreground of consciousness than it is today.

One of the clearest examples of the pre-Hellenistic sense of group identity can be found among the ancient Israelites. At the center of Israelite mythology was the story of the patriarch Jacob and his twelve sons. According to this myth, each of Jacob's sons was the original ancestor of one of the twelve tribes which made up the nation of Israel, and thus every Israelite was ultimately descended from a single person: Jacob. In fact, the book of Genesis contains a story in which Jacob receives a second name: after battling all night with an angel, Jacob is victorious, and in recognition of this is given the new name Israel ("he contended with God"). The nation of Israel itself, therefore, is named after its father Jacob/Israel – the ancestor of all Israelites – and the Hebrew Bible is subsequently permeated with instances in which Jacob comes to be a symbolic figure representing the entire nation.

The process in which Jacob is symbolically transformed into the nation of Israel is described in Genesis 46, where we find the following passage:

> God spoke to Israel [Jacob] in a vision at night. "Jacob, Jacob," he said. "I am here," he replied. "I am God, the God of your father," he continued. "Do not be afraid of going down to Egypt, for I will make you a great nation there."[2]

Here we see the core image of a metamorphosis in which Jacob becomes transformed, in the alchemical crucible of Egypt, into the nation of Israel.

This belief that the nation of Israel was in some mysterious sense a single person pervaded the life of the Israelites. One central manifestation of this was in the relationship between the Israelites and their god Yahweh.

This relationship was always understood as existing fundamentally between Yahweh and the nation as a whole, rather than between Yahweh and individual Israelites. The great covenants that Yahweh decreed took the form of requirements that the entire nation had to obey, in return for which Yahweh would guarantee that the nation as a whole would flourish. Thus, for example, it was forbidden for individuals to erect sacrificial altars for Yahweh – rather, Yahweh commanded that sacrifices could only be made in one central place (the temple in Jerusalem) under the control of the priesthood representing the nation as a whole. Thus each Israelite understood that his or her connection with Yahweh was not an individual one, but that this connection existed only through the intermediation of the collective.

The same pattern held true throughout the ancient world. In Greece, for example, the center of one's identity was lodged in the polis of which one was a citizen. As in Israel, the patron gods of a polis were linked with the polis as a whole rather than with individuals. Sacrifices, festivals, and other forms of connection with these gods were almost always communal rather than individual affairs. As the great historian of Greek religion Martin Nilsson says,

> Greek religion was indissolubly connected with the community and its component parts, State, clan, and family. . . . We may speak of a collective piety. . . . The individual counted simply as a link in the chain of the clan, as one citizen of a State; to be cast out from the clan and the State was, next to death, the heaviest punishment which could be inflicted on anyone. . . . The gods who protected the clan and the State protected also their members and showed kindness to them. Everyone was responsible for paying them reverence and must fulfill their demands, for an offense against them was avenged not only on the criminal but on his clan and State. . . . The individual might find satisfaction and be filled with piety toward the gods, so long as he recognized that he was a link in the chain of the clan, a citizen of his State. He found his satisfaction in the collective piety within the circle of clansmen and of fellow citizens of the community, and knew that his peace was securely made with the gods.[3]

A crucial effect of this sense of corporate identity was in the realm of people's orientation toward death. When the center of identity lay in the group rather than in the individual, there was less motivation for attention to be focused on the question of life after death. As long as identity was lodged in the collective, the fact that the collective would continue after one's personal death was experienced unconsciously as reducing the stress that the knowledge of human mortality might otherwise produce. As Nilsson says, early antiquity was a time

> when conscious individualism was unknown and when the individual was only a link in the chain of the generations. Such an age had no need of a belief in the immortality of the individual, but it believed in the eternity of life in the sense that life flows through the generations which spring from each other.[4]

Thus, for example, there is almost no concern expressed in the Hebrew Bible for the question of what happens after death. Certainly death was feared and struggled against, but speculation about how personal immortality might be achieved is almost completely absent. We do find in the Mesopotamian Epic of Gilgamesh what might seem at first to be an exception to this rule, for in the story, King Gilgamesh does indeed engage in a quest for personal immortality. However, by the time the tale ends it has become a cautionary lesson whose message is precisely that immortality is impossible to attain, and the most one can hope for is to live on in the memory of the collective.

As a consequence of this lack of concern for personal immortality resulting from a sense of corporate identity, among the Israelites, Greeks, and Mesopotamians what happens after death was only rarely described, and when it was it was almost always pictured as a descent to a dark and lifeless underworld, the inhabitants of which, as M.L. West says in his recent comparative study of Greek and Near Eastern mythology,

> are feeble phantoms, sometimes referred to by the phrase "the strengthless heads of the dead." They have lost the power of human speech. . . . Instead they go about twittering like disturbed bats in a cave; in the mass, their noise is like the screaming of birds. . . . The house of the dead was not a desirable residence. It was notably dark and sunless. It is a commonplace of Greek poetry that those who die must leave the light of the sun. . . . The usual Babylonian conception is similar. . . . Job too has been quoted in part: "before I go, not to return, to the land of dark and blackness, the land of caliginous gloom and chaos, that shines [only] gloomily. . . ." The underworld was also a place of accumulated filth and decay, like the tomb. Homer applies to the house of Hades the formulaic epithet *euroeis*, an adjective denoting the presence of physical corruptions such as mould or rust. . . . The house of Ereshkigal [the Mesopotamian goddess of the underworld], as described in a formulaic passage that recurs in several poems, is a place "where dust is their food, their bread clay. . . . Over the door and the bolt is a layer of dust. . . ." In the Old Testament

> we meet phrases such as "those who have gone down to the dust," "dwellers in the dust," "those who sleep in the dusty earth."[5]

Such imagery is, of course, not a picture of immortality, but exactly the opposite: a terrifying symbolic representation of the very absence of life. As such, the effect of this imagery was unconsciously to discourage any attempt to ponder the question of what happens to the individual after death, and thus to redirect people's orientation to death back into the matrix of collective identity.

The prevalence of the kind of corporate identity that I have been describing here depended, of course, on the strength and cohesion of the local group of which one was a member. But it was precisely the strength and cohesion of local societies that were challenged by the coming of the Hellenistic imperial order after Alexander's conquests. As smaller societies became absorbed into the larger Hellenistic empire they lost a significant degree of autonomy, and consequently were unable to provide a sense of collective identity for their members. A universal Hellenistic culture rapidly began to emerge as cities modeled on the Greek polis were established throughout the Mediterranean and Near East, and these cities quickly became centers for the dissemination of Greek language, customs, and ways of thinking. The result of this cultural imperialism was that local societies increasingly lost their sense of self-determination. In this weakened state the local cultures could no longer maintain their powerful hold on the psychologies of their inhabitants, and the pattern of group identity that had previously held sway began to dissolve, leaving individuals suddenly thrown back on themselves. As W.W. Tarn says in his classic work *Hellenistic Civilization*, "With Alexander begins man as an individual."[6]

This trend toward the dissolution of the bond between the group and the individual was also strongly intensified by the dramatic improvements in communication and transportation that accompanied the emergence of the new imperial political order. A decisive leap occurred in the ability of individuals to leave the localities where they were born and move elsewhere in the empire, or at least to become aware (both consciously and unconsciously) of the possibility of doing so. Thus people became increasingly "detachable" from their local societies, and their sense of identity began to shift from being centered in the collective to being centered in their own individuality.

Along with this growing sense of individual independence from the collective went a concomitant experience of a loss of contact with the traditional gods. These gods were, as we have seen, fundamentally related to the group rather than to the individual, and, as local societies lost their clear boundaries in the face of the growing influence of the new imperial political order, so the local gods lost their ability to capture the allegiance of individuals increasingly freed from embeddedness in the collective. The result was a growing feeling of disconnection from the old gods, a feeling that the gods were losing their power and ability to provide an experience of security and meaning. The gods were felt to be withdrawing, becoming more and more distant and difficult to contact.

This loss of connection with the realm of the divine set in motion a pattern of religious questing, as individuals began to search for new sources of ultimate meaning: new gods better able to supply the missing sense of contact with the foundations of life. One obvious requirement of such new forms of divinity was that they no longer be tied to a particular locality, and so we find during the Hellenistic age the emergence of new trans-imperial symbolic systems that could be transported and established anywhere in the empire. One of the most successful of such systems was that of "astral religion," in which the divine forces came to be seen as residing in the realm of the stars. Since the heavens look the same wherever one travels, the stars provided ideal raw material for a portable religious sensibility no longer grounded in a local community. Another common response to the weakening of the old local gods was the phenomenon of "syncretism," which refers to the process of creating composite divinities out of many local gods; where syncretism took place, each local god came to be seen as merely one manifestation of a much larger divine force whose true dominion embraced the entire empire. Such, for example, was the nature of the great Hellenistic goddess Isis who, originally from Egypt, came to be worshipped throughout the empire, and was explicitly understood as unifying all the local goddesses of the smaller societies that had become absorbed into the larger imperial structure.

Of course, the loss of the old group identity also had a profound impact on people's relationship to the problem of death. As we have seen, before the Hellenistic age, anxiety about death was dealt with through identification with the community which would live on after one's death. However, when this sense of corporate identity succumbed to the new individualism of the Hellenistic era, the problem of death moved quickly into the foreground of consciousness. The result was that the search for new ways of coming to terms with one's mortality became intertwined with the search for new symbolic systems that could help achieve an understanding of the divine realm but that were no longer tied to particular localities. This linking of a new religious concern for the problem of mortality with the emergence of new, non-local symbolic systems is strikingly illustrated in the spread throughout the empire of the Christian movement, in which the central image was that of an overcoming of the power of death.

In addition, the intertwined issues of individual identity, personal mortality, and the need for non-local images of the divine became connected with another factor: namely, a longing for experiences of transformation. For Hellenistic culture was a culture in the process of rapid metamorphosis, and one effect of this was the catalyzing of a desire for personal metamorphosis. A tendency emerged for individuals unconsciously to seek experiences of transformation in order to fit into a culture in transformation. It is in this context that we can understand the flourishing in Hellenistic culture of the so-called "mystery religions," which were characterized by the requirement that their members undergo a process of initiation aimed at producing a direct experience of personal transformation. The mystery religions often invoked a symbolism involving the image of death and rebirth, an age-old representation of the process of transformation. The Christian movement as well incorporated this element into its structure in the symbolism of the death and resurrection of Jesus, and in the transformative initiatory ritual of baptism that was required for membership.

The form which such experiences of transformation could take varied from tradition to tradition, but the general trend of a widespread search for the new and unusual – contact with which would create a sense that a personal transformation had indeed taken place – is clear. As the New Testament scholar Dieter Georgi says,

> If I were asked to describe the main characteristic of Hellenistic culture between Alexander and Constantine, I would answer that it was committed to experiment with transcendence, literally as well as metaphorically. It represented a multifarious exploration of the limits and possibilities of humanity. It was a laboratory of the extraordinary.[7]

Perhaps the most extreme response to the emergence of the new Hellenistic culture is to be found among the Jewish people. We saw earlier the extent to which the ancient Israelites lived with a sense of the corporate identity of the nation of Israel. The Jewish commitment to the survival of their national identity was so strong that the dissolving force of the Hellenistic empire came to be understood as constituting a cosmic enemy poisoning reality itself. The result of this was the emergence of thc radical idea that the only way to overcome this enemy was through a transformation of the entire cosmos, and the concept arose that time itself was coming to an end – the so called "apocalyptic" worldview ("apocalypse" means "revelation," and in this context it refers to the revelation that the world was ending). The old world of small, autonomous societies was indeed ending, but the Jews projected their own national anxieties on to the universe as a whole, and produced in their apocalyptic literature an astonishing array of cosmological symbolism and visionary predictions. One can also see in Jewish apocalyptic an unconscious reflection of the search for transformation discussed above, only here the transformation was sought not in the realm of personal experience (since the Jews clung to a collective rather than individual structure of identity) but in a universal cataclysm and metamorphosis. It was, of course, out of this Jewish apocalyptic milieu that the Christian movement was born, for both John the Baptist and his disciple Jesus seem to have presented themselves as apocalyptic prophets, and early Christian texts such as the Gospels and the letters of Paul are saturated with apocalyptic ideas and imagery.

The presence of cosmological imagery in Jewish apocalyptic brings us to another crucial component of the Hellenistic revolution. For the cosmic symbolism in Jewish apocalyptic was merely one manifestation of a decisive shift in the understanding of the nature and structure of the universe that took place in the Hellenistic age, side by side with the cultural shift discussed above.

Beginning with the pre-Socratic philosophers but clarified and publicized for the first time in Plato's dialogues, a radically new vision of the organization of the cosmos began to achieve popular currency in the Hellenistic age (Plato was still alive when Alexander was born, and it is in the Hellenistic age that Plato's ideas became common knowledge). In the old cosmology, which was more or less the same throughout the Mediterranean and Near East, the earth was usually imagined as being a flat disc, with the sky forming a fixed dome above it, and the underworld lying beneath. A great mountain often marked the center of the earth (for example, Mount Olympus or Mount Zion), and was believed to be the dwelling place of the gods. This universe was small, contained, and rather comforting in its effect on the imagination (Figure 13.1).

However, in Plato's dialogues we find publicized for the first time a radically new world picture. In this new cosmology, the earth is no longer conceived of as a flat

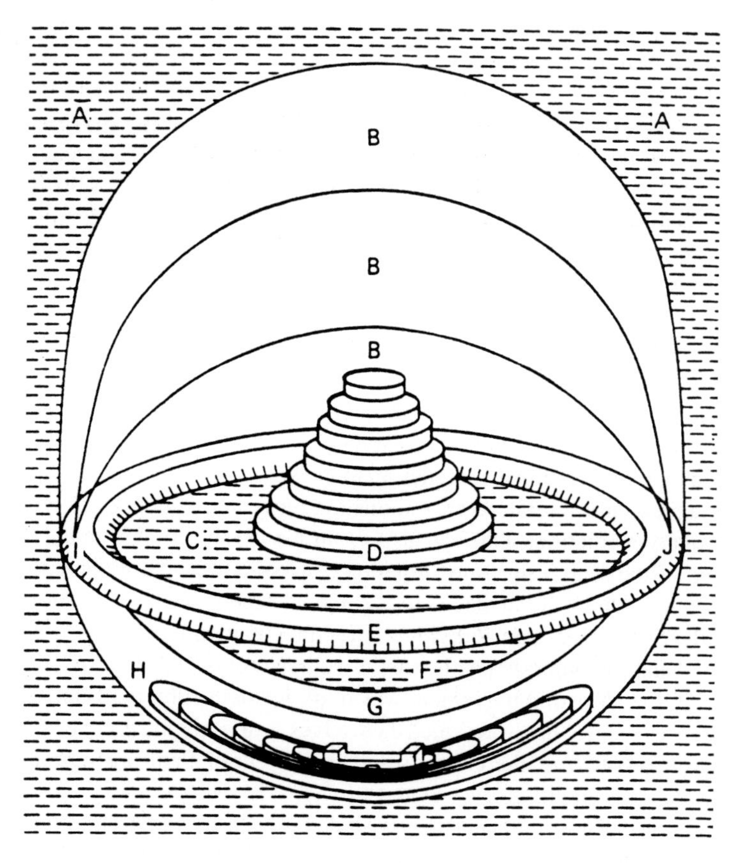

Figure 13.1 Babylonian conception of the universe. A: Heavenly ocean. B: Three heavens. C: Sea surrounding the earth. D: Earth mountain. E: Mountains confining the sea. F: Bottom of the ocean. G: Underworld. H: Palace of the underworld. I: Mountain of the rising sun. J: Mountain of the setting sun.

Source: Introduction to the Old Testament, 2/e, by West, © 1981. Reprinted by permission of Prentice-Hall, Inc., Upper Saddle River, NJ, USA.

disc, but is rather envisioned as being a globe; and the heavens are no longer a fixed dome, but rather constitute an enormous sphere with the stars attached, rotating the earth (located at the sphere's center) once a day. This new cosmology was destined to become Western culture's universally accepted picture of the structure of the universe for almost 2000 years, from the time of Plato to the time of Copernicus.

The fact that this new cosmology arose simultaneously with the political transformation of the Hellenistic age created a synergism in which the questing spirits of the Hellenistic world – those who, in Dieter Georgi's words, were living in a "laboratory of the extraordinary" – could create remarkable new symbolic systems merging cosmological speculations with ideas, intuitions, and images arising from the experience of dwelling in a culture undergoing a tremendous and rapid metamorphosis.

For example, as mentioned above, the old cosmology often located the home of the gods on the top of a great mountain at the center of the earth. But in the new cosmology, in which the earth was understood as a globe dwarfed in magnitude by the great sphere of the heavens, the great mountain of the gods suddenly became merely a microscopic bump on the surface of the earth – no longer a proper habitation for the divine forces which were in control of the universe. As a result, during the Hellenistic age we find the emergence of imagery in which the gods come to be seen as dwelling in the realm of the stars, no longer nearby and accessible but reachable only through extraordinary means (Figure 13.2).

The most common manifestation of this migration of the gods into the heavens was the production of narratives, within many different religious contexts, telling of miraculous journeys to the heavens to experience contact with the divine. For example, many of the Jewish apocalyptic texts announcing the end of the world took the form of tales about ascending to the heavenly realm, where the author would receive a revelation of divine secrets about cosmic history.

But it is crucial to notice that this new understanding of where the gods had gone and how they might be contacted meshed perfectly with the developments, discussed earlier, that arose out of the *social* transformation of the Hellenistic world. For as we saw, the breakdown of the old, local forms of religion created a situation in which the old gods were experienced as withdrawing, their power becoming more and more indistinct and a sense of connection with them becoming more and more difficult to achieve. Here the new cosmology was perfectly situated to play a decisive role; for it provided a compelling response to the unconscious sense of loss of connection with the gods by offering an answer to the question of where the divine powers had gone and how they might once again be contacted.

Similarly, another new concept first publicized by Plato and then rapidly adopted during the Hellenistic period was the idea that the human soul (*psyche* in Greek) is actually immortal, and ascends to the heavens after death. Indeed, for Plato the soul and the heavens were intricately bound together, for he argues that humans souls were created from the same substance as the soul of the entire cosmos itself, and that the number of human souls is equal to the number of stars.[8] This new concept of the soul and its grounding in cosmic reality provided a remarkable basis for

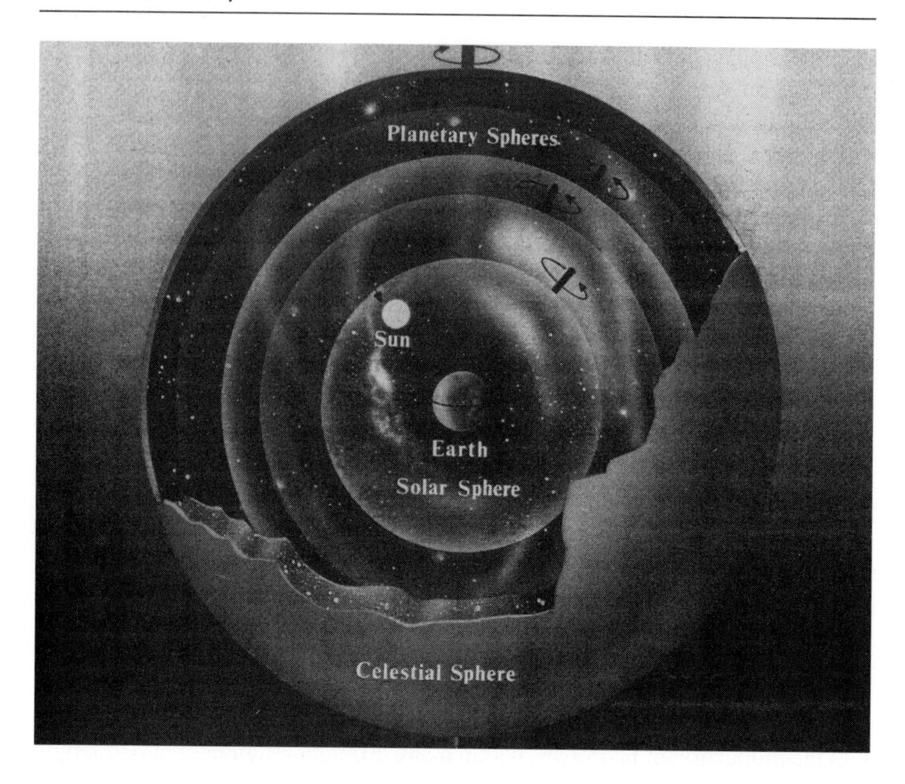

Figure 13.2 Aristotle's universe consisted of spheres nested within spheres, their axes and directions of rotation adjusted to approximate the observed motions of the sun, moon, and stars across the sky (not to scale)
Source: From *Coming of Age in the Milky Way* by Timothy Ferris, copyright 1988 by permission of William Morrow and Company, Inc.

responding to one of the most pressing unconscious anxieties brought on by the Hellenistic political transformation: namely, how the suddenly increased individualism fostered by that transformation was going to deal with the concomitantly increased anxiety over the problem of death. Acceptance of the old picture of a dark and terrifying underworld had been possible when people's fundamental sense of identity was lodged in the eternal collective, but, now that people had become separable from the collective and thrown back on their individual identity, some way of imagining a positive individual afterlife became necessary. Plato's concept of the immortal soul and its inherent connection with the divine heavens of the new cosmology provided a tremendously appealing answer to the problem of death, and during the Hellenistic age it quickly became the dominant conception of what happens to the individual after death.

While discussing Plato's new concept of the immortality of the soul, we should note that for Plato the soul was immortal because it was non-material and separate from the body, and thus would not die when the body died. Indeed, Plato taught a doctrine of the reincarnation of the soul, according to which the soul after death would eventually find itself attached to a new body. Plato's concept of the soul had a profound appeal in the Hellenistic period, since it provided strong support for the movement away from collective and toward individual identity. For if the soul was immortal and separate from the body, it had no inherent connection with the social group into which one was born – one's body might have been born in Athens, but one's soul had lived before in other bodies and in other places, and would do so again after death.

Finally, as we saw earlier, the transformation of the world during the Hellenistic age sparked a growing desire on the part of individuals for experiences of personal transformation, and here too the implications of the social shift became bound up with the new cosmology, for the imagery of the journey to the heavens inspired by the new cosmology almost always presented the heavens as a place where a personal transformation took place. Plato himself had already expressed this idea when he told a myth in his *Phaedrus* about souls rising up to the ultimate boundary of the cosmos, and then described the crossing of that boundary into the realms beyond the universe using imagery directly invoking the supreme moment of initiation in the Eleusinian mysteries: a moment when the initiates experienced a profound sense of individual transformation that permanently changed their relationship with the divine powers of the universe.[9] This linking of the cosmic journey of the soul with the experience of personal transformation found its way into many of the new Hellenistic religious systems, from Jewish apocalyptic to the mystery cults of Mithras and Isis and the esoteric teachings of Gnosticism and Hermeticism.

In ways such as these the new culture and the new cosmology of the Hellenistic age intertwined with and reinforced each other, producing a sudden and simultaneous shift in both life-experience and worldview: a synthesis whose power was far greater than the sum of its parts. Indeed, it is no exaggeration to say that the many-faceted socio-cosmic metamorphosis of the Hellenistic age constitutes one of the great revolutions in the history of human culture.

In the end, the most successful product of this revolution, of course, was the religion of Christianity, which in its early stages is often referred to by scholars as the "Christ cult."[10] The Christ cult was perfectly suited to offer an attractive response to the conditions of the Hellenistic age – indeed, the evolution of its symbolism, ideology, and structure was in many ways conditioned precisely by its need to appeal to people whose consciousness had been shaped by Hellenistic culture.

For example, the Christ cult obviously offered a direct response to the question of death and personal immortality. For it provided its members with a guarantee of a positive afterlife through the claim that its savior figure had permanently conquered death, and that cult adherents could participate in this conquest by undergoing initiation into the movement through the ritual of baptism.

In addition, the Christ cult presented itself as a symbolic community – the "New Israel" – of which people could become citizens without needing to be tied to a particular locality. It thus served as a portable homeland, offering a symbolic substitute for the lost sense of collective identity that had died with the dissolution of the old local groups. Indeed, just as the ancient Israelites had understood themselves as part of the corporate being of "father Jacob," so the members of the Christ cult were taught that they had become part of "the body of Christ."

Further, along with giving its members citizenship in a symbolic homeland, the Christ cult offered to its adherents an almost infinitely intricate symbolic personal genealogy: upon joining this group, one immediately became heir to the extraordinarily complex and elaborate universe of history, myth, and symbol embodied in the texts of the cult – what we now call the Bible. Here was provided – now on a symbolic level – the same rich sense of embeddedness that used to be furnished by one's growing up within the traditions of a local society. In other words, the Christ cult offered a convincing sense of identity to people for whom the old structure of local group identity was no longer available.

Additionally, at the core of the Christ cult was a myth of death and rebirth, an almost universal symbolic representation of the experience of transformation, the longing for which was a central component of Hellenistic psychology. And, like the Hellenistic Jewish tradition out of which it arose, the Christ cult projected this imagery of transformation on to the cosmos itself by perpetuating and elaborating the apocalyptic vision of the end of the world that had been the Jewish response to the Hellenistic revolution.

The new cosmology of the Hellenistic age also found expression in the Christ cult, for example, in the story of Jesus' ascension to the heavens after his resurrection; in the belief in the "second coming," according to which Jesus would descend again from the heavens in the same way he had ascended; in the image of the descent of the spirit-dove through the opened heavens at Jesus' baptism; and in Paul's description of his own journey to the heavens in II Corinthians.[11] In all of these images, and many more that could be mentioned, the need to feel connected to the new cosmic home of the divine manifests itself in the Christ cult just as it does in other religious movements of the Hellenistic period.

Having gained a sense of the overall contours of the Hellenistic age, we may now turn our attention to the nature and significance of the parallels between that age and our own moment in history that I mentioned at the beginning of this chapter. Such parallels have, of course, often been noted before. Tarn, for example, says in *Hellenistic Civilization*, "The resemblance of this world to our own is at first sight startling,"[12] and in the most recent full-scale treatment of the Hellenistic age, Peter Green's *From Alexander to Actium*, Green says,

> As my work proceeded, it acquired an unexpected and in ways alarming dimension. I could not help being struck, again and again, by an overpowering sense of déjà vu. . . . What this parallelism signifies I do not pretend to know, and think it wiser not to speculate; but it does suggest, forcefully, that there may indeed be something more in the Hellenistic age for concerned modern readers than mere antiquarian interest.[13]

What are these parallels? First and foremost, we are currently livi enormous and extremely rapid process of cultural unification resemblin motion by Alexander's conquests, but this time on a much larger – indeed – scale. This planetary cultural unification has been well underway since at lea early part of the twentieth century, and can be instantly discerned in our amus reaction today to the quaint statement from Franz Cumont with which I began this chapter. However, now, at the beginning of the twenty-first century, this tremendous process of cultural unification is suddenly undergoing an additional quantum leap in speed and intensity as a result of the emergence of the global information system of the internet and the World Wide Web, and the anticipation of even more potent developments in planetary networking that lie in the immediate future.

As we have seen, the most significant effect of the cultural unification that characterized the Hellenistic revolution was a decisive shift in the locus of human identity from the collective to the individual, with the subsequent emergence of new symbolic systems that offered responses of various kinds to this shift. Likewise, in our own time a change in the structure of human identity seems to be accompanying the process of planetary cultural unification (at least in the industrial cultures of the West that are at the forefront of this process).

The nature of the alteration in the structure of human identity that is now taking place is most often described as consisting in a "fragmentation" of the self. The sense of a unified center of identity within the individual that has been dominant in Western culture since the Hellenistic age is seen by many contemporary historians, philosophers, and cultural critics as currently undergoing a radical dissolution. Kenneth Gergen, for example, in his book *The Saturated Self: Dilemmas of Identity in Contemporary Life*, notes that the older views of a unified, individual self

> are falling into disuse, and the social arrangements that they support are eroding. This is largely a result of the forces of social saturation. Emerging technologies saturate us with the voices of humankind – both harmonious and alien. As we absorb their varied rhymes and reasons, they become part of us and we of them. Social saturation furnishes us with a multiplicity of incoherent and unrelated languages of the self. For everything we "know to be true" about ourselves, other voices within respond with doubt and even derision. This fragmentation of self-conceptions corresponds to a multiplicity of incoherent and disconnected relationships. These relationships pull us in myriad directions, inviting us to play such a variety of roles that the very concept of an "authentic self" with knowable characteristics recedes from view. The fully saturated self becomes no self at all.[14]

And in his book *The Protean Self: Human Resilience in an Age of Fragmentation*, Robert Jay Lifton says:

> We are becoming fluid and many-sided. Without quite realizing it, we have been evolving a sense of self appropriate to the restlessness and flux of our time. This mode of being differs radically from that of the past. . . . I have named it the "protean self" after Proteus, the Greek sea god of many forms. The protean self emerges from confusion, from the widespread feeling that we are losing our psychological moorings. We feel ourselves buffeted about by unmanageable historical forces and social uncertainties. . . . We are beset by a contradiction: schooled in the virtues of constancy and stability – whether as individuals, groups, or nations – our world and our lives seem inconstant and utterly unpredictable.[15]

The fragmentation of identity described by Gergen and Lifton has also, of course, become a central axiom of "postmodern" philosophy, psychology, and cultural theory as embodied in the work of such thinkers as Michel Foucault and Jacques Lacan. One can hardly read a page of the writings of such authors without coming across a reference to a "fragmented identity" or a "decentered self."

Along with this shift in the structure of personal identity, our own time – like the Hellenistic age – is simultaneously experiencing the sudden emergence of a radically new cosmological vision. To take just one example, it is only since the discoveries of Edwin Hubble in the early 1920s that we have known that galaxies exist beyond the Milky Way – in other words, about eighty years ago the universe as we know it expanded overnight by a factor of *100 billion.* As a result of this and countless other cosmological reorientations, our current vision of the nature of the universe has become that of a reality without a center or boundaries, within which our own existence is entirely without meaning or context. And now, as in the Hellenistic age, a new cosmology and the effects of a dramatic process of cultural unification are interacting with each other – the fragmentation of identity that seems to be resulting from our contemporary cultural transformation is precisely mirrored in the decentered cosmology within which all of us now dwell, leading to a doubly reinforced sense of a loss of contact with the grounding forces of reality.

Indeed, just as the Hellenistic Jews responded to the socio-cosmic transformation of their own time with their vision of ultimate catastrophe and apocalypse, so in our own time apocalyptic ideation permeates our worldview. Whether it be nuclear war or environmental collapse, our culture has been living for a number of decades with the feeling that some sort of cataclysmic event is quickly approaching. Of course, the Jewish apocalyptic vision of the end of the world was in retrospect a fantasy, while nuclear annihilation and the collapse of the biosphere are possibilities that are all too real. However, the difference may in fact lie only in that we are *living out* our projection of a radical metamorphosis, while the apocalyptic Jews simply experienced their projection symbolically – although it must be emphasized that the world of the Hellenistic Jews of Palestine did indeed end when the Roman army destroyed Jerusalem and the Jewish temple in 70 CE.

The inner structure of the new world within which we find ourselves today as a consequence of our current "neo-Hellenistic" cultural metamorphosis is now, at the beginning of the twenty-first century, being clarified in a remarkable way by the emergence of a new global system of communication and interrelationship: the internet or "cyberspace." This spectacular new development, although almost entirely unpredicted a few years ago, can in retrospect be seen as an absolutely natural outgrowth of the dramatic planetary unification characteristic of the modern world in general. It parallels in many ways the sudden appearance in the Hellenistic world, in the aftermath of the conquests of Alexander the Great, of a new trans-imperial matrix of cross-cultural intercommunication.

In addition, the emergence in our time of the phenomenon of cyberspace – and the related technology of "virtual reality" – parallels in some fascinating respects the new impulses introduced by Plato that immediately became part of the Hellenistic worldview. For example, I mentioned earlier that in Plato's new concept of the soul, the soul was understood as being non-material and separable from the physical body, and I pointed out the extent to which this concept of the division of the soul from the body supported the new emphasis on individual identity characteristic of the Hellenistic age.

Like Plato's vision of the separable soul as an entity more connected with the heavens than with the earth, the phenomena of cyberspace and virtual reality provide an extraordinary experience of the state of being a disembodied entity in a non-material realm. When we navigate through the "information-space" of the internet ("surf the Web"), we leave our bodies behind while our consciousness seems to explore an entirely separate universe. As Jennifer Cobb says in *CyberGrace*:

> The center of gravity of the Information Age is not matter, but information and knowledge. According to *A Magna Carta for the Knowledge Age*, coauthored by Esther Dyston, George Gilder, George Keyworth, and Alvin Toffler, the "central event of the 20th century is the overthrow of matter". . . . We are entering a time when the truths of modernism – that the world is made up of discrete, material objects that can be physically mapped, described, and, in theory, controlled – are being replaced by a new set of understandings based on the primacy of nonmaterial events, or packets of information, that are dynamically linked in a vast, invisible terrain known as cyberspace. . . .
>
> A vast, pulsing, electronic world, cyberspace encircles the globe. When we enter it, we go into a place that feels removed from the physical world. It is a space composed of information, images, and symbols. In many ways, this world of pure images is the crowning achievement of a Western trajectory of thought that began with Plato in his apocryphal cave. Plato argued that we are trapped in the cave of matter and can see the real world of intellectual ideas only as the shadows these ideas cast upon the walls of the cave. Plato's call was for us to emerge from the cave and live fully within the world of ideal forms, the life of the mind. Cyberspace can be interpreted as the Platonic realm incarnate.[16]

Obviously the experience of cyberspace has the effect of loosening our ties to our ordinary identities as defined by our bodily presence in the world, and thus dramatically reinforces the fragmented identity characteristic of modern life experience.

It is not difficult to see a similarity between Alexander's unifying conquests of the ancient world and the appearance in the modern world of cyberspace as a force leading to a radical increase in cultural interconnection (and related shifts in patterns of personal identity). However, to conclude this chapter, I would like to suggest that in some ways the emergence of cyberspace can be seen not only as a phenomenon parallel to the process of Hellenistic cultural unification, but also as parallel to the *responses* to cultural integration that emerged in the Hellenistic world. In particular, I would like to propose that the birth of cyberspace in our time bears an intriguing resemblance to the emergence of the Christ cult in the Hellenistic age.

As we saw earlier, the Christ cult provided a symbolic "homeland" to people who were no longer able to experience in reality the ancient sense of being identified with a local traditional community. I believe it is no exaggeration to see in the Christ cult's "New Israel" a kind of *virtual reality*, in which a non-material symbolic structure was able to provide a replacement – and a convincing one, judging by its success – for what had previously been an actual physical reality.

I mentioned earlier a number of reasons for the appeal of the Christ cult in the Hellenistic world. However, I would suggest that an additional crucial factor in the success of the Christ cult's "virtual reality" was the extraordinary *richness and density* of its content: namely, the enormous body of myth, history, and symbol contained in the texts of the Bible. Among ancient Western works of mythic imagination, for sheer size and intricacy the Bible was rivaled only by the epics of Homer. However, whereas the tales of Homer concerned the lives of a single generation of heroes, the Bible presented an unparalleled dramatic panorama of the mythic history of an entire civilization. In addition, while Homer had been widely known for centuries, the Bible had been the obscure possession of an ignored people until the members of the Christ cult suddenly and with tremendous energy brought it to public attention. Through the activity of the Christ cult, in the form of the Bible a hitherto unknown imaginal universe of spectacular dimensions burst unexpectedly into the consciousness of the Hellenistic world.

Beyond its sheer magnitude and richness of detail, however, the Bible as presented by the Christ cult possessed one other remarkable characteristic. For in adding their own "New Testament" to the older, massive Hebrew Bible, the members of the Christ cult produced a new, composite document that can only be described as an almost infinitely complex *hypertext* (i.e., a web-like structure of elements in which each is linked to numerous others in a non-linear fashion – something like the World Wide Web). I am here referring to the fact that at the core of the ideology of the New Testament (and of all subsequent early Christian literature) was the idea that everything in the Bible was connected to everything else through the phenomena of prophecy and "typology."

To begin with, the events in the life of Jesus, according to early Christian writers, all took place as "fulfillments of prophecy" – i.e., they could only be understood by tracing the threads of meaning that connected them back to events described in the much older Hebrew Bible. Further, though, a similar but even more far-reaching "hypertext" effect was achieved by the early Christian practice that scholars call "typology." Here the threads of meaning that were seen as linking things together went far beyond the imagined fulfillment of explicit prophetic promises, for typology refers to the early Christian authors' practice of making connections of meaning between phenomena on the basis of almost any sort of resemblance or relationship: for example, Jesus ("King of the Jews") is born in Bethlehem because that is where King David was born, the watery baptism of Jesus is symbolically connected to the watery flood story of Noah through the symbol of the dove, and Jesus' shining "transfiguration" at the top of a hill is connected to the fiery appearance of Yahweh on Mount Sinai by the presence of a vision of Moses. Examples like these could be multiplied endlessly, both within the New Testament itself and even more ubiquitously in the work of the early Christian interpreters of the Bible.

What, then, was the Bible as presented by the Christ cult if not an infinitely dense, complex, *hyperlinked virtual reality*? And what has been the subsequent history of Christianity if not the story of how the whole of Western civilization, longing for a lost experience of identity and meaningfulness, fell helplessly headlong into that hyperlinked virtual reality and lived within its sparkling matrix for 2000 years?

In his last, great work, *Mysterium Coniunctionis*, Carl Jung described the way in which periodic experiences of disintegration and reintegration characterize human life, both on the individual and collective levels. When, as a result of changing circumstances, a guiding structure of life – a "conscious dominant" – loses its ability to provide a meaningful order, a process of dissolution ensues, an alchemical melting down of previous forms into a formless state, out of which a new conscious dominant then crystallizes into formation.[17] When the new conscious dominant first emerges, says Jung, it attracts to itself all the factors of the human psyche through an irresistible power of fascination and numinosity. The Hellenistic age, as we have seen here, was precisely such a time of breakdown and reconfiguration. The old conscious dominant – the structure of traditional, local corporate identity – was no longer capable of ordering life in a meaningful way, and a process of dissolution unfolded that led, after an extraordinary period of competing alternatives, to the emergence of the new conscious dominant embodied in the uniquely fertile matrix of the Christian mythos, which magnetically attracted into itself, with all of the fascination of the truly numinous, the collective psyche of the West.

Now, in our own time, the alchemical process is once again unfolding. The conscious dominant has lost its ability to guide us – as Yeats put it, "the center cannot hold" – and the great dissolution is well under way. Is the sudden, mysterious, numinous attraction of cyberspace an indication that therein lies the embryonic form of the new conscious dominant? Or are we seeing here merely the first of many competing reality structures that will arise to contend for the new allegiance of the human soul? Indeed, will we even survive at all, or will we succumb to an all too literal living out of our own apocalyptic visions? Only time will tell, of course. But my hope is that in recognizing that we are not alone in our bewilderment

– in recognizing that a similar situation was faced by others like us two thousand years ago – we may gain access to a valuable source of wisdom and courage as we move forward into an uncertain future.

NOTES

1 Franz Cumont, *Oriental Religions in Roman Paganism* (New York: Dover Publications, 1956), pp. 196–197.
2 *The Jerusalem Bible, Readers Edition* (New York: Doubleday and Co, 1968), p. 52.
3 Martin Nilsson, *Greek Piety* (New York: W.W. Norton and Co, 1969), pp. 7–8.
4 Martin Nilsson, *Greek Folk Religion* (Philadelphia: University of Pennsylvania Press, 1972), p. 60.
5 M.L. West, *The East Face of Helicon* (Oxford: Oxford University Press, 1997), pp. 159–162. It is interesting to note that the Egyptian conception of death differed greatly from that of Greece, Israel, and Mesopotamia. However, the Egyptian conception had almost no influence on other cultures. This is because the Egyptian emphasis on the preservation of the physical body and hence on immortality was the result of the unique geographical circumstances of Egypt: in the earliest phases of Egyptian history, the bodies of the dead were buried directly into the desert sands and as a result were naturally dried out and preserved, often with skin and hair intact. The sense of preservation after death that this phenomenon engendered was carried on into later Egyptian culture and artificially reproduced, manifesting in the practice of mummification and the beliefs connected with it. But because other cultures did not share Egypt's peculiar geographical circumstances, its burial practices and beliefs about death were not adopted elsewhere. See Stephen Quirke, *Ancient Egyptian Religion* (London: British Museum Press, 1992), p. 143; A. J. Spencer, *Death in Ancient Egypt* (London: Penguin Books, 1982), pp. 29–30.
6 W.W. Tarn, *Hellenistic Civilization* (New York: New American Library, 1974), p. 79.
7 Dieter Georgi, *The Opponents of Paul in Second Corinthians* (Philadelphia: Fortress Press, 1986) p. 390.
8 Plato, *Timaeus* 41d–e.
9 For Plato's use of Eleusinian imagery in the *Phaedrus*, see Walter Burkert, *Ancient Mystery Cults* (Cambridge: Harvard University Press, 1987), pp. 92–93.
10 For the use of the term "Christ cult," see Burton Mack, *A Myth of Innocence* (Philadelphia: Fortress Press, 1988), pp. 100ff. Cf. Rudolf Bultmann, *Theology of the New Testament* (New York: Charles Scribner's Sons, 1951), pp. 123ff.; Wilhelm Bousset, *Kyrios Christos* (Nashville: Abingdon Press, 1970), pp. 138ff.
11 II Corinthians 12: 1–5.
12 W.W. Tarn, *Hellenistic Civilization* (2nd edn) (New York: New American Library, 1951), p. 3. I have not been able to consult the first edition of Tarn's work, which was published in 1927. If this statement appears in the first edition, then it would appear that during the twenty-one years which had elapsed since the very different statement by Franz Cumont in 1906 with which I began this chapter – years that, of course, include World War I – a crucial shift had taken place in historians' understanding of the significance of the Hellenistic age in the evolution of Western culture.
13 Peter Green, *From Alexander to Actium: The Historical Evolution of the Hellenistic Age* (Berkeley: University of California Press, 1990), p. xxi.
14 Kenneth J. Gergen, *The Saturated Self: Dilemmas of Identity in Contemporary Life* (New York: Basic Books, 1991), pp. 6–7.
15 Robert Jay Lifton, *The Protean Self: Human Resilience in an Age of Fragmentation* (New York: Basic Books, 1993), p. 1.

16 Jennifer Cobb, *CyberGrace* (New York: Crown Publishers, Inc, 1998), pp. 30–31.
17 Carl Jung, *Mysterium Coniunctionis* (Princeton, NJ: Princeton University Press, 1970), pp. 355ff.

Chapter 14

MOOSE, FOOSE, FAMOSE

Judith Grahn

Archeomythology, a genre defined by Marija Gimbutas, catches the imagination by ordering multiple sets of findings from the neolithic into a single origin story. That an origin story rests in the Sacred Feminine is what makes it news. Poets and mythographers, Jungians and many indigenous people and the grassroots Goddess Movement have all put forward female origin stories; but they did not have archeological input or scientific standing. Origin story has been an integral part of archeology but, until archeologist Marija Gimbutas, the underlying Western story consisted of what I call Male-Only-Origin-Story-Example (MOOSE).

By crossing into other fields, which she lists as history, folklore, and mythology, Gimbutas has tied the physical evidence of past civilization to the narrative folklore of its present or recent past. This deepening of story to a prehistory 25,000 years long has a number of uses. By using archeological techniques of turning fragments into motifs – in mythology – she emerged with physical evidence for story itself. It is possible to see how story evolved from physical enactment of major life and idea themes.

Because she brings mythology to bear on her archeological findings, Gimbutas' work emphasizes the sources of how we come to place credence on one story over another. Her methodology also highlights that in science just as surely as in religion, we rely on mythology to make sense of knowledge. We are fortunate that Gimbutas had such a rich unsuppressed folklore from which to draw her own mother lode of feminine story. This strain had not disappeared under the weight of male-only-origin-story, instituted by church, state and literary media within historic times in the geographic region of her investigations.

Thus she mined two previously untouched streams of culture with neolithic roots; the one in clay from deep underground, the other out of official sight in the tales told around winter kitchen tables or whispered in Lithuanian churchyards, and taught to her as a child. Since much of folklore is vested specifically in women's culture, this body of materials is in a sense an "archeology" of women's narratives. In matching the two disciplines of folklore and archeology, Gimbutas produced an extraordinary contribution: Female-Only-Origin-Story-Example (FOOSE).

All archeology makes use of origin story, and story for the most part works from the premise of telling originations. Origination story usually sets consciousness in a context of time, place and cause-and-effect or other relationship. The grammatical structures of Latin languages set events in the context of time and space through tense and adverb; and of course also force gender choice along binary lines. The subject as creative force is rarely "it;" hence creation story has been gendered. The major creation stories have been MOOSE.

To give an example, Louis Leakey caught both scientific and popular imaginations not only by the antiquity of his skull findings at Oldovai Gorge. All due credit should go to the Leakey family and other archeologists who have demonstrated human origins as African. However, the story to which his fragments immediately became attached was already deeply entrenched as gendered: male hunters created culture. Imaginative tales of cavemen and mammoth hunters in the icy slopes of ancient Europe had become doctrine by the time Leakey postulated that the crushed skull of Oldovai Gorge was a result of prehuman male aggression; the vast entrenched panorama of male-only origin story was receiving one more example of its "truth" – the oldest known physical evidence that warfare and aggression is the root of our humanity and our use of stone tools.

Leakey's argument rested on his belief that the broken skull had to have been caused by a deliberate forceful blow. Let us for a moment consider that crushed skull from the point of view of two female narrators, Gimbutas and myself. Suppose that instead of the Leakey family, we found that skull fragment. While Gimbutas' story rests on women's "life-giving" properties, especially of birth, mine rests on the connection between menstrual cycles and the moon, and hence on the "menstrual mind" – a set of relationships – as formulator of culture.

Marija Gimbutas uses the word "symbol" for the motifs in the goddess figures she both studied and unearthed. I use the word "metaform." I consider my term to be a contribution to and a furtherance of the discourse on origin story inclusive of the female that Gimbutas has led. Metaform, briefly, means an embodied or enacted idea with menstruation at its base. While menstruation *per se* is not an overt theme for Gimbutas, it is covertly present in her many references to female moisture, streaming, flow, and energy swirls.

In my imagining of Gimbutas' version the skull was female, and the act of aggression was by a barbaric male member of a barbarian group. The males were overpowering a more advanced, peaceful, female-led group, who had already created complex culture, and were being taken over by the simpler, aggressive, male group (FOOSE). Gimbutas believed that Old Europe consisted of matristic, agrarian communities characterized by a complete absence of weapons of warfare or of fortifications. She hypothesized that invasions by "less civilized" horse-mounted, sky-god worshipping "Kurgan" (barrow-building) people destroyed the thousands of years-long reign of the peaceful mother goddess culture. Her critics point out that the story of barbaric cultures overthrowing civilizations is no longer credible to historians. Nevertheless, Gimbutas' work highlights powerful imagery of the sacred feminine through the paleolithic into the advent of agriculture in the neolithic, in large regions of the European peninsula.

In my metaformic version the skull was not crushed as an act of aggression, but as a blood sacrifice. The force of the blow was not anger or a fight over territory; the intent was to kill the victim quickly, "humanely," since the person was not an enemy, but rather was cherished. The purpose was metaformic, to make the victim's blood flow so that it could be equated with the flow of menstrual blood and therefore become connected to the lunar cycle and other female-centered ideas. In my version, either sex could have delivered or received the blow, though at least one would probably have been male, as the purpose of the rite is to teach males to entrain with lunar and other cycles and thus become encultured human beings.

In Leakey's (*et al.*) origin story, only males participated: men crush other men's skulls for male purposes, territory, sexual competition, using alleged "innate aggression," and this creates culture in the use of stone tools.

In Gimbutas' version, females first created culture and then strange groups of males made war on them, usurped and replaced them; the reasons she cites for the cultural development are the "life-giving" properties of females, and the awe these were given by related males.

In my version, the gender of both the victim and the stone wielder are unknown, but at least one is male, because the assumed purpose was the artificial inducing of blood flow; since in women blood flow is natural, artificially inducing blood flow was for the benefit of the males, to entrain them to the primary metaformic culture as it was developing. In this teaching to men of ideas contained in women's *r'tu* (a Sanskrit word meaning both ritual and menstruation), even if both participants were male the underlying purpose of the act rests on the bedrock of women's *r'tu*. This is Female-And-Male-Origin-Story (FAMOSE).

Note that in my story version "aggression" is not accepted as a fundamental biological innate human trait leading to culture, either formative or barbaric. Rather, my metaformic story implies that what we now understand as male aggression and blood-lust has its roots in imitations of female *r'tu*, and therefore is a construct of our peculiar human formation. Both aggression and the woman-killing relations that sometimes exist between the genders are explained in terms of a cultural dialectic rather than as biology or innateness. The essentialism (about women's innate peacefulness and men's innate aggression) of both Leakey's and Gimbutas' stories are thus turned on end, and a new relational element is added: the bond of blood that is common to both genders, yet accessed differently.

Necessity to witness or experience for themselves blood flow leads to the creation of the use of flint weapons for men; they did this to keep pace with women's developing ideas. And, for that matter, necessity to display blood-based ideas to men and boys leads to the development of cutting tools by women. Metaformic FAMOSE does not imply that males created tools "first," or created a stone clobbering instrument "first," or created anything at all without the participation of women and women's ideas.

Then what of aggression and the measuring of testosterone levels? But glands are evidently sensitive and interact with story. Words spoken and written easily evoke tears, even sobbing. Sexual arousal urgently requiring orgasmic release is a frequent result of certain tales. Women of various cultures report that discussion of menstruation can bring on an unexpected period. So too testosterone-correlated aggression must result from mythic reality. What we construct as "real" follows from our stories – and vice versa, as many philosopher/transformers from Plato to Marx to Jung to Louise Hay have variously pointed out.

The biblical origin story of Eden blames the Mother of humanity, Eve, but at least she is in the story. In the MOOSE directly following and reacting to the origin story of Genesis, the female creative principle has no place at all, no existence. The feminine has no active principle; it is inert, an object to be carried to paleolithic caves, lusted after, used, adored or hated, bought, traded, fought over, and so on.

Gimbutas has not only provided a FOOSE; she is also the first person to back a FOOSE story with physical evidence. She bases her argument in the sacralization of the female body and of women's work, especially in the fertile productions of the body: of pregnancy, of milk, and "flow." She sees in the icons of female figures holding certain creatures a link between women and nature, nature in general. I do not see this, or at least, I frame it differently. From a metaformic standpoint, the connections between women and nature are always cultural connections and contain cognitive content. Gimbutas believed this as well but, by framing so much of her argument in terms of female fertility, she de-emphasized the female conscious mind. She also discounted the masculine as an integral part of cultural creation story.

Meantime, MOOSE is the primary story line in the West, unfolding and grabbing center stage for 2500 years, unchallenged except for Gimbutas and a few mythologists who have seen clues similar to those used by her in her folklore studies.

The horns of MOOSE clash and argue, creating the illusion of variety. In the fight between Christian biblical literalists and secular humanists, everything at issue remains MOOSE. Ideas of Darwin and even Marx, while challenging literalist interpretations of biblical mythology, are two versions of the same story.

Biblical belief established as "real" the myth of exclusively male creation principle. That in monotheism the deity is gendered as only male is the basis of MOOSE in secular theory as well. Darwin and Marx grew from this male root following the Reformation – the doctrine by which everyone can interpret the root MOOSE creation myth for himself. Both Darwin and Marx, even though tempered by Engels' discussions of "early matriarchies," establish rationales for the myth that human males alone have created culture.

Darwin's contribution to MOOSE was his provision of the idea of evolution toward the greater good by means of competition over scarce resources. Since competition is considered a masculine characteristic, "survival of the fittest" (the current doctrine of biological sciences) is a MOOSE myth. This is very much a materialist ideology: the prehuman ape evolved into human by means of aggression, competition, survival of the fittest and innate, genetically endowed "intelligence" (by which is meant qualities displayed primarily by certain classes of males). Social Darwinism grew and inevitably continues to grow directly out of this MOOSE, which also establishes and reinforces a racialized and economic caste system. This myth teaches that the more material culture a man or group acquires, the more superior and evolved he/it is considered to be. Thus the myth is self-proving.

Marx developed his theory of dialectical materialism as a corrective for the gross social inequalities of early capitalism as men followed the dictum "survival of the fittest" and acquisition of material wealth as a sign of superior quality of life. Although he had access to information about female-centered social institutions of the Iroquois people (through Engels and Louis Henry Morgan), both Marx and Engels saw the so-called "matriarchies" as a primitive form which fortunately – in their view – were overthrown and replaced by patriarchies that went on to higher evolution and material civilization. The dismissal in both Marx and Darwin of religion as a useful or desirable social form is a reflection of the degree to which they were challenging, successfully and at cost, the biblical story of origins.

By concentrating on the idea of physical "need" and material well-being as motives for existence, Marx continued MOOSE and justified belief in it. Human beings evolve culture to fulfill material "needs," this version says. The reason we developed culture was to provide ourselves with certain essential bodily necessities. The belief in physical "need" as the prime motivating force of culture is a Marxian foundation, and leads directly to competitive "survival of the fittest" philosophy, and also to the idea of the supremacy of mankind over animals – since they are, by definition, "too unintelligent" to develop material culture, and hence, along with the rest of nature, are part of the raw material of production.

Darwinian/Marxian MOOSE is so pervasive a belief that I want to take time to give a counter-example that directly contradicts both "material need" and survival of the fittest as motivations of human development. The gentle Tasmanian people lived perfectly comfortably for 5000 years in a bitterly cold climate without shoes or coats, without anything considered "proper clothing," and without use of fire for warmth, until they were beaten and tortured to near-genocidal death last century by British sailors and settlers raised on MOOSE.

Darwinian/Marxism forces class categories and conflicts, since by definition those without complex material culture, especially of "use" or "need," are considered stupid or at best "underprivileged"; while those classes and cultures that excel at collecting and producing goods are by definition considered "privileged," and constant efforts are made to "educate everyone" to be "smart" and "advanced" enough to collect lots of material culture.

Freud added the individual's own inner and personal life experience and relationship to the body, especially to the phallus, as his contribution to MOOSE. Little boys have something more, little girls envy them. This MOOSE is so well accepted that even a prominent woman biologist has described the clitoris, not as large and unique and the only organ specifically orgasmic in function, but rather as a "vestigial penis." That is to say, not only do males differentiate critically from the "feminine" in order to individuate, but women do so as well! A friend told me a story illustrating how artificially induced the concept of "penis envy" of little girls is. Her 3-year-old niece began to cry after the girl's mother explained to her that a boy has a penis and a girl does not have one. Responding to the inconsolable sobbing, her mother elicited a tearful explanation: the injustice that little boys get to have "peanuts" while she did not get to have any "peanuts." Therein lies the power of story. And of inequity.

We are surrounded by MOOSE myths, from the classic taming of the West as a shoot-out between two or more men, to the marketing of women's cooking and healing traditions as if they were invented by men: Bayer aspirin, Budweiser Beer, and Colonel Sander's Fried Chicken. Our society holds to the myth that acquisition is a "necessity," the myth of random chance in evolution; the myth of oedipal complex, the myth of the withering away of the state after communism redistributes goods, the myth of intelligence as the ability to retain and regurgitate abstract vocabularies and patterns, and all the myths of race and class characteristics; the myth of a single "building block" of the universe; the "big bang" theory; the mind/body split; and a variety of materialist myths about the nature of time, of spirit, of how the mind is constructed.

We live in a sea of MOOSE. Gimbutas is our first usable raft.

With her brilliant combination of both archeology and mythology, Gimbutas has created the first FOOSE that uses materialist evidence. This particular combination is why hers is such an important myth for our time. She knits together two forms that have been separated. Hard science and mythology are not even in the same schools, departments or buildings in our college system. They are split the same way the mind/body is split. Few scientists admit or perhaps think about how thoroughly origin myth informs their theories, shapes and directs the nature of their inquiries and enables the popular imagination to grasp, admire, and use their conclusions. So authoritarian and exclusive is materialist MOOSE that it has used its narrow vision to nearly destroy the word "myth" itself. The popular media, emulating science leaders, uses the word myth to mean lie or fantasy. This furthers the illusion that one single story is true, is the only possible version.

Nevertheless, Gimbutas gives us a solid foundation of female imagery from the distant past, and a marvelous emblematic language underlying European culture. Also helpful to me is that she emphasizes "female moisture" as a major motif, so menstrual themes are at least implied in her work. That her theory rests so squarely on metaphors of birth and that her belief is that the Kurgan people were male barbarians mounted on horseback produces a more woman-only focus than might otherwise be true, and makes it FOOSE. Men haven't enough to do in her "matristic" ideal world except wait for their barbarian entrance waving the flags of sky gods and authoritarianism overhead. But the sheer variety of her findings and her deciphering of a language of symbol and motif in imagery and incised geometry on the icons of Old Europe give us a way to stand outside of MOOSE and differentiate ourselves from it. And then to formulate new origin stories that are more gender inclusive (swallow MOOSE and FOOSE with FAMOSE) to guide us into the next era.

If we live in a sea of MOOSE and Gimbutas is our first raft, my metaformic theory is new land in a new place.

One reason why men frequently think that women make no contribution to culture is that they see the vast strata of women's contribution as "nature"; and they see this because their own MOOSE philosophers have taught them that the basis of development is "material necessity." So they think that women's accomplishments of home, hoe, and hearth are somehow "natural" when they actually required the most primal and startling originality. FAMOSE teaches that the purposes of all culture were fundamentally the holding of ideas: consciousness, not "material necessity" created culture. Necessity may be the mother of invention, but not of creation. Metaformic thinking is the mother of creation.

My metaformic theory is not the only FAMOSE, of course. All womanism is seeking FAMOSE, and all pagan pantheons are rooted in FAMOSE; the creation stories and rituals of many indigenous peoples have richly FAMOSE content.

However, to the extent that these are local or antiquated myth and ritual, they cannot compete with global MOOSE with its vast myth- and image-producing media, and the formidable resources and persuasive power of the hard sciences with which to exert belief systems.

That MOOSE is being challenged as much as it is is a tribute to both feminism and people of color pluralism. Gimbutas' FOOSE and metaformic theory are both promising as challenges to MOOSE because their theoretical basis rests on science. In my case, as anthropology, archeology, and ethnography effectively spill out more accurate information they contribute to metaformic theory.

Blood is a more universal human experience than almost anything. Blood rites are related to consciousness, to rites of passage and to transformation of all kinds, our group identities and to our deepest national and personal motivations.

Metaformic theory is not Eurocentric; it draws its examples from commonalities of every different human culture and every person's relationship to culture and lineage. By making careful politically and culturally sensitive uses of anthropology, ethnography, mythology, and folklore coupled with electronic group self-reflection (say, through groups making videos of themselves) we could see cultural self-and-other examinations become not "big" but grand "little" science of the twenty-first century.

Metaformic theory says that what differentiates humans from animals is menstruation and its connection to a clearly visible exterior cycle, the lunar cycle. Menstrual rites pulled human consciousness into being. Two non-material necessities are in effect: necessity of the female gender to teach menstrual consciousness to non-menstruating males; and necessity for males to display, use, and re-reflect their understandings of consciousness. They did this by developing their own blood rites and seclusion rites. The results have been cultural artifacts and practices that "contain" our ideas.

In seclusion women sat, lay or stood in sometimes difficult but nevertheless meaningful postures, shunned men and sex, ate simply and developed utensils. These practices came from ideas about separating hands or other parts of the body from the numinous blood. Menstruating women in their seclusion rites developed body arts, shapes, and protections which have become human clothing and cosmetics, and were or even still are credited with awesome capacity to influence natural forces in village life.

In reflecting their own comprehensions of these mysteries, males excelled at public display, developed their own clubs, engaged in grandiose bloodsheds and became big story-tellers.

This dynamic is why so much of humanity appears to have two strata: a female private strata (thought of as nature) and a male public strata (thought of as culture). Both strata are culture if we understand that all distinctly "human" behavior is based in menstrual and other blood rituals.

Metaformic theory teaches that women's culture, the first strata, originates in the containing of consciousness rather than in material necessity. Thus, women gatherers of the ancestral past did not "need" to bring early cultigens home and garden them; this was additional effort, done for the purposes of ritualizing consciousness. Many of the substances carried home to serve as red dyes for ceremonies were originally inedible or poisonous. Some ritual processes such as heating, salting or mixing with other substances enabled them to become edible, and they gradually became the most important foodstuffs for later economic development: agricultural and industrial people. Such cultigens as potatoes, yams, the major grains, carrots, cola, tobacco, turmeric, saffron, chili, honey, olives, and so on were first valued for metaformic purposes – chiefly as red dyes or red paste which could be used for menstrually based performances of cosmological ideas, ideas that tied men and women together and tied both to plants in ritual relationship.

According to this theory, women were first attracted to little red beans metaformically, and only later roasted them for eating. So we see that women first had peanuts.

Metaformic theory promises to be dynamic rather than static, and to posit a dynamic interaction between the genders that propels us in our evolutionary spiral. Sometimes men are predominantly driving new cultural forms, sometimes women are. There is always a dialectic tension between them that will force the next wave.

Metaformic theory is inclusive, both genderwise and cross-culturally; it is relational rather than competitive, and describes some essentials of why we behave in the bizarre and un-animal-like ways we do. According to my metaformic theory, war and aggression are not the central creation principles; they are one disbalanced evolution of male imitations of menstrual rite. Unlike Gimbutas' FOOSE theory, which relegates these male-developed arts to the nefarious netherworld of "barbarian sky-god worshipping" hoodlums, FAMOSE metaformic theory appreciates the cultural contributions and technological accelerations that, in the last few hundred years, were consequences of war. However, warfare has evolved to the edge of the abyss of nuclear annihilation. Even at their "best," wars are vendettas against civilian populations and leave a generation of veterans with shattered psyches. We can glorify it no longer. And what is battle basically if not a parallel menstrual rite of passage, a sacrificial rite, for late adolescent boys? To get their heads shaved, eat simple foods, go without sex, stand and sit in prescribed, uncomfortable postures, bond with each other, act in behalf of the whole, and shed blood. Can we not imagine better puberty initiations that stop short of violent bloodshed?

The phrase "against casting" refers to a recent mass media method of assimilating non-male, non-white groups to MOOSE. A MOOSE myth, such as the shoot-out that perpetually tames the West, features two, usually white men firing bullets at each other until the designated "bad" one dies. If the main hero is suddenly cast as a female or a dark man, this is called "against casting." In a civil war film, "against casting" an African-American man as a judge is historically inaccurate, but helps assimilate African-American people to the traditional MOOSE myth. This also makes the teaching of history an exercise in continually revising revisions, but never changes the MOOSE plot.

MOOSE myth has led us into serious social problems. Men batter women in part because they are taught that they need to be in control of society, since they or a god just like them invented it. In some groups, men taunt each other for failing to "control your woman." MOOSE religious leaders teaching that God is male and controlling enforce this code of male "honor."

Racial and class-based caste systems flourish for lack of FAMOSE myths and rites, which are inclusive of everyone as part of sacred and interactive creation story. Under MOOSE, dark and poor peoples, but especially dark young men, are socially constructed as a shadow side of elite white psyche. Liberal white social policy arranges for many dark young men to be outside the "legitimate" economy, angry, alienated and violently expressive. Conservative white social policy polices this behavior by arranging for this group to be publicly imaged, punished, confined (in latter-day seclusions) and frequently ill-treated, which keeps the cycle – a blood cycle – spinning. Someone needs to say that both policies are inherently racist and classist. FAMOSE asks, "Why does elite white society *need* a socially enacted shadow side?"

We now need "against writing" and theories of new rituals the production of non-shoot-out methods of creating and maintaining societies. Women get tired of the ways men bleed, yet continue in shame to hide the peaceful bleeding and its peaceful ritual potential.

Origin stories direct the courses of societies. The new electronic loom of the internet and television visuals are direct results of MOOSE efforts; but used democratically as we whirl into the next millennia, the media should be an instrument for replacement myths that are FAMOSE, FAMOSE, and more FAMOSE.

BIBLIOGRAPHY

Gimbutas, Marija Alseikait (1982) *The Goddesses and Gods of Old Europe, 6500 to 3500 BC: Myths and Cult Images* (new and updated edn), Berkeley: University of California.

—— (1989) *The Language of the Goddess: Unearthing the Hidden Symbols of Western Civilization*, London: Thames and Hudson.

—— (1991) *The Civilization of the Goddess* (1st edn), San Francisco, CA: HarperSanFrancisco.

Gimbutas, Marija Alseikait and Marler, Joan (1997) *From the Realm of the Ancestors: An Anthology in Honor of Marija Gimbutas*, Manchester, CT: Knowledge Ideas & Trends.

Grahn, Judith (1993) *Blood, Bread, and Roses: How Menstruation Created the World*, Boston, MA: Beacon Press.

Chapter 15

Reasonable Woman/ Reasonable Man

The emergence of a modern archetype of gender equality in political life

Peter Rutter

Unceasing dynamic interaction between inner and outer worlds – in this case more specifically the interaction between what is held inside the individual psyche and what is manifested outwardly in the civic/political life of the community – has in the last decade of the twentieth century bred a new archetypal image: that of the conjoined Reasonable Woman/Reasonable Man. Although new, the archetype of the Reasonable Woman/Reasonable Man is a variant of one of the most fundamental of all archetypes: the *Coniunctio Oppositorum* (Latin for the joining together of the opposites), as is described with such subtlety and complexity by C.G. Jung in *The Psychology of the Transference* (*CW* 16: 163–323).

Thus Reasonable Woman/Reasonable Man, as an archetype, reaches back and forth from the cultural environment, through ego-consciousness, down to the very depths of the unconscious and the psychobiological self, transcending and expanding the meaning of "reasonable" far beyond its sense of the logical, linear or rational. Rather, this archetype manifests a reasonableness beyond reason, and is instead a representation of the best possibilities of our human qualities, in Jungian terminology referred to as the self. Through the emergence in political life of the archetype of Reasonable Woman/Reasonable Man, the psyche has successfully interposed the self-values of integrity, wholeness, and the dignity of the individual into the culture in ways that instill both ancient and new values of relatedness, even compassion, in the daily life of our communities and our civic society.

This chapter describes how the archetype of the Reasonable Woman/Reasonable Man has quite recently emerged as a representation of gender equality, how its presence in the culture affects the individual psyche in some remarkable and inspiring ways, and how it and other new archetypes can germinate in the fertile soil of the meeting place between psyche and politics.

From a conventional psychological understanding there are several unusual aspects to the development of the Reasonable Woman/Reasonable Man archetype. For one, the symbolic imagery of this archetype did not appear directly from the psyche, as would a dream or vision. More like a mature work of art, the psyche needed outward cultural practices and institutions to contain and hone the development of this archetype. Unlike a conventional work of art, however, the Reasonable Woman/Reasonable Man archetype was rendered into form, in 1991, through a quintessentially *political* process: it sprang into its current configuration through word and idea, in this case the words and ideas of a Federal Judge in an opinion he wrote for the United States Court of Appeals in a case called Ellison vs. Brady. The ramifications of this case serve to remind us that the archetypal underpinnings of the Judge and the Law are present in our daily political life.

The case of Ellison vs. Brady itself provided particularly fertile ground for the creation of a new archetype. It was a sexual harassment case, so the central conflict in the case reflected our culture's core anxiety and shadow regarding sexual behavior and its links to inequalities of power. Sexual harassment law is in itself unique in that it begins to apply standards and values for sexual and gender-based behavior that emanate from the public, civic arena into what was previously claimed to be within the exempt zone of private behavior. Sexual harassment law is Civil Rights law, and in itself is revolutionary because it establishes for every individual in our society a civil right not to be subjected to certain kinds of previously allowable sexual behavior – if that behavior unreasonably interferes with one's employment or educational opportunities.

Although the idea of mandating a new standard of sexual behavior as public policy and civic duty may seem to some an intrusion of politics into the psyche, one point that I wish to make here is that this political idea from the outer world also sprang, as did the Reasonable Woman/Reasonable Man archetype itself, from the inner world of the psyche. Indeed, the broader area of Civil Rights law itself is a product of the grand collaboration between psyche and politics that this volume is about.

In describing the evolution of an archetypal image, let me clarify the terminology I am using. Drawing from Jung, I consider an archetype to be a fundamental element of form through which the psyche can experience both itself and the outside world. Archetypal forms both allow and delimit our perception and experience in the world, and can usefully be grouped in pairs of opposites, such as merger or separation, light or dark, danger or safety, anxiety or peace, self or not-self. In my view, archetypes are fundamental units of form that exist in the unseparated body/mind. They are components of the neuropsychological scaffolding, so to speak, that allow the psyche to generate such higher-order functions as consciousness, language, emotion, symbol, thought and meaning. This use of the concept of archetype is congruent with that of Anthony Stevens in his book *Archetypes: A Natural History of the Self*. He defined archetypes as "innate neuropsychic centres possessing the capacity to initiate, control and mediate the common behavioral characteristics and typical experiences of all beings irrespective of race, culture or creed" (1982: 296).

This psychobiological view of archetype is of an indwelling formal capacity for structure through which the organ system called "psyche" functions, in collaboration, of course, with the brain, the nervous system and the neurotransmitter chemicals – much in the way that other organ systems of the body operate. For instance, bone marrow, red cells, white cells, platelets, the heart, blood-vessels and plasma are forms through which the circulatory system functions. Within this biologically grounded definition, in my view everything we can now call an archetype is the product of the evolution of the human species. Furthermore, such evolution of the psyche has always taken place in the cauldron of the meeting place between the individual organism and its environment, just as it has for all the other organ systems of the human species.

A billion years ago the struggle between organism and environment was limited to molecular transactions between blue-green algae cells and the elemental chemical environment of the planet earth's carbon, nitrogen, hydrogen and oxygen. Yet as the organism that became human evolved, it developed more and more capacities through which transactions between organism and environment could take place. At the present time, I contend that the resonating interaction between the psyche and the impact of the cultural environment we have created is akin to our ancient struggle with the physical environment. Now, the dynamic interaction of psyche and culture fuels the evolution of new psychological forms, or archetypes. A parallel dynamic of the evolution in the twentieth century of the "psychological cultural attitude" is described by the Jungian analyst Joseph Henderson in his ground-breaking book analyzing the interaction of psyche and culture, *Cultural Attitudes in Psychological Perspective* (1984).

With that prelude, let me move on to a more specific discussion of how I have come to view the Reasonable Woman/Reasonable Man as a new archetype, and what I see as its unique meaning. Jungian-oriented clinicians and students of analytical psychology are most accustomed to noticing expressions of archetypal forms as they emerge in dreams, in religious and spiritual ritual forms, in visual arts, theater and opera, and in literary forms such as novels and fairy-tales. From this perspective, I am claiming the emergence of an archetypal form from a very different source indeed – in this case, from a judge's opinion in a United States Federal Court.

The story of Ellison vs. Brady is one of the thousands told daily in our court rooms, one that is drawn from the seemingly trivial events, feelings and grievances of everyday modern life, told and retold by lawyers and jurors and judges without any particular awareness that they have often created a story with age-old mythic form. Of course, no court room story, just as no therapy hour, is even remotely trivial when we remind ourselves that both are representations of the struggle of the individual self to live safely and with dignity in the world, despite the wounds and deprivations emanating from both the psyche and the outside world.

The story that led to the articulation of the Reasonable Woman/ Reasonable Man archetype, briefly told, takes place at a United States Internal Revenue Service office in San Mateo, California, where IRS employee Sterling Gray invited fellow employee Kerry Ellison to lunch one day. Ms Ellison went to lunch with Mr Gray, but declined subsequent invitations from him toward any further socializing. Yet, several weeks later, Mr Gray handed Ms Ellison a note which read:

> I cried over you last night and I'm totally drained today. I have never been in such constant term oil [*sic*]. Thank you for talking with me. I could not stand to feel your hatred for another day.

Ms Ellison became frightened by this note and informed her supervisor, who felt it constituted sexual harassment. Ms Ellison, however, chose not to file a formal complaint but simply to ask a male co-worker to clarify with Mr Gray that she was not interested in him. Within a few days, with no further contact from Mr Gray, she left the office for four weeks to begin a prearranged IRS training course in St Louis. But while she was in St Louis, Mr Gray wrote Ms Ellison a letter saying, in part:

> I know that you are worth knowing with or without sex. . . . Leaving aside the hassles and disasters of recent week. I have enjoyed knowing you so much over these past few months. Watching you. Experiencing you from O so far away. Admiring your style and elan. . . . Don't you think it odd that two people who have never even talked together, alone, are striking off such intense sparks . . . I will write another letter in the near future.

Frightened as Kerry Ellison was by this further communication, she did not file a sexual harassment complaint. Instead, after informing her supervisor in San Mateo, she counted on IRS administrative procedures to discipline Mr Gray – who was indeed transferred to a San Francisco IRS office, about twenty miles north of San Mateo – and to inform him yet again not to contact Ms Ellison in any way. She then returned to her office after the training sessions in St Louis were completed, with the problem apparently resolved. However, Mr Gray appealed against the transfer after only three weeks. He requested a return to San Mateo, which he was granted would occur in four months, and he again contacted Ms Ellison with some imputation that they had a relationship.

When Ms Ellison first heard that Mr Gray was to be transferred back to her office she became quite frightened, and only then did she file a sexual harassment complaint, both against her harasser and against her employer for creating a hostile work environment. Clearly, her fear of future events should Mr Gray return to her workplace was central to her complaint. Nevertheless, the Federal District Court rejected her claim because it felt that the IRS had dealt adequately with the original harassment, and that Ms Ellison's fear of future events did not constitute sexual harassment on the basis of a hostile work environment.

This, then, set the stage for Kerry Ellison's appeal. Would her inner state, that of extreme fear on hearing that Mr Gray would be transferred back to her workplace, qualify as a "reasonable" basis for making a hostile environment sexual harassment claim?

On 23 February 1991, Judge Robert R. Beezer of the United States Court of Appeals, Ninth Circuit, handed down his opinion in Ellison vs. Brady. The standard legal citation for this case is: 924 F.2d 872 (9th Circuit 1991), but this opinion is now known in our social and jurisprudential history as the "Reasonable Woman Decision." In it, US Appellate Judges Beezer and Alex Kozinski, both appointed to the bench by President Ronald Reagan and considered to be Republican and Conservative, voted two to one in favor of Ms Ellison's sexual harassment claim against the IRS (personified as the defendant by then Secretary of the Treasury

Nicholas Brady). Judge Beezer's opinion addressed one of the pivotal evolving questions in sexual harassment law and policy: given that sexual harassment law and policy forbids conduct of a sexual nature that creates "an intimidating, hostile or offensive working environment" (US EEOC Guidelines on Discrimination Because of Sex, 1980), from whose perspective should we make the judgment of whether or not there is a hostile environment? If we remain true to the historical standard of the "reasonable man" or "reasonable person," are we perpetuating sex discrimination by not differentiating the perspective of the "reasonable woman?" What transformed Judge Beezer's opinion into the historic Reasonable Woman Decision was the following passage:

> We adopt the perspective of the reasonable woman primarily because we believe that a sex-blind reasonable person standard tends to be male-biased and tends to systematically ignore the experiences of woman. . . . We realize that there is a broad range of viewpoints among women as a group, but we believe that many women share common concerns which men do not necessarily share. For example, because women are disproportionately victims of rape and sexual assault, women have a stronger incentive to be concerned with sexual behavior. Women who are victims of mild forms of sexual harassment may understandably worry whether a harasser's conduct is merely a prelude to violent sexual assault. Men, who are rarely victims of sexual assault, may view sexual conduct in a vacuum without a full appreciation of the social setting or the underlying threat of violence that a woman may perceive.

In issuing this opinion, Judge Beezer installed into the public psyche the personhood of the Reasonable Woman, abandoning the age-old perspective of the "reasonable person," or "reasonable man." The Reasonable Woman takes her place, to be sure, alongside the Reasonable Man – Judge Beezer reminds us that when men allege sexual harassment, "the appropriate perspective would be that of a reasonable man."

Judge Beezer described what he saw as the flaw in the reasonable person standard:

> If we only examined whether a reasonable person would engage in allegedly harassing conduct, we would run the risk of reinforcing the prevailing level of discrimination. Harassers would continue to harass merely because a particular discriminatory practice was common, and victims of harassment would have no remedy.

He also captured the dynamic, evolutionary quality of the interaction of psyche and politics when he observed:

> Conduct considered harmless by many today may be considered discriminatory in the future. Fortunately, the reasonableness inquiry which we adopt today is not static. As the views of reasonable woman change, so too does the . . . standard of acceptable behavior.

The importance of the establishment of a Reasonable Woman as a co-equal to the Reasonable Man should not be underestimated. As a milestone of cultural history, the court opinion in Ellison vs. Brady has brought into stable form the first archetypal image of gender equality in the history of our culture – meaning the cultural history of European–North American Civilization. Whether archetypal images of gender equality exist in other cultures is an important and interesting question beyond the scope of this discussion, but they do not exist in the West. In the evolution of our culture, I find it inspiring and hopeful that a stable archetypal image of gender equality should have arisen in a culture that has until very recent history regarded women as inferior beings and as property. As an archetypal form, it is there to be built upon into the future as a vision, not yet realized, of true social and political equality. As such it is allied with and supports other forms of social and political equalities along other dimensions, such as race, color, religion, sex, national origin, economic status, physical ability or sexual preference.

I want here to describe further the psychological-political dynamic through which I believe a new archetypal form such as the Reasonable Woman/Reasonable Man can evolve. In doing so I hope to clarify why I consider Reasonable Woman/ Reasonable Man to be an archetype, rather than a fleeting cultural form. As I imagine it, the idea that women and men were political and social equals was intuited innumerable times in the history of our culture by countless women and men. But because in the evolution of our culture we developed a social structure that was in such stark contrast to the notion of gender equality, intuitions and articulations of gender equality were sent out to the culture time and again, only to disappear, as do brief vapor trails. For millennia, indeed until only recently, the political and civic life of the culture would not or could not contain and hold in stable form the notion of gender equality, among other equalities.

But the psyche did not give up. No matter how oppressed by even the most monstrous political inequalities – female infanticide, legalized rape, genocide, conquer and wholesale slaughter of defeated peoples, slavery, persecutions based on difference of color, gender, religious or political belief – the undaunted psyche, meaning countless undaunted individual women and men, kept "dreaming" of possible political and social forms that did not yet exist, and in fact had never existed.

I introduce the term "dream" here quite intentionally, to represent what I see as the dynamic source of these persistent notions of equality in a universe where no such outward form existed. To me there is a strong explanation for the ability of people to continually and persistently generate the idea, image, intuition, of equality: that it is an indwelling, psychobiologically based form – an archetype. Equality is a form that the human psyche has carried within itself for millennia, to be dreamed and dreamed again, waiting for a political climate that could recognize it, respond to it, and hold it stably so both cultural and individual growth could be built upon it. It is as if the biosphere had evolved seeds of flowering plants for millions of years (which I surmise that it did) before it also evolved the soil in which such seeds could take root, producing an enduring family of flowers. Thus such seeds had to be "re-invented" by evolution over and over again until they could take root.

So despite its power as an indwelling archetype, capable of being imagined and dreamed, gender equality could never take root. It had to be re-invented, as I believe it was without fail in every society in every era, and cast out into the political environment to see if it could take root.

In our cultural history, the ideas of liberty and equality became institutionalized – fleetingly in the French Revolution, and permanently (thus far) in the Rights cited by the American Declaration of Independence. Although the Declaration of Independence's language was overtly gender-unequal, its spirit created the very political environment that eventually gave life to the archetypal expression of gender equality when it proclaimed:

> We hold these Truths to be self-evident, that all Men are created equal, that they are endowed by their Creator with certain unalienable Rights, that among those are Life, Liberty, and the Pursuit of Happiness.

Nevertheless, its articulation of unalienable Rights began an uninterrupted evolution that has led to very real, stably held forms of equality. This evolution has all occurred in the American Agora – the free marketplace of ideas – through civic discourse, in legislation, in constitutional law and judicial opinions, in jury findings, in political activism from those whose rights were unequal, in the psyches of individual men and women who either dreamed of equality or were confronted with the grievances of those who demanded equality. Some of the signal events in the evolution of these rights were in Lincoln's Emancipation Proclamation abolishing slavery, in the fight for Women's Suffrage, in the union movement of organizing labor, in the 1955 Supreme Court decision in Brown vs. Board of Education that ruled illegal segregation in public schools and other facilities, in the lunch counter sit-ins and freedom rides that were the backbone of the African-American Civil Rights Movement, in the Women's Rights movement that labored for a hundred years against all odds to have the society accept gender equality as real, and in the passage of subsequent Civil Rights legislation that led to what we now know as sexual harassment law. At a certain point, a critical mass is attained of individuals dreaming the same dream (as Martin Luther King invoked so eloquently) of a new political form, and the political landscape is significantly altered. Yet even that cannot occur without the co-evolution, so to speak, of the political soil itself.

One of the most moving and hopeful implications about the partnership between psyche and culture in creating stable images of equality is that those who hold superior political power are able to relinquish some of it in the attempt to create equality – put another way, in an attempt to honor the Archetype of Equality, once it has been elevated to a politically articulated ideal. Lincoln and an all-white/male power elite promulgated the Emancipation Proclamation. Men passed the nineteenth Amendment to the Constitution, providing the basis for women to vote. An all-white male Supreme Court unanimously held racial segregation to be illegal in Brown vs. Board of Education. An overwhelmingly white male Congress – with nearly equal numbers of Republicans and Democrats in support – passed the Civil

Rights Act of 1964, which created a legal basis for naming and eradicating gender discrimination. This in turn has led to the articulation of sexual harassment law, and in a direct line to Judges Beezer and Kozinski (again, appointed by President Reagan) who voted for what became the Reasonable Woman Decision and the creation of the first stable archetypal image of gender equality. A strong recent example of this same dynamic in the political arena was the peaceful handing over of power in South Africa to the Nelson Mandela-led African National Congress by the formerly murderously racist white apartheid regime.

There are other explanations of why people in power might voluntarily cede some of their own in the interests of equality. One could argue that they are motivated only by their perception of self-interest, are bowing to expediency and are cutting the best deal they believe that the political environment allows. To me, such an explanation is not only unduly cynical, but it defies reality. Despite the most barbaric setbacks imaginable having occurred in the twentieth century – I refer to the Holocaust and other genocides, the World Wars and the countless other wars – I do not see how we could have evolved the stable ideas of equality, human rights and civil rights if they were not indwelling archetypal strivings. In fact, it is only from the perspective of these notions of equality that we can be as horrified as we are by such human rights violations. Before ideas of equality took root, genocide, slavery and rape were so culturally syntonic that anyone objecting would be considered to be expressing a psychotic delusion. For that is the fate of an archetypal idea expressed into a culture that cannot contain and positively mirror it. I would like to think that the manifestation of these rights confers some evolutionary advantage on us as a species; some evolutionary capacity not to destroy each other seems to me to have been beneficial to the human race for a long time, not limited to its absolute necessity in the nuclear age.

The soil to contain the seed, then, is as much a product of archetypal psychological-political evolution as is the seed itself. However, the seed tends to precede the soil. The seed of an archetypal dream or intuition, however fleeting, needs only one individual, whereas the soil of cultural evolution needs a stable community of individuals invested in nurturing the archetypal ideas emanating from the seeds. In this case, the community is represented by the American Democracy, at the leading edge of a line of cultural evolution that we call Western civilization. The American Democracy seems capable of stably holding in the community the notion of equality. In order to do so, it counts on and responds to, on both the collective and individual levels, stably held archetypal forms. Gender equality is an idea that many individuals, over the millennia, have attempted to plant in our culture by casting seeds of an archetypal intuition. That the archetype of the Reasonable Woman/Reasonable Man is now stably codified through the opinion in Ellison vs. Brady is of immeasurable importance. It is as if our political psyche has located and created the well, the source of equality to which it can now go back again and again for sustenance and encouragement. And even though the United States Supreme Court in subsequent decisions went back to using the gender-blind language of the "reasonable person standard" in sexual harassment law, the

Court – down to its most conservative Justices Antonin Scalia and Clarence Thomas – now unanimously understands and accepts that the reasonable person standard includes the disparate experiences and perspectives of *both* the Reasonable Woman and the Reasonable Man. Once named, she cannot easily be voided.

Yet there is much work ahead to more fully realize and render into socially concrete form the values of this new archetype. Sustenance and encouragement is what the ideas of gender and other equalities will always need. We are each inescapably involved in both the psychological and cultural levels of conflict between destructive energies and ideas, and the more encouraging, creative, life-sustaining forces. The struggle between light and shadow is played out in both the outer and the inner world. The impact of stably held political and cultural forms such as the Reasonable Woman/Reasonable Man archetype in influencing that struggle cannot be underestimated. When an individual struggles with his or her personal suffering as a result of societal injury, the fact that somewhere it is written that this suffering is unjust can become the first stably held inner container that leads to individual healing.

I have witnessed the healing power of the archetype of Reasonable Woman/ Reasonable Man in working with people on both sides of sexual harassment conflicts and other kinds of boundary violations. The existence of an objective, political standard of equality in our society often helps to ease the suffering of women who have been harassed or sexually assaulted, especially when the politically expressed standard also, as does this archetype, directly invokes the integrity and wholeness of the self. Through this archetype and the whole body of civil rights that it represents, traumatized women have another voice – as well as practical remedies that can be expressed in the outer, legal world – that can begin to answer back to the assaultive internalized self-hatred that is often the deepest and most enduring injury in cases of sexual boundary violation. Likewise, I have worked with men who have harassed women, simply by acting out of long-held behavioral patterns that our culture has for millennia approved of and held out as acceptable. The degraded inner images of women that are introjected by the male psyche from the culture then allow enactments of degrading and violent outer behavior. Yet I have seen men draw upon the messages communicated by the archetype of the Reasonable Woman/ Reasonable Man and begin to reorient in a respectful direction not only their behavior toward women, but their inner attitudes toward the feminine in both themselves and the outer world.

The wake-up call for such men is often through the application of sexual harassment law or policy in their workplace or educational environment. Yet even when inner change is enforced by law through the political process, if the values invoked are supported by the power of an archetypal form, beneath men's resistance to change at the ego level can often lie a positive identification at the level of the self with the idea of gender equality.

Our society threatens to be divided by racial and gender-based conflict and culture wars, with articulated rationales that defend domestic terrorism and personal violence on the basis of race, ethnicity, gender, sexual orientation or child-bearing choice. In the face of this, the archetype of the Reasonable Woman/Reasonable Man is one of many that may emerge through the co-evolution of politics and psyche that will draw from the well of archetypal ideas of equality, thus sustaining and healing us as individuals and as a society. I have on a number of occasions sat in a room together with a man and a woman who had been involved in a damaging sexual boundary violation, attempting against enormous impasses to facilitate a conflict resolution and healing between them. When successful, despite the depth of injury and anger that divides this man and this woman, I know that I have witnessed before me the living transformation of the perpetrator–victim dyad into a living embodiment, in these two previously irreconcilable people, of the Reasonable Woman/ Reasonable Man archetype. In this possibility lies great hope for the future of our psychological and political life.

BIBLIOGRAPHY

Henderson, Joseph (1984) *Cultural Attitudes in Psychological Perspective*, Toronto: Inner City Books.

Jung, C.G. (1966) "Coniunctionis Oppositorum," in *The Psychology of the Transference*, *CW* 16: 163–323.

Stevens, Anthony (1982) *Archetypes: A Natural History of the Self*, New York: William Morrow.

United States Equal Opportunity Commission (EEOC) (1980) *Guidelines on Discrimination because of Sex*, Washington, DC.

Chapter 16

Is the modern psyche undergoing a rite of passage?

Richard Tarnas

> [A] mood of universal destruction and renewal . . . has set its mark on our age. This mood makes itself felt everywhere, politically, socially, and philosophically. We are living in what the Greeks called the *kairos* – the right moment – for a "metamorphosis of the gods," of the fundamental principles and symbols. This peculiarity of our time, which is certainly not of our conscious choosing, is the expression of the unconscious man within us who is changing. Coming generations will have to take account of this momentous transformation if humanity is not to destroy itself through the might of its own technology and science. . . . So much is at stake and so much depends on the psychological constitution of modern man.
>
> C. G. Jung

What are the deep stirrings in the collective psyche of the West today that could affect our public life in the future? Can we discern any larger patterns in the immensely complex and seemingly chaotic flux and flow of our age?

Influenced by the depth psychology tradition founded a century ago by Freud and Jung, and especially since the 1960s and the radical increase in psychological self-consciousness which that era helped mediate, the cultural ethos of recent decades has made us well aware of how important is the psychological task of understanding our personal histories. We have sought ever deeper insight into our individual biographies, looking to recover the often hidden sources of our present condition, to render conscious those unconscious forces and complexes that shape our lives. Many now recognize that same task as critical for our entire civilization.

What individuals and psychologists have long been doing has now become the collective responsibility of our culture: to make the unconscious conscious. And for a civilization, to a crucial extent, *history* is the great unconscious – history not so much as the external chronology of political and military milestones, but as the *interior* history of a civilization: that unfolding drama evidenced in a culture's evolving cosmology, its philosophy and science, its religious consciousness, its art, its myths. For us to participate fully and creatively in shaping our future, we need to better understand the underlying patterns and influences of our collective past.

Only then can we begin to grasp what forces move within us today, and perhaps glimpse what may be emerging on the new millennial horizon.

I focus my discussion here on the West, but not out of any triumphalist presumption that the West is somehow intrinsically superior to other civilizations and thus most worthy of our attention. I do so rather because it is the West that has brought forth the political, technological, intellectual, and spiritual currents that have been most decisive in constellating the contemporary world situation in all its problematic complexity. For better or worse, the character of the West has had a global impact, and will continue to do so for the foreseeable future. Yet I also address the historical evolution of Western consciousness because, for most of us reading these words, this development represents our own tradition, our legacy, our ancestral cultural matrix. Attending carefully and critically to this tradition fulfills a certain responsibility to the past, to our ancestors, just as attempting to understand its deeper implications fulfills a responsibility to the future, to our children.

A paradox confronts every sensitive observer about the West. On the one hand, we cannot fail to recognize a certain dynamism, a brilliant, heroic impulse, even a nobility, at work in Western civilization and in Western thought. We see this in the great achievements of Greek philosophy and art, for example, or in the Sistine Chapel and other Renaissance masterpieces, in the plays of Shakespeare, in the music of Bach or Beethoven. We see it in the brilliance of the Copernican revolution, with the tremendous cosmological and even metaphysical transformation it has wrought in our civilization's worldview. We see it in the unprecedented space flights of a generation ago, landing men on the moon, or, more recently, in the spectacular images of the vast cosmos coming from the Hubbell telescope and the new data and perspectives these images have brought forth. And of course the great democratic revolutions of modernity, and the powerful emancipatory movements of our own era, vividly reflect this extraordinary dynamism and even nobility of the West.

Yet at the same time we are forced to admit that this very same historical tradition has caused immense suffering and loss, for many other cultures and peoples, for many people within Western culture itself, and for many other forms of life on the planet. Moreover, the West has played the central role in bringing about a subtly growing and seemingly inexorable crisis on our planet, a crisis of multidimensional complexity: ecological, political, social, economic, intellectual, psychological, spiritual. To say our global civilization is becoming dysfunctional scarcely conveys the gravity of the situation. For humankind and the planet, we face the possibility of great catastrophe. For many forms of life on Earth, that catastrophe has already taken place. How can we make sense of this tremendous paradox in the character and meaning of the West?

If we examine many of the intellectual and cultural debates of our time, particularly near the epicenter of the major paradigm battles today, it is possible to see looming behind them two fundamental interpretations, two archetypal stories or metanarratives, concerning the evolution of human consciousness and the history of the Western mind. In essence these two metanarratives reflect two deep myths in the collective psyche – and let us define myths here not as mere falsehoods, nor as collective fantasies of an arbitrary sort, but rather as profound and enduring patterns of meaning that inform the human psyche and constellate its diverse realities. These two great myths in the collective psyche structure our historical self-understanding in very different ways. One could be called the myth of progress, the other the myth of the fall.

The first, familiar to all of us from our education, describes the evolution of human consciousness, and particularly the history of the Western mind, as an extraordinary progressive development, a long heroic journey from a primitive world of dark ignorance, suffering, and limitation to a brighter modern world of ever-increasing knowledge, freedom, and well-being. This great trajectory of progress is seen as having been made possible by the sustained development of human reason, and above all by the emergence of the modern mind. We recognize this view whenever we encounter a book or program whose title is something like "The Ascent of Man" or "The Discoverers" or "Man's Conquest of Space," and so forth. The direction of history is seen as onward and upward. Humanity is here often personified as "man," and imaged, at least implicitly, as a solar masculine hero of Promethean character: bold, restless, brilliantly innovative, ceaselessly pressing forward with his intelligence and will, breaking out of the structures and limitations of the past, forever seeking greater freedom and new horizons, ascending to ever higher levels of development. The apex of human achievement in this vision begins with the ascendance of modern science and individualistic democracy. The view of history is one of progressive emancipation and empowerment. It is a vision that emerged fully in the course of the European Enlightenment, in the seventeenth and eighteenth centuries, though its roots are as old as Western civilization itself. In many respects our modern consciousness is so fully identified with this myth that it has become our common sense, the lineaments of our self-image as modern humans.

The other view, whose presence has become much stronger in our cultural discussion in recent years, though it was always present to one degree or another as a compensatory counter-current to the progressive view, describes this story in quite opposite terms. In the form this myth has taken in our era, the evolution of human consciousness and the history of the Western mind are seen as a tragic story of humanity's radical fall and separation from an original state of oneness with nature and with being. In its primordial condition, humankind had possessed an instinctive knowledge of the profound sacred unity and interconnectedness of the world; but under the influence of the Western mind, and especially intensifying with the ascendance of the modern mind, the course of history has brought about a deep schism between humankind and nature, and a desacralization of the world. This development has coincided with an increasingly destructive human exploitation of nature, the devastation of traditional indigenous cultures, and an increasingly unhappy state of the human soul, which experiences itself as ever more isolated, shallow, and unfulfilled. In this perspective, both humanity and nature are seen as having suffered grievously under a long domination of thought and society associated with both patriarchy and modernity, with the worst consequences being produced by the oppressive hegemony of Western industrial societies empowered by modern science and technology. The nadir of this fall is seen as the present time of planetary ecological disaster, moral disorientation, and spiritual emptiness, which is the direct consequence of human hubris as embodied above all in the structure and spirit of the modern Western mind and ego. Here the historical perspective is one which reveals a progressive impoverishment of human life and the human spirit, a fragmentation of original unities, a ruinous destruction of the sacred community of being.

Something like these two interpretations or paradigms of the history of human consciousness, which I have described here in somewhat oversimplified terms for the sake of easy recognition, can be seen to inform many of the more specific issues of our age. One might say that these opposing historical perspectives, with their many variations and compromise formations, constitute the most fundamental argument of our time: Whither humanity? Upward or downward? How are we to view Western civilization, the Western intellectual and spiritual tradition, its canon of great works? How are we to view modern science, the modern era? How are we to view "man"? Is it progress, or is it tragedy? Has the modern Western project brought Enlightenment, or Kali Yuga?

John Stuart Mill, in his splendid essay on Coleridge, once made an observation which I have always considered to be shrewd and perceptive, even wise. He pointed out that in intellectual controversies, both parties to the debate tend to be correct in what they affirm and wrong in what they deny. Mill's insight into the nature of intellectual discourse sheds light on many things: whether it is conservatives debating liberals, parents arguing with their children, or a lovers' quarrel, almost invariably something is being repressed in the service of making one's point. But I believe that this insight applies with particular aptness to the conflict of historical visions I have described above. For I would like to suggest that both parties to this dispute have grasped an essential aspect of the picture: that both mythic visions are in a sense correct, each with compelling arguments within its own frame of reference, but that they are both intensely partial visions, as a result of which they both deeply misread the larger story. And I believe that this larger story is one in which the two opposite interpretations are exactly intertwined to form a complex but integrated whole.

Indeed I believe the two stories actually constitute each other. They underlie and inform each other, make each other possible. One might compare the way these two historical interpretations coalesce, while appearing to exclude each other, to those gestalt-experiment illustrations that can be perceived in two different, equally cogent ways, such as the precisely ambiguous figure that can be seen either as a white vase or as two black faces in profile. By means of a gestalt switch in perception, the observer can move back and forth between the two images, though the figure itself remains unchanged. Niels Bohr's famous dictum, drawn from his experience in quantum physics, that the opposite of a great truth is another great truth, expresses a similar insight.

What is difficult, of course, is to see both images, both truths, simultaneously. But this may be the task we must engage if we wish to gain a deeper understanding of the evolution of human consciousness and the history of the Western mind: to see that long spiritual and intellectual journey, through stages of increasing differentiation and complexity, as having perfectly ambiguously brought about both a progressive ascent to autonomy, and a tragic fall from unity – and as having perhaps prepared the way for a synthesis on an altogether new level. For I believe that the two historical perspectives which I have described reflect opposite but equally essential aspects of an immense dialectical process, an evolutionary drama that has been unfolding for thousands of years, and that now appears to be reaching a critical moment of transformation.

We can gain deeper insight into the polarity of these two historical perspectives, as well as their possible synthesis, by examining carefully the underlying structure of the modern Western world view. If we were to isolate the particular characteristic of the modern world view that distinguishes it from virtually all premodern world views, what we might call primal world views, I believe we would have to say that the fundamental distinction or difference is this: the modern mind experiences the world in such a way as to draw a radical boundary between the human self as subject and the world as object. The subject–object divide, the sense of radical distinction between self and world, which we could call Cartesian for shorthand, is fundamental to the modern mind. The modern mind is constituted upon it. Modern science, from Bacon and Descartes on, is deeply founded upon the conviction that if one is to know the world as it is in itself, one must cleanse one's mind of all human projections, such as meaning and purpose, onto the world.

By contrast, in the primal world view, meaning and purpose are seen as permeating the entire world within which the self is embedded. The primal human walks through a world that is experienced as completely continuous between inner and outer. He or she sees spirits in the forest, perceives meaning in the movement of two eagles across the horizon, recognizes significance in the conjunction of two planets, experiences a world in which the human being is completely embedded in a larger being that is ensouled. The primal world is radically ensouled: it communicates and has purposes; it is pregnant with signs and symbols, implications and intentions. The world is animated by the same psychologically resonant realities that the human being experiences within. The human soul participates in a world soul, or *anima mundi*, and the language that articulates that *anima mundi* in all its flux and diversity is the language of myth, the archetypal language of the human psyche. The many particulars of the empirical world are all intrinsically endowed with an archetypal significance, mythic and numinous, and that significance flows between inner and outer, self and world, without any absolute distinction.

The modern world view considers this to be a naive epistemological error. If I see spiritual presences out in the world – as if the world is communicating with me in some purposeful way, as if it is laden with meaning-rich symbols – then I am projecting human realities on to the non-human world. This is childish and immature, intellectually primitive, delusory, and needs to be outgrown.

In the modern world view, then, the human self is seen as the exclusive repository of conscious intelligence, moral sensibility, and spiritual aspiration in the universe: all meaning in the universe comes from the human subject. Not just modern science but the entire world view of modern humanism is based on this assumption; it underlies, for example, the basic twentieth-century existentialist conviction that essential to the human project, in its unique pathos and courage, is the imperative to bring meaning to a universe that otherwise lacks all meaning.

In retrospect we can see that virtually everything in Western intellectual and spiritual history, from the Hebrew prophets and Greek philosophers on, has in one way or another supported this long bipolar movement. Two basic developments have happened. On the one hand, the human self has been gradually differentiated out of the larger matrix of being; its autonomy, intellectual and moral, has been forged. It is dynamically self-determining, self-aware, self-revising, self-responsible; it even has an impulse toward self-transcendence. The autonomy of the individual rational mind and will is an extraordinary development, and it is precious to every one of us. We value our individual freedom to be able to stand up to a tradition, to our parents, to the world view we were socialized within, to conventional society's values. We value being able to question, to go deeper, to go further than the status quo. We value being able to explore and judge for ourselves whether some other reality is more profound than the one presented to us by the orthodoxy. This is precious to us. We all have an allegiance, often unspoken and unrecognized, to this autonomous self, forged over many centuries of cultural, psychological, and intellectual development.

On the other hand, this autonomy has been purchased at a great price: the disenchantment of the universe. The high cost has been a gradual voiding of all consciousness and intelligence, all soul, all spirit, all meaning, all purpose from the entire world, with all these now relocated more or less exclusively within the human self. This disenchantment has been discerned and lamented almost from the very start of the modern project – "I am terrified by the eternal silence of these infinite spaces," said Pascal as he looked out on the modern universe (Pascal, [1670] 1966: 95). The human soul has not felt at home in that universe – the soul can hold dear its poetry and its music, its moral passion, its private religion and metaphysics, but these find no certain foundation in the empirical cosmos. Our psychological and spiritual predispositions are absurdly at variance with the world revealed by our scientific method. We are, it seems, "by nature" personal, intentional, concerned with value and meaning and purpose, but "nature" itself is understood to be devoid of these qualities. In such a context, all human imagination, religious experience, aesthetic sensibility, moral values, and so on must be seen as idiosyncratic human psychological constructs, as courageous projections. It is a profoundly self-contradictory situation to be in.

The modern experience of a radical division between inner and outer – of a subjective, personal, and purposeful consciousness that is paradoxically embedded in and evolved from a world that is intrinsically unconscious, impersonal, and purposeless – is represented historically in our culture in the great division between the Enlightenment and Romanticism. In the world view of the modern West, the Enlightenment essentially rules the outer cosmos and the objective world, while the Romantic aspirations of our art and music, our spiritual yearnings, rule the interior world of the modern soul. In the Romantic tradition – represented, for example, by Goethe and Rousseau, Blake, Wordsworth and Coleridge, Beethoven and Hölderlin, Emerson and Whitman all the way up to our post-1960s counterculture – the modern soul found profound spiritual and psychological expression. The Enlightenment tradition, by contrast, represented by Newton and Locke, Voltaire and Hume – and more recently by thinkers such as Bertrand Russell or Karl Popper, the cosmologists Stephen Hawking and Steven Weinberg, or the evolutionary biologist Richard Dawkins – has been mainly informed by rational-empirical science. In a sense, the modern soul's allegiance is to Romanticism, while the modern mind's allegiance is to the Enlightenment. There is a kind of schizophrenia within the world view that all of us grew up with in the twentieth century. Our spiritual being, our psychology, is contradicted by our cosmology. Our Romanticism is contradicted by our Enlightenment, our inner by our outer. There is no easy congruence between those two radically different world views; yet, to use Faust's term, they are somehow forced to "cohabit within our breast."

Yet the problem with this condition is not merely internal distress. Since the cosmological context within which all human activity takes place has lost any ground for transcendent values – spiritual, moral, aesthetic – the values of the marketplace and mass media freely colonize the human imagination and drain it of all depth. In the contemporary world, a disenchanted world view essentially empowers the utilitarian mindset to colonize all human subjectivity. The drive for ever greater financial profit, political power, and technological prowess supersedes all other aspirations. The utilitarian impulses of instrumental reason inevitably take over as ends rather than means. In turn, anxiety in the face of a meaningless cosmos and the loss of a coherent world view creates a spiritual hunger, an alienation and disorientation, which leads to an addictive hunger for ever more material goods, a pathological consumerism that cannibalizes the planet in a kind of self-destructive frenzy. Highly pragmatic consequences ensue from the schizoid modern world view.

So many factors have pushed us in this direction. In many ways, not just the Western path but the entire human project can be seen as impelling the differentiation between self and world, between humanity and nature, between autonomy and participation, between part and whole. As soon as our species first used a tool, we began to move as a subject against an object, a human being *vis-à-vis* the world. As soon as we used linguistic and religious symbolization, we began to objectify our experience in such a way that the world acts on us and we act on the world. A memorable image at the beginning of the film *2001: A Space Odyssey* captures this larger coherence in the overall vector of the human epic. In a sequence entitled "The Dawn of Man," a protohuman primate has just made the primal discovery of using a tool; he has used a bone as a weapon to succeed in some life-and-death struggle. And in the ecstasy of that discovery, he hits the bone over and over again on a rock; eventually it shatters and flies up into the air, and in slow motion metamorphoses into a spaceship in the year 2001. In that one image we see the whole Promethean trajectory, the alpha and the omega of the Promethean quest to liberate the human being from the bonds of nature, to differentiate and emancipate the human being through human intelligence and will, to gain control over the matrix from which it emerged. This quest climaxes in modernity, in modern science, where the whole focus of knowledge is prediction and control over a natural world seen as unconscious, impersonal, and mechanistic, lacking all interiority or subjectivity. We humans alone, possess interiority – all else is made up of objects "out there."

The modern Western differentiation of the autonomous human self and disenchantment of the empirical cosmos also has significant roots in certain aspects of the religious traditions that have informed the Western spirit, whereby a transcendent divinity is discerned as being radically separate from the mundane created world of mortal finitude and unredeemed nature, while bearing a special relation to the human being and human history. "Man is made in the image of God," whose ontological separation from and superiority to the world He has created is mirrored in the human being's separation and superiority with respect to the rest of nature. The role of Judaism and Christianity in this larger process of differentiation and disenchantment is crucial. But I wish to focus particularly on secular modernity, which emerged out of the Judaeo–Christian European matrix, and which propelled this process in a dramatic sequence of major paradigm shifts in our intellectual history.

We can of course trace much of this to the Cartesian revolution which separated soul from body, human subject from objective world. But Descartes' philosophy, which basically articulated the emerging awareness of the autonomous modern self, grew out of a prior, even more dramatic and consequential paradigm shift, the Copernican revolution. The Copernican shift of perspective can be seen as a paradigmatic metaphor for the entire modern world view: the massive seeing through of the naive understanding, the discovery of the superiority of the modern mind to all past understandings, the awakening to the world-creating and world-destroying power of human reason, the radical displacement of the human being from the center of the ancient cosmic womb to a relative and peripheral position in a vast and impersonal universe, the ensuing mechanization of the world picture. And this shift has been followed by others. Darwin, in essence, introduced a "Copernican" revolution in biology: whereas Copernicus left the Earth as just another insignificant planet, no longer the noble center of the universe, so Darwin left humans as just another ephemeral species among the animals, no longer the divine focus of creation.

Even the postmodern mind finds its roots in Copernicus's paradigmatic act of deconstructive reflexivity, his recognition that the apparent movement of the objective heavens was being unconsciously caused by the movement of the observing subject on the Earth. Here Kant was the crucial, proto-postmodern figure, with his Copernican revolution in philosophy whereby he recognized that the phenomenal order of the world is constituted by the ordering structures of the human mind. This is where the modern begins its shift to the postmodern. For Kant's insight into the human mind's subjective ordering of reality, and thus, finally, the relative and unrooted nature of human knowledge, has been extended and deepened by a host of subsequent developments, from anthropology, linguistics, sociology of knowledge, and quantum physics to cognitive psychology, neurophysiology, semiotics, and philosophy of science; from Marx, Weber, and Wittgenstein to Heisenberg, Kuhn, and Foucault. The consensus is decisive: the world is in some essential sense a construct. Human knowledge is radically interpretive. There are no perspective-independent facts. Every act of perception and cognition is contingent, mediated, situated, contextual, theory-soaked. Meaning is rendered by the mind and cannot be assumed to inhere in the object, in the world beyond the mind, for that world can never be contacted without having already been saturated by the mind's own nature. That world cannot even be justifiably postulated. Radical uncertainty prevails, for in the end what one knows and experiences is to an indeterminate extent a projection.

It was Friedrich Nietzsche who fully captured the pathos of the existential and spiritual crisis that would befall modern humanity in the aftermath of these revolutions which caused the displacement of the human, the disenchantment of the cosmos, the destruction of the metaphysical world, the death of God. Listen to the hyper-Copernican imagery – and that peculiarly tragic combination of self-determining will and inexorable fate – in this famous passage:

> What were we doing when we unchained this Earth from its Sun? Whither is it moving now? Whither are we moving? Away from all suns? Are we not perpetually falling? Backward, sideward, forward, in all directions? Is there still any up or down? Are we not straying as through an infinite nothing? Do we not feel the breath of empty space? Has it not become colder? Is not night continually closing in on us?
>
> (Nietzsche [1882] 1974: 181)

Here we enter the eye of the needle of the late modern self, of the alienated postmodern self.

Depth psychology enters into this history in a most interesting and consequential way. On the one hand, in a famous passage at the end of the eighteenth of his Introductory Lectures, Freud pointed out that psychoanalysis represented the third wounding blow to the human being's naive self-love and megalomania, the first being Copernicus's heliocentric theory, the second being Darwin's evolutionary theory. For psychoanalysis revealed that not only is the Earth not the center of the universe, and not only is the human being not the focus of creation, but even the human mind and ego, our most precious sense of being a conscious rational self, is only a recent and precarious development out of the primordial id, and by no means master of its house. With his epochal insight into the unconscious determinants of human experience, Freud stood decisively in the Copernican lineage of modern thought that progressively relativized and peripheralized the status of the human being. And again, like Copernicus and like Kant but on an altogether new level, Freud brought the fundamental recognition that the apparent reality of the objective world was being unconsciously determined by the condition of the subject.

But Freud's insight was a sword that cut both ways, and in a significant sense Freud represented the crucial turning point in the modern trajectory. For the discovery of the unconscious collapsed the old boundaries of interpretation. As the post-Cartesian empiricists had emphasized, the primary datum in human experience is ultimately human experience itself – not the material world, and not sensory transforms of that world; and with psychoanalysis was begun the systematic exploration of the seat of all human experience and cognition, the human psyche. What Freud, and more deeply Jung, uncovered was that hidden by the radiant light of modern consciousness was the larger mystery of the psyche, the unconscious, informed and impelled by powerful mythic structures.

Here we see the extent to which depth psychology is rooted in and expressive not only of the solar Enlightenment side of the Western legacy but also the lunar Romantic. Both Freud and Jung were as much influenced by Goethe as by Darwin; they were equally committed to the exploration of the interior mystery of human subjectivity as to the lucid rational analysis of the human animal; their researches focused on myth, religion, dreams, and art, but were carried out with the intellectual rigor of the scientific observer. Moreover, as especially Jung understood, depth psychology engaged the challenge recognized by Kant as it attempted to discern the deep structural principles informing the human subject, those enduring patterns and forms which affect and even constellate our reality. Thus was opened up the radical possibility that even the world of modern science, the Enlightenment project, the self-image of modern man, could be revealed as expressive of underlying archetypal forms, mythic patterns. Even the anti-mythological consciousness of the Enlightenment reflects a mythic impulse at work. Disenchantment is itself a kind of enchantment, a form of consciousness reflecting a particular archetypal gestalt.

If we examine the long journey of differentiation of the human self and disenchantment of the cosmos, beginning with the primal *anima mundi*, we can see that the *participation mystique* – the consciousness of being embedded in an ensouled world, a matrix of living meaning – was gradually transformed into the modern experience of being a separate autonomous conscious self divided from a soulless world, and that this development can also be viewed as a gradual transformation of the *anima mundi* into the individual unconscious. The *anima mundi* has thereby been subjectivized, humanized, individualized, secularized, and repressed by the rational ego. Thus do Freud and Jung represent the great pivot, coming at that stage in the Cartesian development when the ego was able to theorize that from which it had emerged and cut itself off, with pathological consequences which they set out to heal. Freud of course continued many of the Enlightenment's limiting assumptions, and it was Jung who more fully recognized the depth and mystery of the unconscious. Moreover, in his final decades, through his later researches into the nature of archetypes, and particularly into the problem of synchronicities, Jung began to break through the Cartesian-Kantian limitations of his earlier understanding and to overcome the barriers between human interiority and external world. This, combined with his deep insights into the transformational teleology of the psyche, collective as well as individual, into the death–rebirth process, and, finally, into the alchemical sacred marriage, began to bring forth a new potential of participatory wholeness in the Western world view.

Depth psychology has provided countless tools and insights with which we can better comprehend the historical developments described in this chapter, from the discovery of the unconscious to the understanding of the psyche's symbolic modes of expression, the multivalent complexity of archetypes, and the dynamics of psychospiritual transformation. And it is with the aid of these tools and insights that we can begin to recognize that the highly critical situation in which we find ourselves – in our world as well as in our world view – closely resembles a critical phase in an archetypal initiation process of death and rebirth, a process that Jung explored both experientially and theoretically throughout his life, and that was subsequently illuminated by the work of others such as the psychoanalyst and transpersonal psychologist Stanislav Grof and the mythologist Joseph Campbell.

I recall a lecture by Campbell in the late 1960s when he told a story of North American shamanic initiation. Rasmussen, the Danish-Eskimo explorer and ethnologist, in the course of his expeditions through the arctic regions of the North American continent, had conversations with many old shamans. One of them told the story of his own initiation as a young boy. He said that he was taken by an older shaman out on a sled over ice, and placed in a small igloo just large enough for him to sit in. He crouched on a skin, and was left there for thirty days with just a little water and meat brought in occasionally during that period. He said, "I died a number of times during those thirty days, but I learned and found what can be found and learned only in the silence, away from the multitude, in the depths. I heard the voice of nature itself speak to me, and it spoke with the voice of a gentle motherly solicitude and affection. Or it sounded sometimes like children's voices, or sometimes like falling snow, and what it said was, 'Do not be afraid of the universe.'" This discovery, Campbell goes on, became a point of absolute internal security for the initiate, and made possible his return to his community with a wisdom and assurance that was unmatched by everyone there, so that he could help others from that inner place.

This was of course the great death–rebirth initiation that, whether in the form of sacred rites of passage or of ancient mystery rituals, has informed indigenous, traditional, and archaic cultures throughout human history. But our own culture is notable for the utter absence of such an initiatory tradition. The dangerous, bold, risk-taking energies of youth are necessary for an initiatory process to take place, as all primal cultures know. Ours does not. Primal societies use these energies to mediate that great transition of each generation from dependence to independence, from immaturity to maturity, from childhood to adulthood, for the sustaining of the community both materially and spiritually. This initiation consists of a profound, very frightening encounter with the darkest aspects of existence: with death, with utter aloneness, with suffering, with a crisis of meaning, with a sense of despair, a leaving of the community. In a sense, it is a leaving not only of the safety of the maternal, familial, and community womb but of the entire community of life.

This encounter provides a rite of passage for youths who can thereby discover their deeper purpose, their meaning, because in that great encounter with death and rebirth they are able to engage and experience, directly in their bodies, in their souls, the powerful archetypal forces that permeate life and nature and every human being, and they thereby come into direct knowledge of the great mysteries of death and rebirth. From that place, they can re-engage life with a new knowledge; they can bring back to the community an enriched understanding.

Our culture does not provide such an initiation, a rite of passage for youth. But that is just the beginning of it. If all our youth are uninitiated, then of course all our adults are uninitiated too. When one turns on the television, virtually everything one sees is designed for the adolescent mind: *Pow! Zap! Boom!*, explosions, aggression, superficial sex, incessant change, shiny surfaces. There is no sense of the deeper meanings, the profundity of life, no sense of the fact that decisions about the future need to be made not just from the point of view of what is going to show up on the bottom line of the next quarterly report, but what is going to affect the seventh generation from now. This is an awareness much larger than what is available to someone who has not gone through an initiatory transformation.

The reason why our culture does not provide such an initiation, however, is not just that it has somehow simply forgotten, or foolishly abandoned, its traditional wisdom, and myopically asserted a mechanistic material world with no deeper spiritual purpose or significance. I believe the reason why our culture does not provide such an initiation is that it is itself immersed in such an initiation, of the most epochal and profound kind.

I believe the West – humankind – has entered into the most critical stages of a death–rebirth mystery. The entire path of Western civilization has taken humankind and the planet on a trajectory of initiatory transformation, into a state of spiritual alienation, into an encounter with mortality on a global scale – first with the nuclear crisis, followed by the ecological crisis – an encounter with mortality that is no longer personal but rather transpersonal, collective, planetary; into a state of radical fragmentation, into the "wasteland," into that crisis of existential meaning and purpose that has informed so many of the most sensitive individuals of the twentieth century. It is a collective dark night of the soul, a deep separation from the community of being, from the cosmos itself. We are undergoing this rite of passage with virtually no guidance from wise elders because the wise elders are themselves caught up in the same crisis. This initiation is too epochal, too global, too unprecedented, too all-encompassing; it is larger than all of us. Perhaps the very absence of initiatory rites of passage in our culture has served this process by creating a kind of closed container, a pressure cooker, an alchemical vessel that is intensifying the archetypal energies into a collective morphic field of explosive power, acted out on the stage of history with, as it were, the cosmos itself as the tribal matrix of the initiatory drama. It seems that we are all entering into something new, a new development, a crisis of accelerated maturation, a birth, and we cannot really know where it is headed.

But we can draw on those sources of insight that come from the mystical and shamanic epiphanies and writings of those individuals who have undergone a death–rebirth initiation. We can draw as well from our own psychospiritual journeys, which perhaps permit us to glimpse that extraordinary truth which Goethe understood: "Until you know this deep secret, 'Die and be reborn,' you will be a stranger on this dark Earth."

This is the dark Earth that the modern mind has in some sense constructed for itself. Yet, in another sense, perhaps we find ourselves thrown into this dark estrangement because larger forces are at work, larger than the merely human. That is, the selective interpretation of experience that underlies the modern objectification of reality may itself be a highly developed – if largely unconscious – expression of the evolving mythopoeic imagination, operating within a very specific archetypal gestalt, moving toward some new reconfiguration of the human being in relation to the cosmos – a "metamorphosis of the gods."

What is on the other side of being a stranger on this dark Earth? In a speech at Stanford University in 1994, Vaclav Havel suggested an answer:

> Planetary democracy does not yet exist, but our global civilization is already preparing a place for it: It is the very Earth we inhabit, linked with Heaven above us. Only in this setting can the mutuality and the commonality of the human race be newly created, with reverence and gratitude for that which transcends each of us, and all of us together. The authority of a world democratic order simply cannot be built on anything else but the revitalized authority of the universe.
>
> (Havel 1994)

And how is "the authority of the universe" rediscovered? How can we participate in a transformative unfolding that would lead toward a more integral world? One factor, I believe, is that we need to radically expand our ways of knowing, our epistemology. We need to move beyond the very narrow empiricism and rationalism that were characteristic of the Enlightenment and still dominate mainstream science today. We need to draw on – to use a single encompassing term – the wider epistemologies of the heart. We need ways of knowing that integrate the imagination, imaginal and archetypal insight, the intuition, the aesthetic sensibility, the revelatory or epiphanic capacity, the capacity for kinesthetic knowing, the capacity for empathic understanding, the capacity to open to the other, to listen. Indeed, a highly developed sense of empathy is critical if we are to overcome the subject–object barrier. We need to be able to enter into that which we seek to know, and not keep it ultimately distanced as an object. We need, to use biologist Barbara McClintock's phrase, "a feeling for the organism."

Our best philosophy of science has taught us the extent to which our epistemology creates our world. Not only reason and empiricism but hope, faith, and compassion play a major role in constellating reality. And this perhaps is the underlying message of our modern Enlightenment's unexpected darkening of the world: at the heart of cognition is a moral dimension. To assume that purpose, meaning, and conscious intelligence are solely attributes of the human being, and that the great cosmos itself is a soulless void, reflects an invisible act of cosmic hubris on the part of the modern self. In essence, our task may be to move from an I–It relationship with the universe to an I–Thou relationship.

Let us try a thought experiment. Imagine that you are the universe, a deep, beautiful, ensouled universe, and that you are being approached by two different epistemologies, two suitors who seek to know you. Would you open your deepest secrets to the suitor – that is, to the methodology, the epistemology – who would approach you as though you were unconscious, utterly lacking in intelligence or purpose, and inferior in being to him; who related to you as though you were ultimately there for his exploitation, his self-enhancement; and his motivation for knowing you is driven essentially by a desire for prediction and control for his own self-betterment? Or would you open your deepest secrets to that suitor – that epistemology, that methodology – who viewed you as being at least as intelligent and powerful and full of mystery and soul as he is, and who sought to know you by uniting with you to create something new?

The postmodern mind has come to recognize the degree to which our often hidden presuppositions play a crucial role in constellating the reality we seek to know. It is clear to me, if the universe is anything like the mystery I believe it is, that, under duress, it will always render to the mainstream sciences a highly partial and misleading vision of what it is. At the dawn of modern science, Francis Bacon starkly represented what eventually became the dominant form of epistemology in the West. He said that for science to advance we need to wrest the secrets from nature by methods of forceful interrogation comparable to the torture rack; nature must be "put in constraint," "bound into service," made a "slave" (Merchant 1980: 168–169). As we well know from contemporary animal experimentation, this is not a mere metaphor (Schopenhauer once said that animals live in a hell in which human beings are the devils). Compare this ruthlessly objectifying strategy with the esoteric, mystical form of engagement with nature, an entering into a participatory understanding of the universe, characterized by aesthetic delight, intellectual ecstasy, imaginative flourishing, empathic unity, a hermeneutics of trust instead of suspicion. Knowledge becomes an act of love.

I believe we have a choice. There are many possible universes, many possible meanings, floating through us. We are not solitary subjects in a meaningless universe upon which we can and must impose our egocentric will. Nor are we just empty vessels, as it were, on automatic, passively playing out the intentions of the world soul, the *anima mundi*. Rather, we are creative participants, as autonomous yet embedded interpreters, in a co-evolutionary unfolding of reality. It is a complex process where both we and the universe are mutually creators and created. What seems to be unfolding is not only a recovery of the *anima mundi* but a new relationship to it. Something new is being forged; it is not simply a "regression" to a premodern state. We seem to be moving to a world view that is a dialectical synthesis of world and self, a new vision of the universe reflected in the many scientific and philosophical impulses working today toward a participatory holistic paradigm.

From this point of view, epistemologically, we are not ultimately separated from the world, projecting our structures and meanings onto an otherwise meaningless world. Rather, we are an organ of the universe's self-revelation. The human self has been forged into an autonomous intellectual and moral self, and is now in a position to recognize itself as being a creative, intelligent nexus embedded within the larger context of the *anima mundi*. We are beginning to see that we play a crucial role in the universe's unfolding by our own cognitive processes and choices, tied to our own psychological development. And thus our own inner work – our moral awareness and responsibility, our confrontation with our shadow, our integration of the masculine and feminine – plays a critical role in the universe that we can create.

Here, depth psychology can serve the further development of that moral impulse which has been slowly forged in the Western consciousness by its religious traditions. For as the Mexican poet Octavio Paz put it, "the examination of conscience, and the remorse that accompanies it, which is a legacy of Christianity, has been, and is, the single most powerful remedy against the ills of our civilization" (Paz, 1991). I believe that it will take a fundamental moment of remorse – and we know this is an essential element in the death–rebirth experience – a long moment of remorse, a sustained weeping and grief, a mourning. It will be a grief of the masculine for the feminine; of men for women; of adults for what has happened to children; of the West for what has happened to every other part of the world; of Judaeo-Christianity for pagans and indigenous peoples; of Christians for Jews; of whites for people of color; of the wealthy for the poor; of human beings for animals and all other forms of life. It will take a fundamental metanoia, a self-overcoming, a radical sacrifice, to make this transition. Sometimes when we speak about the emergence of a new paradigm and a new world view, we focus on the intellectual dimensions of this shift; these are indeed crucial. But I do not think we can minimize the central importance of the moral dimension for this great transformation to take place.

Let us now return to the original polarity of the two mythic perspectives of history, of heroic progress and tragic fall, that have constituted our self-understanding. I have suggested that part of our task is to be able to see both of these metanarratives at once, to recognize both as truths, both as partial images of the whole. Yet I also believe that for us today it is not just a matter of intellectual understanding of this coincidence of opposites in our historical evolution. Rather, it is a matter of experiencing, suffering through, the struggle of opposites within our consciousness. We must in a sense undergo a kind of crucifixion, become a vessel through which the consciousness of our era, and of the future, works out its contradictions, within our minds and spirits, our bodies and souls. As Jung and others like Marie-Louise von Franz have described, very much in the spirit of Hegel: by suffering to the extreme under the great problem of opposites – by fully accepting the activity of this dialectic within us – we can sometimes become a place in which the divine opposites spontaneously come together. Much of the intensity of our age derives, I believe, from precisely this dialectical activity, this clash of the opposites, pressing relentlessly to bring forth something new.

Are we going to make it? We cannot be completely sure that we will. No authentic initiatory process begins in the certainty of its outcome. It is not at all certain that we will successfully pass through this eye of the needle, this planetary ego death. For the foreseeable future, we seem to be living in an era of high drama. We seem to be engaged now in a kind of race, as H. G. Wells said, between education and catastrophe, but which I would describe as a race between initiation and catastrophe.

Jung once said that "if the encounter with the shadow is the 'apprentice-piece' of psychological development, then that with the anima is the 'masterpiece'" (Jung 1959: 61). I believe this is a statement of profound relevance for our moment in history, pointing not only toward the need for remorse and moral regeneration but also toward the *hieros gamos*, the sacred marriage of masculine and feminine, both of which will require a sacrifice and ego death. What seems to be called for at this threshold in our evolution is a great self-overcoming, a recognition not only of the heroic magnitude but also the hubris of the modern project. We need to integrate the shadow of the solar heroic trajectory, a trajectory whose ascent and decline were profoundly carried by the Copernican revolution in all its complexity, as the modern mind, decathecting from the Earth, now identified itself with the transcendent Sun, the Solar Logos, the new luminous cosmic center, brilliantly illuminating all with its radiant transcendent reason – but eventually descending, as must every sun, to die into the lunar night, returning into the feminine matrix of being, the mystery, the great unconscious, for a new *coniunctio* of the opposites, and thus a new creation.

All of this points to a rereading of our Western narrative of solar heroic progress within a larger context of tragedy and, perhaps, something more – something perhaps Shakespearean in the grandeur of its moral and aesthetic conception. Of course this is itself a myth. But what I am suggesting is that not only the human psyche but the cosmos itself may be archetypal, mythically informed. And perhaps this is the deepest act of trust that is being asked of us at this moment in history, to open up to the possibility that our universe may possess a moral and aesthetic dimension in its unfolding being, that it is not only capable of embodying, say, the intelligence of a Newton or an Einstein, as our Enlightenment view of the universe assumes with its quest for a grand unified equation, but that it may also be capable of embodying the intelligence and imagination and heart of, say, a Shakespeare. For I believe our task is to develop a moral and aesthetic imagination deep enough and wide enough to encompass the contradictions of our time and our history, the tremendous loss and tragedy as well as greatness and nobility, an imagination capable of recognizing that where there is light there is shadow, that out of hubris and fall can come moral regeneration, out of suffering and death, resurrection and rebirth.

BIBLIOGRAPHY

Havel, V. (1994) "Address on the Occasion of the Jackson H. Ralston Prize Ceremony," Stanford University, 29 September.

Jung, C. G. (1959) *Collected Works*, Vol. 9, i, Princeton, NJ: Princeton University Press.

Merchant, C. (1980) *The Death of Nature*, San Francisco, CA: Harper & Row.

Nietzsche, F. (1974) *The Gay Science*, trans. W. Kaufman, New York: Random House. First published 1882.

Pascal, Blaise. (1966) *Pensées*, trans. A. J. Kramer, Harmondsworth: Penguin. First published 1670.

Paz, O. (1991) "Poetry and the Free Market," *New York Times Book Review*, 8 December.

Index

Aboriginals 105–21
absolutism 149, 151; biblical 56; diversity and return to 150
adolescence 47, 48, 239, 262
Aeschylus 116
affective responses 167
aggression 233, 262; innate 234; testosterone-correlated 235
alchemy 56, 58, 64
alcohol 106, 108, 109
Alexander III (the Great), king of Macedonia 213, 214, 217, 218, 220, 227, 228
Alice Springs 105–6, 110, 116, 117
allegory 64, 65, 70, 74
Allen, Woody 79
alliances 47, 48, 66
ambivalence 40, 48, 70
Anderson, B. 182
Angkor Wat 175, 179, 180
anima mundi 260, 265
animus 63, 67, 72, 75, 78
anomie 88
Anthropos term 32
anxiety 40, 64, 65, 73, 242; about death 218, 222; national 219; unconscious 222
apartheid 101, 165, 167, 248
apocalypse 219, 221, 223, 226, 229
Aquarius 52, 54, 61
archaeomythology 232
Aristotle 6, 150
Arlen, Harold 66
Armstrong, K. 142–3, 143–4, 150
Asia 50, 101; southeast *see* Cambodia; Malaysia; Vietnam
astrology 51–2, 54
Atwood, Margaret 45
Australia 50, 105–21; Land Rights cases 112
authoritarianism 128, 150, 237
autonomy 47, 73, 161, 217, 219, 256; rights to 153; struggle for 45
axis mundi 175, 176, 177, 180

Babel, Tower of 141, 142
babies 35–6, 68; murdered 196; unwanted 101
Bacon, Sir Francis 264
Balkanization 88
Balkans 18, 24
baptism 219, 223, 224, 229
Baptists 101, 112
Barr, Roseanne 100
Bateson, Gregory 102
Baum, L. Frank 62–5 *passim*, 69, 70, 74, 77, 78
Beauty and the Beast 70
Beck, Ulrich 38
Becker, E. 195
Bedouins 143
Beethoven, Ludwig van 252, 257
Beezer, Robert R. 244, 245, 248
Beijing 100
belonging 163, 165, 166, 214
Berlin Wall 54
Bernières, Louis de 130–1
Bethlehem 229
Bible 46, 151, 228; Corinthians 224; Eden story 235; Genesis 141, 214, 215, 235; Hebrew 215, 216, 228, 229; New Testament 228; Old Testament 216–17
black men 101, 105–21, 164, 240;

imprisoned 158, 160, 165; *see also* apartheid; race/racism; slavery
Blair, Tony 34, 37
Blake, William 30, 257
body 58, 77; mind split from 237; need to impose on others 68; soul separate from 222–3, 227
Bohr, Niels 254
Bolger, Ray 62, 76
Bosch, F. D. K. 177
Bosnia/Bosnians 127–8, 131, 152, 157, 186
boundaries 182, 217; breaking of 57; cosmological 223; disappearing 101; transgression of 125; violation of 249
bourgeoisie 86
Bradley, Bill 2, 14, 15
Brady, Nicholas 245; *see also Ellison vs Brady*
Brahma 176
Branagh, Kenneth 79
Brecht, Bertolt 26, 37
Brewster, E. H. 173
Brother Klaus (Nicolas von der Flüe) 31–2
Bruni, F. 56, 57
Bryan, William Jennings 63, 64, 74
Buber, M. 145–6
Buddhism/Buddhists 101, 142, 170, 182, 184; *kâthen* festival 183; mythology 175, 178, 179; symbolism 171–3, 174, 176, 183; thought 177; *see also* Zen
Bun Chân Mol 184
Bunhaeng Ung 195–6
Bush, Barbara 26
Bush, George 1, 6, 9

Cambodia *see* Angkor Wat; Khmer; Meru; Phnom Penh
Campbell, Joseph 2, 261
capitalism 14, 48, 86, 92, 187; aggressive 143; early, social inequalities of 236; feudal 186, 188; modern "myth" of 152; patriarchal 90; rampant and ruthless 144
Carlyle, Thomas 25
Carter, Jimmy 37
Cartesian development 260
Castoriadis, C. 147
Catholics: Irish 157, 186; schools 57
Census Bureau (US) 101
Central America 157
Chameau, C. 183
Chan Chakrei 192, 195
Chandler, D. P. 178, 183, 189, 194
chaos 120, 129; order and 101
Chechnya 152
Chhouk (Cambodian Regional Secretary) 195
Chicago 63; riots (1968) 8
children 40, 42, 47, 57, 64; kidnapped 101; murdered 196; parental time spent conversing with 100; parents arguing with 254; welfare of 136, 148; *see also* babies
China 29, 100; P'an a Ku 32; Taoism and Confucianism 142
Chou Ta-Kuan 179
Christian Coalition (US) 57
Christ(ianity) 32, 52, 56, 112, 143, 258; cult of 223, 224, 227; "ecology" person 92; Hellenistic age and 214, 218–19; pivotal ceremonial liturgy 110; Roman Empire's conversion to 213; success of 223–4; *see also* Baptists; Bible; Catholics; God; Protestants
cities: change in 142; destruction of 100, 118
civil rights 151, 166, 242, 247–8
class *see* social class
Clinton, Bill 8–10 *passim*, 13, 27, 34, 84; impeachment possibility 56–7; popularity 101; vaunted empathy 79
Clymer, A. 56
Cobb, Jennifer 227
Cold War 23, 24, 25
Coleridge, Samuel Taylor 254, 257
collectivization 134, 170, 186
Columbus, Christopher 210
Commager, Henry Steele 63–4
communication 48, 117, 148, 217; establishing and maintaining 118; global 141, 227
Communism 14, 23, 54, 55, 99, 237; "great leap forward" 188; Maoist-inspired 170; political purges 191
communities 127, 128–9, 130, 145; identification with 218, 228
compassion 13, 18, 26, 32, 112, 115, 264
"compassionate conservatism" 6
competition 41, 53, 144, 154, 208, 235
compromise 208, 209
concentration camps 186
conflict 57, 118, 119, 152–3, 158, 188;

archetypal 208; associated with masculine principle 151; class 157, 236; good and evil 209; inter-ethnic 122–40; resolution of 147; universality of 150–1
conquest 53, 57, 227, 228
consciousness 53, 54, 67, 68–9, 151, 159, 160, 168; annihilation of 70; anti-mythological 260; body and 227; containing of 239; cultural 35, 163; death and 218; differentiation of 65; ego 241; gender 46; higher 147; interplay of 73; mass 40; menstrual 238; national 79; origination story and 232–3; political 66, 74; psychological 66, 72; ritualizing 239; separate from group 164; shaped by Hellenistic culture 214, 223; streams of 117; symbol of 76; voiding of 256; Western, evolution of 252
consensus 27, 52, 149, 259
conservatives 58, 78, 86, 240, 244
Cook, Capt. James 114
Cooper, Gary 78
cooperation 141, 147; economic 152, 153; group 51
Copernicus, Nicolaus 221, 252, 258, 259–60, 266
cosmology 2, 220–1, 223, 239, 257; Cambodian/Buddhist 171, 173, 174, 176, 178; Hindu 174, 176
cosmos 58, 178, 219, 221, 259, 260; centre of 177, 180; tribal matrix of initiatory drama 263
courage 64, 68, 73, 230, 256
Court of Appeals (US) 242, 244
cowardice 64, 68, 73
creation 101, 102, 151, 258; cultural 235; mythological 108, 110; source of 175; struggles with 118
creativity 85, 176
Croatia/Croats 24, 127, 157
cross-cultural issues 110, 117, 120
cults 53; Christ 223, 224, 227; mystery 223
cultural complex 157–69
cultural transition 213–31
Cumont, Franz 213, 225
cyberspace 227–8
cyclic processes 52, 53, 59, 180, 234, 240
Czech Republic/Czechoslovakia 55
Darwin Charles 208, 235, 236, 258, 259, 260
Davenport, Guy 100
Davis, Bette 72
Davis, Judy 79
death 216, 219, 224, 261–3 *passim*, 267; anxiety about 218, 222; ego 266; God 99, 259; life after 217, 223; near-genocidal 236
Defense Education Act (US, 1958) 24
defenses 70, 73, 76
de Havilland, Olivia 72
deities 51; earthly and celestial 180; moon 53; *see also* God; goddesss; gods
DeLay, Tom 56
democracy 14, 29, 30, 65, 149; "death of" 57; fundamental ideas 55; individualistic 253; introduction of 185; liberal 152; planetary 263; world safe for 78
Democrats (US) 6, 8, 39, 63, 86, 247; matriarchal stance 64
demonic figures 70, 71, 79
Denby, David 56, 57
Denslow, W. W. 65
Depression: (1893) 64; (1930s) 26
desacrilization 253
desires 37, 53, 56, 58, 173; clash of 61
destiny 101–2, 120
dhamma 173, 176, 177, 179
dialectic 236, 239, 255
Diana, Princess of Wales 34, 42
differences 46, 54, 126–8, 130, 160, 162; clarifying 100; creation/destruction of 102; ethnic 157; intolerance of 152; manufacturing 186; religious 157; us/them 167
discrimination 158
disintegration 18, 53, 102, 118, 144, 229; cultural 120; feminine principle and 146, 147; inner 141; of unity 152
diversity 18, 130; acceptance and tolerance of 148; cultural 42; downsized 100; ethnic 42; good emphasizes 102; myth and origins of 141–56; political 90; protecting and privileging 95; "racial" 42; redemption of 129; respect and affection for 90; sexual 42; universality of 150–1
divinities 218; *see also* gods; goddesses
Djakarta 100
dogma 11, 31

dreams 2–3, 12, 14, 69–70, 72, 213; Aboriginal 111, 112, 117; Christian 112; following instruction given in 32; image frequently symbolized in 68; mythic 5; "prison" 158, 160, 165
Drinan, Robert F. 56
drunkenness 106, 108, 109, 110
Dumas, Alexandre 74
Dylan, Bob 37
Dyston, Esther 227

ecofeminism 45, 92
ecological concern 153, 262
ecomasculinism 41
economic myth 207–12
ego 260, 266; conscious collective 150; consciousness 241; development 53, 148; pure 149; rigid identity 132
Egypt 29, 32, 148, 215, 218
Einstein, Albert 101, 102, 266
Electra see Orestes
Eleusian mysteries 223
elitism 149, 247; power-grabbing 54; white psyche 240
Ellison, Ralph 163
Ellison vs Brady case (1991) 242, 243, 244, 246, 248
El Salvador 131, 135
empathy 75, 78, 79, 100, 120; politics of 12, 13; relating and caring 148
energy 73, 159, 180–2, 228; archetypal 262; centres of 174; political 45, 65, 84–7, 94
Engels, Friedrich 235, 236
Enheduanna 54, 59
Enlightenment (Age of Reason) 30, 210, 211, 253, 256–7, 260; characteristics of 263
enlightenment (spiritual) 70; Buddhist 174, 176, 177
environmentalism 86, 89, 91, 210
equality 51; civic and civil 165; gender 241–50; social 26
Erikson, E. H. 162
Eros 40, 146–8, 125, 152
erotic leaders 39–43
Errington, S. 182
ethnic cleansing 165
ethnicity 42, 101, 122–40, 152; conflicts around 157, 159
ethnos logic 165–6, 167–8
evil 12, 70, 72, 102, 124, 135, 148; collective 165; conflict and 209; fascination with 131–2; feminine associated with 151; "pure" 131, 134; struggle between good and 135; victims of 134
evolution 61, 146, 212, 243, 246, 259; cultural 248
existentialism 12, 101, 120, 256
extermination 125, 190, 196
extraversion 66, 68, 71–2, 75–9 *passim*, 95

factionalism 122–40, 143, 188, 193, 194
failure 57, 79, 152; leadership and 36–9, 43, 44
family 47; obliteration by television 100
FAMOSE (Female-And-Male-Origin-Story-Example) 232, 233, 237, 238, 239, 240
fantasies 38, 74, 226, 237; collective 120, 253; grandiose 43, 44; omnipotent 35
Farrakhan, Louis 164–5
Fascism 23, 165
"father" leaders 6
FBIS (Foreign Broadcast Information Service) 186–7
feminine 41, 42, 64, 232; fear of 151; integration of masculine and 265, 266; males differentiate critically from 236; politics and 50–61, 151; power of 74
feminine principle 146–7, 148, 152
feminism 45, 46; gulf between other movements and 91–2
fertility: human 51, 235; land 178
film 257; *see also Wizard of Oz*
Flüe, Nicolas von der *see* Brother Klaus
FOOSE (Female-Only-Origin-Story-Example) 232, 233, 235, 237, 239
Ford, Henry 100–1
Foucault, Michel 132, 226, 259
fragmentation 38, 79, 84, 88, 165; feminine principle and 146, 147; identity 226
Franz, Marie-Louise von 32, 266
Freud, Sigmund 34, 51, 87, 102, 147, 236, 251; Introductory Lectures 259–60
Friedan, Betty 56–7
fundamentalism 94; nationalist 126; political 11, 12, 150; religious 11, 12, 86, 95, 141–2, 153

galaxies 11, 226

Gardner, John 102
Gardner, M. 63
Garland, Judy 62, 66, 76, 78
Gaster, T. H. 141
gays 47, 65, 78, 132
GDP (Gross Domestic Product) 208
gender 45, 46, 87, 89, 242; conflicts around 157, 159; differences 126, 152, 157; equality 241–50; present preoccupation with issues 148
Genet, Jean 41
genocide 157, 167, 170, 171, 186, 248
Georgi, Dieter 219, 221
Gephardt, Richard A. 57
Gergen, Kenneth 225, 226
Gestalt 254, 260, 263
Gilder, George 227
Gilgamesh Epic 216
Gimbutas, Marija 232, 233, 234, 235, 237, 239
Gingrich, Newt 14
global factors: communication 141, 227; information systems 225; martketplace 100; myth 24, 211; unity 153
global warming 101
Gnosticism 223
God 51, 58, 86, 141, 143, 149, 150, 258; Adam encouraged to disobey 151; belief in 162; benevolent 31; death of 99, 259; male 240; rebuilding of *Nekudim* by 147; self and 145; working out of the plan of 207
goddesses 32, 50, 51, 175; archetype 58; Hellenistic 218; lunar dragon 53; mother 233; underworld 216
gods 149, 220; Greek 88, 141, 150, 215, 217, 226; Hindu 175, 176, 179, 180; moon 53; new 99; old 218
Goethe, J. W. von 257, 260, 263
Gold Standard 63–4
good 70, 102, 124, 132, 148, 151; common 210; conflict and 209; self-righteousness of 134; struggle between evil and 135
"good-enoughness" 34–49
Gorbachev, Mikhail S. 23
Gottlieb, F. 147
Gray, Sterling 243–4
Greeks 43, 110, 125, 141, 214, 216, 256
Green, Peter 224
Green parties 91
Grof, Stanislav 261
Guatemala 157
guerrillas 135–7

Haley, Jack 76
Hall, D. 207
Hall, M. G. 53
Hamilton, Margaret 72
Hanks, L. M. 182
Harburg, E.Y. 66
Harms, Danil 136
Harris, A. S. 67
Havel, Vaclav 55–6, 58, 263
Hay, Louise 235
Headley, R. K. 174
healthcare reform 9–10
Hearn, M. P. 63, 64
Hebrew prophets 143, 256
Hegel, G. W. F. 266
Heine-Geldern, R. 180
Heisenberg, Werner 101
Hellenistic age 213–31
Hermeticism 223
heroes 15, 25, 27, 37, 67, 207–9 *passim*, 240; compassionate 26; idealized 56; solar masculine 253
heroines 65, 71
Hildebrand, J. 130
Hillel the Elder, Rabbi 155
Hillman, J. 36
Hinduism 142, 171; cosmology 174, 176; gods 175, 176, 179, 180; mythology 178; thought 177
Hitler, Adolf 37, 102
HIV/AIDS 41, 91
Hock, Dee 101
Holocaust 14–15, 125, 162, 167, 248
Holy War 150, 152, 157
Homer 150, 216, 228; *Iliad* 209
homogenization/homogeneity 17, 18, 100, 152
homosexuality 56, 78; *see also* gays; lesbians
"homosociality" 41
Hubble, Edwin 226
human rights 167, 248
Hun Sen 187
Hunt, Helen 79
Hu Tim 194
Hutus 157, 186

icons/iconography 51, 71, 176, 183, 237
idealism/ideals 57, 90, 91, 144, 208;

Aryan 162; democratic 26, 166; higher 210
identification 38, 100, 120, 159, 160; community 218, 228
identity 88, 106, 135, 151; change in structure 225; civic 165; collective 129, 132, 216, 217, 222–4 *passim*; conscious 125; diverse 152; ego 132; ethnic 157; fragmentation of 226, 228; gender 157; grounded in symbols 162; group 163, 165, 166, 214; homogenized 152; loss of 132; multiple 129; national 127, 128, 152–3, 219; psychological 87; racial 160; religious 128, 157; sexual 40; social 157, 163, 165–6
Ieng Thirith 195
Ignatieff, Michael 126–7, 128, 130
illusion 129, 147, 235
images/imagery 29, 39, 49, 64, 78, 79, 95, 110, 215; apocalyptic 219; archetypal 134, 241, 242; astrological 54; Buddha 173; Christ 52; cosmological 219; cultural complex and 166; decoding 120; dehumanizing 186; divine 58, 59, 61, 149; female 50, 237; film 247–8; God/gods 58, 145, 149, 221, 258; hyper-Copernican 259; ideal 30; initiatory 223; introverted 73, 76; intuition 68; mandala 174; media 123; mythic 125, 129, 130, 135, 136; non-heroic 38; "phantom" 125; poetic 123, 136; prehistoric 51; projected 117; propaganda 73; sacred 50; Shadow 31, 32, 91; touching and absorbing 119; *see also* self
imagination 65, 85, 95, 263, 266; mythic 52, 228; radical 48, 87
imperialism: aggressors 186, 187; order 214, 217
Inanna 54, 59–61
incest 47, 111
India 29, 99, 127; Cosmic Lion Goddess 32; Hinduism and Buddhism 142
individualism 14, 25, 144, 186; new 218
individuality 51, 53, 99, 163, 214; false sense of 132; identity shift to 217
individuation 65, 90–3, 145, 147
inequality 141, 142, 148; political 246; social 236
inferiority 66, 67, 68, 159
initiation 79, 223, 263, 266; puberty 239; shamanic 261–2
inner world 92; class and 93
integration 62, 70; masculine and feminine 265; masculine and feminine principles 148; of opposites 54, 152–4
integrity 62, 66, 71, 74, 78, 79, 88, 241; disintegration and 102; legitimation of 72; mature 65
intellectualism 52, 85, 101, 142, 192, 227
intelligence 68, 71, 253, 255, 264; anxiety over 64; "emotional" 66; genetically-endowed 235; myth of 237; privileged 67; psychological 70; voiding of 256
internet 48, 100, 225, 227, 240
introversion 66, 68, 71–8 *passim*, 95
intuition 73; extraverted 72; introverted 68, 69
Iran 143
Irish people 42; Catholics and Protestants 157, 186
Iroquois people 236
IRS (US Internal Revenue Service) 243, 244
Islam 24, 127–8, 142, 157; Cham (Cambodian) 190; extremist 152; motivating force 143; radical 150
isolationists 65, 77
Israel 148, 153, 157; ancient 214–16, 219, 224; West Bank 152; *see also* Jerusalem
Italy 31

Jackson, Jesse 18
Jackson, Michael 86
Jacob (patriarch) 214–15, 224
James, William 149–50
Jefferson, Thomas 207
Jerusalem 143, 215, 226
Jessup, H. I. 174
Jews 15, 90, 112, 226; commitment to national identity 219; Hellenistic 226; *see also* Holocaust; Israel; Judaism
jihad 150
John the Baptist, St 219
John Paul II, Pope 101
Josephus, Flavius 14
Judaeo-Christianity 56, 265
Judaism 147, 258
judges 112, 117, 243
Jukurrpa 108, 110, 112, 119
Jung, Carl Gustav 2, 6, 11, 31, 52, 56, 65, 87–9 *passim*, 131, 235, 251; alchemical

researches 64; Aquarian Age 54; "bewitching quality of person" 77; collective unconscious 93, 102; ego's function of consciousness 151; extraverted feeling/sensation 66, 68, 69; inferior introverted thinking 66; psyche 160, 161–2, 261; psychic energy 84; psychological types 66; self 149; Shadow concept 30, 91, 148; "superior function" of consciousness 67; symbols of the unconscious 44; synchronicities 261; therapeutic approach 122, 123; typology of character 72, 95; unconscious 260, 261; works: *Aion* 51; *Collected Works* 132, 134, 135, 145, 161, 241, 266; *Man and his Symbols* 32; *Memories, Dreams, Reflections* 147, 154; *Mysterium Coniunctionis* 58, 229
justice 32, 105; economic 93; ethnic 127; origins of 111–16; social 39, 47, 85, 93

Kabbalah 146–7, 151
Kahn, C. H. 144, 153
Kalsched, Donald 70
Kampuchea *see* Cambodia
Kansas 102; *see also Wizard of Oz*
Kant, Immanuel 258–9, 260
Kaplan, A. 148
Keats, John 3
Kennedy, John F. 12, 26
Kennedy, Robert F. 12, 26
Keyworth, George 227
Khmer/Khmer Rouge 175, 178, 187–90 *passim*, 192; purges 170, 171, 186, 191, 194–6 *passim*
Kiefer, Anselm 14–15
Kiernan, B. 190, 194, 195
King, Martin Luther 247
Kosovo 100, 131, 135, 136
Koy Thuon 171, 192, 194
Kozinski, Alex 244, 248
Kumanjai Japaljarri 106–17
Kurgan people 233, 237

Labour Party (UK) 36, 39
Labrador Peninsula 32
Lacan, Jacques 226
Lahr, Bert 62, 68
Langley, N. 70
language 141, 174, 217; archetypal 162; emblematic 237; gender-unequal 247; hybrid 92; Latin 233; mixed-up 107; psychological type 72; universal 100
Laplanche, Jean 42
Lasswell, H. D. 148, 149
Latin America 44, 157
law(s) 165, 242, 247; Mosaic 56, 112; mythic events and 105–21; *see also* justice
leadership 57, 95; business 13; celebrity models of 15; charismatic 64; erotic 39–43; "good-enough" 34–49; heroic 15, 37–8; lack of 209; political 6, 13, 40, 58, 185; reflections on 23–8; suspicious 185
Leakey, Louis 233, 234
Ledgerwood, J. 183
legends 110, 112–16, 141, 178
lesbians 45, 47; baby adoption 101
"Leviathan" (Hobbes) 28, 29
Liberals (UK) 86
Lifton, Robert Jay 225–6
Lincoln, Abraham 25–6, 247
Lithuania 232
Littlefield, Henry M. 63, 64, 65
Livingston, Robert L. 57
Locard, H. 189
"logos" 144, 145, 17
Londonderry 99
Lon Nol regime (Cambodia) 170, 188, 189, 190, 192
love 32, 46, 48, 125; knowledge becomes an act of 264; pure 132; self 40
lunar cycle *see* moon phases
Luria, Isaac 146–7

McClintock, Barbara 263
Machiavelli, Niccolò 35, 43
McKinley, William 63
Magaziner, Ira 9
Malaysia 208
mandala 183, 185, 191; myths 171–80; politics 180–5
Mandela, Nelson 248
Mantegna, Joe 79
Maoists 170, 186, 187
Marduk 53
marital infidelity 56, 57
market economy 24, 91, 93, 95, 152
Marx, Karl 235, 236, 259
masculine principle 148, 151
Maslow, A. 87
Maspero, E. 178–9

materialism 143, 235, 237; dialectical 236
matriarchies 64, 235, 236
May, S. 190
meaning(s) 88, 135, 152, 218, 228–9, 253, 255; crisis of 262; living 260; projection of 51–2; rhetoric about 94; sacred 58; transcendental 62
Mecca 143–4
media 100, 123; concern 39–40
meditation 171–3, 176
Mediterranean 214, 217, 220
"melting pot" phenomenon 152
Meltzer, Donald 58
menstruation 52, 53, 233, 234–5, 238, 239
Merchant, C. 264
Meru, Mt 174–5, 176, 179, 180
Mesopotamia 53, 216
"metaform" 233–4, 235, 237, 238, 239
metanarratives 253
metaphors 66, 171, 237; empty 3; intellectual 101
microbelonging 129
Microsoft 101
Mill, John Stuart 254
mind 6, 252–3, 258–9; adolescent 262; autonomy of 256; body split from 237; conscious 235; managing 118; Meltzer's three "states of" 58; postmodern 264
minorities 86
mistapeo 32
Mithras 223
modernity 252, 254, 258
Mok (Cambodian Military Commander) 192, 195
monotheism 53, 143
Montenegro 136
moon phases 52–3, 59, 234
MOOSE (Male-Only-Origin-Story-Example) 232, 233, 235, 236–7, 238, 239–40
morality 58; based on spiritual principles 56; Buddhist 173; "unobtainable" 57
Morgan, Frank 71
Morgan, Louis Henry 236
Morison, Eliot 63–4
Morrison, Toni 101
Moses 56, 57, 112
mothers 41, 45, 115, 116, 151; good-enough 35; leaders 6; seductiveness of 42; sleeping with 113; unwed 78
movements: anti-war 151; civil rights 151, 166; emancipatory 252; peace 151; political 92, 144, 149; religious 144, 224; revolutionary 150; social 85–6, 91–2
Muhammad (prophet) 143–4
murder 99–100, 107, 111, 115–16, 196
music 86, 252, 256
Muslims *see* Islam
myth(ology) 2, 23, 27, 52, 53, 253; biblical 235; democratic 210; diversity and 141–56; economic 207–12; enduring 8–9; FAMOSE 240; global 24, 211; Greek and Near Eastern 216; hero 25, 207–9 *passim*; invisibility 157–69; law and 105–21; mandala 171–80; materialist 237; MOOSE 239–40; narratives in 122–40; new 56, 58, 59, 61; reflections on 23–8; religious 210; ritual and 12–15; sentimental 62; social attitudes and 30; universal 4, 134; usefulness of 118–19; *see also* archaeomythology; politics and myth

Nagourney, A. 56
narratives 64, 94, 122–40, 159, 164; hero 208; religious 208, 209, 221; social 167; *see also* metanarratives
National Socialism *see* Nazis
nationalism 24, 185; "fiction" of 127; fundamentalist 126; paranoid 127, 128
Nazis 15, 112, 125, 149, 186; Jung and 162
Near East 50, 53, 216; cosmology 220; Hellenistic culture 214, 217
Neolithic Period 50, 232, 233
networking 48; planetary 225
networks 86; "dense" 58–9; espionage, "rubber plantation" 195; informal 128; patronage 192, 193; social and cultural 85
Neumann, E. 148
New Left 91
Ney Sarann 192
Nicholson, Jack 79
Nietzsche, Friedrich 259
Nilsson, Martin 216
Nitze, Paul 99
Nixon, Richard M. 92
norms 144; submission to 51
Northern Ireland 157

nuclear age 248; adversaries 99; bases 46; war/annihilation 226
Nye, R. B. 63

Ocean of Milk 175, 176, 178
Ochwiay Biano 154
Oedipus 112–14, 237
Oldovai Gorge 233
Olympus, Mt 220
opportunism 70; legalistic 101
opposites 52, 53, 73, 130; bridging 62; conflict of 153; containers for holding 133; divine 266; integration of 54, 152–4; joining together of 241; knowledge of reality of 151
oppression 88, 126, 128, 150, 187, 188; political 143
order: chaos and 101; destruction of 152; imperial 214, 217; political 217; social 189; understanding and 123; world 55, 263
"Orestes" 105, 114–16
orgasm 236
Osaka 100

Paine, Tom 212
Pakistan 127
Palaeolithic Age 50, 52
Palestine 148, 152, 153, 157; Hellenistic Jews 226
Papadopoulos, R. K. 126, 128–9, 130
paranoia 188, 193, 194; nationalist 127, 128
parents 48, 93, 94, 256; arguing with children 254; "good-enough" 35–6; pre-adolescent struggle with 47; time spent conversing with children 100
Paris 88, 100
Pascal, Blaise 256
patriarchy 6, 48, 64, 78, 90, 92; domination of thought associated with 254
patronage 171–85
Pauk (Cambodian Military Commander) 192
Paul, St 219
payback 108, 111, 113, 115–16
Paz, Octavio 265
"penis envy" 236
Perentie 106, 107, 108, 111, 112, 114, 115, 117
personality 12; immature 44; opposing 72, 76; typically involved in resacrilization 90–1
Peru 157
phallic symbolism 88
philosophy 226, 252, 258
Phnom Penh 170, 186, 192, 194, 195, 196
Phouk Chhay 94
Pike, Bishop James 143
Pius XII, Pope 31
Plato 6, 29, 30, 219–21, 222–3, 227, 235
pluralism/plurality 150, 153, 154
Plutarch 146
poetry 59, 123–4, 125, 137–8, 256
Pol Pot 170, 188, 191, 192, 193–4, 195
Poland 24
police 106, 117, 131, 188; mistrust of 112
polis 165, 166, 217
"political correctness" 165
politics 1, 6, 38, 39, 53, 65–6, 187; carnival 45; consciousness 69; current problems 214; defining characteristic 24; feminine and 50–61; fundamental question for 23; gender equality in 241–50; identity 166; image that shaped 52; mandala 180–5; narratives in 122–40; professional 34; progressive 48; reflections on 23–8; religion and 142–4; separatist 46; sibling 47, 48; transformation of 84–102; transformative 48; tricksters in 43, 45; turmoil 143; visionary 10, 44; *see also* conservatives; Democrats; Green parties; Labour; Liberals; New Left; politics and myth; Republicans
politics and myth 4, 5, 9, 10, 12, 14, 15; of the person 90, 93–5; power of 51; practising 207–12; unified 29
Polynesia 77
Populist Movement 63
Porée, G. 178–9
postmodernity 8, 259, 264
power 44, 45, 49, 125, 126, 127, 208; black men 165; disintegrating 53; domination in politics 147; equal and shared 10; fear of 128; feminine 74; gracious surrender of 78; inflated use of 73; irrational intuitive 72; motivating, economic 208; patronage and 171–85; political 85, 149; relative 69; struggles for 66; universal 51; wealth and 144, 182; world 65

predictions 55, 90
prejudice 163
priestesses 54, 59
prisons 158, 160, 165; "without walls" 170
projections 51–2, 53–4, 117, 120, 219; negative 148, 157; response to other groups through 159–60
propaganda 73, 78, 125; anti-Semitic 186
prophecy 228, 229
Protestants 157, 186
protestors 45–6, 88, 100
psyche 4, 14, 54, 134, 149, 151; autonomous operation 161; collective 5–13 *passim*, 52; "bad-enough" 39; elite white 240; evolution of 243; group identity in 165; hidden processes in 51; images innate in 32; Jung's idea of 160, 161–2; modern, undergoing rite of passage 251–67; myth and 9–10; political 62–83, 87–90; politics and 9–10, 242; prescience 65; shattered 239; unconscious 52; *see also* collective psyche; soul(s)
psychic activity/forces 42, 54, 134, 135, 160
psychoanalysis 118; *see also* Freud; Grof; Jung; Laplanche; Meltzer; Spence; Winnicott
psychodynamics 47, 161
psychological types 66, 72, 75
psychology 5–6, 12, 37, 58, 88, 90, 217; analytical 84, 122, 159, 243; anti-political biases in 161–3; cognitive 66, 259; depth 145, 149, 152, 260, 261; developmental 36; film characters 66; Hellenistic 224; humanist 87; Jungian 64; political 34; post-Jungian 84; "postmodern" 226; transpersonal 93, 261; *see also* projections; splitting
psychotherapy 34, 37, 45, 70, 84, 86, 87, 89, 128; clinical 90, 122; consciousness 159; contribution of 94; culturally specific myths exchanged in 120; polarities 133–4; subpersonalities and 92; Sugarman project 118; techniques 117
puberty 239
punishment 111, 115, 189
purges 170, 171, 186, 191, 194–6 *passim*
"purification" process 186
Pythagoras 29–30

Quebec 152
Quraysh (tribe) 144

race/racism 26, 27, 42, 118, 119, 163; affective responses for comprehending 167; collective assumptions of 161; conflicts around 157, 158, 159; differences 126, 152; disempowerment 165; expectations mediated by 160; identity 160; myth of 237; *see also* apartheid
Rasmussen, K. J. V. 261
rationalism 52, 120, 143, 263
Reagan, Ronald 27, 244, 248
reality 1, 44, 68, 99, 117, 253; constellating 264; cosmological/cosmic 2, 221; external 126, 147; good and evil 124; illusory 129; loss of contact with 226; mythological/archetypal 4, 5; objectification of 263; poisoning of 219; political 4, 5, 63; psychological 4, 73; social 43, 47; virtual 227, 228, 229; vision and 7–9
reason 32, 241–50
Reasonable Woman/Reasonable Man 241–50
rebirth 53, 173, 218, 224, 261–3 *passim*, 267
Reformation 52, 235
reforms: healthcare 9–10; political 86
reincarnation 223
relatedness 40, 148, 149
religion 4, 8, 64, 221; archetype goddess 58; "astral" 218; beliefs 32, 50, 51, 152; ceremonies 32, 173, 174; conflicts around 157; ecstatic practices 132; fundamentalist 11, 12, 86, 95, 141–2, 153; historical relation between the political and 142–4; image that shaped 52; *see also* Buddhism; Christ(ianity); Hebrew prophets; Hinduism; Islam; Judaism; Kabbalah; Taoism; Zoroaster
Republicans (US) 1, 6, 56–7, 63, 84, 247; isolationist discourse 77; judges 244; patriarchal position 64
resacrilization 87, 90–1
resurrection 219, 224, 267
revelation 89, 219; cross-cultural 110; self 57, 265; unconscious 32
revenge 157, 167; *see also* payback
rhetoric 71, 94
Rhys Davids, T. W. 174

Right: political 151; religious 86
riots 8, 26
ritual 51, 166, 179, 240, 251–67; baptism 219, 223; blood 238, 239; elementary 53; myth and 12–15; sacrificial 239
Romans 143, 154, 209, 213, 214, 226
Romanticism 256, 257, 260; psyche 6; sensibility 44
Roosevelt, Franklin D. 26, 77
Ros Nhim 194–5
Rousseau, Jean-Jacques 30, 257
Roveda, V. 175
Rumania 24, 100
Rushdie, Salman 62, 73, 77
Russia 99, 152; *see also* Soviet Union
Rwanda 131, 157
sacrilization 235; *see also* desacrilization; resacrilization

Samuels, A. 74, 88, 150, 152, 161
Sanskrit 234
Scalia, Antonin 249
Schopenhauer, Arthur 264
sects 143
Seferis, George 123–4
segregation 247
self 31–2, 40, 149–50, 161; archetypal 149; "authentic" 225; basic activities of 33; collective 149; emergence of deeper sense of 132; fully saturated 225; individual's sense of 160; others and 145–6; postmodern 259; protean 226; social 149; wholeness of 15, 241
self-awareness 88, 256; "political" 90, 92
self-determination 217, 256
self-interest 32, 79, 85, 144; economic myth and 208, 211
sensibilities: aesthetic 256, 263; moral 255; political 78; religious 218; Romantic and Bohemian 44
Serbia/Serbs 127, 128, 136, 157, 186
sexual harassment 242–9 *passim*
sexuality 40–1, 52, 87, 151; arousal 234; incestuous 47; maternal 42–3
shadows 30, 31, 32, 70, 71, 72, 91, 148; collective 167; intragroup processes 157
Shakespeare, William 101, 252, 266
shamans 261
Shell Oil Company 25
Shiva 175
sibling leadership 46–8
Siem Reap 192, 194
Sihanouk, Prince Norodom, of Cambodia 185, 192
similarities 126, 162, 185
Simon Magus 143
Simpson, O. J. 14
Sisowath, Cambodian king 180
Six Day War (1967) 125
slavery 160, 163, 165, 168; abolition of 247
Smith, Adam 35
Snodgrass, A. 177
So Phim 192, 195, 196
social class 93; conflicts around 157, 236; myth of 237; worker-peasant 186, 187
social constructivism/constructions 127, 162
Social Darwinism 235
social issues: attitudes 29, 30, 31, 158–9; cohesion 100; consciousness 30; identities 165–6; malaise 86; organization 32, 46; processes governed by cultural complex 166–7; relations 48
"social contract" 30
socialist ideas 86
Sokundara, P. 183
Somalia 44
Sophocles *see Oedipus*; Orestes
soul(s) 6, 32, 88, 256; body separate from 222–3, 227; evil in 132; fragmentary 147; immortality of 221–3; lost 64; new allegiance of 229; rescuing from isolation 58; rhetoric about 94; trek towards wholeness 56; women do not have 89; world 145, 255
South Africa 101, 157, 248; Truth and Reconciliation Commission 167–8
Soviet Union (former) 23, 54, 55, 94, 186; independent republics 150; religious fundamentalism 142; speculators 100
Spence, Donald 94
Spencer, Herbert 210
Spielberg, Steven 13
spirit(uality) 52, 58, 86, 87, 144, 180, 254, 256; archetypal encounters with 4; essence of 146; morality based on 56; quest for 142; transformation 146, 213–31
splitting 53, 54
Stalinism 170, 187
stars 218, 220, 221; *see also* astrology
Stede, W. 174

Steele, Shelby 164
Steiner, Rudolph 102
stereotypes 163, 167, 186
Stevens, Anthony 242
Stone, Sharon 45
struggle 45, 89, 135, 243; control of government 63; military 150; political 47; power 66; pre-adolescent 47
Stuart-Fox, M. 196
Stuttgart 23
subjectivity 162; outlawed 91
suffering 58, 159, 162, 165, 252, 253, 262, 267; origins and elimination 173
Sugarman/Dionysos Project 118
Sumer(ia) 50, 54, 59
sun 32, 51, 64, 180, 259
superiority 66, 67, 258; male 51
Supreme Court (US) 247, 248
survival 144, 160, 191, 208; of fittest 235, 236; of national identity 219
Suryavarman II, Khmer king 175, 179–80
Switzerland 30, 31
symbolism/symbols 44, 51, 52, 218–19, 223–4, 233, 255; Buddhist 171–3, 174, 176, 183; consciousness 76; cosmic 219; eagle 154–5; feminine principle 64; identity grounded in 162; new 225; religious 257
synchronicities 261
syncretism 218
systems approach 25

taboos 53
Tambiah, S. J. 185
Tannenbaum, N. 183
Taoism 142
Taos pueblo 154
Tarn, W. W. 217, 224
Tasmanian people 236
television 100, 208, 210, 262
Ten Commandments 56, 57
Tennessee 100
terrorists 94, 95
testosterone 234, 235
Thanatos 147
Thatcher, Margaret 6, 38
thinking/thought 217, 227, 252; action without 131; confused 120; domination of 254; European, origins of 118; extraverted 71, 78; Hindu-Buddhist 177; introverted 66, 71, 72, 78; metaformic 238; psychological, anti-political biases in 161–3; with heart 154
Third World 44, 94, 95
Thomas, Clarence 158, 249
Thompson, William Irwin 102
Thomson, L. 69
threats 47, 64, 70, 73
Tiamat 53
Tito, Josip Broz 127
Tiv Ol 194
Tocqueville, Alexis de 26
Toffler, Alvin 227
tolerance 58, 59, 148
Toperoff, S. P. 155
torture 170, 236
totalitarianism 78, 149
"traitors" 192, 195
transcendence 62, 129, 144, 256
transference 117, 119–21
"transfiguration" 229
transformation: differences 127; initiatory 262; metaphysical 252; politics of 84–102, 222; religious 143; social 221; socio-cosmic 226; spiritual 146, 213–31
transition 54, 55; cultural 213–31
trauma 70, 88, 137, 162, 167; psychosocial 157, 168; social 168; working out 163
Travolta, John 79
Traxel, D. 62
tricksters 73; as leaders 43–6; female 45
Trow, George W. S. 100
truth 26, 45, 113, 173, 208; absolute 56, 149, 151; "narrative", political 94; opposite of 254;
Tuol Sleng 170, 193, 194, 195
Tutsis 157, 186
"typology" 228, 229

unconscious 39, 54, 69–70, 166, 219, 260; collective 30, 93, 102, 147; discovery of 261; intelligence in 71; revelations 32; symbols of 44
understanding 26, 126, 214, 253, 258, 262; cognitive 37; existential 120; intellectual 265; order and 123
Unio Mentalis 56
United Nations 99; Children's Fund (UNICEF) 135; Development Programme (UNDP) 135
unity 29, 30, 141, 154; disintegration of 152; empathic 264; global 153; inner

145; political 153, 155; search for 143; social 155
universe 55, 58, 144, 171, 220, 264; authority of 263; Big Bang origin 51, 146, 237; creation of 176, 178, 180; disenchantment of 255; expansion of 226; forces in control of 221; imaginal 228; national anxieties projected on to 219
USSR *see* Soviet Union

values 74, 76, 210; clashes of 54; cultural 32, 53, 86; extraverted 78; moral and spiritual 58; peasant 189; political 86; solar masculine 64; traditional 72; transcendent 144; tribal 144
vaudeville 62, 76
victims 134, 186, 191, 196, 234; child 136
Vietnam 26, 100, 122, 187; Cambodia and 170, 186, 188, 190–2 *passim*, 196; *see also* Pol Pot
violence 132, 141, 144, 157, 171; apartheid 167; collective narratives and 128–31; intoxicated, delusional 118; political 122, 185, 186
Vishnu 175, 178, 180

W ("we") word 90
Warlpiri people 105–21
Warshawski, V. I. 45
water 54, 176, 211
Waters, Maxine 57
Watts, J. C. 56
wealth 24, 39, 144, 178, 182, 236
websites *see* World Wide Web
Wells, H. G. 266
West, M. L. 216–17
White, William Allen 64
white supremacy 164
wholeness 15, 65, 241; participatory 261; soul's trek towards 56
Wiesenfeld, Esther 129
Wilde, Oscar 90
"willy-nilly" condition 134
Wilmer, Harry 122
Winnicott, Donald 35, 36, 84
Wizard of Oz, The 62–83
women 89; *see also* ecofeminism; erotic leaders; FAMOSE; female tricksters; feminine; feminists; FOOSE; gender; goddesses; matriarchies; menstruation; mothers; priestesses
Wordsworth, William 101, 157, 257
World Wide Web 100, 225, 227, 228

Yahweh 215, 229
Yappa law 106–10, 115
Yeats, W. B. 229
Yimsut, Ronnie 190–1
Yugoslavia (former) 24, 136; *see also* Bosnia; Croatia; Kosovo; Montenegro; Serbia

Zeitgeist 7, 30
Zen 131
Zephir, T. 174
Zeus 115, 118, 141, 150
Zion, Mt 220
Zipes, J. 77
Zohar, The 151
Zoroaster 143